HOLIDAY
COURSES

FOR LONG WEEKENDS
AND SHORT BREAKS

HOLIDAY
COURSES

FOR LONG WEEKENDS
AND SHORT BREAKS

A guide to the best holiday courses
and workshops in the UK & Ireland

Edited by Adam Barnes & Lisa Plumridge

howto**books**

Published by HOW TO BOOKS LTD,
3 Newtec Place, Magdalen Road,
Oxford OX4 1RE, United Kingdom.
Tel: (01865) 793806. Fax: (01865) 248780.
Email: info@howtobooks.co.uk
http://www.howtobooks.co.uk
Researched, written and managed by The Content Works
www.thecontentworks.com

First edition

British Library Cataloguing in Publication Data
A catalogue record for this book is available from the British Library.

Cover design by Baseline Arts Ltd.
Cover pictures: Front top middle and top right, West Dean College.
Back middle, Rush Matters; top right, Belle Isle School of Cookery.
Design and typesetting by Baseline Arts Ltd, Oxford
Print management: Deer Park Productions Ltd, Tavistock
Printed and bound by L.E.G.O., Italy

Note: The material contained in this book is set out in good faith for general
guidance and no liability can be accepted for loss or expense incurred as a result
of relying in particular circumstances on statements made in the book.

Contents

Photo ©Rush Matters

Acknowledgements

This first edition of Holiday Courses for Long Weekends and Short Breaks, UK and Ireland, would not have been possible without the enthusiasm and hard work of a large team of very dedicated people. Special thanks go to Adam Barnes, whose persistence and expert eye for detail have resulted in a book we can be proud of. Thanks also to John Adam, Jane Anson, Joseph Bindloss, Nick Bruno, David Cawley, Andy Cooke, Rachel Congdon, Helen Earis, Catherine and David Franks, Victoria Gill, Fiona Johnson, Sharon Lougher, Geraldine Mackay, Lisa Madden, Angelique Mulder, Johnny Pym, Annette Sohor, Tika Stefano, and Nigel Couzens and Samantha Langston at Barking Dog Communications, for their invaluable help in all manner of ways.

We would like to give special thanks to Alison Moran at West Dean College for the many beautiful photos, and to Tim O'Flaherty for his assistance with the images in general.

Many thanks to Nikki Read and Giles Lewis at How To Books for having the idea in the first place and for their backing and encouragement, and thanks also to Andy Esson and Nicki Averill at Baseline Arts for their design work; also to Rik Mulder for his unstoppable energy and determination.

Thousands of letters, telephone calls and emails later, we would also like to extend our thanks to all of the course organisers listed within these covers for their enthusiastic input, co-operation with our writers and sales team, and for offering such a wonderful range of courses.

Lisa Plumridge
Editorial Director
The Content Works

Introduction

This book presents you with a gift-wrapped opportunity to make good the intentions that have long cluttered your internal 'to do' list. Be it learning the guitar, taking up embroidery, making jewellery, baking bread, writing a short story, painting watercolours, restoring furniture, flying falcons, starting yoga or a hundred others, we aim to provide you with the wherewithal to try something new, refresh a skill you once had, or take a current skill to a new level. Using this book you should be able to find the course you want at a time, place and price that suits your needs.

We have gathered together almost 500 venues offering several thousand courses, which fall into the following categories:

Arts – essentially drawing, painting and sculpture;
Crafts – ceramics, woodwork, textiles, fabrics, furniture, jewellery and metal;
Food & Drink – cookery and wine-related courses;
Music & Performance – music, theatre and dance;
Writing, Film & Photography – creative writing, film & televisual arts, and photography;
Home & Garden – interior and garden design;
Body & Soul – yoga, t'ai chi, reiki, aromatherapy, healing, meditation;
Outdoors – environmental, birdwatching, wildlife, falconry and guided walks;
Other – bridge, swimming, history, archaeology.

Some venues are small, family-run affairs offering a single area of excellence – photography weekends, for example; others are adult education centres with course smorgasbords serving up every workshop and retreat imaginable, plus a few more besides. In these cases we have supplied a list of categories in an effort to convey the range of what they offer, but we hope the text provides a more nuanced explanation.

This book does not intend to send you back to school. Our emphasis is as much on 'holiday' as it is on 'course'. The courses we feature are keen to retain an emphasis on fun – on the joy of working and learning alongside similarly minded people, usually in beautiful environments, so that you return home feeling both refreshed and inspired.

We have defined 'short course' to mean courses that last at least two days and at most ten. Accommodation for the intervening night(s) may or may not be offered/included in the price. If it is not, organisers can usually recommend suitable local establishments. Many places featured have one-day courses as well, but they are not our focus. You should contact the course organisers for details of one-day offerings.

How to use the book

This is both for those who have a definite idea about what they want to do and for those with an urge to 'use' their weekends and holidays to some productive end. Some participants will be seeking personal development; others will just fancy playing with clay. Whatever your situation is, you should find inspiration in these pages.

We have arranged our courses by region, and – within each region – alphabetically by the name of the course organiser. The symbols in the title denote the category or categories a course falls into:

Arts

 Crafts

 Food & Drink

Music & Performance

 Writing, Film & Photography

 Home & Garden

 Body & Soul

 Outdoors

All the venues were selected on merit by a team of researchers. Those places with larger listings and photographs have paid a fee for a full page layout; we make no bones about that. They did not buy their way into the book: our researchers hand-picked them, then they were offered the chance to upgrade their listing. They do not, however, specifically endorse the places mentioned in the Eating & Sleeping sections unless stated otherwise.

These extended listings have a 'What's Special?' paragraph that expounds why we are particularly impressed by them – either by describing a favourite course or by identifying the stand-out reason for the effectiveness of their courses.

Booking

Phone numbers
To dial a UK number from abroad, dial the international dialling code, then 44 (for the UK) then the listed phone number minus the first 0.

To dial an Irish (not Northern Ireland) number from the UK, dial 00 353 followed by the listed phone number minus the first 0.

Prices
Prices listed in this book are indicative, rather than prescriptive. The book would be twice as long if we listed prices for every individual course, so we have given ranges within which prices should fall. For clarity's sake, we would encourage you to ring or write to the course organisers should you see something that is of interest, and confirm exactly what the price will be and exactly what – in terms of food, accommodation and other items – is included.

The prices of our Irish venues are listed in euros. The exchange rate is in the region of £1 = 1.4.

Dates
Course dates are also indicative: months highlighted in green are the months when the venue will run courses. You should approach the organisers directly to determine exact

dates. Some course dates will be set in stone months in advance, especially at the larger venues; other venues will simply run courses as and when they are needed. A green month will not necessarily indicate that a course will take place that month; it may just mean that the organisers will arrange one in that month if asked. We cannot be held responsible for listed courses that do not ultimately take place; situations change. If the numbers signing up are insufficient, organisers may sometimes postpone until a later date.

Locations

The contact address listed is not necessarily the same as the address of the course venue. It should be clear from the write-ups where this is the case, but it is worth confirming exactly where your holiday course will be happening.

Other 'attendees'

If you want to bring a child or pet to a place listed as child or pet-friendly, please ring ahead to ascertain exactly what the rules are. Children may be allowed to stay on site but not actually attend the course.

What you can do for us

Firstly, we would be grateful if you would inform the venues that you found them through this book.

Secondly, entries will be refined and updated for the second edition. Therefore we would be delighted to receive feedback from readers and organisers about courses that you have attended, as well as recommendations for new courses. You can send comments to:

How To Books
3 Newtec Place
Magdalen Road
Oxford OX4 1RE
United Kingdom
Or send us an email at: editor@holidaycourses.co.uk

Thirdly, if you enjoy a course, look out for the other 'course' titles that we will be producing, covering other subjects such as sports, and other countries such as France, Spain and Italy.

Happy Holidays!

The regions

Greater London

The London courses have an urban focus – nothing surprising there. The city is home to many of the UK's leading arts and educational institutions and many of the courses are more esoteric and more academic than elsewhere in the country; subjects taught range from making films or props to learning bridge or genealogy. These tend not to be residential courses, but the city is awash with places to stay at every budget level and organisers can usually make recommendations.

South East

This wealthy part of England has some lovely countryside, much of it of a more 'homely' scale and style than you will find in, say, the north of England and Scotland. The South East has historic towns and cities by the dozen, from Winchester and Canterbury to Oxford, Chichester and Brighton, and the intervening countryside is littered with historic houses and sumptuous gardens. Accessibility to the region is straightforward, and all the courses are within easy striking distance of London.

South West

Stonehenge, Glastonbury, the Eden Project, Cornish beaches, Exmoor, Dartmoor, the Cotswolds, Bath, Exeter, the Forest of Dean, St Ives and the South West Coastal Path. The South West is a hugely popular part of England, with the country's mildest climate; and it has numerous seaside and alternative lifestyle associations. The courses offered here are varied in style and content, with many run by people who have left city-based jobs to pursue their artistic and cultural dreams in a stunning part of the country.

East Anglia

This flat, low-lying region is the UK's bread basket and has some of its richest farmland. Its early wealth derived from the successful wool trade and it has some splendid 'wool churches' built with the proceeds. Regional highlights include the Fens, the Norfolk Broads, the Suffolk coast (much of which is owned by the National Trust), Cambridge, Ely and Aldeburgh. Artists will enjoy East Anglia's Constable associations – and we feature many watercolour courses; naturalists will find much of interest in the shingle beaches, mudflats and waterways.

East Midlands

The charms of this region include the Peak District National Park where various of the courses take place, Lincoln with its cathedral, and Rutland Water with its water sports. Courses in the East Midlands have a strong craft focus and we can offer stone masonry, blacksmithing, curtain making, sewing and mosaics among a diverse roster of workshops and retreats.

West Midlands

As England heads towards Wales the landscape becomes more rural. After the Black Country this becomes a region of market towns and small cities – Ludlow and Shrewsbury, Hereford and Worcester. Lichfield cathedral is well worth the visit. Many of the courses here are rural-focused, teaching country pursuits. But there is also painting, cookery and even bell ringing to tempt you westwards.

Yorkshire

One of the most charismatic of English counties, home to beautiful, medieval York with its huge Gothic cathedral; lively Leeds, the famous North York moors and dales; the east coast with Whitby and Scarborough; plus Brontë and Herriot country. You might like to try a cookery course in a county famous for its pies, tarts, puddings and cheeses; or use the scenery to help you unwind, relax and release some of your creative potential through painting, writing or – why not – working with sheepdogs.

The North of England

Where to start? The countryside, perhaps is not a bad place: from the crags of the Lake District to the wilderness of Northumberland, the North of England showcases myriad variations on the theme of beautiful landscapes which make suitable backdrops for an array of courses in walking, birdwatching, photography and others. Towns include historic Durham and Chester, and Newcastle and Manchester, while Hadrian's Wall and the Angel of the North should keep your camera happy. This is a region whose constituent parts all have distinct cultures and local identities; food, literary and arts and crafts traditions will colour many of the courses that you do here.

Wales

Wales is a land famous for its valleys and its hills, with three picturesque national parks - Snowdonia in the north, the Pembrokeshire Coast in the south west, and the Brecon Beacons in the south east. Add in the Gower Peninsula, the Black Mountains, and myriad castles and you have a country rich in photographic and painting potential. A high proportion of our Welsh courses are in some way spiritual and are concerned with yoga, meditation, healing or some other means to bring calm into your life.

Scotland

Hugely popular with tourists on account of its rugged scenery and picture-postcard landscapes, Scotland makes an excellent place to 'get away from it all' on a weekend course – or for longer. Add in the whisky, the music, the golf and the Celtic culture, and reasons for visiting Scotland seem endless. It's an excellent place for outdoorsy courses that take you to some of the less visited regions and islands, as well as for those based in Edinburgh that allow you to enjoy the varied charms of the capital city.

Northern Ireland

Less commonly visited by tourists from England, Scotland and Wales than Eire to the south, Northern Ireland offers natural delights such as Giants Causeway, the Sperrin Mountains and Co. Fermanagh's magnificent Lough Erne with its great fishing. There are beautiful coastal villages near Portrush and three thriving cities – Belfast, Londonderry and Armagh. Belfast, in particular, is a vibrant, welcoming place that is starting to attract increasing numbers of visitors

Ireland

With a literary tradition from the lap of the gods, vibrant cities and some spectacular landscapes, Ireland is a wonderful place to do a course – and there are many cheap flights from the UK. The beautiful Burren plateau in Co. Clare is a popular area for landscape-oriented courses; Dublin makes a superb destination for a short break; and Cork is the European Capital of Culture for 2005. Some courses have a particularly strong Irish flavour and will enfold participants in the country's literary, musical and cultural traditions.

LONDON

Greater London

The London courses have an urban focus –
nothing surprising there. The city is home to
many of the UK's leading arts and
educational institutions and many of the
courses are more esoteric and more
academic than elsewhere in the country;
subjects taught range from making films or
props to learning bridge or genealogy. These
tend not to be residential courses, but the
city is awash with places to stay at every
budget level and organisers can usually
make recommendations.

Bridge weekends with Andrew Robson

Bridge has had a makeover in recent years – it is now, so we're told, a cutting-edge 'urban sport', whose complexities can boost your immune system. If you've been beguiled by the game, the Andrew Robson Bridge Club runs a number of weekends throughout the year for all levels of player (one weekend for beginners, one for intermediate and so on), covering rules, tips, duplicates and supervised play sessions. Andrew Robson is one of Britain's top bridge players as well as an accomplished teacher and writer. His international achievements include being the first Briton to win a US 'Major'. He started the club in 1995 and now has dedicated premises near Parsons Green tube.

Contact
Andrew Robson or David Bakhshi
Andrew Robson Bridge Club
31 Parsons Green Lane
Parsons Green
London SW6 4HH
Tel: 020 7471 4626
Web: www.arobson.co.uk

Practical information
Duration: 2 days
Level: beginner &
intermediate
Non-residential

Group size: 3–25+
Price range: £100–£150
Prices include: lunch
Unsuitable for children
Pets not welcome

Courses available in:

Jan	Feb	Mar	Apr	May	Jun	Jul	Aug	Sep	Oct	Nov	Dec
	Feb				Jun				Oct		

Art modernism: know the art of your time

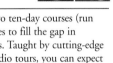

Art History Abroad concentrates mainly on European trips, but they also have two ten-day courses (run over two weeks, not including weekends) in London. 'Modernism in London' tries to fill the gap in students' knowledge of today's art culture vis-à-vis that of more traditional schools. Taught by cutting-edge artists and architects, and including visits to various galleries alongside private studio tours, you can expect to come away with new ideas and a fresh insight into London's contemporary art scene. The other course covers 'Art in Britain 1200 –1914', and contrasts the exhibits in galleries (Saatchi Gallery, Tate Modern, City churches) with associated pictures elsewhere in London, perhaps in other galleries or churches, to ensure a thorough overview.

Contact
Lucie Baird
Art History Abroad (AHA)
179c New Kings Road
Chelsea
London SW6 4SW
Tel: 020 7731 2231
Web: www.arthistoryabroad.com

Practical information
Duration: 10 days
Level: beginner &
intermediate
Residential & non-residential
Group size: 6–20

Price range: £500+
Prices include: lunch
Child-friendly
Pets not welcome

Courses available in:

Jan	Feb	Mar	Apr	May	Jun	Jul	Aug	Sep	Oct	Nov	Dec

International food and wine courses at a Notting Hill favourite

Books for Cooks' legendary day courses are often offered on consecutive days, so you can take two in a weekend. Teachers include French chef and company owner Eric Treuillé, Italian cookbook author Ursula Ferrigno, Japanese-born Kimiko Barber, and others from around the world – an array which gives you some idea of the range of cooking styles on offer. Workshops have different areas of emphasis, from presentation and time management in 'Easy Entertaining', to the all-Italian delights of 'Italian Kitchen'. For the 'Wine and Food of…' evenings, Eric draws upon wine merchants Corney & Barrow to hold an evening dedicated to a particular wine-producing region, with dégustation menu and a tutored tasting.

Contact
Rosie Kindersley or Eric Treuillé
Books for Cooks
4 Blenheim Crescent
Notting Hill
London W11 1NN
Tel: 020 7221 1992
Web: www.booksforcooks.com

Practical information
Duration: 2 days
Level: beginner &
intermediate
Non-residential
Group size: 6–25

Price range: £50–£150
Prices include: lunch,
provided in form of tastings
Unsuitable for children
Pets not welcome

Courses available in:

Jan	Feb	Mar	Apr	May	Jun	Jul	Aug	Sep	Oct	Nov	Dec

Arts with artists in Southwark

The Art Academy, which comprises the Sculpture Academy and the Painting Academy, offers a different dynamic from many art schools. Students work alongside artists and learn as much from their presence as their teaching. The academy prides itself on the fact that by the end of the courses, students are trained vocationally as artists, rather than left requiring direction from future teachers. They have recently moved to a new home in Union Street, near Tate Modern, with five floors of studios and a huge basement gallery.

Courses
Weekend, evening and short courses run throughout the year, covering topics such as 'Painting from Life', 'Introduction to Painting', 'Glass Works', 'Figure Sculpture', 'Life Drawing' and 'Modelling and Mould Making'. As one of Britain's predominantly figurative art schools, the Academy provides classical training, but realigned to today's art world.

What's special?
The wood-carving and stone-carving workshop teaches both traditional and modern techniques. The tutor covers different skills, such as manipulation of tools and working with different woods, and the bulk of the lessons deals with putting these theories into practice.

Eating & sleeping
Café: the Jerwood Space and gallery (020 7654 0171). Pub: Horniman's (020 7407 1991). Restaurant: Oxo Tower (020 7803 3888). Accommodation: Express by Holiday Inn (020 7401 2525), Mercure (020 7902 0800), and the boutique Southwark Rose (020 7015 1480).

Directions
Tube: Southwark (very close) and Borough (five minutes). The Riverside Bus Service (RV1) links Covent Garden, South Bank, Bankside and Tower Hill.

In the area
Southwark is one of London's most vibrant districts: the South Bank, the Globe, Tate Modern, the Clink, Vinopolis and the Royal Festival Hall are all within easy walking distance.

Contact
Course co-ordinator
The Art Academy
201 Union Street
Southwark
London SE1 0LN
Tel: 020 7401 6539
Web: www.artacademy.org.uk
Email: info@artacademy.org.uk

Practical information
Duration: 2–5 days
Level: beginner, intermediate & advanced
Non-residential
Group size: 3–15
Courses available in:

Price range: £50–£300
Prices include: materials
Child-friendly
Pets not welcome

Jan	Feb	Mar	Apr	May	Jun	Jul	Aug	Sep	Oct	Nov	Dec

Soldering and shaping silver at a jewellery workshop

Camberwell College of Art is part of the London University of Arts. Past students have won the Turner Prize, the Jerwood Prize and the BP Portrait Award. In this silver workshop, you learn the essential techniques of soldering, shaping, cutting and piercing – developing designs in base metals before re-creating them in silver. The equipment used on the course can also easily be installed at home, and you can choose what you make – be it bracelet, chain, ring or something bigger. Simple fittings, finishing and polishing are included; stone setting and the cost of the silver is not. Other short courses on offer include printmaking, photography, fine art and still-life drawing.

Contact
Kate Ibbotson
Camberwell College of Arts
c/o Short Course Unit
University of the Arts
John Islip Street
St James, London
Tel: 020 7514 6311
Web: www.camberwell.arts.ac.uk
  – Short courses

Practical information
Duration: 4 days
Level: beginner/intermediate
Non-residential
Group size: 6-10

Price range: £200-£300
Unsuitable for children
Pets not welcome

Courses available in:

Jan	Feb	Mar	Apr	May	Jun	Jul	Aug	Sep	Oct	Nov	Dec

Contemporary jewellery in London and its influences

During Exploring London's Jewellery Design course, you will 'discover contemporary jewellery in a London context'. This means visits to private galleries and designers' exclusive collections, as well as the Victoria and Albert Museum and other leading exhibitions. Each day looks at a different area of jewellery design and the inspirations that shaped it, from its 1950s beginnings to the inspirations from Europe and the hands-on reality of the workshop. Central St Martins School of Art and Design is one of London's most iconic study centres, providing access to some of the most exciting people in the art world. All levels of courses are offered, from beginner to PhD.

Contact
Central St Martins College of Art and Design
Southampton Row
Holborn
London WC1B 4AP
Tel: 020 7514 7015
Web: www.csm.linst.ac.uk

Practical information
Duration: 4 days
Level: beginner
Non-residential
Group size: 3-15

Price range: £200-£300
No lunch provided
Unsuitable for children
Pets not welcome

Courses available in:

Jan	Feb	Mar	Apr	May	Jun	Jul	Aug	Sep	Oct	Nov	Dec

Appreciating the finer things in life at a famous auction house

Many of the courses run by Christie's Education feature visits to the auction house, and all offer exposure to expert teachers and rare artefacts, and the first-hand study of works of art. The 2005 Summer School has a week-long course on Luxury Arts of Russia, looking at, among other things, the history of the Hermitage Collection (which has a strong connection with Christie's). Christie's has been running courses for almost 30 years in Art History, Connoisseurship and the Art Market. Excellent masterclasses include wine, understanding jewellery and how to bid at auction – as well as less usual fare such as 'The Golden Age of Hollywood' and 'The Art of Celebrity'.

Contact
Christie's Education
153 Great Titchfield Street
London W1W5BD
Tel: 020 7665 4350
Web: www.christies.co.uk

Practical information
Duration: 5 days
Level: beginner &
intermediate
Non-residential

Group size: 11-20
Price range: £300-£400
Unsuitable for children
Pets not welcome

Courses available in:

Jan	Feb	Mar	Apr	May	Jun	Jul	Aug	Sep	Oct	Nov	Dec

COURTAULD INSTITUTE OF ART, CENTRAL LONDON

Galleries in history and today at Somerset House

The Courtauld Institute at Somerset House houses a world-famous collection of paintings, prints and drawings. Their Summer School has been running for nine years now, while 2005 will see their first ever Spring School. The week-long courses are taught in small groups and involve visiting galleries, museums and relevant buildings (special access is often allowed to restricted collections) alongside lectures. Topics range from ancient to modern art – for example, 'The Art Museum in History and Today' examines the role that galleries play in the art world, and includes trips to several London galleries. An end-of-the-week drinks party in the neo-classical setting of Somerset House is a spectacular bonus.

Contact
Courtauld Institute of Art
Somerset House
Strand
London WC2R 0RN
Tel: 020 7848 2678
Web: www.courtauld.ac.uk

Practical information
Duration: 5 days
Level: beginners,
intermediate & advanced
Non-residential

Group size: 11–20
Price range: £300–£400
Unsuitable for children
Pets not welcome

Courses available in:

Jan	Feb	Mar	Apr	May	Jun	Jul	Aug	Sep	Oct	Nov	Dec

THE ENGLISH GARDENING SCHOOL, WEST LONDON

Making the best of small gardens in Chelsea Physic Garden

Chelsea Physic Garden, 'London's secret garden', is a wonderful place to study. Founded in 1673, the four-acre plot contains over 5,000 species, and you might never know it existed. On the Really Small Gardens course Jill Billington (20 years a garden designer, and judge at RHS shows) inspires the gardener of even the tiniest patio. You will learn how to plan a layout with scale, balance and harmony, and how to create an atmosphere by selecting plants for form, colour, texture and seasonal effects. The School offers courses for all gardening abilities, including planning and planting, garden photography, painting gardens, and garden transformation.

Contact
Jill Billington
The English Gardening School
66 Royal Hospital Road
Chelsea
London SW3 4HS
Tel: 020 7352 4347
Web: www.englishgardeningschool.co.uk

Practical information
Duration: 2 days
Level: beginner &
intermediate
Non-residential

Group size: 11–20
Price range: £200–£300
Prices include: lunch
Child-friendly
Pets not welcome

Courses available in:

Jan	Feb	Mar	Apr	May	Jun	Jul	Aug	Sep	Oct	Nov	Dec

FONT INTERNATIONAL, CENTRAL LONDON

Writing workshops for budding and experienced writers

Writing workshops are not rare, but Font International's versions offer particularly interesting topics, taught by influential writers. This Dublin-based organisation was founded by novelist Aine McCarthy to stimulate creative talent. The weekends do not deal with the vagaries of, for example, 'writing your first novel', but look in depth at specifics, from improving your non-fiction prose technique, to breaking into travel writing and writing biography. 'You Can Be a Writer' examines the writing life: where to begin, organising your time, writing plans and outlines, etc. The schedule for 2005 also includes 'Writing Non-Creative Fiction', 'Writing Humour' and 'Writing Inspirational Books'. Font offers other services such as manuscript appraisals and career planning.

Contact
Aine McCarthy
Font International
45 Victoria Road
Clontarf
Dublin 3
Tel: 01853 2356
Web: www.fontwriters.com

Practical information
Duration: 2 days
Level: beginner,
intermediate & advanced
Non-residential

Group size: 6–10
Price range: £150–£200
Unsuitable for children
Pets not welcome

Courses available in:

Jan	Feb	Mar	Apr	May	Jun	Jul	Aug	Sep	Oct	Nov	Dec

ARTS EXPRESS, SOUTH LONDON

Stone-carving in Kennington

Arts Express is an educational visual arts charity established in 1999. They run workshops and evening classes in stone carving (usually limestone), which give participants a grounding in the techniques and tools for carving and allow for the completion of individual sculptures. They are suitable for all levels of experience, and groups are small enough to allow for one-to-one tuition, so do take along anything that you feel you particularly want to work on. Marcia Bennett-Male, the tutor, is a stonemason and professional stone carver, and her past students are always describing her as inspirational. Arts Express also works with local communities to produce commissioned pieces of art. They have a number of stone-carving weekends planned for summer 2005.

What's special?

It is unusual to find a course like this in London, offering a great way to get 'hands on' after office life. The studios are beautifully atmospheric, housed in a cobbled mews in converted stables. Definitely an addictive experience all round!

Eating & sleeping

For food: the Doghouse pub on Renfrew Road (020 7820 9310), Thai Silk on Windmill Road (020 7735 9338) and the Lobster Pot (020 7582 5556). For accommodation: the Parkside hotel in Clapham (020 7720 8585) or the Windsor in Tooting Bec (020 8760 0000).

Directions

Kennington is just south of the Thames, with easy access to central London. Nearest tube: Kennington, 5 minutes walk from the Iffiffe Yard studios. Buses include 35, 40, 45, 59, 133, 155.

In the area

Be inspired by the carvings in the Tibetan Peace Garden. Or visit the Imperial War Museum on nearby Lambeth Road, the Oval cricket ground, Kennington Common, Lambeth Palace and the Museum of Garden History.

Contact

Damion Viney
Arts Express
186 Peckham High St
Peckham
London
Tel: 020 7635 6709
Web: www.arts-express.co.uk/courses.html
Email: dv@artsexpress.fsnet.co.uk

Practical information

Duration: 2 days
Level: beginner,
intermediate & advanced
Non-residential

Group size: 6–15
Price range: under
£50–£100
Unsuitable for children
Pets not welcome

Courses available in:

Jan	Feb	Mar	Apr	May	Jun	Jul	Aug	Sep	Oct	Nov	Dec

BERRY BROS. & RUDD WINE SCHOOL, CENTRAL LONDON

Wine courses in beautifully restored 17th-century cellars

World-renowned wine merchant Berry Bros. & Rudd offers a range of wine courses at its 17th-century premises in St James's Street. The Wine, Spirit and Education Trust (WSET) course is available at various London venues, but the Berrys version combines structured learning with a location in one of the capital's most historic buildings. The beautifully restored cellars date back to 1698 and the shopfront is one of few 18th-century examples surviving in London. The courses, which have an optional exam, introduce grape varieties, wine-making methods and the wine regions of the world, along with the development of wine-tasting skills. You will study in the Pickering Cellar, which stretches underneath St James's Street and Crown Passage.

Courses
In addition, Berrys offers day and evening courses, such as An Introduction to Wine Luncheon, Bordeaux's Hottest Wines, The Bollinger Dinner, The Complexity of Riesling, The Port Walk Tasting, One-Day Wine Schools and many others.

What's special?
The WSET wine course is the most thorough in the UK, and Berrys is one of the oldest and most venerated wine merchants. Put them together and you have something special, combining a classic London experience with a wine masterclass.

Eating & sleeping
There are many restaurants and hotels nearby – Dukes (020 7491 4840), Browns (020 7493 6020), the Ritz (020 7493 8181). Local restaurants include Le Caprice, Nobu and the Mirabelle.

Directions
Berrys is located in the heart of St James's. Tube: Green Park or St James's Park. Buses: 83, 72, 19, 10, 14, 137, 9 and 22.

In the area
You don't get much better placed than this, a stone's throw from Jermyn Street, Bond Street, Fortnum & Mason, St James's Palace and the Royal Academy.

Contact
Rebecca Lamont
Berry Bros. & Rudd Wine School
3 St James's St
St James
London
Tel: 0870 900 4300
Web: www.bbr.com
Email: rebecca.lamont@bbr.com

Practical information
Duration: 2 days
LDuration: 5–10 days
Level: intermediate
Non-residential
Group size: 11–20

Price range: £50–£400
Prices include: Lunch
Unsuitable for children
Pets not welcome

Courses available in:

Jan	Feb	Mar	Apr	May	Jun	Jul	Aug	Sep	Oct	Nov	Dec

Georgian buildings study week in Fitzroy Square and Buckinghamshire

As a charity dedicated to preserving Georgian buildings and gardens, the Georgian Group consult on planning permission as well as facilitating talks, trips and courses. Plans for 2005 include a visit to Highgrove, a Devon country house weekend and a trip to Rome. Their annual five-day Georgian Buildings Study Week is split between Fitzroy Square and an overnight trip to a country house in Buckinghamshire. The courses take you to Sion Park, Dom Cruickshank's house in Spitalfields, the Royal Naval College and the Brooking Collection in Greenwich, with private tours around each. Members are given priority on all events, although they are open to the wider public.

Contact
Rachel Kennedy
The Georgian Group
6 Fitzroy Square
Bloomsbury
London W1T 5DX
Tel: 020 7529 8920
Web: www.georgiangroup.org.uk

Practical information
Duration: 5 days
Level: beginner &
intermediate
Residential & non-residential
Group size: 11–20
Courses available in:

Price range: £500+
Prices include: call for details
Unsuitable for children
Pets not welcome

Jan	Feb	Mar	Apr	May	Jun	Jul	Aug	Sep	Oct	Nov	Dec
				May							

Weekend courses at Shakespeare's Globe

Weekend Shakespeare Courses run throughout the Globe's theatre season (May–Sept), exploring meaning and symbolism in the plays. Globe director Mark Rylance, together with Shakespeare teacher Peter Dawkins and astrologer Laurence Hillman, mix both formal presentations and informal explorations, including magic, juggling and writing. Following the Saturday night performance (included in the price), you can sleep under the painted heavens on the stage. On Sunday, Mark gives a presentation on the deeper metaphysical ideas behind the Globe's construction. Globe Education run courses and workshops throughout the year, some aimed specifically at families. These include evening talks, morning workshops, discussions with actors, staged readings and Child's Play sessions.

Contact
Mark Rylance and Laurence Hillman
The Globe Theatre
Bankside
Southwark
London SE1 9DT
Tel: 020 7902 1400 or 020 7401 9919
Web: www.shakespeares-globe.org

Practical information
Duration: 2 days
Level: beginner &
intermediate
Residential & non-residential
Group size: 3–10
Courses available in:

Price range: £50–£100
Prices include:
accommodation
Child-friendly
Pets not welcome

Jan	Feb	Mar	Apr	May	Jun	Jul	Aug	Sep	Oct	Nov	Dec
		Mar		May		Jul		Sep			

Practical plastering for DIY enthusiasts

This plastering course is for builders and DIY enthusiasts, and is an excellent way to learn a skill that could save you substantial amounts of money. You need to be pretty fit, as plaster rendering and pebble-dashing are hands-on trades, and you will finish the weekend understanding how to replace a ceiling and how to make walls flat and ready for a paint finish. Most of the courses are aimed at professionals, equipping you for work as a freelance builder, but all are suitable for enthusiasts with a basic understanding of DIY. Other options include five-day courses in plastering, brick laying, marble plastering and rendering

Contact
Jeff Boot
Goldtrowel Plastering Organisation
Asheton Farm
Tyseas Hill
Stapleford Abbotts
Essex RM4 1JU
Tel: 01708 745935
Web: www.goldtrowel.org

Practical information
Duration: 2 days
Level: beginner &
intermediate
Non-residential

Courses available in:

Group size: 6–10
Price range: £150–£200
Unsuitable for children
Pets not welcome

Jan	Feb	Mar	Apr	May	Jun	Jul	Aug	Sep	Oct	Nov	Dec
Jan	Feb	Mar	Apr	May	Jun	Jul	Aug	Sep	Oct	Nov	Dec

CITY LIT, CENTRAL LONDON

Write a short story in a weekend

In May 2005, City Lit opens in beautiful new buildings in Covent Garden, to become the largest adult education centre in Europe. One of their most interesting courses is 'Write a Short Story in a Weekend', in June. You will be shown how to begin, develop characters, structure the story, find turning points, create themes and conflict, and set up twists, denouements and a good ending. Linda Leatherbarrow, who runs the course, is one of the UK's leading writers of short stories.

Courses
City Lit offers the biggest choice of part-time courses in the capital – from visual and performing arts to languages, computing, complementary therapies and humanities, as well as specialist areas such as speech therapy, courses for deaf people and a programme for people with learning difficulties. On the creative writing courses, many students begin with a short course and then go on to follow a longer, more in-depth study programme.

What's special?
The college is renowned for attracting skilled practitioners – artists, writers and performers – who are passionate about their subjects. A recent Government report described tutors at the City Lit as "not just experts, but the experts".

Eating & sleeping
Café on site. Restaurants: Sarastro (020 7836 0101), Majjo's Foods (020 7831 0138) and Chez Gerard at the Opera Terrace (020 7379 0666). Hotels: the Covent Garden Hotel (020 7806 1000), and One Aldwych (020 7300 1000).

Directions
Tube: Holborn or Covent Garden. Keeley Street is between Drury Lane and Kingsway.

In the area
Covent Garden (for the market and Royal Opera House), Theatreland, the British Museum, the Strand and innumerable shopping opportunities are all close to hand.

Contact
Humanities Department
City Lit
Keeley Street
Covent Garden
London WC2B 4BA
Tel: 020 7831 7831
Web: www.citylit.ac.uk
Email: infoline@citylit.ac.uk

Practical information
Duration: 2 days
Level: beginner & intermediate
Non-residential

Group size: 16–20
Price range: under £50
Unsuitable for children
Pets not welcome

Courses available in:

Jan	Feb	Mar	Apr	May	Jun	Jul	Aug	Sep	Oct	Nov	Dec

THE HANDWEAVERS' STUDIO, EAST LONDON

Loom-weaving, tapestry making, spinning and felting in London's East

Whether you want to create your own Bayeux Tapestry, or stick with a cushion cover for the church bazaar, the Tapestry Making Course at the Handweavers' Studio will set you on your way. Beginners will explore basic tapestry skills, plus more advanced texture and low-relief techniques. More experienced weavers will be able to explore source materials and discuss projects. If you want to develop a particular source material (such as pictures from postcards, magazines, sketches or photos) you can bring it along and work from it. The studio also offers weekend courses in loom weaving, tapestry weaving, spinning and felt making, alongside longer courses and day-long demonstrations.

Contact
William Jeffries
The Handweavers' Studio
29 Haroldstone Road
Walthamstow
London E17 7AN
Tel: 020 8521 2281
Email: handweaversstudio@msn.com

Practical information
Duration: 2 days
Level: beginner &
intermediate
Non-residential

Courses available in:

Group size: 6–10
Price range: £50–£100
Unsuitable for children
Pets not welcome

Jan	Feb	Mar	Apr	May	Jun	Jul	Aug	Sep	Oct	Nov	Dec

HARMONY WORKS, WEST LONDON

Create a news-based musical opera in a weekend

Harmony Works is aimed at those who like singing in the shower but have always secretly thought they were destined for something more. Day, weekend and longer workshops run throughout the year, focusing on singing and performance, mainly for thirtysomethings or older. The company is led by music and theatre professionals who between them have worked at the English National Opera, Royal Opera House and National Theatre. Options available for 2005 include song writing, singalong Shakespeare, How To Sing in Tune, Women's Voice Workshop, Love Songs for Valentine's, and a seven-day course on devising a musical theatre piece from scratch. Some children's weekend workshops are also available.

Contact
Helen Astrid
Harmony Works
61 Bollo Bridge Road
Acton
London W3 8AX
Tel: 0870 774 0486
Web: www.harmonyworks.co.uk

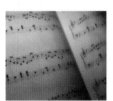

Practical information
Duration: 2 days
Level:
Non-residential
Group size: 6–15

Courses available in:

Price range: £50–£150
Prices include: lunch
Unsuitable for children
Pets not welcome

Jan	Feb	Mar	Apr	May	Jun	Jul	Aug	Sep	Oct	Nov	Dec

INCHBALD SCHOOL OF DESIGN, CENTRAL LONDON

Interior design and decoration at Inchbald

The Inchbald School of Design was founded by Jacqueline Duncan in 1960 when interior design was only just emerging as a recognised profession in Britain. Today, Inchbald offers a number of five-day and two-week courses beside their longer training courses. The five-day 'Interior Design and Decoration' course introduces students to core concepts, from ergonomics, window dressing, upholstery detailing and the transforming of light and space, to understanding colour, texture and pattern. Other courses include a five-day look at lighting design, grounding students in the use of modern lighting techniques to transform interiors, plus drawing courses. MAs and diplomas are available in each subject.

Contact
Alan Hughes
Inchbald School of Design
32 Eccleston Square
Victoria
London SW1V 1PB
Tel: 020 7630 9011 or 020 7730 5508
Web: www.inchbald.co.uk

Practical information
Duration: 2–5 days
Level: beginner
Non-residential
Group size: 6–25

Courses available in:

Price range: £200–£500+
Prices include: Lunch
Unsuitable for children
Pets not welcome

Jan	Feb	Mar	Apr	May	Jun	Jul	Aug	Sep	Oct	Nov	Dec

HEATHERLEY'S SCHOOL OF FINE ART, WEST LONDON

Printmaking workshops in Chelsea

Heatherley's was established more than 150 years ago and is the oldest independent art school in London (and the first to admit women on an equal footing to men). It was one of the first schools to offer courses to the wider public, and its Summer School (11 July to 26 Aug 2005) attracts people from all over the world for an array of one-week courses. It has excellent facilities: a dark room, beautiful studios filled with natural light, dedicated sculpture studios and an excellent arts library. The school regularly organises painting days in nearby parks and galleries, and by the river.

Courses

Heatherley's is among the few art colleges in Britain focusing purely on portraiture, figurative painting and sculpture, so the teaching is particularly specialised. Tuition is offered in Oils, Watercolours, Pastels, Portraiture, Sculpture and Printmaking; all suitable for beginners. Many evening and part-time courses are also available throughout the year.

What's special?

The Printmaking Course is all-encompassing, covering aspects of etching, aquatint, drypoint, woodcut and lithography. Print imagery will be developed both through drawing and more experimental approaches.

Eating & sleeping

Chelsea Harbour has lots of good restaurants, cafés and bars – try Aquasia (020 7376 5249) or Thai on the River (020 7351 1151). For accommodation Heatherley's has arranged a special room rate at Jurys Inn (020 7411 2200). Quote 'Heatherley's'.

Directions

Situated west of Chelsea, by Chelsea Harbour. By tube: Fulham Broadway (District Line). By bus: C3, 19, 49, 239, 319, 345, 11, 22, 328, 14, 211, 414.

In the area

Heatherley's is within striking distance of the King's Road, Chelsea Harbour Design Centre, Victoria and Albert Museum, Leighton House Museum and Linley Sambourne House.

Contact

Richard Thorneycroft
Heatherley's School of Fine Art
80 Upcerne Road
Chelsea
London SW10 0SH
Tel: 020 7351 4190
Web: www.heatherleys.org
Email: info@heatherleys.org

Practical information
Duration: 5 days
Level: beginner &
intermediate
Non-residential

Group size: 11–20
Price range: £100–£150
Unsuitable for children
Pets not welcome

Courses available in:

Jan	Feb	Mar	Apr	May	Jun	Jul	Aug	Sep	Oct	Nov	Dec

Advanced driving weekends: intensive and countrywide

If only all drivers could be made to take this course... The Skills for Life Advanced Motoring Test offers a weekend-long 'Max Driver', which teaches you how to drive more safely. This is not sold as a 'course'; it's more about self-motivation under the eye of experienced driving instructors. The test looks at hazard management and risk assessment, and once completed, your car insurance could reduce. The £85 package comprises Associate Membership of a local Institute of Advanced Motorists (IAM) group, the relevant manual, the test fee, and – once you've passed the test – your first year's IAM membership. Alternatively, there are 208 centres nationwide where you can spread the classes over several weeks.

Contact
Bryan Lunn
Institute of Advanced Motorists
IAM House
510 Chiswick High Road
Chiswick
London W4 5RG
Tel: 020 8983 1885 (CLAM)/020 8996 9620 (IAM)
Web: www.clam.org.uk or www.iam.org.uk

Practical information
Duration: 2 days
Level: intermediate &
advanced
Non-residential

Group size: 1
Price range: £50–£200
Unsuitable for children
Pets not welcome

Courses available in:

Jan	Feb	Mar	Apr	May	Jun	Jul	Aug	Sep	Oct	Nov	Dec

Researching land and manorial records to trace your family history

Genealogy has become one of the nation's favourite pastimes, and the Institute of Heraldic and Genealogical Studies provides academic facilities to support this burgeoning interest. Their 'Tracing Your Family Tree' week offers a very practical look at parish, land, manorial and census records, plus other sources, and shows how to decipher them to reveal your own family tree. Founded in 1961, the Institute was the first school dedicated to the study of genealogy. Weekend courses include Land and Manorial Records, and Intermediate Genealogy, with day courses such as Introduction to Family History and Palaeography (interpreting pre-17th-century handwriting).

Contact
Institute of Heraldic and Genealogical Studies
79–82 Northgate
Canterbury
Kent CT1 1BA
Tel: 01227 768664
Web: www.ihgs.ac.uk

Practical information
Duration: 5 days
Level: beginner &
intermediate
Residential
Group size: 6–20
Courses available in:

Price range: £200–£300
Prices include: meals &
accommodation
Unsuitable for children
Pets not welcome

Jan	Feb	Mar	Apr	May	Jun	Jul	Aug	Sep	Oct	Nov	Dec

An introduction to British sources and archives

Now in its third year, British Archives week will give an intensive introduction to the research sources available in and around London, with visits to the major national repositories, and lectures at the Institute of Historical Research. Participants will be introduced to different libraries and archives, and shown how to use their catalogues and finding aids. The programme will be reinforced by lectures, but students will have plenty of opportunity to pursue their own research interests. There will be professional historians and researchers on this course, but it is open to anyone interested in using London's research facilities. The Institute of Historical Research is part of the University of London.

Contact
Institute of Historical Research
University of London
Senate House
Malet Street
Bloomsbury
London WC1E 7HU
Tel: 020 7862 8740
Web: www.history.ac.uk/training/courses/BritArchives.html

Practical information
Duration: 5 days
Level: intermediate
Residential
Group size: 6–15

Price range: £50–£100
No lunch provided
Unsuitable for children
Pets not welcome

Courses available in:

Jan	Feb	Mar	Apr	May	Jun	Jul	Aug	Sep	Oct	Nov	Dec

THE INTERIOR DESIGN SCHOOL, NORTH LONDON

Interior design in Queen's Park

The Interior Design School's 'Introduction to Interior Design' course is for people who want to understand the design process in order to improve their living environments, and also for those considering interior design as a career. This week-long course concentrates on making over a room, while the two-week London Design Experience offers inspiration from London's top interiors and includes trips to galleries, restaurants and shops. The longer course is aimed at those with a keen interest in travel and design, but is open to all. The Interior Design School was founded in 1991 and is housed in a purpose-designed space in Queen's Park, with a big studio on the first floor, full of natural light.

Courses
The school has introduced several other one day-courses recently, on lighting, sourcing materials and designing a child's bedroom. They also have weekend courses on property renovation/refurbishment, kitchens and bathrooms respectively.

What's special?
Tutors are all working designers who have designed interiors for the likes of Liberty's and Selfridges. They know which design concepts are hot off the press and can arrange for access to them. All courses include talks from leading manufacturers and suppliers.

Eating & sleeping
Excellent cafés and delis in Salusbury Road: Baker & Spice (020 7604 3636), the Salusbury Pub (020 7328 3286) and Hugo's (020 7372 1232). Hotels: the Marriot in Maida Vale (020 7543 6000) or the more intimate House in Hampstead (020 7431 8000).

Directions
The Interior Design School is just outside the congestion-charging zone and five minutes' walk from Queen's Park tube. Buses include 36, 6, 187, 206 and 316. Brondesbury Park station is also walkable.

In the area
Queen's Park has pitch-and-putt and tennis courts. It's ten minutes by taxi to Westbourne Grove's market, boutiques and restaurants, and 20 minutes to Oxford Circus.

Contact
Iris Dunbar
The Interior Design School
22 Lonsdale Rd
Queen's Park
London NW6 6RD
Tel: 020 7372 2811
Web: www.design-school.com
Email: ideas@design-school.com

Practical information
Duration: 2–5 days
Level: beginner
Non-residential
Group size: 6–15

Price range: £150–£500+
Prices include: lunch provided
Unsuitable for children
Pets not welcome

Courses available in:

Jan	Feb	Mar	Apr	May	Jun	Jul	Aug	Sep	Oct	Nov	Dec

Darkroom technique and camera use in Islington

If you are a keen photographer looking to develop your skills, 'Darkroom Technique and Camera Use' is a popular weekend workshop covering processing, printing, print finishing, spotting and presentation. You will also get to review others' photographic work. The course looks at darkroom use, how to print from negatives (bring your own), and tips for taking better photographs. Afterwards, you are eligible for half-price darkroom use for the rest of the year. Courses are based at the Islington Arts Factory, which also has dance, music and art studios, and three galleries. Other courses include a ten-day Painting Summer School, Jazz Dance, Modern Dance, T'ai Chi, Ballet and Working with Clay.

Contact
Kriton Pantelli
Islington Arts Factory
2 Parkhurst Road
Holloway
London N7 0SF
Tel: 020 7607 0561
Web: www.islingtonartsfactory.org.uk

Practical information
Duration: 2–10 days
Level: beginner &
intermediate
Non-residential

Group size: 3–10
Price range: £50–£500+
Child-friendly
Pets not welcome

Courses available in:

Jan	Feb	Mar	Apr	May	Jun	Jul	Aug	Sep	Oct	Nov	Dec

Intensive pottery throwing with a respected commercial potter

Pottery courses are a great way to get hands-on with art and crafts. This intensive Pottery Throwing course is run by artist and potter John Dawson from his South London home. He runs one-day courses during the summer break, when the adult schools close, with intensive two-day courses by arrangement. You will learn the basics of throwing, moulding and firing clay, with all materials and lunch provided. John is a well-known commercial potter, and these courses are a wonderfully intimate way to learn from a terribly enthusiastic and knowledgeable professional. There is room for five students only.

Contact
John Dawson
47 Heathwood Gardens
Charlton
London SE7 8ES
Tel: 020 8316 1919
Email: john16749@btinternet.com

Practical information
Duration: 2 days
Level: beginner &
intermediate
Non-residential

Group size: 3–5
Price range: £100–£150
Prices include: lunch
Unsuitable for children
Pets not welcome

Courses available in:

Jan	Feb	Mar	Apr	May	Jun	Jul	Aug	Sep	Oct	Nov	Dec

Gastronomic appreciation: boulangerie courses in Marylebone

Do you want the aroma of fresh bread wafting through your kitchen every morning? Well, this popular boulangerie course at the Cordon Bleu institute shows you how. The bread-baking introduction covers flour selection, the use of fresh yeast and dough making. You will learn how to make country-style loaves, baguettes, croissants and brioche. And never fear: your creations accompany you home each day. Established in 1895, Le Cordon Bleu promotes worldwide appreciation of the culinary arts. Among other courses in London are the Chocolate Workshop, Desserts for Entertaining, Introduction to French Cuisine, Vegetarian Dinner Party and Fish Dinner Party.

Contact
Le Cordon Bleu Insitute
114 Marylebone Lane
Marylebone
London W1U 2HH
Tel: 020 7935 3503
Web: www.cordonbleu.edu/

Practical information
Duration: 3 days
Level: beginner &
intermediate
Non-residential

Group size: 6–10
Price range: £300–£400
Prices include: lunch
Child-friendly
Pets not welcome

Courses available in:

Jan	Feb	Mar	Apr	May	Jun	Jul	Aug	Sep	Oct	Nov	Dec

LEAD AND LIGHT, NORTH LONDON

Decorative glass and stained glass windows in Camden

This Stained Glass Window (Lead Work) course explains the traditional method of assembling glass into a lead light or stained glass window. You will develop your own design and adapt this into a working pattern, then cut and lead your pattern into a completed panel. The course is run by Lead and Light, a small company based in Camden Lock, which has been a working studio for over 30 years. There are a number of courses on offer, including longer ones at Easter and summer, and weekend courses throughout the year. Short courses and weekend workshops in traditional and contemporary glass-making techniques cover sandblasting, leading, painting, copper foiling and fusing.

Contact
Lynette Wrigley
Lead and Light
35A Hartland Rd
Camden
London NW1 8DB
Tel: 020 7485 0997
Web: www.leadandlight.co.uk

Practical information
Duration: 3 days
Level: beginner
Non-residential

Group size: 3-10
Price range: £150-£200
Unsuitable for children
Pets not welcome

Courses available in:

Jan	Feb	Mar	Apr	May	Jun	Jul	Aug	Sep	Oct	Nov	Dec

LEITH'S SCHOOL OF FOOD AND WINE, WEST LONDON

Cookery and wine courses in Chelsea Harbour

Leith's School of Cookery in Chelsea Harbour is one of London's most famous cookery schools. They have good links with many of London's best restaurants, and renowned chefs, cookery writers and Masters of Wine often demonstrate here. Many of the courses are for 'enthusiastic amateurs', and the week-long version is particularly comprehensive, covering topics such as pasta making, chicken boning, sauce preparation, shellfish and delicate desserts. Courses are for up to 48 people in three kitchens. Many of the one–day workshops are held over two consecutive days (Italian Cooking Saturday, followed by Thai Cooking Sunday) and could be combined in a weekend.

Contact
Judy Wilkinson
Leith's School of Food and Wine
21 St Alban's Grove
Chelsea Harbour
London W8 5BP
Tel: 020 7229 0177
Web: www.leiths.com

Practical information
Duration: 5 days
Level: beginner &
intermediate
Non-residential

Group size: 25+
Price range: £500+
Prices include: lunch
Unsuitable for children
Pets not welcome

Courses available in:

Jan	Feb	Mar	Apr	May	Jun	Jul	Aug	Sep	Oct	Nov	Dec

LEWISHAM ARTHOUSE, SOUTH LONDON

Summer pottery workshop with Shirley Stewart

A professional potter who has held exhibitions throughout the UK, Shirley Stewart has been teaching pottery since 1989. She runs courses at Lewisham Arthouse, a charitable co-operative in a Grade II listed building. All levels of experience are welcome to the ten-day Summer Pottery Workshop which immerses participants in pot making, and covers hand-building, throwing, glazing and firing. The course fee includes a certain amount of clay per day – if you go pot crazy, there's an extra charge. Apart from this there are glazing workshops, pottery-throwing workshops and children's workshops, where children can make one or two pieces to pick up at a later date. All work is bisque-fired, glazed and refired.

Contact
Shirley Stewart
Lewisham Arthouse
140 Lewisham Way
New Cross
London SE14 6PD
Tel: 020 8692 2513 (home)/020 8694 9011 (studio)
Web: www.shirli-stewart.co.uk

Practical information
Duration: 10 days
Level: beginner &
intermediate
Non-residential
Group size: 6-10

Price range: £500+
Prices include: lunch & some
clay
Child-friendly
Pets not welcome

Courses available in:

Jan	Feb	Mar	Apr	May	Jun	Jul	Aug	Sep	Oct	Nov	Dec

LONDON ACADEMY OF RADIO, FILM AND TV, NORTH LONDON

Acting masterclass at a respected media school

The London Academy was founded in 1999 by radio and media expert Andrew Parkin, and in five years has built up an impressive client list, including the BBC, Channel 4, Scottish Television and the British Film Institute. It is now one of London's most respected media schools, offering an extensive range of courses, many of which are taught by household names such as Peter Purves and Charles Brescia. It is this quality of teachers that stands the London Academy apart from its competitors. For 2005, the academy will offer a range of courses in Pembrokeshire, South Wales with the same high-quality teaching served up in beautiful surroundings.

Courses
Weekend and week-long courses include Acting, Filmmaking, Photography, Radio Production, TV Presenting, Make-up, Video Editing, Voice Training and many others; see website for the complete list.

What's special?
The one-week masterclasses on acting or TV presenting are particularly interesting. You will learn all the important techniques, gain practical experience and receive a DVD showreel of your new talent to show casting agents. Past students have gone on to work for the BBC and other well-known broadcasters.

Eating & sleeping
Novotel Euston (020 7666 9000) opposite the British Library, the Dorset Square Hotel (020 7723 7874), or the Holiday Inn by Camden Lock (020 7485 4343). For food try The Great Nepalese (020 7388 6737), Bertorelli's (020 7636 4174) by Goodge Street station, or the excellent Villandry (020 7631 3131).

Directions
London: left out of Euston Station (towards Eversholt St) and Lancing St is directly opposite the steps. Buses include 168, 390, 18, 30, 476, 73, 10, 59 and 91. Wales: see website for details.

In the area
Don't miss the British Library with its excellent exhibitions. The Camley Street Natural Park is also close and is good for birdwatching. Or head to Camden for the markets.

Contact
Andrew Parkin
London Academy of Radio, Film and TV
1 Lancing St
Euston
London NW1 1NA
Tel: 020 8408 7158
Web: www.media-courses.com
Email: talent@btconnect.com

Practical information
Duration: 2–5 days
Level: beginner,
intermediate & advanced
Non-residential

Group size: 3–10
Price range: £300–£500+
Child-friendly
Pets not welcome

Courses available in:

Jan	Feb	Mar	Apr	May	Jun	Jul	Aug	Sep	Oct	Nov	Dec

LONDON BUDDHIST CENTRE, EAST LONDON

Meditation weekend retreats with London Buddhist Centre

The London Buddhist Centre holds mediation courses, Buddhism courses and introductory day retreats in London, and weekend retreats (or longer) in London and Suffolk. The centre is one of the largest urban Buddhist Centres in the West; it opened in 1978 in a former Victorian fire station and is now part of the East End landscape. Plenty of courses are available for beginners, with something interesting on offer almost daily, throughout the year. For those who want to retreat on their own, the centre even provides two huts for absolute privacy. Courses cover a wide range of meditation and Buddhism disciplines, and several Buddhist festivals are celebrated here.

Contact
London Buddhist Centre
51 Roman Road
Bethnal Green
London E2 0HU
Tel: 0845 458 4716
Web: www.lbc.org.uk

Practical information
Duration: 2 days
Level: beginner &
intermediate
Residential & non-residential
Group size: 25+

Courses available in:

Price range: £150–£200
Prices include:
Accommodation provided if
in Suffolk
Unsuitable for children
Pets not welcome

Jan	Feb	Mar	Apr	May	Jun	Jul	Aug	Sep	Oct	Nov	Dec

LONDON COLLEGE OF COMMUNICATION, CENTRAL LONDON

Screen-printing courses in Elephant and Castle

Screen Printing is an unusual art-and-craft skill, and the London College of Communication, near the South Bank, is a well-regarded place to learn. Formerly the London College of Printing, it hosts courses in a variety of media-related subjects, from journalism and photography to advertising and design. For the screen printing course you do not require any prior knowledge, and over the weekend you will choose, prepare and print a screen artefact from start to finish. You should try to come up with your own image for the design, so have a rummage through your drawers before you arrive. Other courses include Alternative Photography, Creative Thinking, Illustration and Broadcast TV Journalism.

Contact
London College of Communication
Elephant and Castle
London SE1 6SB
Tel: 020 7514 6578
Web: www.lcc.arts.ac.uk

Practical information
Duration: 2 days
Level: beginner
Non-residential

Group size: 6–15
Price range: £100–£150
Unsuitable for children
Pets not welcome

Courses available in:

Jan	Feb	Mar	Apr	May	Jun	Jul	Aug	Sep	Oct	Nov	Dec

LONDON COLLEGE OF FASHION, CENTRAL LONDON

An introduction to footwear design and history

Spend a week learning about shoes. One of over 130 specialist courses offered at the London College of Fashion, an Introduction to Footwear Design looks at everything from understanding the foot's physiology to making mock-ups of the shoe. At the end of the week, you will have a final design, which you could then complete on the LCF's pattern and cutting course. Each of their study areas (shoes, hats, accessories, clothes, etc) has courses for all abilities. Students can choose from a vast array of subjects, from fashion design and technology to marketing and image creation. The formats vary from weekend, day and evening classes to longer professional qualifications.

Contact
Sophia Raja
London College of Fashion
20 John Princes Street
Oxford Circus
London W1G 0BJ
Tel: 020 7514 7566
Web: www.fashion.arts.ac.uk

Practical information
Duration: 5 days
Level: beginner &
intermediate
Non-residential

Group size: 25+
Price range: £300–£400
Unsuitable for children
Pets not welcome

Courses available in:

Jan	Feb	Mar	Apr	May	Jun	Jul	Aug	Sep	Oct	Nov	Dec

Down-to-earth London wine courses

The London Wine Academy aims to take the stuffiness out of wine appreciation. They offer 11 different one-day workshops and run a variety of workshops on consecutive Saturdays and Sundays. Saturday will cover the basics of grapes and regions, followed by more advanced work (such as food and wine matching) on Sunday. Tutors include many Masters of Wine and other well-known industry professionals. The academy also runs wine tours, evening tastings, six-week wine courses and a particularly lovely Italian Food and Wine Matching Day – expect to sample Tuscan sausages with a good glass of southern Italian red.

Courses
Visit their website for an up-to-date itinerary of all the different courses. Weekends planned for 2005 include 'Old and New World Wines' at the beginning and end of the year, plus 'Champagne and New World Wines', a Bordeaux and Burgundy workshop and a 'Dessert and Rhone Workshop'. Courses are £99 per day.

What's special?
The teaching is refreshingly down-to-earth – spitting your wine out after tasting is purely optional, and there's plenty of time for questions. You are also getting access to an impressive array of teachers from around the world.

Eating & sleeping
Accommodation near the Atlas: Ibis Earl's Court (020 7610 0880). Nearby Fulham has plentiful eating options – try Il Pagliaccio (020 7371 5253). Restaurants around Kensington: Itsu (020 7584 5522) and Bibendum (020 7581 5817).

Directions
The main offices are in Farringdon. Weekend courses are held at the Atlas pub (020 7385 9129), near West Brompton/Earls Court tube, The Drapers Arms in Islington or Mju Restaurnt in the Millennium Hotel (020 7437 4370 – special rates negotiated), near Knightsbridge tube.

In the area
You are close to the Royal Albert Hall, the museums of South Kensington, the markets of Notting Hill and the open spaces of Holland Park.

Contact
Leta Bester
London Wine Academy
Garden Floor
6 Coldbath Square
The City
London EC1R 5NA
Tel: 0870 1000 100
Web: www.londonwineacademy.com
Email: info@londonwineacademy.com

Practical information
Duration: 2 days
Level: beginner & intermediate
Non-residential
Group size: 11–25

Price range: £150–£200
Prices include: wine and food. Lunch often included in their wine days.
Unsuitable for children
Pets not welcome

Courses available in:

Jan	Feb	Mar	Apr	May	Jun	Jul	Aug	Sep	Oct	Nov	Dec

THE LONDON COLLEGE OF MASSAGE, NORTH LONDON

An introduction to massage for beginners in Camden

The London College of Massage's Beginners' Introduction to Massage is a weekend affair which promises an 'easy-to-learn technique for the back, neck and shoulders, head and face' plus introduction to essential oils. A maximum of 12 students ensures a high level of individual tuition; and because the college has professional affiliations with the British Massage Therapy Council and British Complementary Medicine Association, you get a thorough grounding. The college also offers a full Beginners' Course over three weekends, and other courses from Indian Head Massage and Baby Massage to Manual Lymphatic Drainage, Remedial Massage for Injuries and Thai Massage. Courses range from introductions to advanced classes.

Contact
The London College of Massage
Diorama Arts Centre
34 Osnaburgh Street
Camden
London NW1 3ND
Tel: 020 7813 1980
Web: www.massagelondon.com

Practical information
Duration: 2 days
Level: beginner, intermediate
& advanced

Non-residential
Group size: 11-15
Price range: £100-£150
Unsuitable for children
Pets not welcome

Courses available in:

Jan	Feb	Mar	Apr	May	Jun	Jul	Aug	Sep	Oct	Nov	Dec

LONDON SCHOOL OF ANIMAL CARE AND SADDLERY, GREATER LONDON

Dog-training weekends at Capel Manor

The London School of Animal Care and Saddlery offers one of the few week-long dog-care courses in London. Separation anxiety, over-dominance, aggression and obsessive-compulsive disorders are just a few of the terms explained in this insight into the canine mind. The sessions include practical work away from the couch, so come prepared with a collar and lead. The centre also offers ongoing courses, one day per week, and classes may be suitable for families. You can do two-day Puppy Care Courses, Backyard Poultry Care, Introduction to Fish Keeping... even a four-week Dog Massage Course. The school reserves the right to exclude animals that may pose a safety risk.

Contact
Paul Bryant
London School of Animal Care and Saddlery
Capel Manor College
Bullsmoor Lane
Enfield
Middlesex EN1 4RQ
Tel: 020 8366 4442
Web: www.capel.ac.uk

Practical information
Duration: 5 days
Level: beginner
Non-residential
Group size: 6-10

Price range: £100-£150
Prices include: no food, but café on site.
Child-friendly
Pet-friendly

Courses available in:

Jan	Feb	Mar	Apr	May	Jun	Jul	Aug	Sep	Oct	Nov	Dec

THE MAKE-UP CENTRE, SOUTHWEST LONDON

Make-up courses from basic to special effects

Founded almost 20 years ago, The Make-Up Centre trains professionals for stage and screen make-up, while also offering courses of more general interest. Their Basic Make-up Course can be applied to personal make-up, since it looks at methods of application and how to emphasise (or not) specific features and flaws. You can also join several of the longer courses for a week, to learn about a specific area of make-up: bridal fashion is particularly popular with non-professionals. Courses range from the year-long to shorter courses on Beauty and Fashion Make-up, Hairstylist Fashion, Film Make-up and Special Effects. Delamar Academy is the only make-up school in Britain whose graduates have gone on to win Oscars.

Contact
The Make-up Centre
The Old Church
52a Walham Grove
Fulham
London SW6 1QR
Tel: 020 7381 0213
Web: www.themake-upcentre.co.uk

Practical information
Duration: 5 days
Level: beginner
Non-residential

Group size: 6-10
Price range: £500+
Unsuitable for children
Pets not welcome

Courses available in:

Jan	Feb	Mar	Apr	May	Jun	Jul	Aug	Sep	Oct	Nov	Dec

Genealogy and other courses in a central London square

Mary Ward was a Victorian whose bestselling novels earned her fame and riches. She established the Mary Ward Settlement to provide cultural and educational opportunities to the poor, and played a key role in setting up Somerville College, Oxford's first women's college. Today, the Mary Ward Centre teaches over 7,000 students each year. One of their most interesting courses is a two-day introduction to sources for genealogical research – family records, stories, Census returns, newspapers, etc – which looks at how to access, assess and interpret these records. Other courses include computing, languages, music, and a programme designed for the over–60s, covering subjects such as bridge, creative writing, debates and dance.

Contact
Suzanna Jackson
Mary Ward Centre
Short Course Admissions
42 Queen Square
Holborn
London WC1N 3AQ
Tel: 0870 3814412
Web: www.marywardcentre.ac.uk

Practical information
Duration: 2–6 days
Level: beginner,
intermediate & advanced
Residential & non-residential
Group size: 1–5

Price range: £150–£500+
Prices include: meals &
accommodation
Child-friendly
Pets not welcome

Courses available in:

Jan	Feb	Mar	Apr	May	Jun	Jul	Aug	Sep	Oct	Nov	Dec

Understand the world around you in one of London's finest museums

The Natural History Museum is one of London's most prestigious museums, ideally placed next to the Victoria and Albert Museum. It runs a range of adult-education classes through the year, mainly on Saturdays, but also offers some weekend events based around exhibitions. Day courses planned for 2005 include 'Museum Photoshop Photography', 'Winter Gardens', 'Drawing Geological Landscapes', 'Woodlice, Millipedes and other Garden Creepy Crawlies' and a look at weeds. Weekend sessions might include painting courses, run over two consecutive weekends, looking at how to illustrate using pigments produced from natural materials. It is rare to find accessible, science-based short courses such as these.

Contact
Natural History Museum
Education Department
Cromwell Road
South Kensington
London SW7 5BD
Tel: 020 7942 5555
Web: www.nhm.ac.uk

Practical information
Duration: 2 days
Level: beginner
Non-residential
Group size: 16–20

Price range: under
£50–£100
Unsuitable for children
Pets not welcome

Courses available in:

Jan	Feb	Mar	Apr	May	Jun	Jul	Aug	Sep	Oct	Nov	Dec

Chinese brush and watercolour with the National Trust

Osterley House is set in extensive park and farm land, with gardens and neo-classical buildings. It's an inspiring place to spend a weekend and just eight miles from Piccadilly Circus. There are a number of arts weekends planned throughout the year, and you're not going to be short of inspiration setting up your easel against this beautiful setting. Subjects include Chinese Brush Painting, Watercolour Painting and Garden Painting. They vary according to which experts are available. The house has a wide-ranging educational programme, with a variety of day events. Options include guided garden tours, local history courses, and a day looking at Osterley Park's time as a guerrilla warfare training school.

Contact
Osterley House
National Trust
Jersey Road
Isleworth
London TW7 4RB
Tel: 020 8232 5052
Web: www.nationaltrust.org.uk/places/osterley

Practical information
Duration: 2 days
Level: beginner
Non-residential

Group size: 11–15
Price range: under £50
Unsuitable for children
Pets not welcome

Courses available in:

Jan	Feb	Mar	Apr	May	Jun	Jul	Aug	Sep	Oct	Nov	Dec

Writing workshops underneath the London Eye

Morley College dates back to the early 1880s, when Emma Cons was busy turning the Old Vic into one of London's most prominent theatres. Public lectures held there created a demand for more systematic instruction for local working men and women, so Samuel Morley bankrolled the opening of a college next door. Today Morley College is one of London's most prominent adult education colleges, welcoming over 15,000 students a year. Their Writing Workshops run over three separate weeks (beginner, intermediate, advanced) in July, aimed at prose writers of all experience levels. The weeks involve workshops, discussions, individual tuition and plenty of writing opportunities. Intermediate and advanced participants submit work before the course, which will be individually discussed by the Literary Consultancy, an independent group offering manuscript assessment and editorial advice.

Courses
Alongside these excellent weeks, Morley runs an impressive array of short and long courses year round in Visual Arts, Languages & Humanities, Music, Dance & Drama and Exercise & Health.

What's special?
Morley's writing workshops are very clearly targeted. You choose what level your writing is at, and the classes are designed to give inspiration and advice to allow you to progress upwards.

Eating & sleeping
The Marriott at County Hall (020 7928 5200), the Mad Hatter in Stamford St (020 7401 9222) and Days Hotel, Waterloo (020 7922 1331). Food is available in the College's excellent refectory and on the South Bank: try The People's Palace (020 7928 9999).

Directions
Near Westminster Bridge and Waterloo International station. Tube: Lambeth North, Elephant & Castle, Waterloo. Many buses.

In the area
Morley is just south of the Thames, near the South Bank, the London Eye, the National Theatre and Tate Modern. Lambeth Palace is a five-minute walk.

Contact
Morley College
61 Westminster Bridge Road
Southwark
London
Tel: 020 7450 1889
Web: www.morleycollege.ac.uk
Email: enquiries@morleycollege.ac.uk

Practical information
Duration: 5 days
Level: beginner, intermediate & advanced
Non-residential

Group size: 16–20
Price range: £50–£100
Unsuitable for children
Pets not welcome

Courses available in:

Jan	Feb	Mar	Apr	May	Jun	Jul	Aug	Sep	Oct	Nov	Dec

Floristry and flower-arranging for weddings and pleasure

Out of the Bloom emphasise that they are flower teachers, not flower sellers, and they teach flower-arranging and floristry comprehensively. Their day-long, week-long and month-long courses operate throughout the year. The week-long classes cover flowers for weddings and funerals, hand-tied flowers, loose flowers and tall vases… in fact most aspects of floristry design. Class sizes are very small, usually two teachers to five students, and Joanna will inspire you to draw on you own emotions to discover the beauty of flowers. The course covers the principles of design, and the importance of symmetry and colour co-ordination, but you will also be encouraged to use your intuition to create arrangements.

Contact
Out of the Bloom
89/91 Bayham Street
Camden
London NW1 0AG
Tel: 0207 482 3301
Web: www.outofthebloom.com

Practical information
Duration: 5 days
Level: beginner &
intermediate
Non-residential
Group size: 3–5

Price range: £500+
Prices include: lunch
Unsuitable for children
Pets not welcome

Courses available in:

Jan	Feb	Mar	Apr	May	Jun	Jul	Aug	Sep	Oct	Nov	Dec

Make the most of your digital camera

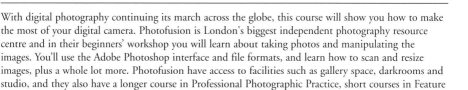

With digital photography continuing its march across the globe, this course will show you how to make the most of your digital camera. Photofusion is London's biggest independent photography resource centre and in their beginners' workshop you will learn about taking photos and manipulating the images. You'll use the Adobe Photoshop interface and file formats, and learn how to scan and resize images, plus a whole lot more. Photofusion have access to facilities such as gallery space, darkrooms and studio, and they also have a longer course in Professional Photographic Practice, short courses in Feature Writing for Photographers and Architectural Photography, and ongoing courses in Understanding the Camera and Discovering Photography.

Contact
John Phillips
Photofusion Photography Centre
17a Electric Lane
Brixton
London SW9 8LA
Tel: 020 7738 5774
Web: www.photofusion.org

Practical information
Duration: 2 days
Level: beginner &
intermediate
Non-residential

Group size: 6–10
Price range: £150–£200
Unsuitable for children
Pets not welcome

Courses available in:

Jan	Feb	Mar	Apr	May	Jun	Jul	Aug	Sep	Oct	Nov	Dec

Dance and movement in a multitude of styles in Camden

The Place is a London centre dedicated to dance and movement. You can watch, perform and learn a range of dances and related disciplines, either buying tickets for individual performances or studying up to postgraduate level. Easter Organics is an intensive week of classes, teaching styles ranging from Jazz through to Contemporary, mixed with yoga and Pilates; you choose which classes you want to take (up to four). There's also a Summer Intensive, which allows you to combine classes from an extensive range of different dance styles using both traditional and contemporary techniques.

Contact
Andy Papas
The Place
Part-time School
17 Duke's Road
Camden
London WC1H 9PY
Tel: 020 7388 8430
Web: www.theplace.org.uk

Practical information
Duration: 5 days
Level: beginner &
intermediate
Non-residential

Group size: 16–20
Price range: £50–£300
Unsuitable for children
Pets not welcome

Courses available in:

Jan	Feb	Mar	Apr	May	Jun	Jul	Aug	Sep	Oct	Nov	Dec

NATIONAL MARITIME MUSEUM, SOUTH LONDON

Maritime History Summer School: The Sea and History 1700-1805

In the year that commemorates the bicentenary of the Battle of Trafalgar and the death of Admiral Nelson, this two-week maritime history course examines the growth of oceanic trade, naval power and scientific exploration in the 18th century. Topics will include exploration, the growth of the Royal Navy, the social and technological aspects of maritime life, the slave trade, history of navigation and maritime art.

Courses
This accredited course is run jointly by the National Maritime Museum, Greenwich Maritime Institute (University of Greenwich) and King's College London. It is designed for those wishing to develop existing interests in maritime history and who may want to undertake higher study in this field. Seminars will be delivered by such distinguished maritime historians as Professors NAM Rodger, Andrew Lambert and Roger Knight, the authors of recently published seminal works on the Royal Navy and Nelson.

What's special?
Greenwich's rich maritime heritage makes it an unrivalled place in which to study maritime history – Nelson's body lay in state there before his funeral, and the town is now a World Heritage Site. As part of the nationwide 'SeaBritain' festival commemorating the Trafalgar bicentenary and Britain's wider maritime heritage, Greenwich will host various exciting events including a major National Maritime Museum exhibition, 'Nelson & Napoléon' and a Trafalgar conference. Students will be able to attend the conference's keynote lectures and dinner reception.

Eating & sleeping
Greenwich has a huge variety of restaurants, notably the Spread Eagle (020 8853 2333) and the historic Trafalgar Tavern (020 8858 2909). For accommodation, Devonport House Hotel (020 8269 5400) and the Ibis Hotel (020 8305 1177) are very close.

Directions
Mainline rail services from London Bridge to Greenwich. Docklands Light Railway: Cutty Sark. Tube to North Greenwich and bus 188. Cruises to Greenwich from Central London piers.

In the area
Greenwich's many attractions include the glorious architecture of the Queen's House and Old Royal Naval College; the Royal Observatory; National Maritime Museum; the tea clipper 'The Cutty Sark'; and picturesque Greenwich Village.

Contact
Sally Archer
National Maritime Museum
Greenwich
London SE10 9NF
Tel: 020 8312 6772
Web: www.nmm.ac.uk/openmuseum
Email: openmuseum@nmm.ac.uk

Practical information
Duration: 10 days
Level: intermediate
Non-residential

Group size: 6–20
Price range: £500+
Unsuitable for children
Pets not welcome

Courses available in:

Jan	Feb	Mar	Apr	May	Jun	Jul	Aug	Sep	Oct	Nov	Dec
						Jul					

POINT BLANK, NORTH LONDON

Learn to DJ in a weekend

Based in Islington – so plenty of bars and clubs for 'field work' – this crash course in Learning to DJ offers a fun and very different way to spend a weekend. Professional tutors, all active in the music business, teach mixing, compiling a play list and other essentials to classes ageing from 15 to 50. The longer courses leave you with a mix tape but the weekend courses are often too short; you'll have the skills to make one at home though. Decks and mixers are provided at individual work stations, as are records. Point Blank also run longer courses on music production, radio production, sound engineering, editing and song writing.

Contact
Dave Pine
Point Blank
23–28 Penn Street
Old Street
London N1 5DL
Tel: 020 7729 4884
Web: www.pointblanklondon.com

Practical information
Duration: 2 days
Level: beginner
Non-residential
Group size: 3–10

Price range: £300–£400
Child-friendly
Pets not welcome

Courses available in:

Jan	Feb	Mar	Apr	May	Jun	Jul	Aug	Sep	Oct	Nov	Dec

PRESCOTT & MACKAY SCHOOL OF FASHION AND ACCESSORY DESIGN, CENTRAL LONDON

Millinery courses in Broadway Market

Prescott & Mackay started life as a handmade-shoe company before branching into tuition in 1998. Since then they have added further courses in related subjects. For example, the two-day 'Introduction to Blocked Hats' covers techniques for constructing a 'blocked' hat in various materials, from moulding and stitching to decorative trimmings. And you will have a hat to take away at the end of it. The fee includes some very basic materials, but the main fabrics for the hats are selected and purchased individually from the shop on-site. Other subjects on offer include soft/structured bag making, pattern cutting, shoe making and corsetry.

Contact
Kirsty Prescott and Melissa Mackay
Prescott & Mackay School of Fashion and
Accessory Design
74 Broadway Market
London E8 4QJ
Tel: 020 7923 9450
Web: www.prescottandmackay.co.uk

Practical information
Duration: 2 days
Level: beginner &
intermediate
Non-residential
Group size: 2–5

Price range: £200–£300
Prices include: basic
materials
Unsuitable for children
Pets not welcome

Courses available in:

Jan	Feb	Mar	Apr	May	Jun	Jul	Aug	Sep	Oct	Nov	Dec

RACHEL CLARK'S LIFE PAINTING & DRAWING SCHOOL, EAST LONDON

Life-painting and drawing weekends with a well-known portrait artist

Rachel Clark is a well-known portrait artist who offers highly recommended portrait and life drawing classes from her East London studio. She has been teaching students of all abilities since 1976, and because she keeps her class sizes so small (max 8), they are a great way to learn skills from a successful artist. Easels and drawing boards are provided, and further materials are available to purchase (charcoal, putty rubbers, papers, fixative, turpentine and a small supply of oil paints). Besides weekend courses, Rachel offers one-week courses, Saturday life classes, corporate courses and private tuition. Classes are held at her light and airy studio not far from Canary Wharf.

Contact
Rachel Clark
Rachel Clark's Life Painting & Drawing School
25 Limehouse Cut
46 Morris Road
Bromley by Bow
London E14 6NQ
Tel: 020 7987 8776
Web: www.rachelclark.com

Practical information
Duration: 2 days
Level: beginner &
intermediate
Non-residential

Group size: 3–8
Price range: £150–£200
Unsuitable for children
Pets not welcome

Courses available in:

Jan	Feb	Mar	Apr	May	Jun	Jul	Aug	Sep	Oct	Nov	Dec

RAINDANCE, CENTRAL LONDON

Film making for beginners

Raindance holds Britain's largest independent film festival and is dedicated to promoting independent film. It runs a number of weekend courses aimed at first-time film makers. Led by Elliott Grove (Raindance founder), who has produced over 100 short films and four feature films, this particular course looks at how to make then sell a movie. You will learn how to shoot a 90-minute, 35mm colour film, with soundtrack, for as little as £10,000. Close attention will be paid to the tools available to low-budget film makers, such as lighting techniques and capturing sound, plus topics such as storyboarding and editing, and how to get investment. The company also offers a range of courses for intermediate film makers, covering techniques for writing, directing, filming, producing and editing. Some evening courses are available as well.

What's special?

The writers, directors or producers of Lock, Stock & Two Smoking Barrels, Lighthouse, Waking Ned, Sliding Doors and Memento all attended this intensive seminar before making their first films. Guy Ritchie and Matthew Vaughn met here, so make sure you're nice to your neighbour.

Eating & sleeping

Raindance recommends Grange Hotels (020 7233 7888). Food-wise, try Yauatacha (020 7494 8888) on Broadwick Street, and Randall and Aubin (020 7287 4447) and Fresh and Wild supermarket (020 7434 3179), both on Brewer Street.

Directions

Head office on Berwick Street (off Oxford St). Tube: Oxford Street, Piccadilly or Tottenham Court Road. Other venues include the London Film School (24 Shelton Street; Covent Garden tube) and elsewhere in Soho or Covent Garden.

In the area

You're in the heart of Soho, an area full of bars, restaurants and boutique shops, and within walking distance of the National Gallery, the Royal Academy, Green Park and Hyde Park.

Contact

Emma Luckie
Raindance
81 Berwick Street
Soho
London W1F 8TW
Tel: 020 7287 3833
Web: www.raindance.co.uk/courses
Email: info@raindance.co.uk

Practical information

Duration: 2 days
Level: beginner,
intermediate & advanced
Non-residential

Group size: 6–25+
Price range: £150–£300
Unsuitable for children
Pets not welcome

Courses available in:

Jan	Feb	Mar	Apr	May	Jun	Jul	Aug	Sep	Oct	Nov	Dec

Scenic art and making props for the stage at London's RADA

Spend a week studying at the Royal Academy of Dramatic Art (RADA), where Ralph Fiennes, Anthony Hopkins, et al, learnt their craft. Unlike students on the longer courses, those on the week-long courses require no experience, but places do fill up quickly. 'Making Props for the Stage' provides an overview of the skills needed by RADA staff, and then gives you the chance to try for yourself. Courses in both scenic art and props are offered, using skills such as modelling, furniture upholstery and carving. RADA offers a range of excellent day-, week- and two week- workshops, aimed at interested members of the public as well as aspiring actors.

Contact
Neil Fraser
RADA
62–64 Gower Street
Bloomsbury
London WC1E 6ED
Tel: 020 7636 7076
Web: www.rada.org

Practical information
Duration: 5 days
Level: beginner
Non-residential
Group size: 3–10

Price range: £300–£400
Lunch not provided
Unsuitable for children
Pets not welcome

Courses available in:

Jan	Feb	Mar	Apr	May	Jun	Jul	Aug	Sep	Oct	Nov	Dec

Workshops and masterclasses at the World Music Summer School

Right in the centre of London, the world-famous School of Oriental and African Studies (SOAS) hosts an annual World Music Summer School with courses in an array of arts. For Summer 2005, the courses will be Bollywood-themed, with a combination of workshops, master classes, concerts and lectures. In the past there have been courses in Cuban drumming, Noh theatre, Mongolian singing, Indian and Chinese dancing. Besides the Summer School, courses are run throughout the year from undergraduate to postgraduate levels, covering subjects as diverse as Arts and Society in Africa, Ancient Chinese Civilisation, Japanese Calligraphy and Cinemas of Asia and Africa.

Contact
School of African and Oriental Studies (SOAS)
University of London
Thornhaugh Street
Russell Square
Bloomsbury
London WC1H 0XG
Tel: 020 7898 4081
Web: www.soas.ac.uk

Practical information
Duration: 5 days
Level:
Non-residential
Group size: 3–25+

Price range: £50–£100
No lunch provided
Unsuitable for children
Pets not welcome

Courses available in:

Jan	Feb	Mar	Apr	May	Jun	Jul	Aug	Sep	Oct	Nov	Dec

Weekend workshops in screenwriting

Set up in 1983 to help writers find work in film and television, the Screenwriters' Workshop offers a number of one-and two-day courses. Weekends established for Spring 2005 include Screenwriting (12–13 March), where you will read scripts from feature films and television drama, and use writing exercises. Other topics include Writing Comedy, Producer Training and 'Does It Have Legs?' – a look at how to create a long-running series. All courses are suitable for both new and experienced writers, and take place around the country; all bookings should be directed through the London office.

Contact
Paul Gallagher
The Screenwriters' Workshop
Suffolk House
1–8 Whitfield Place
London W1T 5JU
Tel: 020 7387 5511
Web: www.screenwritersworkshop.co.uk

Practical information
Duration: 2 days
Level: beginner
Non-residential

Group size: 6–10
Price range: £50–£100
Unsuitable for children
Pets not welcome

Courses available in:

Jan	Feb	Mar	Apr	May	Jun	Jul	Aug	Sep	Oct	Nov	Dec

SHEPHERDS BOOKBINDERS, SOUTHEAST LONDON

Book-binding, restoration and box-making in Bankside

In 1998, Shepherds Bookbinders joined forces with Zaehnsdorf, one of the leading 19th-century bookbinders, and Sangorski & Sutcliffe, whose jewelled bindings are coveted by collectors worldwide. The resulting company offers Saturday courses in various aspects of bookbinding and book conservation, and weekend courses in leather restoration and refurbishment of leather bindings. For those just starting out, the most suitable would be the 'Bookbinding for Beginners' course. Classes are limited to six people and each class has a technical assistant working alongside the tutor to provide personal tuition. Courses are run from the company's large workshop in the Bankside area of London.

Contact
Linda Watts
Shepherds Bookbinders
Units 107–108,
30 Great Guildford Street
Southwark
London SE1 0HS
Tel: 020 7620 0060
Web: www.bookbinding.co.uk

Practical information
Duration: 5 days
Level: beginner
Non-residential

Courses available in:

Jan	Feb	**Mar**	Apr	May	**Jun**	Jul	Aug	Sep	Oct	**Nov**	Dec

Group size: 3–10
Price range: £200–£300
Unsuitable for children
Pets not welcome

SOTHEBY'S INSTITUTE OF ART, CENTRAL LONDON

All that glisters: the identification of material at Sotheby's

The Sotheby's Summer School offers various courses, and 'All that Glisters: The Identification of Material', under the leadership of Robert Child of the National Museums and Galleries of Wales, is one you could never find elsewhere. Workshop participants consider various rare and not-so-rare materials, exploring the identification and uses of materials such as ivory, tin, gold and plastic. Copies and fakes are also assessed and inferior methods explored. No scientific knowledge is necessary and students are encouraged to bring objects in for discussion. Summer School 2005 also includes 'Jewellery Design', 'Making Jewels', 'Introduction to Fine Art', and 'Introduction to Contemporary Art'.

Contact
Sotheby's Institute of Art
30 Oxford Street
West End
London W1D 1AU
Tel: 020 7462 3232
Web: www.sothebysinstitutelondon.com/

Practical information
Duration: 5 days
Level: beginner &
intermediate
Non-residential
Group size: 11–15

Courses available in:

Jan	Feb	Mar	Apr	May	**Jun**	**Jul**	Aug	Sep	Oct	Nov	Dec

Price range: £400–£500
No lunch provided.
Unsuitable for children
Pets not welcome

SPREAD THE WORD, SOUTH EAST LONDON

The mind's eye: writing and the place of the imagination

Spread The Word was established in 1995 to aid the development of new writing in London. It offers a wide range of events for writers, including reading groups, creative writing workshops, seminars, one-to-one feedback sessions and live literature seasons twice a year. Not to be missed are the week-long poetry and fiction course for experienced writers, run in conjunction with the Arvon Foundation's Totleigh Barton Centre, and numerous weekends looking at, among other topics, comic timing, memoir writing and fiction writing. They attract numerous well-known writers as tutors, including, recently, Booker-prize nominee Romesh Gunesekera.

Contact
Nick Murza
Spread the Word
77 Lamberth Walk
Lamberth
London SE11 6DX
Tel: 020 7735 3111
Web: www.spreadtheword.org.uk

Practical information
Duration: 2–7 days
Level: beginner
Non-residential

Courses available in:

Jan	Feb	**Mar**	**Apr**	**May**	Jun	Jul	Aug	**Sep**	**Oct**	Nov	Dec

Group size: 11–15
Price range: under £50
Unsuitable for children
Pets not welcome

Building conservation and repair in Spitalfields

The Society for the Protection of Ancient Buildings was founded by William Morris in 1877 to counteract the destructive 'restoration' of medieval buildings by many Victorian architects. These days SPAB holds weekend courses at the 18th-century Artworkers' Guild in Bloomsbury, London and in several wonderful locations around the country, where home owners and people with a general interest in historic buildings can learn more about how such properties function and how to repair them.

Courses

Other Society activities include six-day courses aimed largely at professionals, held at its Georgian headquarters in Spitalfields, plus 'Introduction to Lime' day courses for builders (20 per cent of all British buildings were constructed with lime and cement repairs can be damaging), and a series of lectures on repair, conservation and architectural history.

What's special?

The society fields a range of speakers, including Marianne Suhr from the BBC's 'Restoration' series. The weekend courses are meticulously delivered – and you'll get a chance to do some repairs. The Home Owners' Courses for 2005 are in London, Devon, the Scottish Borders, Derbyshire, Kent and Brecon, with the building traditions of the surrounding area being a component of each course.

Eating & sleeping

There are plenty of places to eat in Bloomsbury. Abeno (020 7405 3211) is an interesting Japanese restaurant, while the Townhouse Brasserie (020 7636 2731) has good, inexpensive French food. Nearby hotels include the smart Montague on the Gardens (020 7637 1001) and the feng shui inspired Myhotel, Bloomsbury (020 7667 6000).

Directions

The London weekend course is held at the Artworkers' Guild, 6 Queen Square, WC1N 3AT. Nearest tubes: Russell Square and Holborn. Many buses to Bloomsbury Square and Russell Square.

In the area

Bloomsbury is packed with Georgian squares (such as Bedford Square and Russell Square), making it a lovely area to explore on foot. The British Museum houses some of London's finest artefacts, and there are many antique book shops in the area.

Photo ©Mark Barrett

Contact

Isla Campbell
Society for the
Protection of Ancient Buildings (SPAB)
37 Spital Square
Spitalfields
London E1 6DY
Tel: 020 7377 1644
Web: www.spab.org.uk
Email: isla@spab.org.uk

Practical information

Duration: 2 days
Level: beginner & intermediate
Non-residential
Group size: 25+

Price range: £100–£200
Prices include: Lunch
Unsuitable for children
Pets not welcome

Courses available in:

Jan	Feb	Mar	Apr	May	Jun	Jul	Aug	Sep	Oct	Nov	Dec

ST JOHN'S AMBULANCE, LONDON
Learn to save lives with St John Ambulance

St John Ambulance has over 900 years of history, dating back to Jerusalem. If you are interested in learning first aid, there is no better forum. With venues around the country, their basic lifesaving course requires two eight-hour classes, often run on consecutive days. This introductory course will teach you how to handle an emergency situation and covers vital lifesaving and resuscitation techniques. You receive certification at the end. Students who complete the introductory course can undertake the Lifesaver Plus module, which covers further techniques. Courses are also available in first aid for babies and children, plus safety in the workplace. The website has details of all venues.

Contact
Sally Davidson
St John Ambulance
27 St John's Lane
London EC1M 4BU
Tel: 08700 10 49 50/020 7324 4220
Web: www.sja.org.uk/training/courses/

Practical information
Duration: 2 days
Level: beginner
Non-residential

Group size: 11–15
Price range: under £50
Unsuitable for children
Pets not welcome

Courses available in:

Jan	Feb	Mar	Apr	May	Jun	Jul	Aug	Sep	Oct	Nov	Dec

TASTING PLACES, WEST LONDON
Masterclasses in food and wine with the capital's celebrated chefs

Tasting Places was founded 12 years ago, to celebrate the notion that enjoyment of food and drink should be one of life's essentials. To that end, they offer the chance to learn cooking skills from some of London's most celebrated chefs. These day-long classes, with Michelin-starred chefs from Nobu, Bibendum, Moro and other leading London restaurants, are an amazing opportunity to work with, and learn from, the head chefs in their own kitchens. Classes will be informative and fun, with recipe packs and lunch or dinner included. The company also offers cooking holidays in Italy, France, Spain and other European locations. They hope to reinstate Oxfordshire cooking weekends in 2006.

Contact
Sarah Robson or Sara Schwartz
Tasting Places
Unit 108 Buspace Studios
Conlan Street
London W10 5AP
Tel: 020 7460 0077
Web: www.tastingplaces.com

Practical information
Duration: 2 days
Level:
Residential & non-residential
Group size: 6–15
Price range: £150–£300

Prices include: lunch or dinner
Unsuitable for children
Pets not welcome

Courses available in:

Jan	Feb	Mar	Apr	May	Jun	Jul	Aug	Sep	Oct	Nov	Dec

TRIYOGA, NORTH LONDON
Yoga workshops in Primrose Hill and farther afield

A variety of yoga workshops run throughout the year in TriYoga's beautiful space in North London's Primrose Hill. One of the best things about the set-up is that there are classes taking place between 6.30am and 10pm virtually every day. They run some weekend workshops here, plus plenty of day workshops and longer courses, and the guest teachers are among the best in the world. The centre also runs yoga weekends and retreats outside London. These are usually run by Simon Low, a TriYoga director and one of London's most respected teachers, in places such as Yorkshire's Ampleforth Abbey. The weekends combine active yoga with meditation and breathing.

Contact
Simon Low
TriYoga
6 Erskine Road
Primrose Hill
London NW3 3AJ
Tel: 020 7483 3344
Web: www.triyoga.co.uk

Practical information
Duration: 2 days
Level: beginner,
intermediate & advanced
Residential & non-residential
Group size: 16–25+

Price range: under
£50–£150
Child-friendly
Pets not welcome

Courses available in:

Jan	Feb	Mar	Apr	May	Jun	Jul	Aug	Sep	Oct	Nov	Dec

UNIVERSITY COLLEGE, CENTRAL LONDON

London's Art and Architecture

History of Art is a department of University College, London, teaching a wide variety of undergraduate, postgraduate and short courses. Their popular Summer School offers two weeks of courses during which at least half the teaching takes place in galleries, museums and places of architectural interest.

Courses
The week-long courses cover topics including Italian Renaissance art in London, public and private architecture, and aspects of Modern Art. Course director Gilly Hatch is a freelance lecturer who works for the National Gallery, Wallace Collection and Courtauld Institute Gallery, as well as teaching in UCL's History of Art Department.

What's special?
The Summer School is designed for anyone wanting to know more about London's staggering array of international art and historical and modern architecture. Expect to cover the city's parks, gardens, housing, post-1945 sculptures, archaeological sites and historical artefacts.

Eating & sleeping
UCL has its own refectory and bars. Or try Pied a Terre (020 7636 1178) in Charlotte Street. For accommodation try Myhotel Bloomsbury (020 7636 0076), the Gower House Hotel (020 7636 4685) and the Crescent Hotel (0870 752 2235). Ask about student accommodation.

Directions
Gower Street runs parallel to Tottenham Court Road in central London. Nearest tubes include Goodge Street and Warren Street. Buses include 10, 24, 29, 73 and 134. The department is located in Gordon Square.

In the area
UCL's Bloomsbury location is perfect for a history of art student: the Percival David Foundation for Chinese Art is a few doors away; the British Museum and the National Gallery are just up the road. Classes are often held in these and other museums.

Contact
Gilly Hatch
University College, London
History of Art Summer School
43 Gordon Square
Camden
London WC1E 6BT
Tel: 020 7679 3000
Web: www.ucl.ac.uk/art-history/summerschools.htm
Email: hoa-summerschool@ucl.ac.uk

Practical information
Duration: 5 days
Level: beginner,
intermediate & advanced
Non-residential
Group size: 11–15

Price range: £300–£400
Prices include: lunch on the
first day; party on the final
night.
Unsuitable for children
Pets not welcome

Courses available in:

Jan	Feb	Mar	Apr	May	Jun	Jul	Aug	Sep	Oct	Nov	Dec

THE WALLACE COLLECTION, CENTRAL LONDON

Practical art classes at one of the city's little-known treasures

As if being one of London's most special galleries was not enough, the Wallace Collection also offers practical art classes. The two-day Still Life Workshop looks at 17th-century Dutch paintings, exploring the qualities and surfaces of the foods and fruits, and examining other commonly used still-life motifs. In the first session, you make studies for a still life of your own, using a selection of black and white materials. The next day you turn these objects into a more finished piece of work using coloured pastels. The Collection's Education Department offers a range of courses from one-day workshops and lectures to postgraduate studies in the History and Business of Art.

Contact	**Practical information**	Group size: 6–15
Emma Bryant	Duration: 2 days	Price range: £50–£100
The Wallace Collection	Level: beginner	Unsuitable for children
Hertford House	Non-residential	Pets not welcome
Manchester Square		
London W1U 3BN	Courses available in:	
Tel: 020 7563 9500		
Web: www.wallacecollection.org		

Courses available in:

Jan	Feb	Mar	Apr	May	Jun	Jul	Aug	Sep	Oct	Nov	Dec

WIMBLEDON SCHOOL OF ART, SOUTHWEST LONDON

A hands-on week of jewellery making in Wimbledon

Wimbledon School of Art was founded in 1890 and has a reputation as one of the capital's major art schools. Their 'Simply Earrings, Bracelets and Necklaces' course offers a hands-on week of jewellery making, teaching basic techniques –suitable for beginners– that could be taken on to further study. You learn basic stringing and wire-wrapping techniques, how to use the tools, and how to assemble your masterpiece, whether hoop or drop earrings, bracelets or necklaces. There are other week-long courses in arts, photography and fashion, and courses at foundation, undergraduate, postgraduate and doctorate level in fine art, stage and screen design, special effects design and costume design. They also run a popular Summer School.

Contact
Wimbledon School of Art
Palmerston Road
Wimbledon
London SW19 1PB
Tel: 020 8408 5000
Web: www.wimbledon.ac.uk

Practical information	Price range: £200–£300
Duration: 5 days	No lunch provided
Level:	Unsuitable for children
Non-residential	Pets not welcome
Group size: 3–10	

Courses available in:

Jan	Feb	Mar	Apr	May	Jun	Jul	Aug	Sep	Oct	Nov	Dec

ZEN SCHOOL OF SHIATSU, EAST LONDON

Intensive shiatsu massage courses in Shoreditch

Shiatsu is a hands-on Japanese healing art which aims to re-balance the body and mind. For those wanting to learn more, the Zen School offers five-day intensive shiatsu courses five times a year. And since the school is a member of the General Shiatsu Council, any certification you receive will be recognised externally. Their ongoing evening and weekend classes don't even have to be booked in advance: just turn up five minutes before and join at any part of the cycle. Intensive courses, however, need to be reserved. They also offer Beginners' Intensive T'ai Chi, Taoist Meditation for Beginners and Zen Insight Meditation for Beginners.

Contact	**Practical information**	Group size: 11–20
Kris	Duration: 5 days	Price range: £300–£400
Zen School of Shiatsu	Level: beginner	Unsuitable for children
19–21 Phipp Steet	Non-residential	Pets not welcome
London EC2A 4PN		
Tel: 0700 078 1196/0700 078 1195	Courses available in:	
Web: www.learn-shiatsu.co.uk		

Jan	Feb	Mar	Apr	May	Jun	Jul	Aug	Sep	Oct	Nov	Dec

Oxford

Maidstone

Southampton

Folkstone

Brighton Hastings

The South East

This wealthy part of England has some sumptuous lovely countryside, much of it of a more 'homely' scale and style than you will find in, say, the north of England and Scotland. The South East has historic towns and cities by the dozen, from Winchester and Canterbury to Oxford, Chichester and Brighton, and the intervening countryside is littered with historic houses and sumptuous gardens. Accessibility to the region is straightforward, and all the courses are within easy striking distance of London.

ANDREW JOHN STUDIO, EASTBOURNE

Watercolour by the sea

Throughout the year, Andrew John runs short painting breaks with a full programme of watercolours, food and wine. Students can stay in his spacious Edwardian home and look forward to tailored demonstrations, plenty of painting practice and individual advice, home-cooked meals and, in summer, excursions to paint by the sea or in the surrounding countryside. Guests are invited to turn up the night before the course for a welcoming drink and meal with other students, followed by a demonstration. Non-painting partners are also welcome to stay and share full-board accommodation at 50 per cent of the normal course fee.

Contact
Andrew John
Andrew John Studio
23 Baslow Rd
Eastbourne
E Sussex BN20 7UL
Tel: 01323 736745
Web: www.andrewjohn.co.uk

Practical information
Duration: 2–4 days
Level: beginner,
intermediate & advanced
Residential & non-residential
Group size: 1–10

Price range: £200–£300
Prices include: meals &
transport.
Unsuitable for children
Pets not welcome

Courses available in:

Jan	Feb	Mar	Apr	May	Jun	Jul	Aug	Sep	Oct	Nov	Dec

ART ON TILES STUDIO, WALBERTON, NR ARUNDEL

Dutch Delft-style tile-painting

The Dutch town of Delft, famous for developing ceramic glazing, is also synonymous with blue and white tile designs. These weekends introduce the history of Delft tile painting, while giving students the chance to produce a number of their own tiles. This is a detailed skill, but with a maximum of seven students per class, even the most unpainterly will end up with tiles they enjoy. Completed pieces need to be fired overnight, so anything finished on the second day will be posted. The course fee includes lunches and a meal on Saturday evening and B&B accommodation is offered at an extra charge of £30.

Contact
Jonathan Waights
Art on Tiles Studio
2 Orchard Terrace
The Street
Walberton
Nr Arundel
W Sussex BN18 0PH
Tel: 01243 552346
Web: www.artontiles.co.uk

Practical information
Duration: 2 days
Level: beginner,
intermediate & advanced
Non-residential
Group size: 3–10

Price range: £100–£150
Prices include: meals &
materials
Unsuitable for children
Pets not welcome

Courses available in:

Jan	Feb	Mar	Apr	May	Jun	Jul	Aug	Sep	Oct	Nov	Dec

THE BASKETMAKERS' ASSOCIATION, HURST

Basket-making on Dinton Pastures

Incorporating eight lakes, two rivers, black swans and 350 acres of woodland and meadow, Dinton Pastures Country Park is an ex-gravel extraction site turned beauty spot. The park offers several basket-making courses throughout the year, where participants learn to weave willow and rushes into unique creations. There will also be discussions about willow management and the traditional methods to manage it for basketry and wildlife. The courses are run by Christine Brewster, a seasoned tutor, who also runs workshops from her studio near Reading and around the country. Previous experience is not a requirement for these weekends, but those looking to improve their skills are also welcome.

Contact
Grace Gray
The Basketmakers' Association
Dinton Pastures Country Park
Nr Wokingham
Berkshire RG10 0TH
Tel: 01344 354443
Web: www.basketassoc.org

Practical information
Duration: 2 days
Level: beginner &
intermediate
Non-residential
Group size: 6–15
Courses available in:

Price range: under £50
Prices include: materials
Unsuitable for children
Pets not welcome

Jan	Feb	Mar	Apr	May	Jun	Jul	Aug	Sep	Oct	Nov	Dec

BRIGHTON INDEPENDENT PRINTMAKING, BRIGHTON

Traditional and contemporary print crafts in Brighton

Brighton Independent Printmaking was established in 2000 to help firm up the future of traditional printmaking techniques, and support the development of new printmaking technology. In continuation of this commitment, the studio offers a comprehensive programme of workshops on all aspects of printing and printmaking. They have weekends in Collagraph, Etching and Lino Cutting prints, as well as courses in techniques from Letterpress, the original method of printing newspapers, through to Photo Etch, a modern printmaking approach that uses photo images. Basic materials are included in the tuition fee, and specialist tools and materials are available to buy.

Contact
Brighton Independent Printmaking
Module B1
Enterprise Point
Melbourne St
Brighton
E Sussex BN2 3LH
Tel: 01273 691496
Web: www.brightonprintmaking.co.uk

Practical information
Duration: 2 days
Level: beginner,
intermediate & advanced
Non-residential

Group size: 3–10
Price range: £50–£150
Child-friendly
Pets not welcome

Courses available in:

Jan	Feb	Mar	Apr	May	Jun	Jul	Aug	Sep	Oct	Nov	Dec

BRIGITTE TEE, LYMINGTON

Everything you ever wanted to know about wild mushrooms

Brigitte Tee is the UK's leading wild mushroom expert and chef. The programme of the two day-breaks depends on the season (best from August to January) but usually includes morning tuition, lunch, afternoon foraging in the New Forest, a gourmet mushroom-based meal in the evening and a night in the Gorse Meadow Guest House, followed by a second day's un-guided mushroom forage at no extra charge. Mushrooms will be inspected at the end of each day and poisonous varieties extracted. Out of concern for the forest's wildlife, neither small children nor pets are allowed. All uncontaminated, edible mushrooms that participants have picked can be taken home.

Contact
Brigitte Tee
Mrs Tee's Wild Mushrooms
Gorse Meadow
Sway Rd
Lymington
Hampshire SO41 8LR
Tel: 01590 673354
Web: www.wildmushrooms.co.uk

Practical information
Duration: 2 days
Level: beginner &
intermediate
Residential & non-residential
Group size: 6–15
Price range: £50–£150

Prices include: meals,
accommodation &
mushrooms
Child-friendly
Pets not welcome

Courses available in:

Jan	Feb	Mar	Apr	May	Jun	Jul	Aug	Sep	Oct	Nov	Dec

BUTSER ANCIENT FARM, WATERLOOVILLE

Introduction to archaeological excavation & recording

Butser Ancient Farm is part museum, part research project. Their archaeological aims are to discover and teach what life was like in Roman and prehistoric eras, and their findings have reshaped understanding of prehistoric life. Research undertakings include building ancient structures in line with contemporary techniques, and growing and processing Roman crops according to the technology of the time. The learning programme includes a two-day introduction to basic archaeology where each participant is given one square metre of training trench to excavate. They will also learn about the methods and equipment used in archaeological discovery and recording, as well as receiving guidance in interpreting finds.

Contact
Chris Ellis and Joyce Herve
Butser Ancient Farm
Nexus House
Gravel Hill
Waterlooville
Hampshire PO8 0QE
Tel: 023 9259 8838
Web: www.butser.org.uk

Practical information
Duration: 2 days
Level: beginner
Non-residential

Group size: 6–15
Price range: £50–£100
Unsuitable for children
Pets not welcome

Courses available in:

Jan	Feb	Mar	Apr	May	Jun	Jul	Aug	Sep	Oct	Nov	Dec

CLARITY BOOKS & WORKSHOPS, CARISBROOKE

Retreats and workshops on the Isle of Wight

Clatterford House is a spacious family home hosting workshops and retreats, where visitors are respected as personal guests. The workshops explore emotional intelligence and help guests to develop a sense of their own spiritual natures, enabling more fulfilling relationships and lives. Psychologist and hypnotherapist Sylvia Clare has written a number of self-development and parenting books and is an acknowledged leader in her field. The courses that she runs with David Hughes, a musician and meditation instructor, draw on the foundation principles of metaphysics, shamanism and Buddhism, as well as contemporary psychological methods. The workshops help people reshape aspects of their lives, focusing on awareness of self and others.

Courses
Courses include 'Auras, Chakras and Energy', 'Self Esteem in Families', 'Maximise Your Potential' and 'Love and Relationships'. Meditation is incorporated into all workshops, as are trips to the beach and castle. All workshops and retreats are based on unconditional confidentiality, honesty and acceptance, to allow people to explore any aspect of their lives. Course durations are negotiable.

What's special?
Sylvia and David offer around 30 different themes for their workshops and organise six set weekends per year. The rest of the time, course content is open to negotiation, with participants choosing from retreat time, gentle meditation and individual therapy. They also offer relationship counselling retreats.

Eating & sleeping
Participants can stay on site or in B&B accommodation nearby. Meals are made by Sylvia, who holds a diploma in advanced cookery; they will be vegetarian and, usually, organically home-grown.

Directions
Ferries connect the Isle of Wight to Southampton, Portsmouth and Lymington, all of which are served by trains from London. The organisers will pick up and drop off at the ferry. By car, Clatterford is on the B3323 south of Newport.

In the area
Clatterford House has wonderful views of Carisbrooke Castle and the beautiful Bowcombe Valley. There are plenty of local walking opportunities including the start of the Tennyson Trail.

Contact
Sylvia Clare
Clarity Books & Workshops
Clatterford House
Clatterford Shute
Carisbrooke
Isle of Wight PO30 1PD
Tel: 01983 537338
Web: www.claritybooks.co.uk
Email: sylvia.clare@btinternet.com

Practical information
Duration: 2 days
Level: beginner,
intermediate & advanced
Residential & non-residential
Group size: 1–10

Price range: £150–£200
Prices include: meals &
accommodation
Child-friendly
Pet-friendly

Courses available in:

Jan	Feb	Mar	Apr	May	Jun	Jul	Aug	Sep	Oct	Nov	Dec

CLARIDGE HOUSE, DORMANSLAND

Quaker retreat for non-Quakers

Claridge House is a Quaker-run retreat centre in the village of Dormansland. The 150-year-old house runs a residential programme of relaxing weekends most of which are not religiously based, and which are simply open to anyone interested in spirituality and learning in a peaceful environment. There are 12 bedrooms (which can either be single occupancy or shared), two lounges and a Quiet Room. Full board is provided, and all the home-cooked meals are vegetarian and vegan. The course programme includes both weekend and mid-week breaks, featuring such varied themes as an Introduction to Homeopathy, Chinese Brush Painting, Creative Writing, Alexander Technique, Singing, Meditation and Circle Dance.

Contact
Claridge House
Dormansland
Dormans Rd
Lingfield
Surrey RH7 6QH
Tel: 01342 832150
Web: www.claridgehouse.quaker.eu.org

Practical information
Duration: 2–4 days
Level: beginner &
intermediate
Residential
Group size: 6–20
Courses available in:

Price range: £100–£300
Prices include: meals &
accommodation
Unsuitable for children
Pets not welcome

Jan	Feb	Mar	Apr	May	Jun	Jul	Aug	Sep	Oct	Nov	Dec

CUTTING EDGE FOOD & WINE SCHOOL, ROBERTSBRIDGE

Wine-tasting weekends and cookery courses

The Cutting Edge Food & Wine School's remit is this: take London's top chefs and wine experts, put them in a 16th-century Sussex farmhouse, and unleash their teaching skills on the general public. The experts include Tom Kline (Jamie Oliver's boss at The River Café), Curtis Stone (Head Chef at Marco Pierre White) and Henri Chapon (Europe's third-ranked sommelier). As well as running a large number of mid-week cookery courses, both at general foundation level and as themed cookery days, the school offers a wine-tasting weekend. The property includes a vineyard producing sparkling wine, so the emphasis is on champagne, sparkling wines and red wines.

Contact
Cutting Edge Food & Wine School
Ryth & Mike Edwards
Hackwood Farm
Robertsbridge
Sussex GU9 8EN
Tel: 01580 881281
Web: www.cuttingedgefoodandwineschool.co.uk

Practical information
Duration: 2–5 days
Level: beginner &
intermediate
Residential & non-residential
Group size: 6–20

Courses available in:

Price range: £100–£500
Prices include: meals &
accommodation
Unsuitable for children
Pets not welcome

Jan	Feb	Mar	Apr	May	Jun	Jul	Aug	Sep	Oct	Nov	Dec

THE CUTTING GARDEN, ROBERTSBRIDGE

Organic gardening with Sarah Raven

Sarah Raven's Cutting Garden is a gardening and cookery school run from Perch Hill Farm in East Sussex. As well as a number of one-day courses taught by published chefs and gardeners, Sarah runs seasonally themed, two-day, vegetable-gardening courses. The autumnal Grow Your Own Veg course starts with the fundamentals of designing a vegetable garden, then covers planting dates and suggestions for which vegetables and salads to grow. Other gardening themes include ornamental vegetable growing, vegetables for beginners, and garden design; for non-gardeners there's painting, basket-making and cookery. Home-grown lunches provided.

Contact
Sarah Raven
The Cutting Garden
Perch Hill Farm
Brightling
Robertsbridge
Sussex TN32 5ER
Tel: 0845 0504849
Web: www.thecuttinggarden.com

Practical information
Duration: 2 days
Level: beginner &
intermediate
Non-residential
Group size: 6–25

Courses available in:

Price range: £150–£300
Prices include: (meals &
lunch only)
Unsuitable for children
Pets not welcome

Jan	Feb	Mar	Apr	May	Jun	Jul	Aug	Sep	Oct	Nov	Dec

THE DAIRY STUDIO, LEWES

Landscape painting at the Dairy Studio

The Dairy Studio is on the rural fringes of Lewes at Old Malling Farm. It is a well-equipped art studio, incorporating the studios of two working artists and providing a large space from which classes and workshops are run. Susie Monnington-Dasent, the studio's founder, has been running workshops since 1991 and her artwork reflects her interest in light and colour within landscapes. The studio has a strong 'green' ethos, with natural wool insulation. It has recently been renovated to make the most of its natural northern light and to provide space both for teaching and Susie's own work. The studio also has excellent print facilities and a large etching press.

Courses
The emphasis is on drawing, painting and print-making, and weekends are themed by subject matter – flowers, life drawing, the sea etc – with inspiration drawn from the surrounding countryside. All levels of experience can be catered to, from absolute beginners to degree-holders looking for new approaches. Susie runs a number of other courses including installations, plus one-day courses in landscapes, life drawing or print workshops, where a variety of print processes can be explored.

What's special?
The seasonal Landscape Painting class is a particular pleasure. Students go onto the South Downs and practise in remote areas which are only accessible to the Dairy Studio, producing around four or five small paintings in any chosen media.

Eating & sleeping
The Shelleys Hotel (01273 472361) in Lewes and Kington Cottage B&B (01273 858431) in Itford. For food, Bill's café/deli in Lewes (01273 476918) and the Hungry Monk restaurant in Jevington (01323 482178).

Directions
Take A26 from Lewes (Uckfield direction). Left at traffic lights into Church Lane, through Malling, past the police headquarters. Right into Church Lane/Old Malling Way. Left after half a mile, over old railway, and on to the Dairy Studio.

In the area
It's a beautiful area for walking and wildlife-spotting, destined to become a National Park. Lewes, with its castle and history, and Brighton, with its pier and shopping, are both near.

Contact
Susie Monnington-Dasent
The Dairy Studio
Old Malling Farm
Lewes
E Sussex BN7 2DY
Tel: 01273 858438
Web: www.dairystudio-artcourses.co.uk
Email: susiemd@btinternet.com

Practical information
Duration: 2–6 days
Level: beginner,
intermediate & advanced
Non-residential
Group size: 3–15

Price range: under
£50–£150
Prices include: some
materials
Child-friendly
Pet-friendly

Courses available in:

Jan	Feb	Mar	Apr	May	Jun	Jul	Aug	Sep	Oct	Nov	Dec

DIMBOLA LODGE MUSEUM, FRESHWATER BAY

Photographic courses in Julia Margaret Cameron's former home

A range of photography courses are organised by this foundation, based at Dimbola Lodge Museum, which is dedicated to the photographic work of Julia Margaret Cameron. Born in Calcutta in 1815, she lived in Europe and South Africa before moving to the Isle of Wight in 1869. Here she bought Dimbola Lodge from a smuggler and converted the hen house into a photography studio and the coal hole into her dark room.

Courses

Cameron's work is celebrated in the range of photography courses that Dimbola offers to both amateurs and professionals. 2005 courses include a wildlife photography Masterclass with Gary d'Aquitaine (4th June, £100) landscape photography with Charlie Waite (30th July, £150) and Koo Stark's 'Opening the Eye' (TBC, £100). Portrait photographer Chris Burfoot will also hold several weekend courses during the year, and there will also be weekend courses in darkroom techniques.

What's special?

Dimbola gives you the rare opportunity to try out some historic photographic processes. There are workshops in albumen, callitype, cyanotype and gum bichromate printing, alongside workshops in general photography techniques, from pinhole cameras through to digital software.

Eating & sleeping

Accommodation is available at Ruskin Lodge (01983 756604) and the Sandpipers Hotel (01983 758500), where many rooms have sea views. For food, try the Fat Cat on the Bay restaurant or the Red Lion pub (01983 754925) at Freshwater. The museum has a tea room.

Directions

Freshwater Bay is on the western tip of the Isle of Wight, off the A3055, two miles from Yarmouth. A car ferry runs between Southampton and East Cowes; passenger ferries between Southampton and Cowes, Lymington and Yarmouth, Portsmouth and Fishbourne, and Portsmouth and Ryde.

In the area

There is a beach by Freshwater Bay, plenty of golf courses, riding stables, the Tennyson Trail for good hiking and lots of wonderful coastal footpaths. Cowes Week is a particular draw.

Contact

Mary Jennings
Dimbola Lodge Museum
Terrace Lane, Freshwater Bay
Isle of Wight PO40 9QE
Tel: 01983 756814
Web: www.dimbola.co.uk
Email: mary@dimbola.freeserve.co.uk

Practical information
Duration: 2 days
Level: beginner &
intermediate
Non-residential

Group size: 11–15
Price range: £100–£150
Child-friendly
Pets not welcome

Courses available in:

Jan	Feb	Mar	Apr	May	Jun	Jul	Aug	Sep	Oct	Nov	Dec

DENMAN COLLEGE, ABINGDON
Learning with the Women's Institute

A Georgian house set in 17 acres of gardens and countryside, this well-established, residential course centre is run by the Women's Institute. Having upheld 'diversity' as the watchword when designing its varied programme of short courses, Denman has now opened to non-members. The college actively appreciates the perspectives brought by students who are not WI members. And while Denman does run workshops in subjects stereotyped as the preserve of the WI (lace making, mah-jong, flower arranging), it also offers courses in topics such as theatre history, Celtic design, public relations and garden design. Denman has disabled facilities, though you should advise of requirements when booking.

Contact
Amanda Roach
Denman College
Marcham
Abingdon
Oxfordshire OX13 6NW
Tel: 01865 391991
Web: www.womens-institute.co.uk/college

Practical information
Duration: 2–5 days
Level: beginner,
intermediate & advanced
Residential & non-residential
Group size: 2–10

Price range: £100–£400
Prices include: meals &
accommodation
Unsuitable for children
Pets not welcome

Courses available in:

Jan	Feb	Mar	Apr	May	Jun	Jul	Aug	Sep	Oct	Nov	Dec

THE EARNLEY CONCOURSE, CHICHESTER
Residential study breaks by the sea

The Earnley Concourse combines purpose-built modern facilities and buildings with the history of 18th-century Earnley Place. The centre is specifically geared towards residential study breaks in comfortable surroundings, and boasts state-of-the-art equipment and studios, as well as a vast programme of courses across music and art disciplines. When residents are not learning, they can use the on-site swimming pool, games rooms, bar and snooker room and ten acres of grounds. Alternatively, the sea is a short walk away, and it's a few miles to the Roman town of Chichester. Earnley prides itself on its home-cooked food, and non-participating partners are welcome to stay. There are also week-long summer schools.

Contact
Gwen Ryan
The Earnley Concourse
Earnley
Chichester
W Sussex PO20 7JL
Tel: 01243 670392
Web: www.earnley.co.uk

Practical information
Duration: 2–7 days
Level: beginner,
intermediate & advanced
Residential & non-residential
Group size: 6–15
Courses available in:

Price range: £100–£500
Prices include: meals &
accommodation
Unsuitable for children
Pets not welcome

Jan	Feb	Mar	Apr	May	Jun	Jul	Aug	Sep	Oct	Nov	Dec

ELDA ABRAMSON, EASTBOURNE
Ink-painting and tapestry in an Eastbourne studio

Elda Abramson is an illustrator, painter and tapestry weaver. She lives and works on the South Coast, running regular workshops in ink painting and the occasional tapestry weaving week from her spacious Eastbourne studio. These embody the idea that guided practice is as important as basic talent in the development of painting skills and a sense of colour. Both beginners and improving painters looking to extend their knowledge are welcome on her ink-painting weekends, with special workshops in landscape and life drawing also on offer for those with some previous experience in ink. Lunch is included in the fee, and students will receive a list of recommended B&Bs upon booking.

Contact
Elda Abramson
The Studio
9a Old Orchard Rd
Eastbourne
E Sussex BN21 1DD
Tel: 01323 648494
Web: www.elda-abramson.com/courses/eastbourne.htm

Practical information
Duration: 2 days
Level: beginner,
intermediate & advanced
Non-residential
Group size: 6–15

Price range: £100–£150
Prices include: meals &
materials
Unsuitable for children
Pets not welcome

Courses available in:

Jan	Feb	Mar	Apr	May	Jun	Jul	Aug	Sep	Oct	Nov	Dec

THE EMBEX STUDIO, NEW MILTON

Papermaking and traditional crafts in Hampshire

Elli Woodsford combines the crafts of papermaking, textiles, machine sewing, origami, dyeing and traditional arts into fantastically unusual, creative courses. Recent two-day adventures include making a book out of your own handmade paper, the idea being to teach students how to incorporate dried flowers and other natural materials into papermaking, while also focusing on machine stitching a silk paper book cover. Another popular two-day course is based on creating a medieval tile panel. Participants learn how to use walnut shell to dye natural fabrics, and then go on to design and make a panel based on authentic medieval tiles found at Winchester, Beaulieu and Netley Abbey.

Contact
Elli Woodsford
The Embex Studio
46 Barton Court Road
New Milton
Hampshire BH25 6NR
Tel: 01425 617650
Email: embexstudio@yahoo.com

Practical information
Duration: 2 days
Level: beginner,
intermediate & advanced
Non-residential
Group size: 3–10

Price range: £50–£100
Prices include: meals &
materials
Unsuitable for children
Pets not welcome

Courses available in:

Jan	Feb	Mar	Apr	May	Jun	Jul	Aug	Sep	Oct	Nov	Dec

EMBROIDERERS' GUILD, HAMPTON COURT PALACE

Embroidery at Hampton Court Palace

The Embroiderers Guild, a charity dedicated to the history, appreciation and study of all things stitched, runs a varied programme of weekday workshops at their premises in the grounds of Hampton Court Palace. The main courses are embroidery-related, with each workshop themed on a design technique, fabric, colour or motif. Recent versions include Stencilling on Fabric, Flowers in Stitch and Transparency (which explored the use of gauzy materials). However, the Guild also offers less obvious courses on, for example, drawing and plastic art. They have a list of local B&B accommodation, materials and refreshments are not included in the fee.

Contact
Dorothy Tucker
Embroiderers' Guild
Apt 41
Hampton Court Palace
Surrey KT8 9AU
Tel: 020 8943 1229
Web: www.embroiderersguild.com

Practical information
Duration: 2–5 days
Level: beginner,
intermediate & advanced
Non-residential

Group size: 6–20
Price range: £50–£150
Unsuitable for children
Pets not welcome

Courses available in:

Jan	Feb	Mar	Apr	May	Jun	Jul	Aug	Sep	Oct	Nov	Dec

EVOLUTION ARTS, BRIGHTON

Mosaic-making by the sea

Evolution Arts is a Brighton pit stop for recreational learning in the arts, music and alternative health. Located two minutes from the sea, but running courses and workshops all over the city, Evolution also offers a few weekend courses. There's a regular Mosaic Weekend, where participants explore the potential for turning household objects into mosaic work. Tuition in the simplest techniques is given, and basic materials are provided, although students should bring items they would like to practise on. Among the alternative health workshops, there are Life Coaching weekends where participants learn techniques to instigate change in their lives, and creativity-tapping courses based on dream interpretation.

Contact
Ben Dew
Evolution Arts
2 Sillwood Terrace
Brighton
E Sussex BN1 2LR
Tel: 01273 204204
Web: www.evolutionarts.co.uk

Practical information
Duration: 2 days
Level: beginner
Non-residential
Group size: 6–15

Price range: £50–£100
Prices include: (materials)
mosaic course
Unsuitable for children
Pets not welcome

Courses available in:

Jan	Feb	Mar	Apr	May	Jun	Jul	Aug	Sep	Oct	Nov	Dec

EMERSON COLLEGE, FOREST ROW

Summer and weekend courses in creative arts and self-development

Emerson College was founded in the early 1960s as an adult education college based on the work of Rudolf Steiner, combining social, psychological and environmental ideas into a creative approach to education. Their programme of courses is concerned with the environment, self development and what they call 'social and artistic renewal' and has groundings in story-telling, creative writing and performance. The college is set in the Sussex countryside and incorporates 15 acres of land.

Courses
'Lifeways' in July is a very popular course for families, with crèches and camps for children, and artistic and study groups for adults. There are many courses in storytelling throughout the summer such as 'Storytelling in the Celtic World', and several summer courses in sculpture, as well as a week of oil painting. There are also courses in biodynamic organic gardening and herbalism, while 'With Art and Soul' gives a general introduction to the college's work.

What's special?
Poetry Otherwise is a week-long series of workshops and readings for poets of all levels of experience, which emphasises freeing up the individual's creativity. There are a number of guest speakers, and students will be encouraged to read their work aloud in groups.

Eating & sleeping
During the summer, most participants stay on site, where meals reflect Emerson's commitment to biodynamic and organic farming. Otherwise there is Brambletye Hotel (01342 824144), Ashdown Park Hotel (01342 824988) or B&Bs. For simple pizza, try Java and Jazz (01342 826699).

Directions
Train to East Grinstead then taxi or 291 bus (first stop after Post Horn Lane; half-mile walk to college). By car: A12 to Forest Hill; B2110 towards Hartfield; 1.5 miles to college on your left.

In the area
Ashdown Forest is the setting for the Winnie the Pooh stories. Standen House is an arts and crafts house designed by Phillip Webb and decorated by William Morris.

Contact
Emerson College
Forest Row
E Sussex RH18 5JX
Tel: 01342 822238
Web: www.emerson.org.uk
Email: mail@emerson.org.uk

Practical information
Duration: 2–6 days
Level: beginner & intermediate
Residential & non-residential
Group size: 6–20

Price range: £50–£400
Unsuitable for children
Pets not welcome

Courses available in:

Jan	Feb	Mar	Apr	May	Jun	Jul	Aug	Sep	Oct	Nov	Dec
				May	Jun	Jul	Aug				

FISHING BREAKS, NETHER WALLOP, STOCKBRIDGE

Fly-fishing at Nether Wallop Mill

These fly-fishing foundation courses take place at Nether Wallop Mill, Hampshire, a fishing school with 15 years' experience. Fully equipped and well situated to make the most of both stream and lake fishing, the school gives hands-on tuition in all aspects of trout fishing. Students will get fishing as soon as possible, since the emphasis is on gaining confidence and skills through practical learning. There will be tuition in selecting the right tackle, casting, hooking and landing a fish, and many other considerations throughout the course. No more than four students are taken at any one time, to allow for close personal instruction.

Contact
Fishing Breaks Ltd
The Mill
Heathman St
Nether Wallop
Stockbridge
Tel: 01264 781988
Web: www.fishingbreaks.co.uk/school.htm

Practical information
Duration: 2 days
Level: beginner &
intermediate
Non-residential

Group size: 1–5
Price range: £200–£300
Unsuitable for children
Pet-friendly

Courses available in:

Jan	Feb	Mar	Apr	May	Jun	Jul	Aug	Sep	Oct	Nov	Dec

HANDSPUN EXOTICS, MAIDENHEAD

Tailor-made spinning, dyeing and felting breaks

Sue McNiven is a spinner with 20 years' experience and a world record holder for the longest thread ever made. She spins the wool of her own cashmere rabbits and teaches the skill to others. Classes can be geared towards students' specific requirements, or Sue will suggest themes for those with a general spinning interest. The beginners' course gives a comprehensive introduction to spinnable fibres, covering purchasing, preparation, using a spinning wheel, and finished yarns. Spinners with experience may be more interested in the courses covering exotic fibres or specialist techniques. Charged by the day, students may specify their preferred dates. Lunch can be provided if requested in advance.

Contact
Sue MacNiven
Handspun Exotics
34 College Rise
Maidenhead
Berkshire SL6 5BP
Tel: 01628 412548
Web: www.handspun-exotics.co.uk

Practical information
Duration: 2–4 days
Level: beginner,
intermediate & advanced
Non-residential

Group size: 1–5
Price range: £100–£300
Unsuitable for children
Pets not welcome

Courses available in:

Jan	Feb	Mar	Apr	May	Jun	Jul	Aug	Sep	Oct	Nov	Dec

HERBS AT WALNUT, HAMPTON HILL

Using herbs nutritionally and medicinally

Penelope Ody is a herbalist with many years of experience and study, both in Britain and China. She runs day courses in how to use herbs medicinally and nutritionally, with the option of taking different courses on consecutive days. The more theoretical courses, such as 'Herbs and Healthy Eating', or the 'Herbal Traditions' day provide an overview of the uses and properties of herbs in certain contexts, and practical advice on how to incorporate the lessons in your daily life. There are also more hands-on workshops where participants make their own herbal creams and ointments, or remedies for specific ailments. Penelope has a few B&B rooms.

Contact
Penelope Ody
Herbs at Walnut
Walnut Cottage
Hampton Hill
Upper Swanmore
Hampshire SO32 2QN
Tel: 01489 819055
Web: www.herbcourses.co.uk

Practical information
Duration: 2 days
Level: beginner
Residential & non-residential
Group size: 3–10
Price range: £50–£150
Courses available in:

Prices include: meals &
lunch often included
Unsuitable for children
Pets not welcome

Jan	Feb	Mar	Apr	May	Jun	Jul	Aug	Sep	Oct	Nov	Dec

FELICITY FAIR THOMPSON, SANDOWN

Writing workshops on the Isle of Wight

This summer writing course accepts a maximum of five students to enable intimate group workshopping sessions and allow each individual some one-on-one tuition. Each day consists of three hours of discussion, where themes addressed include story shape, characterisation, rewriting and editing, as well as approaches to your own creativity and imagination. The rest of the day is open time for writing and exploring the Isle of Wight. Accommodation is provided in the house of Felicity Fair Thompson, course organiser, filmmaker and creative writing tutor. A help-yourself breakfast is included, but no other meals. In spring Felicity also organises An Introduction to Screenwriting: two intensive, linked and non-residential weekends providing skills for writing short films (supported by the UK Film Council and Screen South). In October there's the flagship Writers' Weekend Conference (see below).

What's special?
Boasting a range of seminars, lectures and panel-led discussion groups, the Writers' Weekend Conference brings together experts, professionals and budding writers. There are workshops on everything from writing for children's television to finding an agent. One-to-one sessions enable writers to discuss their work with an objective mentor. £230 residential; £130 non-residential.

Eating & sleeping
The Trouville Hotel in Sandown is the conference hotel. The two spring weekends are non-residential. Summer-course students stay in Felicity's cliff-path home. For food: Saffrons Restaurant in Shanklin (01983 861589) and Clancy's Café Bar (01983 401551) in Sandown.

Directions
Ferries from Southampton, Lymington and Portsmouth, then there's a train to Sandown (conference) or Lake (spring and summer courses). Drivers should take the A3055 to Sandown.

In the area
Apart from the beaches and cliff walks, there is plenty to enjoy on the island such as Queen Victoria's Osborne House, the Needles and the thatched cottages of Godshill.

Contact
Felicity Fair Thompson
39 Ranelagh Rd
Sandown
Isle of Wight
Tel: 01983 407772
Web: www.writeplot.co.uk
Email: felicity@writeplot.co.uk

Practical information
Duration: 3–5 days
Level: beginner,
intermediate & advanced
Residential & non-residential
Group size: 1–5

Price range: £100–£300
Prices include: meals &
accommodation
Unsuitable for children
Pets not welcome

Courses available in:

Jan	Feb	Mar	Apr	May	Jun	Jul	Aug	Sep	Oct	Nov	Dec

FLUX 'N' FLAME, MOCKBEGGAR, RINGWOOD

Jewellery making by the New Forest

This jewellery workshop is located in the village of Mockbeggar on the edge of the New Forest. The courses aim for a relaxed, creative atmosphere where participants of all abilities can learn at their own pace while experimenting with techniques for crafting jewellery. Jess Dickson, who trained in jewellery, and Al Marshall, who is a metal sculptor, run the courses and will cover the basics of soldering, stone setting and forging, but tuition in more unusual techniques is also available. One of the workshop's specialities is helping people to design and make their own wedding rings, and Jess and Al have just made their own! Students build confidence on a practice ring before creating the final one. Materials are not included, but the workshop has a range of gold, silver, copper and semi-precious stones for sale.

What's special?

The maximum number of students on any course is six, and since both Jess and Al will teach, this means real flexibility in terms of the projects and techniques that students can undertake and learn.

Eating & sleeping

Chewton Glen in New Milton (01425 375341) or Picket Hill House B&B in Ringwood (01425 476173). The Three Lions Inn in Stuckton (01425 652489) has serious food; the Red Shoot in Ringwood (01425 475792) something more informal.

Directions

A31 to Ringwood, then A338 towards Salisbury. Turn right before The Old Beams pub. Left at lane end, and Cherry Tree House is 3rd on right. Or National Express coach to Ringwood, X3 bus to Ibsley, then walk to house.

In the area

The New Forest offers plenty for walkers and wildlife enthusiasts. Stonehenge, Avebury, the National Motor Museum at Beaulieu and the ornamental gardens at Exbury are all nearby.

Contact

Jess Dickson & Al Marshall
Cherry Tree House
Gorley Road
Mockbeggar
Ringwood
Hampshire
Tel: 01425 461182
Web: www.fluxnflame.co.uk
Email: aj2kad@yahoo.co.uk

Practical information

Duration: 2–4 days
Level: beginner &
intermediate
Non-residential
Group size: 1–10

Price range: £100–£300
Prices include: meals &
lunch only
Unsuitable for children
Pets not welcome

Courses available in:

Jan	Feb	Mar	Apr	May	Jun	Jul	Aug	Sep	Oct	Nov	Dec

Outdoorsy and craft courses in country houses

Ten miles from the Sussex coast, Abingworth Hal, Thakeham, is a country house hotel whose grounds sprawl over eight acres of parkland. It is one of the bases for the music, dance, arts and cultural courses run by HF Holidays. Participants come to relax – note the heated swimming pool and proximity of a golf course – while also learning about anything from Digital Photography and Belly Dancing to Cartoon Drawing and T'ai Chi. HF Holidays owns similar properties all over the country, literally from the Isle of Wight to the Isle of Arran. Each country house has its own broad programme of learning breaks, and walking breaks are run from each property.

Contact
Chris Helps
HF Holidays
Imperial House
Edgware Rd
London NW9 5AL
Tel: 020 8905 9556
Web: www.hfholidays.co.uk

Practical information
Duration: 3-5 days
Level: beginner &
intermediate
Residential
Group size: 6-20

Price range: £150–£400
Prices include: meals &
accommodation
Child-friendly
Pets not welcome

Courses available in:

Jan	Feb	Mar	Apr	May	Jun	Jul	Aug	Sep	Oct	Nov	Dec

Yoga and mosaics at Hourne Farm

This annual break is a collaboration between Liz de Ath of Brighton-based Inspired Mosaics, and yoga teacher Simon Owen. They offer a relaxing weekend combining mosaic-making (a Zen-like activity in itself) with interludes of yoga and meditation. It takes place every August at Hourne Farm, a charity-run property dedicated to workshops. The farm is surrounded by 100 acres of farmland and woodland on the Kent–Sussex border near Tunbridge Wells. Two nights' accommodation is provided on site and meals will be home-cooked vegetarian, created on the farm's self-catering facilities. Inspired Mosaics also runs mosaic weekends in Brighton; for more details of Simon Owen's yoga holidays, go to www.yoga-breaks.com.

Contact
Liz de Ath
Inspired Mosaics
5a St John's Place
First Avenue
Brighton & Hove
E Sussex BN3 2FJ
Tel: 01273 775350
Web: www.inspiredmosaics.co.uk

Practical information
Duration: 2 days
Level: beginner,
intermediate & advanced
Residential
Group size: 6–25

Price range: £100–£150
Prices include: meals &
accommodation
Unsuitable for children
Pets not welcome

Courses available in:

Jan	Feb	Mar	Apr	May	Jun	Jul	Aug	Sep	Oct	Nov	Dec

Travel photography for beginners

This is a course specifically designed for those wanting to improve the quality of their holiday photos. Students will spend time exploring the aspects of light and composition that affect their pictures, as well as learning some practical camera mechanics. Both theoretical discussion and actual practice are included in the course, which is led by Doug McKinlay, a professional travel photographer whose work is regularly published in national newspapers and abroad. He will also give advice to those interested in getting their pictures published. Accommodation is not included in the fee, but is available at the course venue, while Oxford itself has plenty of choice for avid B&Bers.

Contact
i-to-i
Woodside House
261 Low Lane
Leeds
W Yorkshire LS18 5NY
Tel: 0870 787 2375
Web: www.weekendtravelphotography.com

Practical information
Duration: 2 days
Level: beginner
Non-residential

Group size: 11–20
Price range: £200–£300
Unsuitable for children
Pets not welcome

Courses available in:

Jan	Feb	Mar	Apr	May	Jun	Jul	Aug	Sep	Oct	Nov	Dec

LE MANOIR AUX QUAT' SAISONS, GREAT MILTON

Cookery at Raymond Blanc's hotel

Raymond Blanc's Le Manoir is the only country house hotel and restaurant in the UK to obtain and retain two Michelin stars. L'Ecole de Cuisine was added in 1991 to give foodies a chance to learn the secrets of the kitchens. The fee for the two-day courses covers two nights' accommodation and all meals, including a seven-course Menu Gourmand each evening. The Fish and Seafood course focuses on every aspect of fish cookery, from visiting fishmongers to preparation and filleting. Raymond is particularly passionate about the Vegetarian Cuisine course, which features many signature dishes, as well as a tour of the hotel's enormous organic herb garden.

Contact
Le Manoir aux Quat' Saisons
Church Rd
Great Milton
Oxford
Oxfordshire OX44 7PD
Tel: 01844 278881
Web: www.manoir.com

Practical information
Duration: 2 days
Level: beginner &
intermediate
Residential
Group size: 3–10

Price range: £500+
Prices include: meals &
accommodation
Unsuitable for children
Pets not welcome

Courses available in:

Jan	Feb	Mar	Apr	May	Jun	Jul	Aug	Sep	Oct	Nov	Dec

LESLEY GEORGE, SOUTHSEA

Creative embroidery and machine sewing in Southsea

Lesley George is a Southsea-based fashion designer specialising in creative embroidery and sewing machine use, and she runs a number of weekend courses that explore their possibilities and techniques. These are for people who want to expand their sewing machine skills, and students are asked to bring their own machines to the classes. (There are, however, two machines available for hire). 'Working with Velvets' looks at ways of transfer printing, foiling, burning, embossing and stitching into velvets with a view to creating a set of cards or a small bag. In addition to her roster of stitching classes, Lesley also runs workshops in pattern cutting and garment design.

Contact
Lesley George
21 Fawcett Rd
Southsea
Hampshire PO4 0BZ
Tel: 023 9275 1988
Web: www.lesleygeorge.designer.btinternet.co.uk

Practical information
Duration: 2 days
Level: beginner,
intermediate & advanced
Non-residential

Group size: 3–10
Price range: £50–£100
Child-friendly
Pets not welcome

Courses available in:

Jan	Feb	Mar	Apr	May	Jun	Jul	Aug	Sep	Oct	Nov	Dec

THE LITTLE SHOE WORKSHOP, NEW MALDEN

Making a pair of handmade shoes

This course provides an opportunity to enthusiastic followers of fashion and anyone else who has ever wanted to handmake their own pair of shoes. Using the straightforward elegance of the classic pointy-toed, two-inch-high mule as a template, students are given free creative rein to design and put together a unique pair of shoes in two days. Brides-to-be are invited to make their own wedding shoes. Small classes mean that participants can be guided through the process step-by-step and should come away with some knowledge of traditional cobbling techniques and the confidence to pursue the hobby at home. A list of nearby accommodation is available.

Contact
Kirsty Prescott
The Little Shoe Workshop
Unit 238 Kingspark Buisness Centre
152-178 Kingston Rd
New Malden
Surrey KT3 3ST
Tel: 020 8540 1300
Email: Prescottkirsty@hotmail.com

Practical information
Duration: 2 days
Level: beginner &
intermediate
Non-residential
Group size: 6–15

Price range: £150–£200
Prices include: all materials
Unsuitable for children
Pets not welcome

Courses available in:

Jan	Feb	Mar	Apr	May	Jun	Jul	Aug	Sep	Oct	Nov	Dec

LOW IMPACT LIVING INITIATIVE, WINSLOW

Sustainable living near the Chilterns

The Low-Impact Living Initiative is an undertaking that aims to respect the balance between humans and their environment. Based at the Redfield Community, a programme of weekend courses forms part of a large variety of activities and sustainable-living projects. Among them are an Introduction to Herbalism, DIY for Beginners, Beekeeping, Wind and Solar Energy, and How to Build an Earth Oven. There is also a regular course that serves as a general introduction to Low-Impact Living. Saturday evening activities depend on the weather: either a barbecue or a trip to the local pub. Arrival by bicycle or public transport is encouraged, so there's a £5 levy for cars.

What's special?
The introductory bee-keeping course gives a good theoretical and practical grounding to those interested in keeping a hive. It covers basic health and safety, plus how to start and manage a hive. Participants receive teaching on bees and plants, bee behaviour and swarming, and basic aspects of honey extraction and production. There will be opportunities to handle bees too.

Eating & sleeping
Participants will be housed in a converted stable whose facilities include a solar-powered shower, home-built beds, compost toilets and central heating. Meals are home-cooked and vegetarian, and much food is produced organically on site.

Directions
The community is based just outside the Buckinghamshire town of Winslow. Full directions will be sent out on booking.

In the area
The community is an interesting place in itself, comprising orchards, wood and farmland. The surrounding Buckinghamshire countryside is also a treat for ramblers, very near the Chiltern Hills and featuring many thatched cottages.

Contact
Low Impact Living Initiative
Redfield Community
Winslow
Buckinghamshire
Tel: 01296 714184
Web: www.lowimpact.org
Email: lili@lowimpact.org

Practical information
Duration: 2 days
Level: beginner
Residential
Group size: 6–25

Price range: £100–£200
Prices include: meals & accommodation
Child-friendly
Pets not welcome

Courses available in:

Jan	Feb	Mar	Apr	May	Jun	Jul	Aug	Sep	Oct	Nov	Dec

Drawing and painting the Hampshire countryside and coast

Magic Flute Artworks run a variety of drawing and painting holidays, each designed for a different level of expertise – including many for beginners. The classes are led by Bryan Dunleavy, an experienced adult educator and painter. Weekend courses focus on technique and are themed by medium: acrylics, watercolours or pastels. If the weather is good, students will paint outside, with the Hampshire coast and countryside for inspiration. For those who have mastered the fundamentals, there are five-day holidays themed by subject matter: Shore & Sky, Buildings or Landscape. Students either stay in the Dunleavys' spacious house or in a nearby B&B, although there is a non-residential option if wanted.

Contact
Bryan Dunleavy
Magic Flute Artworks
231 Swaniwck Lane
Lower Swanick
Southampton
Hampshire SO31 7GT
Tel: 01489 570283
Web: www.magicfluteartworks.co.uk/courses.htm

Practical information
Duration: 2–5 days
Level: beginner &
intermediate
Residential & non-residential
Group size: 3–10

Courses available in:

Jan	Feb	Mar	Apr	May	Jun	Jul	Aug	Sep	Oct	Nov	Dec

Price range: £100–£400
Prices include: meals &
accommodation
Unsuitable for children
Pets not welcome

Aga workshops with Mary Berry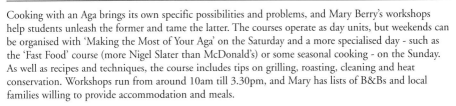

Cooking with an Aga brings its own specific possibilities and problems, and Mary Berry's workshops help students unleash the former and tame the latter. The courses operate as day units, but weekends can be organised with 'Making the Most of Your Aga' on the Saturday and a more specialised day - such as the 'Fast Food' course (more Nigel Slater than McDonald's) or some seasonal cooking - on the Sunday. As well as recipes and techniques, the course includes tips on grilling, roasting, cleaning and heat conservation. Workshops run from around 10am till 3.30pm, and Mary has lists of B&Bs and local families willing to provide accommodation and meals.

Contact
Mary Berry
Watercroft
Church Road
Penn
Buckinghamshire HP10 8NX
Tel: 01494 816535
Web: www.maryberry.co.uk

Practical information
Duration: 2 days
Level: beginner &
intermediate
Non-residential
Group size: 11–21

Courses available in:

Jan	Feb	Mar	Apr	May	Jun	Jul	Aug	Sep	Oct	Nov	Dec

Price range: £150–£300
Prices include: meals
Unsuitable for children
Pets not welcome

Oil painting with Peter Turner

Peter Turner is a well-travelled artist who has lived, painted, taught and exhibited all over the world. He now runs regular painting and photo-editing workshops from his studio in Berkshire. The classes are aimed primarily at beginners – particularly his watercolour workshops which introduce students to the effects of paper choice, colour, planning and speed. The oil painting course is also for the less experienced, and covers what equipment to buy/avoid, how to use paints, and how to work without creating a mess. Peter is passionate about painting and believes that more people should be doing it. These workshops are his way of spreading this enthusiasm. Lunch provided each day.

Contact
Peter Turner
Marsh Studio
126 Strongrove Hill
Hungerford
Berkshire RG17 0SJ
Tel: 01488 681366
Web: www.anglowebs.com

Practical information
Duration: 2–5 days
Level: beginner &
intermediate
Residential & non-residential
Group size: 3–10
Courses available in:

Jan	Feb	Mar	Apr	May	Jun	Jul	Aug	Sep	Oct	Nov	Dec

Price range: £100–£400
Prices include: meals &
accommodation
Unsuitable for children
Pets not welcome

MISSENDEN ABBEY, GREAT MISSENDEN

Learning in the beautiful Chilterns

Missenden Abbey can trace its roots back to 1133, when it was founded as a working monastery. Since that time it has served as both aristocratic home – it was heavily 'Gothicised' in the 19th century – and, post-1947, adult learning centre. The abbey sits in ten acres of parkland in the Chiltern village of Great Missenden and delivers an innovative programme of courses backed up by first-class facilities and tutors. The building incorporates a library, sauna and bar, and participants can be accommodated on site, with meals included.

Courses
There are around ten courses running every weekend, and for those wanting more depth there are week-long courses at the Easter and Summer schools. The range of courses is absolutely vast: Chinese Painting, Textiles, Honiton Lace, Creative Writing, Celtic Design, Drawing, Singing etc. Course fees range from £35 (one-day tuition only) to £550. Prices indicated below are all-inclusive rates. Please ring for the detailed brochure.

What's special?
Following the building of two new art rooms and a dark room, Missenden Abbey has also introduced a series of courses which take place midweek, on one day a week, over six weeks. The range of courses offered includes watercolours, upholstery, basketry, calligraphy, machine embroidery and many more exciting subjects. You can easily do one course on Mondays and another on Tuesdays.

Eating & sleeping
There are 56 rooms on site, all with en-suite bathrooms, phones and broadband. All meals are provided in the restaurant. Meals for non-residents are also available at weekends and during the Easter and Summer Schools.

Directions
30 miles north-west of London on the A413. M40 and M25 are just 20 minutes away. Or train from London Marylebone to Great Missenden, then a seven-minute walk.

In the area
There are National Trust sites such as Waddesdon Manor and Chenies Manor nearby, plus Amersham, Beaconsfield and various pretty villages and walks around the Chilterns.

Contact
Missenden Abbey Information Centre
Great Missenden
Buckinghamshire HP16 0BD
Tel: 0845 0454040
Web: www.adultlearningbcc.ac.uk
Email: adultlearning@buckscc.gov.uk

Practical information
Duration: 2–5 days
Level: beginner,
intermediate & advanced
Residential & non-residential
Group size: 6–15

Price range: £150–£500+
Prices include: meals &
accommodation
Unsuitable for children
Pets not welcome

Courses available in:

Jan	Feb	Mar	Apr	May	Jun	Jul	Aug	Sep	Oct	Nov	Dec

Weaving workshops on an Oxfordshire nature reserve

Janet Phillips shines a light into the complex world of weaving with a number of different workshops at her studio in this Oxfordshire nature reserve. Whether students are starting out or looking for guidance, Janet offers expertise, flexibility and small classes. Most classes are themed by technique or weaving structure, some are focused on design or on dyeing, and some are determined by finished product, with rug and scarf tuition suggested. In the introductory course, students use the simplest weaves to get a feel for the craft and ensure they can finish a cushion cover in the weekend. Lunches and a home-cooked supper on Saturday are an extra £22.50.

Contact
Janet Phillips
Natural Time Out
Warden's House
Bix Bottom
Henley-on-Thames
Oxfordshire RG9 6BL
Web: www.janetphillips.clara.net

Practical information
Duration: 2 days
Level: beginner,
intermediate & advanced
Non-residential
Group size: 1–10

Courses available in:

Jan	Feb	Mar	Apr	May	Jun	Jul	Aug	Sep	Oct	Nov	Dec

Price range: £50–£150
Prices include: meals &
materials
Child-friendly
Pets not welcome

Birdwatching, botanical and natural history holidays

This relaxed natural history tour explores what Nature Trek suggest is England's most significant inland wildlife habitat. The diversity of the New Forest means that all six species of British reptile live here, and the region also boasts a variety of birds, butterflies and dragonflies. With dusk and daytime walks, participants will be encouraged to learn about, marvel at and photograph the bird life and uniquely local bog flora that they will inevitably encounter. Led by expert ornithologists and botanists, Nature Trek wildlife holidays take place around the world and they also have a more botany-focused weekend in Hampshire in June. Both breaks include accommodation in a local hotel.

Contact
Naturetrek
Cheriton Mill
Cheriton
Alresford
Hampshire SO24 0NG
Tel: 01962 733051
Web: www.naturetrek.co.uk

Practical information
Duration: 3 days
Level: beginner &
intermediate
Residential
Group size: 6–15

Courses available in:

Jan	Feb	Mar	Apr	May	Jun	Jul	Aug	Sep	Oct	Nov	Dec

Price range: £200–£300
Prices include: meals &
accommodation
Unsuitable for children
Pets not welcome

Falconry on the Isle of Wight

Appuldurcombe House, an 18th-century Baroque mansion, is part of a 300-acre estate which also incorporates a falconry centre and self-catering cottages on the south side of the Isle of Wight. The Falconry Centre's weekend course introduces students to the birds of prey and the equipment and techniques for handling them. Each day's programme concentrates on flying one type of bird, so that by the end students will have experience of both hawk and falcon, and an understanding of the different approaches for each. Lunch is included, and accommodation for students and their families can be arranged in one of the estate's cottages. Five-day courses also available.

Contact
Owl & Falconry Centre
Appuldurcombe Farm
Wroxhall
Isle of Wight PO38 3EW
Tel: 01983 852484
Web: www.appuldurcombe.co.uk

Practical information
Duration: 2–5 days
Level: beginner &
intermediate
Non-residential
Group size: 3–15
Courses available in:

Jan	Feb	Mar	Apr	May	Jun	Jul	Aug	Sep	Oct	Nov	Dec

Price range: £100–£400
Prices include: meals &
lunch only
Unsuitable for children
Pets not welcome

Porcelain restoration courses in Oxfordshire

Taught by Michaela Coppola, an experienced professional, these weekend or week-long courses give instruction in the most up-to-date methods of china and porcelain restoration as used by the British Museum. Open to all levels of expertise and interest, the classes take a maximum of four students to ensure that each participant gets sufficient individual guidance in this most delicate of crafts. Each student should bring their own item of porcelain, and can expect to see it gradually restored over the weekend through practical demonstrations and plain old practice. Lunch and materials are provided in the tuition fee and B&B accommodation is offered at £20 per night.

Contact
Micky Coppock
Oxford China Restoration Studio
Bewick House
89 Bicester Rd
Kidlington
Oxfordshire OX5 2LD
Tel: 01865 376046
Web: www.oxfordchinarestoration.co.uk

Practical information
Duration: 2–4 days
Level: beginner,
intermediate & advanced
Residential & non-residential
Group size: 3–4
Courses available in:

Jan	Feb	Mar	Apr	May	Jun	Jul	Aug	Sep	Oct	Nov	Dec

Price range: £150–£300
Prices include: lunch and
materials
Unsuitable for children
Pets not welcome

Botanical illustration in a countryside manor

This popular two-day course in Botanical Painting and Drawing takes place at Pashley Manor Gardens. A previous winner of the Christie's English Garden of the Year award, the Grade I listed manor exemplifies the traditional English country house. The gardens bear the mark of many eras of garden history and design, and were recently reworked by landscape architect Anthony du Gard Pasley. Students will produce watercolours or studies of plants under the tuition of Valerie Baines, founder member of the Society of Botanical Artists. She aims to give individual attention to each student, and will demonstrate her own techniques for mastering the 'fear of the white page'.

Contact
Pashley Manor Gardens
Ticehurst
Nr Wadhurst
Sussex TN5 7HE
Tel: 01580 200 888
Web: www.pashleymanorgardens.com

Practical information
Duration: 2 days
Level: beginner &
intermediate
Non-residential
Group size: 6–15
Courses available in:

Jan	Feb	Mar	Apr	May	Jun	Jul	Aug	Sep	Oct	Nov	Dec

Price range: £100–£150
Prices include: meals &
lunch only
Unsuitable for children
Pets not welcome

Weekend workshops on the site of the Battle of Hastings

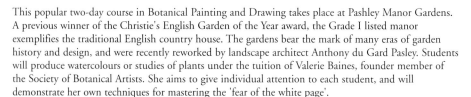

Housed in three 15th-century cottages, Pyke House stands on the site of the Battle of Hastings, now the Sussex village of Battle. The organisers of Pyke's residential courses are as concerned with what students learn, as with creating a relaxing and social atmosphere for them to learn in. Consequently, Pyke boasts about its food and the standard of accommodation. The premises also incorporate a number of communal lounges and some large gardens. Weekends range from textile courses such as lace-making, embroidery and sewing to other pursuits such as painting, yoga or history. All courses may be taken on a non-residential basis, though lunch and dinner will still be included.

Contact
Alison Martin
Pyke House Residential Education Centre
Upper Lake
Battle
E Sussex TN33 0AN
Tel: 01424 772495
Web: www.aredu.org.uk/pykehouse

Practical information
Duration: 2 days
Level: beginner &
intermediate
Residential & non-residential
Groups size: 6-15
Courses available in:

Jan	Feb	Mar	Apr	May	Jun	Jul	Aug	Sep	Oct	Nov	Dec

Price range: £50–£150
Prices include: meals &
accommodation
Child-friendly
Pets not welcome

Dance weekend in March

The Rebel Roc annual dance weekend is an extensive three-day event dedicated to Modern Jive and many other forms of partner dancing. The weekend caters for everyone from absolute beginners with two left feet through to experienced enthusiasts looking for something different. You can come alone or with friends: partners are not required as the teaching methods ensure that everyone mixes. Masterclasses from an international group of tutors cover styles such as Modern and Classic Jive, Salsa, Jitterbug, Tango, Tap, Lindy Hop, Blues and Boogie Woogie. There are Modern Jive improvers' workshops and a 'Learn to Dance in a Weekend' programme focusing on participants' particular needs. Each night features three floors of dancing with live bands and cabaret performances, and the emphasis on fun and socialising is strong: there's even a 'Dance with a Stranger' competition which is open to everyone. All this takes place at Camber Sands - real white-cliff country on the Sussex coast.

What's special?
The 'Learn to Dance in a Weekend' programme is for complete newcomers and enables seasoned jivers to bring along non-dancing family and friends to try something new. Participants will learn from experienced teachers and be jive-proficient by Sunday night.

Eating & sleeping
Accommodation is in the Pontin's self-catering chalets, supported by an on-site grocery shop. There is a self-service restaurant, fast-food options and nearby Rye has plenty of alternatives. Chalets are usually shared but single occupancy is available.

Directions
Camber Sands is two hours' drive from London down the M20. It's accessible from Ashford on the A2070, and Folkestone and Hastings on the A259. The nearest train station is Rye in East Sussex.

In the area
Rye is famous for its potteries, and there are many shops selling antiques, crafts and antiquarian books. The 1066 battleground is nearby, and the coastal landscape makes for some dramatic walks.

Contact
Katy Baxter
Rebel Roc
PO Box 614
Haywards Heath
W Sussex RH17 5WZ
Tel: 01444 411177
Web: www.rebelroc.com
Email: enquiries@rebelroc.com

Practical information
Duration: 3 days
Level: beginner,
intermediate & advanced
Residential
Group size: 25+

Price range: £50–£150
Prices include:
accommodation
Unsuitable for children
Pets not welcome

Courses available in:

Jan	Feb	Mar	Apr	May	Jun	Jul	Aug	Sep	Oct	Nov	Dec
		Mar									

Painting watercolour on the Thames

Rebecca Hind is an exhibiting watercolourist who writes about art and is a qualified teacher. She runs weekend courses at the Dorchester Abbey Guest House, and in good weather, students will be encouraged to paint outside to gain maximum benefit from the picturesque setting – either in the Abbey grounds or around the village. Themes for the courses change; they could be based on seasonal ideas – 'Painting the Autumn Landscape' for example – or technical ones, such as 'Drawing for Painters'. Students are asked to bring their own materials, although Rebecca offers a beginners' kit for £25. Non-participants will have plenty to do in the area, with walking, fishing, bird-watching and Oxford all nearby.

Contact
Rebecca Hind
Dorchester Abbey Guest House
Dorchester-on-Thames
Oxfordshire OX10 7HH
Tel: 01865 340633
Web: www.rebeccahind.com

Practical information
Duration: 2 days
Level: beginner &
intermediate
Residential & non-residential
Groups size: n/a

Price range: £50–£150
Prices include: meals &
accommodation
Child-friendly
Pets not welcome

Courses available in:

Jan	Feb	Mar	Apr	May	Jun	Jul	Aug	Sep	Oct	Nov	Dec

Richard Farrington, Alton
Metal sculpture in a Hampshire barn studio

Richard Farrington is a metalwork sculptor who offers tailor-made courses from his stone-and-timber barn studio near a tributary of the River Wey. He provides an introduction to the skills, equipment and practicalities of working with metal, so that students can produce their own concept under supervision. The specifics of the programme are worked out according to students' needs, but should include welding, plasma cutting, rolling, bending, drilling, sawing, etc. Individuals are taught at £250 a day, £350 for parties of up to three, so it is in students' interest to book as a group. Insurance should be arranged separately, but stock materials are included.

Contact
Richard Farrington
The Studio
42 Whitedown
Alton
Hampshire GU34 1LU
Tel: 01420 542949
Web: www.richardfarrington.co.uk

Practical information
Duration: 2–3 days
Level: beginner &
intermediate
Non-residential

Group size: 1–5
Price range: £200–£500+
Prices include: materials
Unsuitable for children
Pets not welcome

Courses available in:

Jan	Feb	Mar	Apr	May	Jun	Jul	Aug	Sep	Oct	Nov	Dec

ROYAL BOTANIC GARDENS, KEW
Botany, botanical illustration and photography at Kew

Beautiful Kew Gardens hosts a number of short courses. The Creative Plant Photography course gives specialised advice on the appropriate composition and lighting techniques for drawing out the beauty of plants on film. The five-day course allows for plenty of hands-on practice, and processing is available throughout. Other five-day courses include Botanical Illustration, which focuses on drawing and watercolour, and a general Botany for Beginners course which instructs through a programme of lectures, demonstration and practice, covering topics such as classification, cell functions and the major vegetative areas of the world. This has a maximum of 15 students and costs £325.

Contact
Viv Hinks
Royal Botanic Gardens
Kew
Richmond
Surrey TW9 3AB
Tel: 020 8332 5000
Web: www.rbgkew.org.uk

Practical information
Duration: 2–5 days
Level: beginner &
intermediate
Non-residential

Group size: 6–15
Price range: £100–£400
Unsuitable for children
Pets not welcome

Courses available in:

Jan	Feb	Mar	Apr	May	Jun	Jul	Aug	Sep	Oct	Nov	Dec

Needlework at Hampton Court

Founded in 1872 by Princess Christian, one of Queen Victoria's daughters, the Royal School of Needlework (RSN) plays an active part in the long tradition of hand embroidery. Apart from undertaking prestigious embroidery commissions, from the football World Cup logo to the monarch's coronation robes, the RSN's main goal remains the teaching and preservation of hand embroidery skills.

Courses

They run one- to three-day classes, at beginners' and improvers' levels. Students can choose from a variety of techniques, including Beadwork, Silk Shading and Goldwork. There are also workshops based around the creation of specific pieces such as decorative boxes and a concession to modernity in the Machine Embroidery class. All workshops take place at their premises in Hampton Court Palace overlooking the formal gardens. The one-day courses introduce the various techniques.

What's special?

The course in Goldwork (a tradition over 1000 years old) is a particular speciality. Gold and other metal threads are 'couched' (stitched down) into a fabric such as velvet or silk. This is a very good-looking, versatile effect.

Eating & sleeping

Accommodation at the Carlton Mitre Hotel (020 8979 9988) and the Lion Gate Hotel (020 8977 8121). Dining at Le Petit Nantais (020 8979 2309) and Kingston's Riverside Vegetariana (020 8546 7992).

Directions

Trains every half-hour from London Waterloo. Buses from Kingston and Richmond. Between April and October students should report to the Reception Office for a pass giving them free entrance to the gardens.

In the area

The RSN is in Hampton Court Palace and there is much to enjoy here, including the notorious maze. Kew Gardens at Richmond are also worth a visit.

Contact

Royal School of Needlework
Apt 12a
Hampton Court Palace
Surrey
Tel: 020 8943 1432
Web: www.royal-needlework.co.uk
Email: enquiries@royal-needlework.co.uk

Practical information

Duration: 2–3 days
Level: beginner,
intermediate & advanced
Non-residential

Courses available in:

Group size: 6–15
Price range: £100–£200
Unsuitable for children
Pets not welcome

Jan	Feb	Mar	Apr	May	Jun	Jul	Aug	Sep	Oct	Nov	Dec

Residential yoga weekends held nationwide

Ruth White is one the country's foremost yoga teachers. She teaches the principles of Iyengar yoga, which focuses on the form of the postures and the experience of the individual whilst in them. The programme includes breathing exercises and practice, as well as talks, demonstrations and time to pursue other activities. Heythrop Park, Chipping Norton, is the 400-acre site of an 18th-century mansion, and all Ruth's weekends take place in carefully chosen countryside locations, with on-site accommodation included in the price. Day participants are welcome. Similar weekends, and slightly longer breaks, are offered at Epsom College, Eastbourne College, Eden Hall in Kent and Shipton-under-Wychwood in Oxfordshire.

Contact
Ruth White
Church Farm House
Springclose Lane
Cheam
Surrey SM3 8PU
Tel: 020 8641 7770
Web: www.ruthwhiteyoga.com

Practical information
Duration: 2–3 days
Level: intermediate
Residential & non-residential
Group size: 6-25
Price range: £150–£300
Courses available in:

Prices include: meals & accommodation
Unsuitable for children
Pets not welcome

Jan	Feb	Mar	Apr	May	Jun	Jul	Aug	Sep	Oct	Nov	Dec

Thai massage in leafy Gerrards Cross

This two-day course is open to anyone interested in developing Thai massage skills for personal or professional use. Taking a different approach from Swedish massage, Thai massage theorises that the body's energy and tensions run down specific lines. It aims to release or redistribute that energy by applying pressure using techniques that have evolved over 2000 years. Conditions that may particularly benefit from the treatment include back pain, asthma, stressed muscles and prolonged coughs and colds. All tutors are experienced practitioners and often have backgrounds in anatomy, physiology and standard medicine. The school is located in a leafy area of Gerrards Cross, within walking distance of the train station.

Contact
School of Complementary Therapies
16 Dukes Wood Drive
Gerrards Cross
Buckinghamshire SL9 7LR
Tel: 01753 882660
Web: www.complementary-therapies.com

Practical information
Duration: 2 days
Level: beginner
Non-residential

Group size: 3–10
Price range: £50-£100
Unsuitable for children
Pets not welcome

Courses available in:

Jan	Feb	Mar	Apr	May	Jun	Jul	Aug	Sep	Oct	Nov	Dec

Water confidence in Southsea

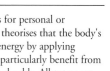

These learn-to-swim courses concentrate first on establishing water confidence, then on swimming technique, because for many adult non-swimmers, confidence is the real hurdle. The school uses a very calm approach, working on a one-to-one basis in the private pool at the Seacrest Hotel in Southsea, Hampshire. Courses last two and a half or five days, with seven or 14 hours of tuition respectively. Consequently, participants can reinforce their previous lesson's work, and build new attitudes and techniques, very quickly. Accommodation and breakfast are in the Seacrest Hotel, overlooking the Solent, with views of the Isle of Wight. Facilities include a restaurant, bar and parking.

Contact
Blaine Perkins
The Southsea School of Swimming
Clarence Road
Southsea, Portsmouth
Hampshire PO5 2LQ
Tel: 023 9282 0609

Practical information
Duration: 2–4 days
Level: beginner
Residential
Group size: 1–2

Price range: £300–£500+
Prices include: accommodation
Unsuitable for children
Pets not welcome

Courses available in:

Jan	Feb	Mar	Apr	May	Jun	Jul	Aug	Sep	Oct	Nov	Dec

SQUIRES INTERNATIONAL SCHOOL OF CAKE DECORATING & SUGARCRAFT, FARNHAM

Cake Decorating

Squires Kitchen is an internationally renowned school dedicated to the craft of cake decorating. Welcoming students and industry professionals from around the world, Squires runs courses for those of all skill levels – from the complete beginner to the advanced – interested in sugar craft and cake decoration. There are two-day courses designed to introduce participants to the use of royal icing, both in covering the cake smoothly and also in creating piped decoration. The Beginners' Sugarpaste workshop covers similar basic skills, and there are also novelty cake-decorating courses to give ideas for all kinds of celebration cakes, including children's birthdays. There are several weekend courses throughout the year where students learn to hand-model flowers out of sugar. An accommodation list is available on request, and students are required to bring certain materials and equipment with them.

What's special?

The bi-annual five-day school in cake decorating is Squires Kitchen's flagship course. Participants learn a range of different skills from expert guest tutors, including sugar modelling, floral work and royal icing techniques. The programme includes two evening demonstrations, plenty of hands-on practice and a dinner.

Eating & sleeping

B&B at Sleepy Hollow (01252 721930); the Bush Hotel (01252 715237) serves traditional English food; the restaurant at the Bishop's Table Hotel (01252 710222) has two AA rosettes.

Directions

The historic market town of Farnham is worth exploring. Sightseeing includes Farnham Castle, established in the Norman era with a few original features still intact, and an array of Georgian architecture.

In the area

Squires is opposite Farnham train station, to which there are regular services from London Waterloo. If driving, take the A3 towards Guildford then the A31 to Farnham. In Farnham, follow signs for the station.

Contact

Squires International School of Cake
Decorating & Sugarcraft
Squire House
3 Waverly Lane
Farnham
Surrey GU9 8BB
Tel: 01252 711749 / 727572
Web: www.squires-group.co.uk
Email: school@squires-group.co.uk

Practical information

Duration: 2–5 days
Level: beginner,
intermediate & advanced
Non-residential

Group size: 3–15
Price range: £100–£400
Unsuitable for children
Pets not welcome

Courses available in:

Jan	Feb	Mar	Apr	May	Jun	Jul	Aug	Sep	Oct	Nov	Dec

Ecologically sustainable living and working: permaculture courses

The Sustainability Centre was set up to promote and develop ecologically sustainable ways of living and working. Their educational programme spans woodland-related skills, traditional rural crafts such as felt making and spinning, and sustainable gardening skills. They also run several permaculture courses. The five-day version introduces the principles and techniques, with students learning to design their own garden and gaining hands-on experience at the Centre's 55-acre site. Students can camp, use the Centre's hostel, or stay at a local B&B. The hostel is located at the top of the South Downs, with views over Hampshire. Breakfast is included, and packed lunches/evening meals are available. There is also a self-catering kitchen.

Contact
Janet Hayes
The Sustainability Centre
Droxford Rd
East Meon
Petersfield
Hampshire GU32 1HR
Tel: 01730 823166
Web: www.earthworks-trust.com

Practical information
Duration: 2-5 days
Level: beginner &
intermediate
Residential & non-residential
Group size: 6-25+

Courses available in:

Jan	Feb	Mar	Apr	May	Jun	Jul	Aug	Sep	Oct	Nov	Dec

Price range: £50-£300
Prices include: meals &
accommodation
Unsuitable for children
Pets not welcome

Cookery classes near Brighton

Run by Graham Funnell, a former head chef at a London restaurant, Thackerys is a small, hands-on cookery school which aims to de-complicate the mysteries of sophisticated cooking. Located near Brighton and the coast, the school is housed in a 350-year-old building where the Funnells' own restaurant used to be. Practice menus vary according to seasonal produce, but have previously included dishes such as home-made prosciutto ravioli, duck with kumquats and rosemary, and whisky and honey ice-cream. Each day students prepare and share lunch, and create dishes to take home. Thackerys takes a maximum of four students per class, with discounts offered on bookings by a group of four.

Contact
Graham Funnell
Thackerys
3 Malling St
Lewes
E Sussex BN7 2RA
Tel: 01273 474634
Web: www.thackerys.co.uk

Practical information
Duration: 2 days
Level: beginner &
intermediate
Non-residential
Group size: 2-4
Courses available in:

Jan	Feb	Mar	Apr	May	Jun	Jul	Aug	Sep	Oct	Nov	Dec

Price range: £200-£300
Prices include: meals &
lunch with wine included
Unsuitable for children
Pets not welcome

Printmaking with Tor Hildyard in her Kent farmhouse

A graduate of the Kent Institute of Art and Design, Tor Hildyard is an exhibiting printmaker with eight years' experience of teaching her craft. She runs two-day courses regularly throughout the year, with special seasonal workshops for those wanting to create their own Christmas cards. Themed according to different techniques, weekend workshops cover Lino Cutting, Paper Litho and 'Intaglio', which covers the etching, dry point and collagraph forms of printmaking. Tor encourages an experimental use of these techniques to help students find what they feel most comfortable with. Non-residential courses take place at her farmhouse home in Kent, and lunch is included in the tuition fee.

Contact
Tor Hildyard
Hawkridge Farmhouse
Cranbrook
Kent TN17 2AD
Tel: 01580 712756
Email: torty@tinyworld.co.uk

Practical information
Duration: 2 days
Level: beginner,
intermediate & advanced
Non-residential
Group size: 2-10
Courses available in:

Jan	Feb	Mar	Apr	May	Jun	Jul	Aug	Sep	Oct	Nov	Dec

Price range: £50-£100
Prices include: lunch and
materials
Unsuitable for children
Pets not welcome

STONEY PARSONS, TUNBRIDGE WELLS

Stained glass techniques with Stoney Parsons

Stoney Parsons is an architectural glass artist whose panels and windows can be seen in St Mary's Hospital, Paddington and the Royal Berkshire Hospital, Reading. Combining techniques first used in medieval times with modern glass techniques, she runs regular weekend workshops teaching participants how to produce a piece of stained glass while giving full vent to their creativity. Over two days beginners are given the techniques, materials and confidence to complete a stained glass panel, progressing from initial design to finished product. There are also courses for more experienced students and others specialising in the basic techniques of painting and firing glass for more detailed effects. All tuition takes place at Stoney's studio on a country park estate in the High Weald. For examples of Stoney's own work and the possibilities of stained glass art, look at her website.

What's special?

Stoney's courses are based on her belief that everybody is creative. She is a gifted teacher who combines 20 years' experience, expertise and love of her craft. Pattern books are banned in the workshop, so people's own ideas are given free reign in a non-prescriptive environment, with Stoney giving guidance where necessary. She creates a safe, fun and welcoming environment with good lunches and refreshments. Class size is limited to eight, so there is plenty of individual guidance.

Eating & sleeping

Tunbridge Wells has the fashionable Hotel du Vin (01892 526455) and the more traditional Swan (01892 543319); dining options include a branch of Raymond Blanc's Le Petit Blanc (01892 559170) and a Wagamamas.

Directions

Eridge is just south of Tunbridge Wells on the A26 towards Crowborough. There are regular trains from London Charing Cross to Tunbridge Wells (about an hour) and taxis are available from the station.

In the area

Nearby Tudeley church has stained glass windows by Chagall. Tunbridge Wells has the historic Pantiles walkway and the Spa Valley railway to nearby Groombridge Place.

Contact

Stoney Parsons
The Glass Studio
Eridge Park
Tunbridge Wells
Kent TN3 9JS
Tel: 01892 750099
Web: www.stoneyparsons.co.uk
Email: stoney@stoneyparsons.co.uk

Practical information

Duration: 2–5 days
Level: beginner,
intermediate & advanced
Non-residential
Group size: 3–10

Price range: £150–£200
Prices include: lunch and
materials
Unsuitable for children
Pet-friendly

Courses available in:

Jan	Feb	Mar	Apr	May	Jun	Jul	Aug	Sep	Oct	Nov	Dec

Learning by ear and singing for pleasure

These are twice-yearly events for anyone interested in singing for pleasure. Following the oral tradition, participants are not required to read music, but simply learn new songs by ear. Each workshop has a different theme and is therefore led by different musicians. The harmony singing workshops, for example, are led by one of the UK's foremost vocal harmony groups. Future weekends will focus on English, Lithuanian and African folk songs, protest songs and gospel music. A concert takes place on the Saturday evening in the 140-seat theatre at the Arts Centre. The course is non-residential and organisers can provide an accommodation list. Participants must be over 16.

Contact
Traditional Arts Projects
Fairfield Arts Centre
Council Rd
Basingstoke
Hampshire RG21 3DH
Tel: 01256 474014
Web: www.tradarts.org

Practical information
Duration: 2 days
Level: beginner,
intermediate & advanced
Non-residential
Group size: 11–25+
Courses available in:

Price range: under
£50–£100
Prices include: concert
Unsuitable for children
Pets not welcome

Jan	Feb	Mar	Apr	May	Jun	Jul	Aug	Sep	Oct	Nov	Dec

Birds and wildlife in the New Forest

The New Forest is one of the most diverse natural habitats in the country, home to Britain's largest population of deer. This four-day holiday explores the New Forest landscape – its woodland, acid bogs, heaths and grazed lawns – and also incorporates trips to the coastal marshes to seek breeding terns and returning waders. The emphasis will be on the wide spectrum of bird types in the area, but there are also trips to ponds and bogs to look at dragonflies and rare plant species, and evening excursions for close-range deer-spotting. This is a fully residential course, with all meals and three nights' accommodation in a small country hotel included.

Contact
The Travelling Naturalist
Wildlife Holidays
PO Box 3141
Dorchester
Dorset DT1 2XD
Tel: 01305 267994
Web: www.naturalist.co.uk

Practical information
Duration: 4 days
Level: beginner &
intermediate
Residential
Group size: 6–15

Courses available in:

Price range: £400–£500
Prices include: meals &
accommodation
Child-friendly
Pets not welcome

Jan	Feb	Mar	Apr	May	Jun	Jul	Aug	Sep	Oct	Nov	Dec

Glyndebourne Operatic Experience

A four-day immersion in the operatic event of the year, with tickets to one of Glyndebourne's productions and a full programme of discussion and lectures to assist your appreciation. Topics given closer examination include use of orchestra, characterisation, and musical and dramatic structure. The operas under discussion depend on Glyndebourne programming, and participants can withdraw if the confirmed production is not to their liking. Accommodation is in a hotel in nearby Lewes, with the course fee covering four nights' stay and a number of meals. There will be opportunity to explore Lewes, and evening transport to and from Glyndebourne is provided. Early booking recommended.

Contact
University of Nottingham Study Tours
School of Education
The Dearing Building
University of Nottingham
Jubilee Campus
Wollaton Rd
Nottingham NG8 1BB
Tel: 0115 951 6526
Web: www.nottingham.ac.uk

Practical information
Duration: 4 days
Level: beginner &
intermediate
Residential
Group size: 16–25

Courses available in:

Price range: £300–£400
Prices include: meals,
accommodation & opera
tickets, transport
Unsuitable for children
Pets not welcome

Jan	Feb	Mar	Apr	May	Jun	Jul	Aug	Sep	Oct	Nov	Dec

TANTE MARIE SCHOOL OF COOKERY, WOKING

Cordon Bleu Cookery

Housed in a Victorian mansion, the Tante Marie School of Cookery has 50 years' experience training the world's top cooks. The school boasts five fully equipped teaching kitchens and one demonstration theatre. While best known for career and gap year courses, the school is today equally famous for a variety of shorter options, such as the Two-Day Modular courses. All courses are taught in small groups (maximum nine students) with the emphasis on learning professional skills in a friendly environment.

Courses
Two-day modular courses include 'Dazzling Desserts', 'Mastering Meat', 'Fish and Shellfish' and 'Working with Yeast'. Students take away a personalised recipe folder and most of the food cooked. Lunch with wine is included. Accommodation advice can be given.

What's special?
The Easy Entertaining course takes the stress out of entertaining – students go home armed with a three-course dinner party for eight having learnt new techniques and presentation skills. The Creative Christmas course takes the pressure off at Christmas – students take home the festive essentials and a two-course, freezer-friendly, seasonal dinner for eight.

Eating & sleeping
The family-run The Dutch (01483 724255) is two minutes' walk. For greater luxury try the Foxhills Country Club (01932 872050). For restaurants Tante Marie recommends the modern French cuisine at Drake's in Ripley (01483 224777). There are also plenty of restaurants in Guildford.

Directions
Junction 10 off M25 and A245 to Woking; or junction 11 and A320. At the Six Crossroads roundabout take either of these A-roads as Carlton Rd runs between them. The turning is soon after the roundabout. The school is near Woking station (27 minutes from London Waterloo). See mapfinder on www.tantemarie.co.uk.

In the area
Guildford is an historical university town with its own castle, cathedral, riverside walks and great shopping. Woking has an impressive theatre, cinema complex and sports centre. The Royal Horticultural Society Gardens at Wisley are also close by.

Contact
Tante Marie School of Cookery
Carlton Rd
Woking
Surrey
Tel: 01483 726957
Web: www.tantemarie.co.uk
Email: info@tantemarie.co.uk

Practical information
Duration: 2 days
Level: beginner &
intermediate
Non-residential
Group size: 3–10

Price range: £200–£300
Prices include: meals &
ingredients
Unsuitable for children
Pets not welcome

Courses available in:

Jan	Feb	Mar	Apr	May	Jun	Jul	Aug	Sep	Oct	Nov	Dec

Rural crafts in historic setting on the South Downs

Weald Downland Open Air Museum is a dedicated living-history project situated within the landscape of the South Downs. The 50-acre site features over 40 historic buildings that have been accurately restored and rebuilt. The museum also has an expansive educational programme with a wide range of courses dedicated to rural crafts and traditional countryside skills. These include workshop weekends that focus on such varied skills as stone-carving, watercolour painting and building garden gates out of oak. The Leaded-Light Stained Glass course lasts three days, and teaches the centuries-old craft of stained glass composition, giving students the opportunity to create their own piece.

Contact
Diana Rowsell
Weald Down Open Air Museum
Singleton
Chichester
W Sussex PO18 0EU
Tel: 01243 811363
Web: www.wealddown.co.uk

Practical information
Duration: 2-5 days
Level: beginner &
intermediate
Non-residential
Group size: 6-15

Courses available in:

Jan	Feb	Mar	Apr	May	Jun	Jul	Aug	Sep	Oct	Nov	Dec

Price range: £50–£300
Prices include: meals &
lunch included on some of
the courses
Child-friendly
Pets not welcome

Watercolours on the Isle of Wight

Kate Bolton, a qualified adult education teacher and exhibiting painter, runs three-day watercolour breaks from an 18th-century former vicarage. Participants are invited to arrive in the afternoon of the first day to share an evening meal and attend an introductory evening session. Two full days of painting follow, with some outdoors work if the weather is good. Accommodation is on site in the vicarage, which has been extended to incorporate three studio apartments (with catering facilities). These are open to painters and their partners both during and beyond the course. Non-residents will be offered help with alternative accommodation on request. Materials are not included in the fee.

Contact
Kate Bolton
Wightwatercolour Painting Holidays
Mulberry Lawn
2 Quay Lane
Brading
Isle of Wight PO36 0AT
Tel: 01983 405209
Web: www.wightwatercolour.co.uk

Practical information
Duration: 3 days
Level: beginner &
intermediate
Residential & non-residential
Group size: 3-10

Courses available in:

Jan	Feb	Mar	Apr	May	Jun	Jul	Aug	Sep	Oct	Nov	Dec

Price range: £100–£200
Prices include: meals &
accommodation.
Unsuitable for children
Pets not welcome

Woodcarving and antique restoration near Burnham Beeches

Colin Mantripp's Lillyfee Arts & Crafts Barn prides itself on the workmanship that goes into its wood designs, in resolute opposition to the style-over-substance approach. Their client list includes Elton John and the Queen, so it's clearly working. Colin, who has exhibited at the V&A museum in London, runs weekend courses in Wood Carving or Antique Restoration for students of all levels of experience. Wood Carving courses cover design, tool care and all aspects of carving itself. Students may choose their subject matter, including 3-D sculpture, figure carving and lettering. Lillyfee is committed to environmentally-friendly ways of working, using wood from sustainable forests and recycling all waste to use as fuel.

Contact
Colin Mantripp
The Woodcarving Studio
Lillyfee Farm Lane
Wooburn Common
Nr Beaconsfield
Buckinghamshire HP10 0LL
Tel: 01494 671690
Web: www.lillyfee.co.uk

Practical information
Duration: 2-5 days
Level: beginner,
intermediate & advanced
Non-residential

Courses available in:

Jan	Feb	Mar	Apr	May	Jun	Jul	Aug	Sep	Oct	Nov	Dec

Group size: 11-20
Price range: £50–£200
Unsuitable for children
Pet-friendly

WEST DEAN COLLEGE, CHICHESTER

Wide-ranging arts weekends

This 19th-century manor house and surrounding 6000 acres used to belong to Edward James, aesthete and co-designer of Dalí's famous Lips sofa. The Edward James Trust, an educational charity, converted the estate into West Dean College, which aims to further James's cultural aims by running a programme of full-time or short courses in music, gardening and the visual and applied arts. The College's wide-ranging short courses are taught by leading professionals and may be taken both residentially and non-residentially. The premises are set among award-winning landscaped gardens which, together with the library, are open to students.

Courses

Courses cover a number of different angles, combining traditional techniques in the arts and crafts with progressive trends. They include subjects such as drawing, painting, pastels, creative writing, wood engraving, basket making, bookbinding, gardening, mosaics, stained glass, blacksmithing, enamelling, opera, guitar playing, jazz appreciation, photography, pottery, sculpture and furniture making. One-day taster courses are also available.

What's special?

West Dean's annual six-day summer school allows students intensive, specialist learning in their chosen field combined with structured forays into other, ongoing courses. With so many people studying, there are great opportunities to interact and swap experiences, and social events are organised.

Eating & sleeping

Accommodation is provided in the Main House or the Vicarage. Guests can choose single or twin rooms, and some are en-suite. There is a licensed bar and a restaurant serving breakfast and three-course meals. Food will always include a vegetarian option.

Directions

Six miles north of Chichester, just off the A286, which lies between the A3 and the M27. Chichester is the closest station.

In the area

Chichester has Roman heritage, a famous cathedral and the renowned Festival Theatre. West Dean is very close to the cliffs and beaches of the south coast, and walkers will enjoy exploring the South Downs.

Contact

Admissions Office
West Dean College
West Dean
Chichester
W Sussex PO18 0QZ
Tel: 01243 811301
Web: www.westdean.org.uk
Email: short.courses@westdean.org.uk

Practical information

Duration: 2–9 days
Level: beginner,
intermediate & advanced
Residential & non-residential
Group size: 6–25+

Price range: £100–£500+
Prices include: meals &
accommodation
Unsuitable for children
Pets not welcome

Courses available in:

Jan	Feb	Mar	Apr	May	Jun	Jul	Aug	Sep	Oct	Nov	Dec

Creative writing in the New Forest

Kathryn Haig is a romance author with five published novels; A Time To Dance is the most recent. She runs three-day novel-writing workshops at her home, a thatched farmhouse in the New Forest. The course offers intensive tuition and skill development, running either Tuesday to Thursday or Friday to Sunday. Every aspect of novel writing is covered, from plotting and characterisation to targeting your reader and finding an agent. With a maximum of ten students, the courses encourage full participation and attention for each individual. Those who have already started a novel may send in their first chapter in advance and will receive a one-to-one session (included in the price).

Contact
Kathryn Haig
Write in the Forest
Haywards Farm House
Boldre
Lymington
Hampshire SP41 5PG
Tel: 01590 624098
Web: www.nettrends.com/kathrynhaig/writeintheforest.htm

Practical information
Duration: 3 days
Level: beginner &
intermediate
Non-residential
Group size: 3–10

Price range: £100–£150
Prices include: lunch
Unsuitable for children
Pets not welcome

Courses available in:

Jan	Feb	Mar	Apr	May	Jun	Jul	Aug	Sep	Oct	Nov	Dec
	Feb		Apr					Sep	Oct		

Writing weekend in 13th-century Oxfordshire abbey

These breaks are arranged by Writers Inc, a London organisation dedicated to the development of writers and the exchange of ideas. Writers of all levels of experience gather in a 13th-century Oxfordshire abbey to take part in an encouraging yet challenging weekend that aims to advance their ideas. In-house tutors are Mario Petrucci, a former poet-in-residence at the Imperial War Museum, and poet, lecturer and journalist Sue Hubbard, but the writing retreats are often led by guest writers. Recent themes included Life Studies, a weekend about writing from personal experience. Weekends are residential, but evening meals are not included. A limited number of assisted places are available.

Contact
Morag McRae
Writers Inc
14 Somerset Gardens
London SE13 7SY
Tel: 020 8305 8844
Web: www.writersinc-london.org.uk

Practical information
Duration: 2 days
Level: beginner,
intermediate & advanced
Residential
Group size: 6–15

Price range: under
£50–£200
Prices include: breakfast,
lunch & accommodation.
Unsuitable for children
Pets not welcome

Courses available in:

Jan	Feb	Mar	Apr	May	Jun	Jul	Aug	Sep	Oct	Nov	Dec
			Apr	May					Oct		

The South West

Stonehenge, Glastonbury, the Eden Project, Cornish beaches, Exmoor, Dartmoor, the Cotswolds, Bath, Exeter, the Forest of Dean, St Ives and the South West Coastal Path. The South West is a hugely popular part of England, with the country's mildest climate; and it has numerous seaside and alternative-lifestyle associations. The courses offered here are varied in style and content, with many run by people who have left city-based jobs to pursue their artistic and cultural dreams in a stunning part of the country.

Pottery and painting holidays in St Ives

John Buchanan's 40 years as a potter and 27 as a ceramics teacher probably earn him guru status in the world of pot-throwing. He works just outside St Ives, from a studio in Halsetown that he rescued from dereliction, and will teach slab-building or modelling if wanted. No one-trick pony, he also teaches painting, particularly watercolours, either from Halsetown or from his chalet overlooking the Hayle estuary. All courses are eminently flexible, and the first morning is spent discussing what you want to learn. Accommodation is available at the chalet and the centre, and John has a minibus to take you to the destinations you need.

Contact
John Buchanan
Anchor Pottery
The St Ives Craft Centre
Halsetown
St Ives
Cornwall TR26 3NB
Tel: 01736 795078
Web: www.cornishceramics.com/panchor.htm

Practical information
Duration: 5-10 days
Level: beginner,
intermediate & advanced
Residential & non-residential
Group size: 3-10

Courses available in:

Jan	Feb	Mar	Apr	May	Jun	Jul	Aug	Sep	Oct	Nov	Dec

Price range: £150-£500+
Prices include: meals &
accommodation
Unsuitable for children
Pets not welcome

Trompe l'oeil painting

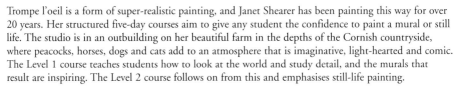

Trompe l'oeil is a form of super-realistic painting, and Janet Shearer has been painting this way for over 20 years. Her structured five-day courses aim to give any student the confidence to paint a mural or still life. The studio is in an outbuilding on her beautiful farm in the depths of the Cornish countryside, where peacocks, horses, dogs and cats add to an atmosphere that is imaginative, light-hearted and comic. The Level 1 course teaches students how to look at the world and study detail, and the murals that result are inspiring. The Level 2 course follows on from this and emphasises still-life painting.

Contact
Janet Shearer
The Art of Illusion
Higher Grogley Farm
Withiel
Nr Bodmin
Cornwall PL30 5NP
Tel: 01208 831926
Web: www.trompeloeil.co.uk

Practical information
Duration: 5 days
Level: beginner,
intermediate & advanced
Non-residential

Courses available in:

Jan	Feb	Mar	Apr	May	Jun	Jul	Aug	Sep	Oct	Nov	Dec

Group size: 2-10
Price range: £400-£500
Prices include: lunch
Unsuitable for children
Pets not welcome

Salmon and trout fishing on the River Tamar

The Arundell Arms know what they're doing when it comes to fly-fishing tuition because they have been teaching for over 60 years. With 20 miles of private fishing on the River Tamar and its tributaries, and a three-acre lake, it is easy to understand why fishing is so well established here. The hotel offers courses for anglers of all experience levels. The general beginners' course looks at both river and lake fishing, but other courses are more specific – river or lake fishing, casting, fly-tying, etc. All courses are taken by two fully qualified instructors so the teaching is very personalised. Accommodation and meals are available in the hotel.

Contact
Anne Voss-Bark
The Arundell Arms Hotel
Lifton
Devon PL16 0AA
Tel: 01566 784666
Web: www.arundellarms.com

Practical information
Duration: 5 days
Level: beginner,
intermediate & advanced
Non-residential

Group size: 2-10
Price range: £400-£500
Prices include: lunch
Unsuitable for children
Pets not welcome

Courses available in:

Jan	Feb	Mar	Apr	May	Jun	Jul	Aug	Sep	Oct	Nov	Dec

BRAMBLES ART RETREAT, LIFTON

Art retreat deep in the Devon countryside

Janet Brady and Peter Davies teach some of the most relaxed, easygoing art courses you will find. They met at art school 25 years ago and moved to this beautiful part of West Devon in 1999. Their 17th-century cottage offers an idyll for those wanting to rest, recharge and paint. Courses take place in a house party atmosphere, and are taught in converted stables in the garden. When not painting, you can walk the dogs, explore the countryside or just relax.

Courses
Janet teaches watercolours and life drawing, Peter oils and acrylics, and they both teach drawing and mixed media work, in the studio and at local locations. You can work with different media and different subjects during a single stay, with courses generally combining people of similar levels of experience. The 'Freedom Course' is tuition-free.

What's special?
The courses are hugely flexible: participants can pursue their own interests, and Janet and Peter work hard to analyse the artists' needs. Secondly, this is a retreat, a holiday. You really do paint as much or as little as you like.

Eating & sleeping
They have three guest rooms in the cottage and use a local B&B if there is overspill. Janet also does all the cooking and many's the guest who has asked her to provide cookery courses.

Directions
A30 from Exeter past Okehampton. 7 miles before Launceston take 'Dingles Steam Village' exit. Left at end of slip road. Go to the end, over crossroads, passing 'Rydons' on left. Right at T-junction and Brambles is second on right.

In the area
Sail at nearby Redford Lake; swim at the beach at Bude; shop in Plymouth; National Trust properties at Lydford Gorge, Cotehele and Lanhydrock; 45 minutes to the Eden Project.

Contact
Janet Brady and Peter Davies
Brambles Art Retreat
Sprytown
Lifton
Devon
Tel: 01566 784359
Web: www.bramblesartretreat.com
Email: info@bramblesartretreat.com

Practical information
Duration: 2–10 days
Level: beginner,
intermediate & advanced
Residential & non-residential
Group size: 1–10

Price range: £150–£500+
Prices include: meals &
accommodation
Child-friendly
Pet-friendly

Courses available in:

Jan	Feb	Mar	Apr	May	Jun	Jul	Aug	Sep	Oct	Nov	Dec

Cookery courses in a Dartmoor town

The pretty town of Ashburton is the site of this intimate, hands-on cookery school. Students choose from a variety of courses where they learn techniques with multiple uses. The main teacher is chef Darrin Hosegrove, who has run a restaurant and lectured in catering. Two-day courses include Seafood, Italian, Gastro, French, Gentlemen's Relish (game and meat) and Beginners; plus a Chef Skills course for the more experienced. They are also introducing five-day courses aimed at people with differing levels of experience. The kitchen is in a converted outhouse and has a farmhouse feel with slate floors and granite work surfaces. The main Georgian townhouse offers accommodation from £65 for a double/twin.

Contact
Stella West-Harling
Ashburton Cookery School
Hare's Lane Cottage
76 East Street
Ashburton
Devon TQ13 7AX
Tel: 01364 652784
Web: www.ashburtoncookeryschool.co.uk

Practical information
Duration: 2–5 days
Level: beginner,
intermediate & advanced
Residential & non-residential
Group size: 3–10

Courses available in:

Jan	Feb	Mar	Apr	May	Jun	Jul	Aug	Sep	Oct	Nov	Dec

Price range: £150–£500
Prices include: meals
Unsuitable for children
Pets not welcome

Pottery courses in a North Cornish fishing town

Barbara is a qualified ceramics teacher who runs courses from a studio in the garden of her old coastguard's house-cum-B&B. From this position on the north Cornwall coast, there are wonderful views towards Tintagel Head, and the rock formations of the surrounding landscape are vital for Barbara's – and often her students' – work. She generally teaches hand-building, rather than throwing on a wheel, because she believes you will achieve more in a shorter, more relaxed time frame. She devises the content of each course around the participants, moving swiftly through baking and decorating techniques. People can usually produce three or four pieces in a two-day course.

Contact
Barbara Bell
Signal Field Studio
New Road
Port Isaac
Cornwall PL29 3SB
Tel: 01208 880075
Web: www.portisaacbay.com

Practical information
Duration: 2–10 days
Level: beginner,
intermediate & advanced
Residential & non-residential
Group size: 1–5

Courses available in:

Jan	Feb	Mar	Apr	May	Jun	Jul	Aug	Sep	Oct	Nov	Dec

Price range: £100–£500+
Prices include:
accommodation & lunch
Unsuitable for children
Pets not welcome

Family-run pottery workshop in Devon countryside

Weekend courses at Barton Pottery place emphasis on fun and relaxation – you're pampered while you potter. Colin Horne introduces coil, slab and throwing techniques, plus some glazing, and by the end you could have five completed pieces which the Hornes will send to you after firing. Group size is limited to six to ensure one-to-one attention, and students – many of whom are first-timers – can make real progress. Colin has been a full-time potter for 16 years, having spent over four years learning the trade, and has a showroom from which he sells his pieces. He organises courses on adhoc basis, but the Hornes always provide accommodation and meals.

Contact
Colin and Diane Horne
Barton Pottery
South Barton
Canonsleigh
Burlescombe
Devon EX16 7JW
Tel: 01823 672987
Web: www.bartonpottery.co.uk

Practical information
Duration: 2 days
Level: beginner
Residential
Group size: 1–10
Price range: £100–£150

Courses available in:

Jan	Feb	Mar	Apr	May	Jun	Jul	Aug	Sep	Oct	Nov	Dec

Prices include: meals,
accommodation & one
evening meal
Unsuitable for children
Pets not welcome

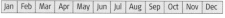

THE BLACKTHORN CENTRE SCHOOL OF PHOTOGRAPHY, CRICKLADE

Photography courses for all abilities near Cricklade

The photography courses at the Blackthorn Centre offer an excellent-value introduction to beginners and show new techniques to those with some competency. Teaching is of a very high standard, and all tutors are working photographers: Chris Milne's background is in travel and wildlife photography. Courses cover all aspects of photography and printing, and combine technical study indoors with location shooting around Wiltshire. Beginners will find the courses particularly useful, especially Starting Photography, which explains the camera's controls and teaches about medium, light and composition. Blackthorn also has courses in landscape, wildlife, portrait and digital photography.

Contact
Chris Milne
The Blackthorn Centre School of Photography
Whitehall Farm
Purton Road
Cricklade
Wiltshire SN6 6HY
Tel: 01454 416937
Web: www.photography-courses.com

Practical information
Duration: 2 days
Level: beginner,
intermediate & advanced
Non-residential

Group size: 6–10
Price range: £50–£100
Unsuitable for children
Pets not welcome

Courses available in:

| Jan | Feb | Mar | Apr | May | Jun | Jul | Aug | Sep | Oct | Nov | Dec |

South West

BUSHHAMMER, SLAUGHTERFORD

Introduction to stone sculpture, based on a Wiltshire farm

It's 'two for the price of one' here, as the cost of the stone sculpture course on this Wiltshire farm also includes annual membership of the workshop. John runs five-day courses that teach you to move, prepare and cut stone with confidence. By the end, you will probably have produced a sculpture, but that is a bonus, not the aim: this is all about learning. You can come back whenever you want to use the facilities and put your new skills to use, exchanging ideas with other sculptors and enjoying this beautiful area with its long history of stone mining and carving. Lots of accommodation and eating possibilities locally.

Contact
John Sait
Bushhammer
Honeybrook Farm
Slaughterford
Wiltshire SN14 8RJ
Web: www.bushhammer.co.uk

Practical information
Duration: 5 days
Level: beginner &
intermediate
Non-residential
Group size: 1–10

Price range: £200–£300
Prices include: large piece of
stone & year's membership
Child-friendly
Pets not welcome

Courses available in:

| Jan | Feb | Mar | Apr | May | Jun | Jul | Aug | Sep | Oct | Nov | Dec |

CARADOC OF TREGARDOCK, DELABOLE

Yoga in Cornwall

This B&B-cum-yoga centre is set in an inspiring location on the north Cornwall coast with uninterrupted sea views. It is based upon two adjacent barns, and the studio is in a converted 60-foot stable. This is yoga the smart way: the Friday evening class leads to champagne and canapés then a three-course meal. On Saturday and Sunday there are two yoga sessions, and in between you can take a picnic lunch and explore the area (the coastal path is very near), have massage or reiki treatments, or relax in the library or garden. All accommodation is en-suite, and groups can hire Caradoc for their own yoga or painting breaks.

Contact
Janet Cant
Caradoc of Tregardock
Treligga
Delabole
Cornwall PL33 9ED
Tel: 01840 213300
Web: www.tregardock.com

Practical information
Duration: 3 days
Level: beginner,
intermediate & advanced
Residential
Group size: 6–15

Price range: £200–£300
Prices include: meals &
accommodation
Unsuitable for children
Pets not welcome

Courses available in:

| Jan | Feb | Mar | Apr | May | Jun | Jul | Aug | Sep | Oct | Nov | Dec |

Painting and drawing in a quiet Cotswold village

Richard Kenton Webb takes a very non-prescriptive approach to the students on his drawing and painting courses. He wants participants to find their own painting voice and express themselves through their art. He usually begins by focusing on drawing, forcing students to concentrate on what is in front of them, rather than on colour. The subject matter is often landscape-oriented to take advantage of the surrounding Cotswold scenery. Richard has been a professional artist for almost 20 years and still teaches undergrad and postgrad art in London. His wife Tessa is very involved in the courses and cooks fantastic lunches and dinners for participants. Accommodation is supplied in two local B&Bs.

Contact
Richard Kenton Webb
Colour in the Cotswolds
The Coach House
Fraziers Folly
Siddington
Cirencester
Gloucestershire GL7 6HR
Tel: 01285 651790
Web: www.colourinthecotswolds.com

Practical information
Duration: 2–4 days
Level: beginner,
intermediate & advanced
Residential & non-residential
Group size: 6–10

Courses available in:

Price range: £200–£500
Prices include: meals &
accommodation
Unsuitable for children
Pets not welcome

Jan	Feb	Mar	Apr	May	Jun	Jul	Aug	Sep	Oct	Nov	Dec

Cookery courses in renovated Wiltshire manor farmhouse

Caroline Yates runs Confident Cooking from her Wiltshire home. Attendees learn three main meals and a light lunch, with emphasis on techniques, special tips, flavour combinations and presentation. At Friday's dinner you watch Caroline in action – take good note because she has taught cookery for 18 years. On Saturday you create lunch and dinner thanks to a combination of demonstrations and your own practice, before you learn a third meal on Sunday. Two chefs guide eight participants so the level of personal attention is exceptional. The eating of the dinners is part of the fun, with wine flowing at Caroline's dining-room table. Everyone stays on site in the Georgian farmhouse.

Contact
Caroline Yates
Confident Cooking
PO Box 841
Devizes
Wiltshire SN10 4UX
Tel: 01380 812846
Web: www.confidentcooking.fsbusiness.co.uk

Practical information
Duration: 2 days
Level: beginner &
intermediate
Residential
Group size: 6–10

Courses available in:

Price range: £300–£400
Prices include: meals &
accommodation
Unsuitable for children
Pets not welcome

Jan	Feb	Mar	Apr	May	Jun	Jul	Aug	Sep	Oct	Nov	Dec

Creative landscape painting in a spectacular Dorset setting

These five-day watercolour courses are run by artist Helen Halliday from the Cromwell House Hotel in Lulworth Cove. They benefit from the enormous range of maritime subject matter in the area – the rock structures at Stair Hole, the bay at Lulworth Cove, Durdle Dor, not to mention cliffs, beaches, boats, stones and seaweed. Most are accessible on foot from the hotel, and Helen gets her students painting outside as much as possible. She encourages copious sketching to provide material for use back home, although participants will also complete a couple of paintings. All meals and accommodation are provided by the hotel and the group usually eat dinner together.

Contact
Catriona Miller
The Cromwell House Hotel
Lulworth Cove
Dorset BH20 5RJ
Tel: 01929 400253
Web: www.lulworthcove.co.uk

Practical information
Duration: 5 days
Level: beginner,
intermediate & advanced
Residential

Courses available in:

Group size: 3–10
Price range: £400–£500+
Prices include: meals &
accommodation
Unsuitable for children
Pets not welcome

Jan	Feb	Mar	Apr	May	Jun	Jul	Aug	Sep	Oct	Nov	Dec

FOOD OF COURSE, SHEPTON MALLET

Tailored cookery courses in a Somerset long house

Lou offers relaxed, residential cooking courses in her beautiful 16th-century Somerset farmhouse. Informality is a key part of the experience, and the domestic setting helps underline this. The courses are intense but huge fun, with discussions in the garden or round the fire in the evening. Lou has been teaching cookery for nearly 18 years (four at this location) and has also run her own catering business.

Courses
The five-day 'New Food' courses are aimed at those who have already done some cooking, but who are feeling stale and want new recipes and a dash of inspiration. The four-week Foundation Course aims to turn you into a competent host possessing real culinary confidence and the course is ideal for those wanting to go back to basics and broaden their cooking knowledge. 'New Food' £790; Foundation £2450-£2650.

What's special?
'New Food' is great if you like to cook but don't want to spend hours in the kitchen. Lou will show you about boning and filleting, sauces and pastries... all you need to reawaken your inner Delia.

Eating & sleeping
En-suite accommodation is available in the Farm House and students also have their own sitting-room. You won't want to eat out because lunch and supper are the products of your daytime exertions.

Directions
Turn west off A371 at Brook House Inn (north of Castle Cary Station), towards Alhampton. Left to Sutton. Through Sutton, down No Through Road to farm on your left.

In the area
Bath, Wells and Glastonbury are nearby, offering historic architecture, abbeys, alternative lifestyles and shopping.

Contact
Louise Hutton
Food of Course
Middle Farm House
Sutton
Shepton Mallet
Somerset BA4 6QF
Tel: 01749 860116
Web: www.foodofcourse.co.uk
Email: louise.hutton@foodofcourse.co.uk

Practical information
Duration: 5-10 days
Level: beginner &
intermediate
Residential & non-residential
Group size: 3-10

Price range: £500+
Prices include: meals &
accommodation
Unsuitable for children
Pets not welcome

Courses available in:

Jan	Feb	Mar	Apr	May	Jun	Jul	Aug	Sep	Oct	Nov	Dec

Painting breaks on a Devon farm

In the middle of the Dart Valley, one of the South-West's most scenic areas, the Reddaways host four-day art courses on their dairy farm. Anne is an artist herself, but the tuition, in an 18th-century cottage in the idyllic farm grounds, is undertaken by experienced teachers. There is a landscape course using watercolours, and another using mixed media, plus two still-life courses and a silk painting week. Much course content relates to the surroundings, although in bad weather, the focus moves indoors. Participants can stay in the main farm or the cottage, where there are four bedrooms. Breakfast is served on site and other meals happen at the local pub.

Contact
Anne Reddaway
Dart Valley Art Holidays
Lower Yetson Farm
Ashprington
Totnes
Devon TQ9 7EG
Tel: 01803 732386
Web: www.dartvalleyartholidays.co.uk

Practical information
Duration: 4 days
Level: beginner &
intermediate
Residential
Group size: 3–10
Courses available in:

Price range: £300–£500
Prices include: meals &
accommodation
Unsuitable for children
Pets not welcome

Jan	Feb	Mar	Apr	May	Jun	Jul	Aug	Sep	Oct	Nov	Dec
		Mar		May				Sep			

Rural crafts in the Forest of Dean

The Dean Heritage Centre is an educational trust set up to preserve the culture and heritage of the Forest of Dean, which lies between the rivers Severn and Wye. To that end, they run workshops throughout the year teaching some of the crafts associated with the area. There are weekend courses in hurdle-making, knife-making, stone-carving and stool-making, and a five-day course in coppice management. The Centre is in the forest, near a millpond and a stream, and the setting is a bonus on top of a good-value course. There are often two or even three tutors with a group of just six students, so you receive lots of good advice.

Contact
Tom Haverly
Dean Heritage Centre
Camp Mill
Soudley
Forest of Dean
Gloucestershire GL14 2UB
Tel: 01594 822170
Web: www.deanheritagemuseum.com

Practical Information
Duration: 2–5 days
Level: beginner &
intermediate
Non-residential

Courses available in:

Group size: 3–10
Price range: £50–£200
Unsuitable for children
Pets not welcome

Jan	Feb	Mar	Apr	May	Jun	Jul	Aug	Sep	Oct	Nov	Dec
			Apr	May			Aug		Oct	Nov	Dec

Tai Chi and Qi Gong in a stunning part of Devon

Tai Chi and Qi Gong retreats at Sharpham House will soon have any participant feeling rejuvenated and relaxed. The retreats are run by Devon Tai Chi, which was established in 1999 by Matthew Rochford, after he had studied Tai Chi for nine years and done a six-year professional training course. The retreat combines the two practices, which have complementary emphases on body, mind and soul, with guided meditation. The house contributes hugely to the relaxed ambience. Built in the 18th century, it has gardens designed by Capability Brown and some of the best views in Devon. Bedrooms are not en-suite. Devon Tai Chi bring their own chef.

Contact
Matthew Rochford
Devon Tai Chi
1 Hillside
Frogmore
Kingsbridge
Devon TQ7 2NR
Tel: 01548 531447
Web: www.devontaichi.co.uk

Practical information
Duration: 2 days
Level: beginner,
intermediate & advanced
Residential
Group size: 3–10
Courses available in:

Price range: £200–£300
Prices include: meals &
accommodation
Unsuitable for children
Pets not welcome

Jan	Feb	Mar	Apr	May	Jun	Jul	Aug	Sep	Oct	Nov	Dec
			Apr	May		Jul			Oct		

DEVON YOGA, DARTMOOR
Workshops through the year in various Devon venues

Devon Yoga runs residential yoga weekends at magnificent Throwleigh House on the eastern edge of Dartmoor. Sitting in 30 acres of gardens, with its own wooded lake, excellent studio, accommodation and food, this makes an ideal yoga venue. Duncan Hulin has been teaching yoga since the early '80s and his approach is both holistic and eclectic; he does not pursue one particular style and so is able to respond to participants' needs. The courses have up to seven and a half hours' yoga each day, and are aimed at those with previous experience. The longer seven-day weekend is more of a retreat, with an emphasis on silence and meditation as well.

Contact
Duncan Hulin
Devon Yoga
1 Barton Cottages
Sowton Village
Exeter
Devon EX5 2AF
Tel: 01392 444727
Web: www.devonyoga.com

Practical information
Duration: 2–7 days
Level: intermediate
Residential
Group size: 6–20

Price range: £150–£500
Prices include: meals &
accommodation
Unsuitable for children
Pets not welcome

Courses available in:

Jan	Feb	Mar	Apr	May	Jun	Jul	Aug	Sep	Oct	Nov	Dec

DILLINGTON HOUSE, ILMINSTER
Arts centre with a huge variety of courses

One of the finest manor houses in Somerset, Dillington has been hosting adult education courses since 1949. The atmosphere is very 'country house', with the main building dating back to the 16th century. Dillington is run by Somerset County Council and is five-star rated by the British Tourism Council. The centre hosts a smorgasbord of courses in the arts, crafts, music and writing, all of them promoting the joys of lifelong learning. There's Scrabble, film, paper-making, recorder-playing… anything and, we suspect, everything you could wish for. Most courses last a weekend, although there are some three- and four-day versions for the keen. Transport and entrance fees, where appropriate, are included.

Contact
Barbara Shaw
Dillington House
Ilminster
Somerset TA19 9DT
Tel: 01460 52427
Web: www.dillington.co.uk

Practical information
Duration: 2–4 days
Level: beginner,
intermediate & advanced
Residential & non-residential
Group size: 6–25+

Price range: £150–£400
Prices include: meals &
accommodation
Unsuitable for children
Pets not welcome

Courses available in:

Jan	Feb	Mar	Apr	May	Jun	Jul	Aug	Sep	Oct	Nov	Dec

DOREEN HOLMES, MINEHEAD
Needlelace in a 16th-century Exmoor farmhouse

Catherine of Aragon brought needlelace to Britain, and after a period of dormancy it was revived in the mid-1980s. Now Doreen Holmes is one of those leading the needlelace charge, teaching many different styles on her courses. Beginners will be given an overview – point de gaz, stumpwork, 3-D flowers and coloured shading – so they can work out which to take further. Those with more experience can turn up with specific ideas and receive tuition in a particular field. You sew, sleep and eat chez Holmes in their 16th-century farmhouse in Exmoor National Park. It's a beautifully rural setting, complemented by home cooking, open fires and lots of walks.

Contact
Doreen Holmes
Higher Golsoncott Farmhouse
Golsoncott
Nr Rodhuish
Minehead
Somerset TA24 6QZ
Tel: 01984 641006
Web: www.needlelace.com

Practical information
Duration: 4 days
Level: beginner,
intermediate & advanced
Residential
Group size: 2–15

Price range: £200–£300
Prices include: meals &
accommodation
Unsuitable for children
Pets not welcome

Courses available in:

Jan	Feb	Mar	Apr	May	Jun	Jul	Aug	Sep	Oct	Nov	Dec

Digital filmic arts tuition in the Quantocks

Peter Goldfield is a professional photographic artist who specialises in one-to-one and two-to-one tuition in digital filmic arts. This can be digital photography, video, multimedia or web-based art. You discuss with Peter what you want to get out of the tuition and he will give you an overview of the possibilities. He demystifies the subject, guiding you through processes and programs, showing you how to get images into a computer, how to process them, and how to get them out again. You work from the studio at his peaceful farmhouse up in the Quantock hills and can stay locally. Suitable for photographers, artists and digital beginners.

Contact
Peter Goldfield
Duckspool
Duckspool Farm
Broomfield
Bridgwater
Somerset TA5 2EG
Tel: 01823 451305
Web: www.duckspool.com

Practical information
Duration: 2 days
Level: beginner,
intermediate & advanced
Non-residential

Group size: 1–2
Price range: £300–£400
Prices includes: lunch
Unsuitable for children
Pets not welcome

Courses available in:

Jan	Feb	Mar	Apr	May	Jun	Jul	Aug	Sep	Oct	Nov	Dec

Landscape painting around the West Country

Claire Smith runs four landscape painting weeks in different parts of the West Country and one in France. She has run courses since 1987 and places particular emphasis on colour. Her West Country courses cover the Teign Valley (sheltered moorland), Dartmoor bluebells (wide variety of sites), Appledore (seascapes) and Postbridge (the High Moor). Days start with a talk, where Claire introduces a technical point, tells students what to expect from the day, and gives hints on sites. As much work as possible is done outside, but there is a studio at the course base. Claire books accommodation in local cottages, hotels or B&Bs, and the group usually eats together.

Contact
Claire Smith
Greenawell
Greenawell Farm
Moretonhampstead
Devon TQ13 8QJ
Tel: 01647 440361
Web: www.greenawell.co.uk

Practical information
Duration: 5 days
Level: beginner &
intermediate
Residential
Group size: 3–10

Price range: £400–£500
Prices include: meals &
accommodation
Unsuitable for children
Pets not welcome

Courses available in:

Jan	Feb	Mar	Apr	May	Jun	Jul	Aug	Sep	Oct	Nov	Dec

Short courses in many arts in a beautiful Cotswold setting

Hawkwood is a dynamic, friendly, independent adult education centre set in glorious Cotswold countryside with views of the Severn Vale. Established in 1948 and very well respected, the college offers an impressive roster of courses throughout the year. Subjects include arts and crafts (it's a leading Japanese embroidery school), music, astrology, nature, healing and therapies, writing and poetry, parenting, yoga, mythology and many more. They also hold subject-specific summer schools looking at music, Kabbalah and yoga. Tutors come from all over Britain and the courses are often aimed at a particular experience level. There are 51 beds at the college, and home-cooked meals are part of the Hawkwood charm.

Contact
Richard Brinton
Hawkwood College
Painswick Old Road
Stroud
Gloucestershire GL6 7QW
Tel: 01453 759034
Web: www.hawkwoodcollege.co.uk

Practical information
Duration: 2–7 days
Level: beginner,
intermediate & advanced
Residential & non-residential
Group size: 2–25+

Price range: £100–£500
Prices includes: meals &
accommodation
Child-friendly
Pets not welcome

Courses available in:

Jan	Feb	Mar	Apr	May	Jun	Jul	Aug	Sep	Oct	Nov	Dec

JOANNA SHEEN, STOKEINTEIGNHEAD

Flower-related activities in Devon

Joanna Sheen trained as a florist with Constance Spry before establishing a business in dried and pressed flowers 25 years ago. Since then she has written over 30 books on the subject and established a Joanna Sheen school in Japan with 40 teachers. During the week she produces crafts for sale, but during spring and autumn weekends she runs courses from her 14th-century Devon farm just outside the Teign Estuary. The setting is very special and Joanna serves cordon bleu lunches in her farm kitchen. The studios are converted barns where course participants undertake four projects, all using the highest quality ingredients, which are provided as part of the course.

Courses
Courses may focus on particular flowers, seasonal themes, card-making, soap-making or candle-making. The weekends are a mixture of demonstration, chat and practical project time to ensure you know how to repeat the techniques at home.

What's special?
Joanna, who personally teaches every class, has had a 100 per cent rebooking rate for her Christmas course. Almost all her clients are now friends who come back each year, so she never runs the same course two years running.

Eating & sleeping
Thomas Luny House, Teignmouth (01626 772976); Virginia Cottage, Shaldon (01626 872634); Potters Mooring Hotel, Shaldon (01626 873225); Sampsons Farm, Preston (01626 354913). Good food at the Church House Inn (01626 872475) and Maidencombe's English House Hotel (01803 328760).

Directions
Head downhill into Stokeinteignhead. At the bottom, the road bears left and then, as it bears right, you see a large, white, thatched house, which is Victoria Farm. Directions on website.

In the area
Becky Falls Woodland Park, with its walks and waterfalls, is not far, and neither is Totnes Castle. The only working malthouse in the West Country is Tucker's Maltings in Newton Abbot.

Contact
Joanna Sheen
Joanna Sheen
Victoria Farm
Stokeinteignhead
Newton Abbot
Devon
Tel: 01626 872405
Web: www.joannasheen.com
Email: joannas@btinternet.com

Practical information
Duration: 2 days
Level: beginner & intermediate
Non-residential
Group size: 3–15

Price range: £150–£300
Prices include: meals & all ingredients
Unsuitable for children
Pets not welcome

Courses available in:

Jan	Feb	Mar	Apr	May	Jun	Jul	Aug	Sep	Oct	Nov	Dec

Art, music and relaxation near Totnes

Fantastic views across the Avon Valley, a truly peaceful setting and a diverse range of activities: Hazelwood is an idyllic spot. This 67-acre estate offers B&B in the main house and self-catering in three cottages. They run weekend courses in watercolours, life drawing, mixed media and Georgian singing, and have a full roster of concerts, talks and other events. The estate was bought by Janie Bowman and her partners in 1988; intending to buy one cottage, they could not bear the thought of the valley being spoilt and ended up purchasing the entirety. This is much more home than hotel, with lots of walking, excellent food and time to relax.

Contact
Janie Bowman
Hazelwood House
Loddiswell
Nr Kingsbridge
Devon TQ7 4EB
Tel: 01548 821232
Web: www.hazelwoodhouse.com

Practical information
Duration: 2 days
Level: beginner &
intermediate
Residential & non-residential
Group size: 3–15

Price range: £150–£200
Prices include: meals &
accommodation
Unsuitable for children
Pet-friendly

Courses available in:

Jan	Feb	Mar	Apr	May	Jun	Jul	Aug	Sep	Oct	Nov	Dec

Interior decorating courses near Stonehenge

Val Maclay is a specialist painter and a master of creating wall and furniture finishes to enhance homes. She runs tailor-made interior decorating courses from her Wiltshire farmhouse, aimed either at those wanting to learn how to paint their own homes or wanting to begin their own careers in interior decorating. She will assemble groups of five people with similar interests, be it wall finishes, frames or professional careers, and teach them about marblising, faux stone, faux silk, wood-graining and other techniques. Students can stay in Val's Georgian home: she does B&B as well as the courses, and serves evening dinners where all guests eat together.

Contact
Val Maclay
Hilcott Farm House
Hilcott
Marlborough
Wiltshire SN9 6LE
Tel: 01672 851372
Email: maclay@hilcott.com

Practical information
Duration: 2–5 days
Level: beginner &
intermediate
Residential

Group size: 3–5
Prices available on
application
Unsuitable for children
Pets not welcome

Courses available in:

Jan	Feb	Mar	Apr	May	Jun	Jul	Aug	Sep	Oct	Nov	Dec

Mandala designs in North Cornwall

You may not know very much about mandalas and their subtle designs, but a course with Jane Blonder will put that to rights. These unusual textiles – forms within circles – are common to many cultures, from Tibetan to Native American. Jane has been designing them for the last 10 years and specialises in geometric designs. On her five-day course students should complete a mandala, while the shorter courses will enable them to understand their design and begin production. The courses are based at Jane's farmhouse, where she provides full-board accommodation. The farm promotes sustainable living and has two studios, one producing mandalas, the other involved in hemp manufacture.

Contact
Jane Blonder
Beeston Farm
Marhamchurch
Bude
Cornwall EX23 0ET
Tel: 01288 381638
Web: www.threadsoftime.co.uk

Practical information
Duration: 2–5 days
Level: beginner
Residential
Group size: 6–25

Price range: £50–£300
Prices include: meals &
accommodation
Unsuitable for children
Pets not welcome

Courses available in:

Jan	Feb	Mar	Apr	May	Jun	Jul	Aug	Sep	Oct	Nov	Dec

HOTEL TRESANTON, ST MAWES

Bridge, painting and physio in a beautiful Cornish hotel

One of Cornwall's most special hotels, Tresanton offers various courses as an extra enticement to bring guests down to this beautiful peninsula. The hotel is made up of a group of old houses on the edge of St Mawes and was bought in 1997 by Olga Polizzi. She redesigned the interiors, imbued the whole place with a Mediterranean feel, and turned it into the destination it is today.

Courses
All-inclusive courses include bridge, painting, yoga and back-oriented physiotherapy. Jonathan Tetley's painting courses include trips to local galleries; Paul Mendelson's bridge week finishes with a weekend of poker. Then there's a detoxifying yoga retreat with Jean Hall, and Sarah Key's 'back in a week' course.

What's special?
Bridge tuition doesn't come any better than this. Paul is a two-time national champion and the four-day course will set you on the road to greatness. Afterwards you can stay on for the weekend poker course. As for the backs, Sarah not only treats participants, but also gives them a technical, personal report and teaches them what to do to sort out their own problems.

Eating & sleeping
There are 29 rooms individually furnished with antiques and Cornish art, and all have sea views. The restaurant specialises in seafood – with a hint of Italian – under head chef Paul Wadham.

Directions
A3078 or B3289 to St Just in Roseland; follow signs to St Mawes; after water tower turn right towards St Mawes Castle; hotel is 200 yards past the castle on the left. Alternatively, plane to Newquay or train to St Austell.

In the area
45 minutes to Truro and St Austell; 45 minutes to the Lost Gardens of Heligan and the Eden Project; 1 hour to Padstow. Trelissick, Trebah and Glendurgan gardens are all nearby.

Contact
Federica Bertolini
Hotel Tresanton
27 Lower Castle Road
St Mawes
Cornwall TR2 5DR
Tel: 01326 270 055
Web: www.tresanton.com
Email: info@tresanton.com

Practical information
Duration: 4–6 days
Level: beginner,
intermediate & advanced
Residential
Group size: 2–20

Price range: £500+
Prices include: meals &
accommodation
Child-friendly
Pets not welcome

Courses available in:

Jan	Feb	Mar	Apr	May	Jun	Jul	Aug	Sep	Oct	Nov	Dec

Canal art on the Kennet

Jane Clements runs two-day courses in Canal Art on the Kennet and Avon Canal in Devizes. The subject matter is traditional 'roses and castles' (landscapes surrounded by floral designs), a style developed in English boat yards for decorating the interior and exterior of canal boats and the objects they contain. During the course, participants will decorate a pre-painted background, learning skills that will enable them to go home and paint boats if they have them, and watering cans and buckets if they don't. And many participants don't. Previously a science teacher, Jane has been teaching Canal Art for five years.

Contact
Jane Clements
45 Buckingham Road Lawn
Swindon
Wiltshire SN3 1HZ
Tel: 01793 615898
Web: spengi@ntlworld.com

Practical information
Duration: 2 days
Level: beginner
Non-residential
Group size: 3–10

Price range: £50–£100
Prices include: lunch
Unsuitable for children
Pets not welcome

Courses available in:

Jan	Feb	Mar	Apr	May	Jun	Jul	Aug	Sep	Oct	Nov	Dec

Kiln-formed glass workshop in Porthtowan

Kiln-formed glass-making is a relatively new art form and Vanessa Langley is one of the few people in Britain offering classes. Her two- or three-day courses are suitable for beginners and those with previous experience of glass-making. The technique is more forgiving than stained glass and first-time students can achieve excellent results. Vanessa has been practising for eight years in the Truro area, moving to this new studio in Porthtowan in late 2004. She organises courses on an ad hoc basis. The two-day version introduces handling, cutting and firing glass, and the piece you produce on Day One is fired overnight, ready for appraisal on Day Two.

Contact
Vanessa Langley
Java Glass
Causilgey Manor
Tregavethan
Truro
Cornwall TR4 9EP
Tel: 01872 561376
Web: www.javaglass.co.uk

Practical information
Duration: 2–3 days
Level: beginner,
intermediate & advanced
Non-residential

Group size: 2–10
Price range: £100–£200
Unsuitable for children
Pets not welcome

Courses available in:

Jan	Feb	Mar	Apr	May	Jun	Jul	Aug	Sep	Oct	Nov	Dec

Drawing classes in the centre of Salisbury

Sight-size is a way of drawing that involves putting the canvas next to the subject and retiring to a distance to decide on your next mark. Jonathan Tetley learnt this naturalistic method, which has been used since the days of Van Dyck, while training in Florence, and since 1997 has been teaching it to course participants. He teaches with a colleague to ensure excellent levels of personal attention, and also runs life classes which focus on anatomy by using longer poses (as do the sight-size classes). Courses take place in a studio in the cathedral close in Salisbury, a beautiful spot with many accommodation and eating possibilities nearby.

Contact
Jonathan Tetley
51 Wiltshire Road
Harnham
Salisbury
Wiltshire SP2 8HT
Tel: 07771 906948
Email: jptetley@f2s.com

Practical information
Duration: 5 days
Level: intermediate
Non-residential

Group size: 6–5
Price range: £200–£400
Unsuitable for children
Pets not welcome

Courses available in:

Jan	Feb	Mar	Apr	May	Jun	Jul	Aug	Sep	Oct	Nov	Dec

JACKDAWS EDUCATIONAL TRUST, FROME

Classical music performance courses in the Vallis Vale

Jackdaws is a friendly place that preaches the joys of classical music performance to participants on its courses. The organisation developed out of a classical music festival that Maureen Lehane Wishart was running nearby, but really took off after funds were raised to buy a house in a stunning part of rural Somerset, and convert it to a permanent base. The emphasis is on group learning, and while courses are undoubtedly fun, you should come prepared to be industrious!

Courses
There are masterclasses in voice, piano, strings, and wind instruments with specific courses aimed at specific playing abilities: frightened, faltering or fluent. Tutors are all top-class teachers and performers. If you're not a player, you could try one of the 'listening courses' where you learn about particular composers and pieces over a weekend.

What's special?
The voice workshops – such as 'Discover your voice', which lays the physical and vocal foundations for a better singing technique, or 'Singing for the Over 60s', aimed at those who have not sung for some time or who want to keep their voices in decent condition.

Eating & sleeping
Jackdaws can arrange B&B in houses in the village for £22 per person. Lunches and dinners are taken together at Jackdaws, with lots of home-made dishes.

Directions
A362 from Frome towards Radstock. Left after half a mile towards Hapsford/Great Elm. Into Great Elm and left after half a mile to Jackdaws. Or train to Frome, then taxi to Great Elm.

In the area
Wells, Salisbury and Bath are all within an hour's drive, and there are plenty of nearby walks in this rural area.

Contact
Maureen Lehane Wishart
Jackdaws Educational Trust
Great Elm
Frome
Somerset
Tel: 01373 812383
Web: www.jackdaws.org.uk
Email: music@jackdaws.org

Practical information
Duration: 2 days
Level: beginner,
intermediate & advanced
Residential & non-residential
Group size: 3–25

Price range: £100–£150
Unsuitable for children
Pets not welcome

Courses available in:

Jan	Feb	Mar	Apr	May	Jun	Jul	Aug	Sep	Oct	Nov	Dec

THE KINGCOMBE CENTRE, DORCHESTER
Wildlife, music and art in west Dorset

This independent environmental study centre in west Dorset is an ideal spot for those wanting to learn about conservation and rural matters in a relaxed, picturesque setting. Surrounding the Centre, the Dorset Wildlife Trust owns 430 acres which have never been treated with chemicals, creating an excellent setting for nature-oriented learning. As well as conservation, Kingcombe offers day-long and residential courses in music, drawing/painting, crafts/photography, writing, geology and others, with tutors coming from all over the country. The Kingcombe Centre comprises a beautiful main barn, the Cowshed, which has been sensitively converted and luxurious Beech Cottage 300 metres up the lane. The Centre has a reputation for the high standard of its catering using local and organic produce.

What's special?
Ecological efforts made in the Lower Kingcombe Valley have ensured that it feels almost unaffected by modern life. There are small pastures, flower meadows, traditional hedgerows and an abundance of wildlife that inspire the courses. The Centre has excellent facilities for the visually impaired and people with disabilities, with wheelchair paths to all parts of the grounds. An electric buggy gives access to most parts of the reserve.

Eating & sleeping
There are two lovely local pubs – the Spyway Inn (01308 485250) in Askerswell and the Marquis of Lorne (01308 485236) in Nettlecombe. For accommodation, there is a holiday cottage nearby sleeping 4 to 6 (01300 321537).

Directions
The Kingcombe Centre is next to the Dorset Wildlife Trust visitor centre in Lower Kingcombe. Turn off the Dorchester-Crewkerne Road (A356) to Toller Porcorum, and turn right in the village along Kingcombe Road. Nearest stations are Maiden Newton or Dorchester South; pick-ups available.

In the area
West Dorset is beautiful, with plenty of walking, cycling and birdwatching opportunities. Other attractions nearby include Maiden Castle, the waterfalls at Athelhampton House, the Dorset County Museum and a complete Roman townhouse in Dorchester.

Contact
Pauline Lowry
The Kingcombe Centre
Toller Porcorum
Dorchester
Dorset DT2 0EQ
Tel: 01300 320684
Web: www.kingcombe-centre.demon.co.uk
Email: kingcombe@kingcombe-centre.demon.co.uk

Practical information
Duration: 2–7 days
Level: beginner,
intermediate & advanced
Residential & non-residential
Group size: 6–25+

Price range: £100–£300
Prices include: meals &
accommodation
Unsuitable for children
Pets not welcome

Courses available in:

Jan	Feb	Mar	Apr	May	Jun	Jul	Aug	Sep	Oct	Nov	Dec

LIQUID GLASS CENTRE, TROWBRIDGE

Traditional and contemporary glassmaking near the River Frome

The Liquid Glass Centre teaches a variety of glass-making skills. They have weekend courses dedicated to glass-blowing, kiln-casting and 'fusing and slumping' where glass is merged by melting. If you're unsure which to pursue, there's a one-day taster course, or try the week-long version at the Spring School, which introduces all the techniques before you decide where to specialise. The centre is run by three professional glass artists who do the vast majority of the teaching. It's a very hands-on experience, very creative and very fun. The Glass Centre is based at Stowford Manor, a Tudor farm near Bath whose outbuildings have been taken over by various craft enterprises. When the glass blowing gets too hot, you can cool off in the river that runs past outside. Local pubs serve lunches, and cream teas are available on site.

What's special?

This is one of the few places in England to offer such an extensive array of glass techniques – certainly on such a friendly basis. The setting is unbeatable, surrounded by workshops housing a stonemason, a furniture maker, a studio gallery... and there is a folk festival held here every summer.

Eating & sleeping

For food: the Thai Barn in Bradford on Avon (01225 866443) or The Poplars pub (01225 752426). There is summer camping at the farm, B&B at Stowford Mill (01225 775919) and Home Farm (01225 764492), both in Wingfield, or self-catering at Church Farm Cottages (01225 722246) in Winsley.

Directions

Stowford Manor Farm sits between Wingfield and Farleigh Hungerford on the A366. It is 3 miles west of Trowbridge and 8 miles from Bath. Stations: Bradford on Avon, Trowbridge and Bath.

In the area

Farleigh Hungerford has a 14th-century castle within walking distance and Castle Combe is also worth a visit. Bath is 15 minutes away.

Contact

Kim Atherton
Liquid Glass Centre
Stowford Manor Farm
Wingfield
Trowbridge
Wiltshire
Tel: 01225 768888
Web: www.liquidglasscentre.com
Email: kim@angelmedia.co.uk

Practical information

Duration: 2–5 days
Level: beginner & intermediate
Non-residential
Group size: 3–10

Price range: £200–£500
Prices include: all materials
Unsuitable for children
Pets not welcome

Courses available in:

Jan	Feb	Mar	Apr	May	Jun	Jul	Aug	Sep	Oct	Nov	Dec

Cotswold photography and painting courses

Kel Portman runs courses in photography and painting from a beautiful part of the Cotswolds. The courses are landscape-based, drawing inspiration from the limestone hills of the Cotswold Edge. The photography courses focus on subject matter and are more about art than technology, although Kel will also run courses geared to the editing of digital pictures. The painting courses will be partially studio-based, but will mainly focus on the outdoors, capturing market towns, farms and, of course, landscapes. Kel is a practising artist who began his career as a print-maker. He was an art lecturer in London before 'retiring' to the West Country to paint, run courses… and teach windsurfing!

Contact
Kel Portman
Boundary Cottage
Back Edge Lane
The Edge
Gloucestershire GL6 6PE
Tel: 01452 812224
Web: www.artbreaks.ndo.co.uk

Practical information
Duration: 2 days
Level: beginner,
intermediate & advanced
Non-residential

Group size: 3–10
Price range: £100–£150
Unsuitable for children
Pets not welcome

Courses available in:

| Jan | Feb | Mar | Apr | May | Jun | Jul | Aug | Sep | Oct | Nov | Dec |

Craft courses on the Somerset Levels

This is a new arts and crafts operation offering courses in a pretty location on the Somerset Levels, near the River Parrett. Cherry Dobson has been teaching upholstery for 20 years and offers tuition in traditional and modern techniques. Students should bring their own project to work on or ask for one to be provided. Cherry also runs courses in patchwork and loose covers, while external experts provide instruction in quilting and oil painting. The studio is in a converted barn in a corner of Cherry's property and looks out into the garden. Guests can stay on a farm B&B nearby where the farmer will arrange walks for non-crafting partners.

Contact
Cherry Dobson
Lilac Barn
Lilac Cottage
Stathe Road
Burrowbridge
Somerset TA7 0JH
Tel: 01823 690134
Web: www.lilacbarn.co.uk

Practical information
Duration: 5 days
Level: beginner &
intermediate
Residential
Group size: 3–10

Price range: £300–£400
Price includes: meals &
accommodation
Unsuitable for children
Pets not welcome

Courses available in:

| Jan | Feb | Mar | Apr | May | Jun | Jul | Aug | Sep | Oct | Nov | Dec |

Falconry week near Bideford Bay

Jonathan Marshall's falconry courses offer a thorough introduction to the hobby. Each participant works with their own bird and progresses from handling a new bird through to hunting – learning enough to acquire and look after a bird of their own, should they be interested. There is a written exam at the end of the week, which people usually pass. Beginners' courses use Harris hawks, but Jonathan also runs an advanced course using 'long wings' (falcons). He has been a professional falconer since 1986 and trains birds for films. He uses the Hoops Inn near Clovelly as his base (accommodation discounts possible), and there is a cliff nearby for flying the birds.

Contact
Jonathan Marshall
Marshall Falcons
Coombe Cottage
Lake, Nr Tawstock
Devon EX31 3HU
Tel: 01271 373309
Web: www.marshallfalcons.co.uk

Practical information
Duration: 5 days
Level: beginner &
intermediate
Non-residential

Group size: 3–5
Price range: £200–£300
Unsuitable for children
Pets not welcome

Courses available in:

| Jan | Feb | Mar | Apr | May | Jun | Jul | Aug | Sep | Oct | Nov | Dec |

MINSTRELS MUSICAL HOLIDAYS, LAUNCESTON

Music-making in the North Cornwall countryside

Friendly, informal and fun… this is what music-making should be about. You spend a week rehearsing and sightseeing in North Cornwall, building up to a last-night concert. The Minstrels courses give participants the chance to perform in front of a supportive audience. It's a family-run business based on a former dairy farm in a rural setting, and the Music Centre is a purpose-built conversion of the old milking parlour. Andrew Barclay is an experienced conductor; wife Penny teaches strings and piano; and her parents Raymond and Veronica Jones run the centre.

Courses
Mornings are spent preparing your pieces; afternoons are 'holiday', when you can visit local sites in the Minstrels minibus; and in the evenings you can meet to discuss your progress. Courses include 'Pianists' and 'Strings' - separate courses for those of (roughly) Grade 4 and higher; 'Village Orchestra', which introduces the pleasures of ensemble playing; and 'Choral Singers'.

What's special?
Our favourite course is 'Choral Singers' which encapsulates the ethos of the Minstrels. It's a large, mixed ability group, so no experience is needed, and participants sing a range of pieces from classical to popular.

Eating & sleeping
Trencreek Farmhouse (01840 230219) offers B&B, and Cherry Tree Cottage (01288 362000) is self-catered. Minstrels hosts an informal music supper mid-week, with a private farm dinner on another night.

Directions
On the north Cornwall coast ten miles north of Launceston, ten miles south of Bude. Map on website.

In the area
Local attractions include the Eden Project, Tintagel, Lost Gardens of Heligan, Camel Valley Wine Centre, Padstow, the coastal path and various beaches. Famous local houses include Cotehele, Lanhydrock.

Contact
Andrew and Penny Barclay
Minstrels Musical Holidays
Rosendale Cottage
Canworthy Water
Launceston
Cornwall
Tel: 01566 781284/781491
Web: www.travellingminstrels.co.uk
Email: enquiries@travellingminstrels.co.uk

Practical information
Duration: 3–6 days
Level: beginner & intermediate
Non-residential
Group size: 3–20

Price range: £100–£300
Prices include: lunches
Unsuitable for children
Pets not welcome

Courses available in:

Jan	Feb	Mar	Apr	May	Jun	Jul	Aug	Sep	Oct	Nov	Dec
			Apr			Jul	Aug		Oct		

Wide range of weekend jewellery courses in St Austell

The Mid Cornwall School of Jewellery (MCSJ) has the widest range of jewellery courses in the UK. Classes are kept small so that all participants advance at their own pace. The eight tutors specialise in different fields, so, if your interest is silverwork, enamelling, engraving, glass-fusing, repair or any other jewellery-related discipline, you will find a suitable course. You can even make your own wedding ring. Courses are aimed at particular skill levels, and MCSJ can often be flexible about running them consecutively. In 2005 the school will begin masterclasses aimed at professionals, and come the spring they will be moving to a rural location six miles outside St Austell.

Contact
Lisa Cain
Mid Cornwall School of Jewellery
19-21 High Cross St
St Austell
Cornwall
Tel: 01726 73319
Web: www.mcsj.co.uk

Practical information
Duration: 2–5 days
Level: beginner,
intermediate & advanced
Non-residential

Group size: 3–10
Price range: £150–£500
Unsuitable for children
Pets not welcome

Courses available in:

Jan	Feb	Mar	Apr	May	Jun	Jul	Aug	Sep	Oct	Nov	Dec

Rural crafts on the Devon-Somerset border

This venue for craft courses is full of the enthusiasm of youth, having only started operations in 2004. It is located in an Area of Outstanding Natural Beauty in the Blackdown Hills and is a very easy-going environment. Much of the work is done outside, inspired by views across the valley, past the alpacas and the sheep. Tracey teaches tassemetrie (tassels and trimmings) and uses experienced craftspeople – full-time artists, rather than full-time teachers – for the other courses. There are two-day courses in, among other subjects, jewellery, chair-making, pewter-casting, stone-carving, stained glass and basket-making (trugs and apple-pickers). Prices are extremely reasonable and there is lots of local accommodation.

Contact
Tracey Bell
The Old Kennels
Stentwood
Dunkeswell
Devon
Tel: 01823 681138
Web: www.theoldkennels.co.uk

Practical information
Duration: 2–3 days
Level: beginner &
intermediate
Non-residential

Group size: 3–15
Price range: £50–£150
Unsuitable for children
Pets not welcome

Courses available in:

Jan	Feb	Mar	Apr	May	Jun	Jul	Aug	Sep	Oct	Nov	Dec

Arts and crafts breaks in an old chapel

Nancy Pickard's home a few miles from Land's End is a converted Wesleyan Chapel more than 200 years old and is a fantastic place to stay (in an adjoining chapel) and learn new skills. She leads enamelling, silverwork and jewellery workshops in the main space, which also doubles as her gallery. And having worked in community arts for 15 years, she knows how to inspire students. The enamelling course gives students confidence in red-hot metals, and the speed of the firing provides plenty of opportunity to create different items. 'Silverwork' focuses on ways to make and join shapes, 'Junk jewellery' on how to make items from inexpensive materials.

Contact
Nancy Pickard
Old Sunday School
Cape Cornwall Street
St Just-in-Penwith
Cornwall
Tel: 01736 788444
Web: www.oldsundayschool.co.uk

Practical information
Duration: 3 days
Level: beginner &
intermediate
Residential
Group size: 3–10

Price range: £200–£300
Prices include: meals,
accommodation & lunch not
included
Unsuitable for children
Pets not welcome

Courses available in:

Jan	Feb	Mar	Apr	May	Jun	Jul	Aug	Sep	Oct	Nov	Dec

Seafood school attached to Rick Stein's famous restaurant

Owned by Rick Stein, whose famous restaurant sits next door, this cookery school specialises in (what else!) fish and shellfish. The central Padstow location has views of the Camel Estuary from where most of the fish comes. Lessons are taught by top-class chefs from the restaurant, and you sleep either in rooms above the restaurant or in a nearby hotel. In the signature Fish and Shellfish course you watch demonstrations, make a seafood lunch and learn other relevant techniques, while the Food Heroes course is based on Rick's TV series. There are also two-day courses in Thai & Chinese, French & Italian, Australian and South Indian seafood.

Contact
Debbie Hill
Padstow Seafood School
The Seafood Restaurant
Riverside
Padstow
Cornwall PL28 8BY
Tel: 01841 533466
Web: www.rickstein.com

Practical information
Duration: 2–4 days
Level: beginner &
intermediate
Residential & non-residential
Group size: 11–20

Courses available in:

Jan	Feb	Mar	Apr	May	Jun	Jul	Aug	Sep	Oct	Nov	Dec

Price range: £300–£500+
Prices include: meals
Unsuitable for children
Pets not welcome

South
West

Bread-making in working Dorset flour mill

Paul is the South-West's bread guru, teaching, consulting and generally doing everything possible to train the world to appreciate a proper loaf. He has been in craft (not industrial) baking for 30 years, and ran a bakery in Australia for 10 years before coming to south-west England. He now runs courses from Cann Mills, a working watermill near Shaftesbury, where the (fifth-generation) miller will show participants around. The Basic Course introduces yeast, fermentation, kneading, gluten, flours; Continental courses concentrate on baguettes, ciabatta, pains de campagne, croissants and brioche, British Traditional courses on bloomers, cottage loaves, malted breads and rye breads. Accommodation can be arranged.

Contact
Paul Merry
Panary
6 Empire Road
Salisbury
Wiltshire SP2 9DF
Tel: 01722 341447
Web: www.panary.co.uk

Practical information
Duration: 2–4 days
Level: beginner &
intermediate
Non-residential
Group sizes: #N/A

Courses available in:

Jan	Feb	Mar	Apr	May	Jun	Jul	Aug	Sep	Oct	Nov	Dec

Price range: £200–£500
Prices include: dinner one
day, lunch each day
Unsuitable for children
Pets not welcome

French polishing and furniture restoration in Cornwall

Peter Thomson is a fourth-generation furniture restorer who has worked for the National Trust, Sotheby's and the Jordanian royal family. He runs courses in hand-finishing and restoration from a converted 19th-century chapel in beautiful countryside near Fowey. Participants can bring their own pieces to work on, but Peter recommends that beginners learn the techniques first and practise on pieces that he will provide. In the polishing course you use traditional methods and learn about stains, chemicals and pigments. The cabinet-making course teaches you basic skills, such as planing, cutting and sharpening before moving on to dismantling, gluing and veneering. Skilled practitioners are welcome, or they can attend the intermediate and professional classes.

Contact
Peter Thomson
The Retreat
Lanteglos Highway
Nr Fowey
Cornwall PL23 1ND
Tel: 01726 870048

Practical information
Duration: 5 days
Level: beginner,
intermediate & advanced
Non-residential

Courses available in:

Jan	Feb	Mar	Apr	May	Jun	Jul	Aug	Sep	Oct	Nov	Dec

Group size: 3–10
Price range: £300–£400
Unsuitable for children
Pets not welcome

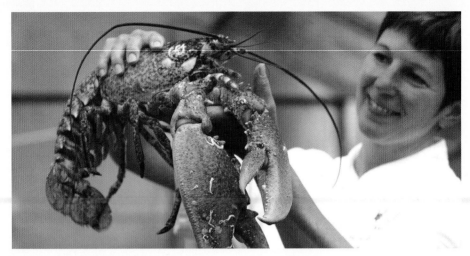

PERCY'S COUNTRY HOTEL AND RESTAURANT, VIRGINSTOW

Informal workshops with Devon's top female chef

Combine one of Devon's finest hotels with one of its top chefs, and a cookery course at Percy's becomes a feast in every sense. Since opening in 1996, Tina Bricknell-Webb has let her cooking be determined by what grows around her: organic, home-reared lamb, eggs and pork plus some of the freshest fish to be found in the county. Tina's cookery workshops have an ambience more akin to a home kitchen than a classroom, with participants discussing in advance what they want to learn. The hotel is cocooned amidst 130 organic acres on the Devon-Cornwall border and offers stunning walks, enchanting wildlife and tranquillity.

Courses
Courses usually happen on Monday and Tuesday (although other weekdays are available) and are themed by subject: fish, game, lamb, meat, desserts and gluten-free. The kitchens have been recently fitted with state-of-the-art induction hobs. Bespoke courses are available.

What's special?
The fish course is the most popular, and involves an optional early-morning trip to bid for the catch at nearby Looe market, fish preparation techniques, dinner party dishes and sauces. The gluten-free course is very useful for coeliacs as it introduces an array of innovative ways to make cakes, breads, puddings and sauces.

Eating & sleeping
Full-board accommodation is provided in one of the 11 luxuriously appointed rooms, most of which have jacuzzis. Participants' lunch is the fruit of their morning labours, while dinner is a special, three-course Percy's effort. Percy's has a mail-order service for its organic and gluten-free offerings: www.organicmeat.co.uk

Directions
From Launceston: A388 towards Holsworthy. Right at St.Giles-on-the-Heath. 2.2 miles to Percy's on the right. From Okehampton: A3079 for 8.3 miles to Metherell Cross. Left and 6.5 miles to Percy's on the left.

In the area
40 minutes to the Eden Project or the North Cornwall coast. 15 minutes to Launceston. Many National Trust properties in the area: Lydford Gorge, Saltram House, Cotehele, Buckland Abbey and Lanhydrock Gardens. Within five minutes of Percy's, Roadford Lake offers excellent water sports and fishing.

Contact
Tina Bricknell-Webb
Percy's Country Hotel and Restaurant
Coombeshead Estate
Virginstow, Devon EX21 5EA
Tel: 01409 211236
Web: www.percys.co.uk
Email: info@percys.co.uk
Web: www.learningstone.net
Email: psqt@learningstone.net

Practical information
Duration: 2 days
Level: beginner, intermediate & advanced
Residential
Group size: 3–10

Price range: £300–£500
Prices include: meals, accommodation & ingredients, knives and aprons
Unsuitable for children
Pet-friendly

Courses available in:

Jan	Feb	Mar	Apr	May	Jun	Jul	Aug	Sep	Oct	Nov	Dec

Stone workshops on the Isle of Portland

In an inspiring, historic quarry setting on the Isle of Portland, the Portland Sculpture and Quarry Trust runs stone-carving and sculpture workshops as part of its effort to regenerate the quarry landscape, and keep alive the stone-working skills and quarrying heritage. The UK's first sculpture quarry and a Site of Special Scientific Interest, it is coloured by rare grasses, butterflies and orchids. If you need inspiration you can wander around and admire the 50 or so works in situ, including a sculpture by Antony Gormley.

Courses

The workshop is in the heart of the quarry, surrounded by sea, sky and stone. The quality of light is superb and is essential to carving. Portland stone is an excellent medium for beginners, and for many a week here is the start of a lifetime hobby, even a full-time pursuit. The tuition provided ensures you will achieve a high quality of work to take home with you.

What's special?

The links between the workshop, the history of working stone on Portland, the geology and the quarrying process. You carve using the same tools as stone masons and carvers 300 years before you, surrounded by the stacked stone that the old quarrymen left behind. (In winter, you work indoors.)

Eating & sleeping

Self-catering at The Old Lower Lighthouse Portland Bird Observatory (£9 per person, 01305 820553); B&B en-suite at The Old Vicarage (01305 824117) or the Portland Heights Hotel (01305 821361).

Directions

Train to Weymouth, then taxi or bus to Portland. By car: follow signs to Portland from Weymouth.
3 hours from London: M3, M27 west, A31 Ringwood/Dorchester, A354 Weymouth, then signs to Portland.

In the area

Non-participants should explore the contrasting quarry environments such as Kingbarrow and Broadcroft butterfly reserve, and visit the Learningstone Centre with its interpretation of the unique local geology (Jurassic), quarrying heritage and the uses of Portland stone. There is also climbing, abseiling, sailing and diving, plus coastal walks.

Contact

Hannah Sofaer
Portland Sculpture and Quarry Trust
Learningstone Centre
The Drill Hall, Easton Lane
Portland
Dorset DT5 1BW
Tel: 01305 826736
Web: www.learningstone.net
Email: psqt@learningstone.net

Practical information

Duration: 3–5 days
Level: beginner, intermediate & advanced
Non-residential
Group size: 6–15

Price range: £200–£300
Child-friendly
Pet-friendly

Courses available in:

Jan	Feb	Mar	Apr	May	Jun	Jul	Aug	Sep	Oct	Nov	Dec

Cider-making and willow craft in the Forest of Dean

Ragmans Lane is a small farm in a glorious Forest of Dean setting right by the River Wye. Run on permaculture principles, the farm produces apple juice (from unsprayed trees) and shiitake mushroom logs. They also run courses in cider-making and play host to others. The cider-making involves collecting the apples, pressing them, various tastings and a look at perry-making, before participants head home with samples of their juice and cider. The Willow Bank organises weekend courses in living willow structures on the same site, and there are also permaculture design courses lasting a fortnight. Participants can stay in the bunk house or in local B&Bs; meals are provided on site.

Contact
Matt Dunwell
Ragmans
Ragmans Lane Farm
Lower Lydbrook
Gloucestershire
Tel: 01594 860244
Web: www.ragmans.co.uk

Practical information
Duration: 2 days
Level: beginner
Residential & non-residential
Group size: 6–15

Courses available in:

Jan	Feb	Mar	Apr	May	Jun	Jul	Aug	Sep	Oct	Nov	Dec

Price range: £100–£150
Unsuitable for children
Pets not welcome

Pottery courses in the village of Queen Camel

Doug Phillips's five-day 'General Throwing' course shows students the potter's complete working cycle, while they make their own pot. They see how clay is taken from the ground, then spend three days working on the wheel, followed by a day decorating and a day firing. Your pot goes home with you. Doug's approach is holistic and he will also teach about the history and chemistry of pottery. He and wife Jennie are both practising potters (Doug since 1968) with Jennie focusing more on decorating. They can arrange accommodation in private houses in this beautiful old village; there are lots of pubs for evening meals and Jennie does a fantastic lunch.

Contact
Douglas and Jennie Phillips
Ridge Pottery
Queen Camel
Yeovil
Somerset
Tel: 01935 850753
Web: www.mud2fire.co.uk

Practical information
Duration: 2–5 days
Level: beginner,
intermediate & advanced
Non-residential
Group size: 2–10

Courses available in:

Jan	Feb	Mar	Apr	May	Jun	Jul	Aug	Sep	Oct	Nov	Dec

Price range: £50–£300
Prices include: lunch
Unsuitable for children
Pets not welcome

Watercolour painting courses by artist Paul Riley

This peaceful spot, beside a stream just outside Dittisham, is an ideal place for an all-inclusive, relaxing, rural art course. Paul Riley teaches oils, pastels and drawing, but specialises in watercolours, especially flowers and still life. He exhibited at the Royal Academy's Summer Exhibition aged 15, the youngest person ever to have done so, and has been a professional artist all his life. In the mornings Paul demonstrates, then guides the students in their practice. In the afternoons students go and explore the area or paint by themselves, before a late-afternoon session with either demonstration or critique. Accommodation is based around a courtyard, and meals are eaten together.

Contact
Paul Riley
Riley Arts
Coombe Farm Studios
Dittisham
Devon
Tel: 01803 722352
Web: www.rileyarts.com

Practical information
Duration: 3–5 days
Level: beginner,
intermediate & advanced
Residential
Group size: 3–15
Courses available in:

Jan	Feb	Mar	Apr	May	Jun	Jul	Aug	Sep	Oct	Nov	Dec

Price range: £200–£500
Prices include: meals &
accommodation
Unsuitable for children
Pets not welcome

All types of fishing tuition and guiding in Somerset

Robin Gurden offers all sorts of fishing tuition in Somerset where he has exclusive rights on parts of the River Barle and Upper Exe. He tailors courses to individual needs, be it a half a day's tuition or three. Beginners will usually specify river or lake fishing and Robin can teach competency in two to three days; he has use of three stocked training pools. If you already have some skill, Robin will demonstrate more advanced techniques and fish craft – casting for salmon, sea trout, etc. He can run all-inclusive courses, arranging accommodation and meals as desired. Tuition is £120 per long day for one person; £140 for two.

Contact
Robin Gurden
3 Edbrooke Cottages
Winsford
Nr Minehead
Somerset TA24 7AE
Tel: 01643 703728
Web: http://freespace.virgin.net/complete.angling

Practical information
Duration: 2–3 days
Level: beginner,
intermediate & advanced
Non-residential

Group size: 1–10
Price range: £100–£300
Unsuitable for children
Pets not welcome

Courses available in:

Jan	Feb	Mar	Apr	May	Jun	Jul	Aug	Sep	Oct	Nov	Dec

South West

Batik Courses on Bodmin Moor

Batik is an art form involving the manipulation of wax and dye, and Robin Paris discovered its joys in Malaysia in 1990. She has been spreading the word ever since, exhibiting around Europe and running courses. These courses happen at various Cornish venues – some residential, some not; see her website for more details – and are aimed at differing levels of batik expertise. Robin uses inspirations from her travels and the Cornish countryside in her work, and the courses incorporate wildlife, cultural and environmental themes. Mornings will often be spent out in the landscape sketching and finding inspiration for batik activities later in the day.

Contact
Robin Paris
4 The Row
Five Lanes
Launceston
Cornwall PL15 7RX
Tel: 01566 86465
Web: www.robinparis.co.uk

Practical information
Duration: 2–4 days
Level: beginner,
intermediate & advanced
Residential

& non-residential
Group size: 3–10
Price range: £50–£200
Unsuitable for children
Pets not welcome

Courses available in:

Jan	Feb	Mar	Apr	May	Jun	Jul	Aug	Sep	Oct	Nov	Dec

Creative and reflective writing courses on the banks of the Tamar

Roselle Angwin runs creative and reflective writing weekends on the banks of the River Tamar. A widely published writer, she has the gift for filling others with confidence in their own efforts, which is why so many people keep coming back. Courses are participatory, but you only read if you're comfortable. Based in a beautiful location in the Tamar Valley, you will eat and write with views of the river and the oystercatchers. The main courses are: Writing from Life; poetry retreat; Writing for Self-discovery; and short stories. Non-participants can amuse themselves in Plymouth, Dartmoor or Bodmin. Roselle also runs courses on Iona and in mid-Wales.

Contact
Roselle Angwin
PO Box 17
Yelverton
Devon PL20 6YF
Tel: 01822 841081
Web: www.roselle-angwin.co.uk

Practical information
Duration: 2 days
Level: beginner &
intermediate
Residential
Group size: 3–10

Price range: £200–£300
Prices include: meals &
accommodation
Unsuitable for children
Pets not welcome

Courses available in:

Jan	Feb	Mar	Apr	May	Jun	Jul	Aug	Sep	Oct	Nov	Dec

Stone-carving and 3-D sculpture in rural Somerset

Shute Farm Studio was established to provide access to a variety of art forms, such as stone-carving, bronze-casting, calligraphy and papier mâché, for those who might not otherwise get the opportunity. This former dairy farm in the Somerset countryside aims to link art with agriculture, promoting some of the less modern arts so that new practitioners can help invigorate the tradition. Non-residential courses are run by specialist tutors in studios converted from old farm outbuildings You can try: stone-carving – designing a sculpture, learning carving techniques and producing your own work; bronze-casting – create two finished bronze sculptures; portrait-modelling – life-sized terracotta portraits; hand-built ceramics – coiling, slabbing and other decorative methods.

Contact
Fran Britten
Shute Farm Studio
Downhead
Nr Shepton Mallet
Somerset BA4 4LQ
Tel: 01749 880746
Web: www.shutefarmstudio.org.uk

Practical information
Duration: 2–5 days
Level: beginner &
intermediate
Non-residential

Courses available in: not applicable

Group sizes: 3–15
Price range: £100–£300
Unsuitable for children
Pets not welcome

Photography holidays on Dartmoor and Devon coast

If you're passionate about photography, you'll find a kindred spirit in Lee Pengelly. He has been a full-time freelance photographer since 2000 and runs three courses that use the Devon countryside as a teaching studio. Discover the South Coast concentrates on fishing villages, estuaries and coastlines; Discover Dartmoor explores the wilderness; and Discover Devon combines the two. You stay in a Dartmoor hotel and visit four to five places each day, learning about techniques, composition, filters and camera types. Devon born and bred, Lee will drive you to hidden parts of the county that visitors might not otherwise find, to photograph subject matter encompassing landscape, architecture and nature.

Contact
Lee Pengelly
Silverscene Photography
31 Fleet Street
Keyham
Plymouth
Devon PL2 2BX
Tel: 01752 500346
Web: www.silverscenephoto.co.uk

Practical information
Duration: 3–5 days
Level: beginner,
intermediate & advanced
Residential & non-residential
Group size: 3–10

Courses available in:

Price range: £300–£500
Prices include: meals &
accommodation
Unsuitable for children
Pets not welcome

Jan	Feb	Mar	Apr	May	Jun	Jul	Aug	Sep	Oct	Nov	Dec

Saucery and fishcraft with one of Britain's top chefs

Sonia Stevenson has now moved on from the Horn of Plenty Restaurant where she became Britain's first Michelin-starred female chef. However, even in retirement, she is continuing to offer two-day courses for cooks of all abilities from the kitchen of her Cornwall home. The courses are very hands-on: Sonia does not start with a grand demonstration but encourages students to get stuck in. There are three courses: sauces (with an emphasis on bases), fish (may include early-morning trips to the fish market) and entertaining (often seasonally themed). The atmosphere in Sonia's kitchen is very relaxed, but because class sizes are small, a huge amount gets done. One-to-one tuition also available.

Contact
Sonia Stevenson
The Old Chapel
Bethany
Trerulefoot
Nr Saltash
Cornwall PL12 5DE
Web: www.soniastevenson.com

Practical information
Duration: 2 days
Level: beginner,
intermediate & advanced
Non-residential

Courses available in:

Group size: 3–10
Price range: £200–£300
Prices include: lunch
Unsuitable for children
Pets not welcome

Jan	Feb	Mar	Apr	May	Jun	Jul	Aug	Sep	Oct	Nov	Dec

STEPPY DOWNS STUDIO, HAYLE

Bird carving courses in West Cornwall

Be warned: this could be life-changing. 18 years ago Roy Hewson went to the studio of a man who carved wooden birds, was converted on the spot, and this is how he has made his living ever since. On his five-day courses participants will carve a beautiful, two-thirds-scale mallard. They work in a studio which looks towards both the north and south Cornwall coasts; a fine place to learn a new skill. Roy delights in passing skills on to new learners and the courses are as popular with women as with men.

Courses
The mallard is created in three stages – carving the outline, texturing the surface and painting it fully. There are no mallets, no chisels; just a seat, a block of wood and a knife. For the texturing Roy uses a pyrography ('fire writing') machine he designed himself.

What's special?
Participants are always amazed by what they are able to produce. Roy has been teaching for 18 years and has fine-tuned the course so that rank amateurs can create a genuinely impressive carving inside five days.

Eating & sleeping
Nearby Blanche B&B (01736 756623) offers full-board accommodation. Alternatively, the Hewsons have a holiday bungalow in the garden which you can book. Lunches taken in local pubs.

Directions
Train: Roy will pick up from St Erth station. Car: leave westbound A30 at St Erth station. Go to T-junction. Left to village. Into village, to top of hill. Studio on left.

In the area
St Ives with all its art associations is four miles away. Falmouth is 12 miles. The Eden Project is 40 minutes away. Plus beaches, coastal walks etc.

Contact
Roy Hewson
Steppy Downs Studio
13 St Erth Hill
Hayle
Cornwall TR27 6EX
Tel: 01736 753342
Web: www.wildlifewoodcarver.co.uk
Email: roy@wildlifewoodcarver.co.uk

Practical information
Duration: 5 days
Level: beginner
Non-residential
Group size: 2–10
Price range: £300–£400

Prices include: lunch
Unsuitable for children
Pets not welcome
Pet-friendly

Courses available in:

Jan	Feb	Mar	Apr	May	Jun	Jul	Aug	Sep	Oct	Nov	Dec

THOMAS HARDY AND WEST COUNTRY LITERATURE, TEIGNMOUTH

Tours around Thomas Hardy country

Literature lovers will revel in the tours that Brian Davidson runs around the West Country. This is an area rich with literary associations and Brian will take participants to the haunts, and tell the stories, of Hardy, Christie, Galsworthy, Tennyson, Coleridge, du Maurier, Conan Doyle, RD Blackmore, Herrick and others. 29 years as a teacher have shown Brian how to convey his passion to others; he knows the area thoroughly and can tell you all about both its literature and history. Please phone to confirm tour dates and availability.

Courses
The course begins with discussions chez Davidson, where group members explain their interests so that a programme can be mapped out. The courses are one or two weeks in duration, although shorter periods can be arranged. Days are spent visiting literary sites, be it Dorchester and Boscastle for Hardy, Torquay for Christie, and Dartmoor for Galsworthy and Conan Doyle.

What's special?
Seeing the landscapes that inspired these literary figures can help to inspire the participants. Not only does your own reading of the writers' work gain resonance but you might find yourself compelled to create as they did.

Eating & sleeping
Participants stay with local families who provide B&B and evening meals within walking distance of the house. Packed lunches are eaten on the road.

Directions
You can come by bus/train to Newton Abbot, where Brian will pick you up. If you come by car, the house is 250 yards from Teignmouth's County Garage – ask for more details..

In the area
Exeter and Plymouth have historical associations from medieval times through the Elizabethan era on to World War II. Dartington Hall and Buckfast Abbey also make excellent day trips.

Contact
Brian Davidson
Thomas Hardy and West Country Literature
60 Third Avenue
Teignmouth
Devon
Tel: 01626 772068
Web: www.hardythomas.co.uk
Email: brian@hardythomas.co.uk

Practical information
Duration: 2–10 days
Level: beginner &
intermediate
Residential
Group size: 1–10

Courses available in:

Jan	Feb	Mar	Apr	May	Jun	Jul	Aug	Sep	Oct	Nov	Dec

Price range: £100–£500+
Prices include: meals &
accommodation
Unsuitable for children
Pets not welcome

Painting school in the old quarter of St Ives

Founded in the 1930s, the School of Painting has long been a focus of St Ives's artistic community. Courses suit all abilities, although those who have not drawn for some time might enjoy the general week best. The six tutors share the teaching pleasures, exposing you to a variety of perspectives and techniques. The general week provides an overview of different subject matters and media, the Life Week includes an array of poses, while the Life-Landscape workshop is more abstract. The School is in the historic part of the town, in an old sail loft, and you paint in a room where generations of local artists have painted before you.

Contact
James Barry
St Ives School of Painting
Porthmeor Studios
Back Road West
St Ives
Cornwall TR26 1NG
Tel: 01736 797180
Web: www.stivesartschool.co.uk

Practical information
Duration: 5 days
Level: beginner,
intermediate & advanced
Non-residential

Group size: 2–20
Price range: £50–£200
Unsuitable for children
Pets not welcome

Courses available in:

Jan	Feb	Mar	Apr	May	Jun	Jul	Aug	Sep	Oct	Nov	Dec

Woodcarving courses near Wadebridge

Tino Rawnsley runs courses in woodcraft and woodland management on an ad-hoc basis from his Cornwall workshop. He knows what he's about, having spent the last eight years making and selling a range of hand-crafted wooden furniture from sustainably harvested materials, and will teach students how to make a longbow or greenwood chair. The course lasts three days during which time students will progress from raw material to finished product. He also runs one-day courses in sustainable woodland management and permaculture, and two-day courses in charcoal-burning. Students are usually welcome to stay and eat chez Rawnsley – it's a friendly, family environment – or there are local B&Bs.

Contact
Tino Rawnsley
Rawnsley Woodland Products
Waverley
Burlawn
Wadebridge
Cornwall PL27 7LD
Tel: 01208 813490
Web: www.cornishwoodland.co.uk

Practical information
Duration: 2–3 days
Level: beginner &
intermediate
Residential & non-residential
Group size: 1–10

Price range: £150–£500+
Prices include: meals &
accommodation
Unsuitable for children
Pets not welcome

Courses available in:

Jan	Feb	Mar	Apr	May	Jun	Jul	Aug	Sep	Oct	Nov	Dec

Unpretentious vegetarian cookery in beautiful Bath

Unpretentious and uncomplicated are the watchwords at the Vegetarian Cookery School. Rachel Demuth runs the courses from her beautiful Bath home, teaching techniques and recipes (both vegetarian and vegan, Mediterranean or Far Eastern) inspired by her travels round the world. The cooking is very communal: students don't produce their own version of every dish, so beginners feel less intimidated. And recipes are only given at the end of the course, so you learn by listening, watching and tasting. Rachel started the school in response to customers at her nearby vegetarian restaurant, Demuth's, which she has run for 18 years. Some of the restaurant's chefs help in the classes.

Contact
Rachel Demuth
The Vegetarian Cookery School
30 Belgrave Crescent
Bath
Somerset BA1 5JU
Tel: 01225 789682
Web: www.vegetariancookeryschool.com

Practical information
Duration: 2 days
Level: beginner &
intermediate
Non-residential

Group size: 3–10
Price range: £200–£300
Prices include: lunch
Unsuitable for children
Pets not welcome

Courses available in:

Jan	Feb	Mar	Apr	May	Jun	Jul	Aug	Sep	Oct	Nov	Dec

URCHFONT MANOR, DEVIZES

Arts, crafts, music and literature in the Wiltshire countryside

This magnificent, 17th-century, red-brick building on the edge of Pewsey Vale offers a vast array of adult education courses. Owned by the county of Wiltshire since the mid-1940s, Urchfont Manor offers year-round courses in art, craft, music, literature and others. Participants come as much for a holiday as for the opportunity to learn, and Urchfont attracts many return visitors with its historic ambience and friendly vitality. The 10-acre parkland grounds overlooking Salisbury Plain are perfect for painters and sketchers, and there are two croquet lawns, walled gardens and a 35-acre wood for quiet rambles.

Courses
Courses are grouped under seven headings: history and archaeology, literature, music, writing, art, craft and miscellaneous. To pick some of 2005's offerings at random, you could try calligraphy, hand-knitting, Edward Elgar, jewellery, Honiton lace, bridge, the Aztecs, driftwood sculpture and bookbinding. Ring for a brochure.

What's special?
Apart from its courses, Urchfont has three main draws: the beautiful location on the edge of a thatched village, the home-made food and the welcoming atmosphere. This is not a faceless institution. Non-participants are entirely welcome.

Eating & sleeping
Accommodation is provided in 36 bedrooms in the manor house or the buildings in the grounds. Rooms with shared bathrooms cost less. The kitchens serve food for which Urchfont is well renowned – no ice cream from a tub here! – and much of the produce comes from the kitchen garden.

Directions
By car: Urchfont is on the B3098, which heads south off the A342 between Devizes and Andover. By train: go to Bath or Westbury and take a taxi or bus.

In the area
The area is rich in pre-historic sites such as Stonehenge and Avebury, while Bath and Wilton House are also easily accessible. There is some excellent local walking, with various white horses carved in the chalk hillsides.

Contact
Susan Delaney
Urchfont Manor
Urchfont
Nr Devizes
Wiltshire
Tel: 01380 840495
Web: www.aredu.org.uk/urchfontmanor/urchfont.htm
Email: urchfontmanor@wiltshire.gov.uk

Practical information
Duration: 2–5 days
Level: beginner,
intermediate & advanced
Residential & non-residential
Group size: 6–20

Price range: £100–£300
Prices include: meals & accommodation
Unsuitable for children
Pets not welcome

Courses available in:

Jan	Feb	Mar	Apr	May	Jun	Jul	Aug	Sep	Oct	Nov	Dec

WESTCOURT BOTTOM, BURBAGE

Painting and sculpture in a 17th-century thatched cottage

Bill Mather is a professional painter, sculptor and caricaturist who runs informal art classes from the 17th-century thatched Wiltshire home he shares with wife Felicity. You pay by the hour, and many B&B guests enjoy a couple of hours' art per day chez Mather. Bill has two studios – one for plaster and clay work, one for painting and drawing – housed in the old stables. He usually has a painting or a sculpture on the go and will work alongside students, teaching and offering advice while at the same time encouraging them to 'take ownership' of the work. Stonehenge, Avebury, the Avon Canal and Savernake Forest are all nearby.

Contact
Bill Mather
Westcourt Bottom
Burbage
Wiltshire SN8 3BW
Tel: 01672 810924
Web: www.westcourtbottom.co.uk

Practical information
Duration: 2–3 days
Level: beginner &
intermediate
Residential & non-residential
Group size: 1–10

Price range: under £50
(students are charged per
hour)
Unsuitable for children
Pets not welcome

Courses available in:

Jan	Feb	Mar	Apr	May	Jun	Jul	Aug	Sep	Oct	Nov	Dec

THE WYE VALLEY ARTS CENTRE, LYDNEY

Various arts courses in a country house near Tintern Abbey

Sandwiched between the Forest of Dean and the Wye Valley, this privately run arts venue offers intimate courses in painting, drawing, sculpture and creative writing. The atmosphere is that of a country house you're sharing with friends. Accommodation is in one of three atmospheric buildings and home-cooked meals are available on site; non-participating partners are welcome. Tutors are all practising artists who have been chosen for their teaching and motivational talents and there is much personal attention. Courses include drawing and painting for beginners and improvers, life drawing, watercolour (often painting images of the Wye Valley), silk painting, sculpture (creating a head in clay) and fiction workshops.

Contact
Valerie Welham
The Wye Valley Arts Centre
The Coach House
Mork, St Briavel's
Lydney
Gloucestershire GL15 6QH
Tel: 01594 530214
Web: www.wyeart.cwc.net

Practical information
Duration: 2–5 days
Level: beginner &
intermediate
Residential & non-residential
Group size: 3–15

Price range: £150–£400
Prices include: meals &
accommodation
Unsuitable for children
Pet-friendly

Courses available in:

Jan	Feb	Mar	Apr	May	Jun	Jul	Aug	Sep	Oct	Nov	Dec

YARAK BIRDS OF PREY, CULLOMPTON

A private falconry school near Cullompton

In the middle of the Devon countryside Yarak offers a unique falconry experience where all tuition is one-to-one or two-to-one. The school is not open to the public and there are no group sessions, so your exposure to, and time flying the birds is that much greater. The school is run by John Pitson who has been a falconer for more than 40 years and teaching for 25 of those. The two-day/two-night course, which includes B&B accommodation, is for those wanting to experience the thrill of handling the hawks, owls and kestrels. The four-day course (accommodation extra) is for those considering falconry seriously and goes into greater detail. Sensible 8-year-olds (and upwards) allowed.

Contact
John Pitson
Yarak Birds of Prey
Langford Mill Farm
Langford
Cullompton
Devon EX15 1RG
Tel: 01884 277297
Web: www.yarakbirdsofprey.co.uk

Practical information
Duration: 2–4 days
Level: beginner,
intermediate & advanced
Residential & non-residential
Group size: 1–2

Price range: £300–£500+
Prices include:
accommodation & lunch and
breakfast
Child-friendly
Pets not welcome

Courses available in:

Jan	Feb	Mar	Apr	May	Jun	Jul	Aug	Sep	Oct	Nov	Dec

THE WAGON HOUSE, ST AUSTELL

Botanical illustration in the Lost Gardens of Heligan

If you want to try a course in Botanical illustration, then a studio in the middle of the world-famous Lost Gardens of Heligan must be the perfect location. Your tutor, Mally Francis, has been painting plants for 15 years – she paints for Heligan Gardens and the Eden Project – and running courses for six years. Her home is one of the estate's original farm buildings, set in a private area at the end of a rhododendron-lined drive. The large, well-lit studio was converted from the adjacent saw-pit in 1999. Lunches, provided by a brilliant caterer, are a daily highlight and can be eaten in the garden, weather permitting.

Courses
Botanical illustration can be learned and this course guides you through a five-stage process from initial drawing to finished article. You can either bring your own flowers or choose from those provided. A list of recommended art materials will be sent.

What's special?
Only a limited number of Botanical illustration courses are held in Britain, but this one has the added advantage of a beautiful Cornish location where like-minded people can acquire new skills from an expert tutor.

Eating & sleeping
The best option is to stay on site but, failing that, local B&B is available with Kathy Lobb (01726 842159) or Vicky Lobb (01726 842001). For evening meals, try the Crown Inn at St Ewe or the School House at Pentewan.

Directions
Detailed directions will be sent when you book. The nearest train station is about 5 miles away in St Austell, but you would need to hire a car.

In the area
The delights of Heligan Gardens are within walking distance and there are numerous other gardens open to the public, as well as the Eden Project (10 miles), Padstow (20 miles), the Cornish Coast Path and various beaches (nearest 2 miles).

Contact
Mally Francis
The Wagon House
Heligan Manor
St Ewe
St Austell
Cornwall
Tel: 01726 844505
Web: www.thewagonhouse.com
Email: thewagonhouse@mac.com

Practical information
Duration: 3 days
Level: beginner,
intermediate & advanced
Residential & non-residential
Group size: 1–10

Price range: £150–£200
Prices include: lunch
Unsuitable for children
Pets not welcome

Courses available in:

Jan	Feb	Mar	Apr	May	Jun	Jul	Aug	Sep	Oct	Nov	Dec

Yoga retreat in Dick Whittington's old home

Based at beautiful Pauntley Court, formerly home to Dick Whittington, Yogabubble nourishes both body and spirit. The weekends are run by Anton Simmha and Kat Moore who both had life-changing experiences on yoga retreats and who hope to recreate that effect. Anton is the principal teacher and specialises in Ashtanga yoga. He teaches with humour, not forcing the spiritual aspect of yoga, but without neglecting it either. The courses are supremely relaxed and allow time for wandering in the gardens (400 acres of grounds) and swimming in the pool, as well as massage-based therapies. This is a private home and there will be no 'strangers' present, so relaxation is complete.

Contact
Kat Moore
Yogabubble
The Dovecote
Pauntley Court
Redmarley
Gloucestershire GL19 3JA
Tel: 01531 821573
Web: www.yogabubble.com

Practical information
Duration: 2 days
Level: beginner,
intermediate & advanced
Residential
Group size: 6–10

Price range: £200–£300
Prices include: meals &
accommodation
Unsuitable for children
Pets not welcome

South West

Courses available in:

Jan	Feb	Mar	Apr	May	Jun	Jul	Aug	Sep	Oct	Nov	Dec

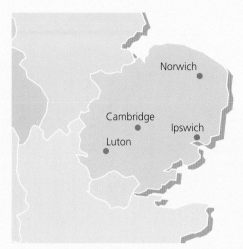

Norwich

Cambridge

Ipswich

Luton

East Anglia

This flat, low-lying region is the UK's bread basket and has some of its richest farmland. Its early wealth derived from the successful wool trade and it has some splendid 'wool churches' built with the proceeds. Regional highlights include the Fens, the Norfolk Broads, the Suffolk coast (much of which is owned by the National Trust), Cambridge, Ely and Aldeburgh. Artists will enjoy East Anglia's Constable associations – and we feature many watercolour courses; naturalists will find much of interest in the shingle beaches, mudflats and waterways.

Cookery courses at renowned Aldeburgh school

This is a sociable course for enthusiasts of all levels wanting to cook, eat, drink and discuss with food journalist Thane Prince and chef Sarah Fox. Make bread, sauces and mouth-watering desserts and learn, in depth, the whys and wherefores of good cooking. There are courses in 'Flavours of Italy', 'Modern British Food', 'Seafood' and 'Mediterranean'. You visit local producers, buy fish from the beach and indulge in olive oil and balsamic vinegar tastings. And busy though the weekend is, there is still a chance to walk on the beach. The course includes five dedicated cooking sessions and all main meals, plus lunch at Sarah's acclaimed restaurant The Lighthouse.

Contact
Thane Prince
Aldeburgh Cookery School
84 High Street
Aldeburgh
Suffolk IP15 5AB
Tel: 01728 454039
Web: www.aldeburghcookeryschool.com

Practical information
Duration: 3 days
Level: beginner &
intermediate
Non-residential

Group size: 6-10
Price range: £400–£500
Prices include: meals
Unsuitable for children
Pets not welcome

Courses available in:

| Jan | Feb | Mar | Apr | May | Jun | Jul | Aug | Sep | Oct | Nov | Dec |

Master stone-carving techniques on the Suffolk coast

Rosemary Elliott, an exhibiting artist and Royal Academy postgraduate with 40 years' teaching experience, shows you how to carve stone over a weekend geared towards relaxation, creative inspiration and physical activity. Workshops take place in the art centre of Bawdsey Manor, a stunning Edwardian folly with water sports, racquet courts, walks and cycle rides. Working with Portland and Bath stone, students receive demonstrations on tools and techniques before group and one-on-one practical sessions. The first day is dedicated to 'roughing out' the stone, the second to refining and the third to polishing and sanding down the figurative or abstract work ready to take home.

Contact
Rosemary Elliott
Bawdsey Manor
Bawdsey
Nr Woodbridge
Suffolk IP12 3AZ
Tel: 01394 411633
Web: www.sculptureinstone.co.uk

Practical information
Duration: 3 days
Level: beginner,
intermediate & advanced.
Residential
Group size: 6-10

Price range: £300–£400
Prices include: meals,
accommodation & materials,
stone and tools
Unsuitable for children
Pets not welcome

Courses available in:

| Jan | Feb | Mar | Apr | May | Jun | Jul | Aug | Sep | Oct | Nov | Dec |

Learn to play the recorder or sing; absolute beginners & kick-start piano

With a long history of running residential music courses for adults, Benslow offers one of the most wide-ranging programmes in the country. Covering early music through to jazz and music technology, their courses cater for all abilities, from the novice through to those seeking to turn professional. Expert tuition is provided by distinguished visiting musicians, who combine a fun, informal approach with enthusiasm and verve. They offer beginners' courses in singing, piano and recorder, and more advanced courses in improvising jazz, 'hot fiddle', chamber music (wind and strings), big band and symphonic band. The Benslow Trust is situated in an elegant Victorian house and grounds at Little Benslow Hills.

Contact
Lisa Railton
Benslow Music Trust
Little Benslow Hills
Ibberson Way, Hitchin
Hertfordshire SG4 9RB
Tel: 01462 459446
Web: www.benslow.org

Practical information
Duration: 2–7 days
Level: beginner,
intermediate & advanced
Residential & non-residential
Group size: 1–25+
Courses available in:

Price range: £100–£400
Prices include: meals &
accommodation
Child-friendly
Pets not welcome

| Jan | Feb | Mar | Apr | May | Jun | Jul | Aug | Sep | Oct | Nov | Dec |

Birdwatching weekends on the North Norfolk coast

Beautifully located at the head of a winding creek on the North Norfolk coast, the 17th-century building which houses the Brancaster Millennium Activity Centre boasts spectacular views. It looks over salt marshes, sand dunes and harbour, which you will explore with an RSPB birdwatching guide in a series of coastal walks. Leisurely and inspirational, the weekends' themes depend on the season: you may watch flocks migrating, identify wintering flocks arriving or observe individual birds. Expert tuition, comfortable bedrooms, a wood-burning stove and fresh, local produce cooked on the premises are just some of this National Trust Centre's charms. The attractions of Norwich, Burnham Market and stunning, sandy beaches lie nearby.

Contact
Joanna Johnson
Brancaster Millennium Activity Centre
Dial House
Brancaster Staithe
King's Lynn,
Norfolk PE31 8BW
Tel: 01485 210719
Web: www.nationaltrust.org.uk

Practical Information
Duration: 2 days
Level: beginner,
intermediate & advanced
Residential
Group size: 6–15

Courses available in:

Jan	Feb	Mar	Apr	May	Jun	Jul	Aug	Sep	Oct	Nov	Dec
	Feb							Sep			

Price range: £150–£200
Prices include: meals &
accommodation
Unsuitable for children
Pets not welcome

East
Anglia

Soft furnishing courses in picturesque village

Learn the skills and workshop secrets needed to produce curtains and complementary soft furnishings, whether for your own satisfaction or as industry training. Classes are highly intensive, yet run in an informal atmosphere, and are available in curtains (foundation, intermediate and advanced), blinds, tassels, lampshades, headboards, cushions and loose covers. The college, which has been featured in Country Living magazine, is set in an attractively restored barn in the picturesque village of Henham; facilities are spacious and the equipment first class. All tutors are highly experienced and well regarded in their fields. It is ten minutes from Bishop's Stortford, with Saffron Walden and Thaxted also nearby.

Contact
Georgina Willett
College of Soft Furnishing
3 The Courtyard
Pledgdon Hall
Henham
Hertfordshire CM22 6BJ
Tel: 01279 851911
Web: www.collegeofsoftfurnishing.co.uk

Practical information
Duration: 2–3 days
Level: beginner,
intermediate & advanced
Non-residential
Group size: 3–10

Courses available in:

Jan	Feb	Mar	Apr	May	Jun	Jul	Aug	Sep	Oct	Nov	Dec
Jan	Feb	Mar	Apr	May	Jun	Jul	Aug		Oct		Dec

Price range: £150–£300
Prices include: meals &
materials – though
participants must buy or
bring sewing kit
Unsuitable for children
Pets not welcome

Cookery school in Suffolk

Cook, solve problems and visit local food producers with Annie and Mark David (chef, radio guest and food writer). You arrive on Friday to a cooked dinner, then spend Saturday preparing the evening's dinner, cooking with Agas and conventional ovens in the custom-built kitchen, with plenty of breaks to discuss and swap ideas. Sunday is 'cookery surgery', where you can solve any problems you might have. Courses are theme-based and include 'Seafood Extravaganza, 'Quick & Easy Entertaining', 'Italy', 'Indian' and 'Christmas without Tears'. The Davids live in the historic market town of Hadleigh, where plenty of beautiful river walks lie on the edge of Constable country.

Contact
Mark David and Emma Crowhurst
The Cooking Experience Ltd
The Chapel House
9 High Street, Hadleigh
Suffolk IP7 5AH
Tel: 01473 827568
Web: www.cookingexperience.co.uk

Practical information
Duration: 2 days
Level: beginner,
intermediate & advanced
Residential
Group size: 3–10

Courses available in:

Jan	Feb	Mar	Apr	May	Jun	Jul	Aug	Sep	Oct	Nov	Dec
Jan	Feb	Mar	Apr	May	Jun	Jul	Aug	Sep	Oct	Nov	Dec

Price range: £300–£400
Prices include: meals &
accommodation
Child-friendly
Pets not welcome

Ceramic restoration in a 19th-century barn

Maureen Aldridge, a ceramic restorer for 22 years, leads specialist courses for all abilities from her 19th-century brick and flint barn studio on the Hatfield House Estate, one of Britain's most magnificent Jacobean mansions. The programmes include gilding, basic china mending and porcelain and ceramic restoration, and are ideal for those seeking a leisure interest while restoring their damaged collectables. Demonstrations are given before the fully supervised, hands-on practical workshops begin; on the gilding course you work with precious metals and learn to restore items, either from a practical angle, such as picture frame restoration, or a creative one. Challenging and fun ways to learn new skills, these accredited courses come recommended by a wide range of antiques and interiors magazines.

What's special?

The three-day china-mending course shows you how best to mend those much-loved ornaments. A post-completion helpline is offered for any queries, and there is a follow-up summer school should you need a refresher.

Eating & sleeping

Orchard Cottage near Hertford (01992 583494); Steward's Cottage in Hatfield (01707 642091). Mowbray can offer accommodation with local families. Those looking for traditional afternoon tea could stop at Abigail's Tea Rooms in St Albans.

Directions

Eight-minute taxi from Potters Bar station. By car, leave M25 at junction 24 and follow signs to Hatfield, then Essendon (off the A1000). The B158 takes you to the top of West End Lane.

In the area

Many stately homes nearby including Knebworth House and Hatfield House (open Mar–Oct). The Roman city of St Albans, with its Abbey, Garden of the Rose and Verulamium is also close.

Contact

Maureen Aldridge
Mowbray Ceramic Restoration
Flint Barn
West End Lane
Essendon
Hatfield
Hertfordshire AL9 5RQ
Tel: 01707 270158/020 8367 1786
Web: www.mowbrayrestoration.com
Email: mowbraycourses@btopenworld.com

Practical information

Duration: 3–10 days
Level: beginner,
intermediate & advanced
Non-residential
Group size: 3–10

Price range: £150–£500+
Prices include: meals &
materials and course manual
Unsuitable for children
Pets not welcome

Courses available in:

Jan	Feb	Mar	Apr	May	Jun	Jul	Aug	Sep	Oct	Nov	Dec

Pottery courses in coastal Suffolk with Deborah Baynes

Expert and friendly pottery tuition in hand building, throwing, decorating, raku and salt glaze is offered in a 16th-century hall by the stunning Orwell Estuary. The course begins with an excellent three-course dinner (with wine) where you meet your fellow potters. Each day starts with demonstrations, followed by tuition and making. One of the highlights is the raku-firing evening, a fun and sociable finale to the course, from which you leave with an impressive array of mugs, jugs, jars, bowls and teapots. Tutor Deborah Baynes is a founder member of the East Anglian Potters Association; her pots can be seen in collections both in the UK and abroad.

Contact
Deborah Baynes
Nether Hall
Shotley
Ipswich
Suffolk IP9 1PW
Tel: 01473 788300
Web: www.potterycourses.net

Practical information
Duration: 2–7 days
Level: beginner,
intermediate & advanced
Residential & non-residential
Group size: 6–15

Price range: £150–£500
Prices include: meals &
accommodation
Child-friendly
Pets not welcome

Courses available in:

Jan	Feb	Mar	Apr	May	Jun	Jul	Aug	Sep	Oct	Nov	Dec

East Anglia

Painting watercolour on the Norfolk coast and broads

Top tuition in the most inspiring of locations. Ian King, TV presenter and Fellow of the British Watercolours Society, pastels expert John Tookey and Robbie McDonald, a leader in the field of loose washes, are among those teaching these intensive yet relaxing courses in the breathtakingly beautiful Norfolk Broads and North Norfolk coast – think Blakeney seascapes and Walberswick watercolours. Demonstrations are followed by closely supervised on-location painting, before participants return to base for afternoon tea and critiques. Courses are designed to suit all abilities, with hands-on tuition combined with a friendly and caring approach. The use of different locations ensures that each course is unique.

Contact
Elaine Allsop
East Coast Arts
5 Woodgate
Cringleford
Norwich, Norfolk NR4 6XT
Tel: 01603 456157
Web: www.norfolkwatercolour.co.uk

Practical information
Duration: 2–4 days
Level: beginner,
intermediate & advanced
Non-residential

Group size: 6–15
Price range: £100–£300
Prices include: meals
Unsuitable for children
Pet-friendly

Courses available in:

Jan	Feb	Mar	Apr	May	Jun	Jul	Aug	Sep	Oct	Nov	Dec

Keeping and flying a bird of prey

Learn to look after a bird of prey at an inspirational site that carefully recreates their natural woodland home. There are species from across the globe living here, including falcons, hawks, owls, eagles and vultures. The courses are led by Phil Gooden, who has been handling birds of prey for over 50 years, and daughter Emma. They offer an insight into how to look after, train and feed these enchanting creatures, as well as teaching how to free-fly different species. The Centre is located in the magnificent grounds of Shuttleworth in Old Warden Park, home to the Swiss Gardens and a wonderful collection of vintage aeroplanes.

Contact
Phillip Gooden
The English School of Falconry
Old Warden Park
Shuttleworth
Nr Biggleswade
Bedforshire SG18 9EA
Tel: 01767 627527
Web: www.shuttleworth.org

Practical information
Duration: 2–5 days
Level: beginner,
intermediate & advanced
Non-residential
Group size: 1–5

Price range: £150–£500
Prices include: Information
pack
Child-friendly
Pet-friendly

Courses available in:

Jan	Feb	Mar	Apr	May	Jun	Jul	Aug	Sep	Oct	Nov	Dec

Hedgelaying in Epping Forest

Epping Forest, famous for its ancient woodland and wildlife, hosts an annual November hedge-laying course taught by a local warden from the nature reserve. The first day is based at the Field Centre, where seminars are given on hedge-laying theory, history, decline and uses, culminating with a minibus tour examining hedge types around the area. On the second day students travel to the Roding Valley Nature Reserve, an Area of Outstanding Natural Beauty with its water meadows and sprawling grassland, where they will be taught practical hedge-laying. The nearby Green Belt makes this a fascinating area for nature-lovers.

Contact
Steve Bunce
Epping Forest Field Centre
High Beach
Loughton
Essex IG10 4AF
Tel: 020 8502 8500
Web: www.field-studies-council.org/eppingforest

Practical information
Duration: 2 days
Level: beginner
Non-residential
Group size: 3–20

Price range: £50–£100
Prices include: light
refreshments
Unsuitable for children
Pets not welcome

Courses available in:

Jan	Feb	Mar	Apr	May	Jun	Jul	Aug	Sep	Oct	Nov	Dec
										Nov	

Shiatsu with Liz Welch

Come back from your holiday revitalised and stay that way. Liz Welch, an alternative health journalist, senior teacher at the European Shiatsu School and energy awareness guru, will teach you all you need to be able to practise basic Shiatsu on family and friends, leaving them de-stressed and relaxed. In addition to the application of practical techniques for joint opening and spinal alignment, you'll receive an introduction to Chinese medicine, Qi energy awareness and first-aid acupressure points. Classes take place in a light and airy converted barn close to the river; local attractions include Ware Ancient Gazebos, Hatfield House and Knebworth. Liz also runs a private Shiatsu practice in Hertford.

Contact
Liz Welch
The European Shiatsu School
c/o 9 The Spinney
Ware
Hertfordshire SG13 7JR
Tel: 01992 550405
Web: www.lizwelch.co.uk

Practical information
Duration: 2 days
Level: beginner
Non-residential
Group size: 3–20

Price range: £50–£100
Prices include: Light
refreshments
Unsuitable for children
Pets not welcome

Courses available in:

Jan	Feb	Mar	Apr	May	Jun	Jul	Aug	Sep	Oct	Nov	Dec
				May				Sep			

Introduction to bookbinding on a Norfolk farm

Situated in the Waveney Valley, adjacent to the Redgrave and Lopham Fin – areas of rugged beauty and scientific interest – is this tranquil and isolated 18th-century farmhouse. The adjacent barn is home to Alan Fitch's intensive and hands-on bookbinding classes. A practitioner for over 20 years, he and his wife welcome you into the fold for the week, by the middle of which you'll have learnt how to bind a book in three different styles. The process is approached in a step-by-step manner, with demonstration followed by closely supervised practice. This ensures you'll have learnt vast amounts by the week's end and have your own completed project to take home.

Contact
Alan Fitch
Farthing Press & Bindery
Ten Farm
Low Common
South Lopham
Diss
Norfolk IP22 2JR
Tel: 01379 687 364

Practical information
Duration: 5 days
Level: beginner &
intermediate
Residential & non-residential
Group size: 1–5

Price range: £200–£400
Prices include: meals &
all materials
Unsuitable for children
Pets not welcome

Courses available in:

Jan	Feb	Mar	Apr	May	Jun	Jul	Aug	Sep	Oct	Nov	Dec
Jan	Feb	Mar	Apr	May	Jun	Jul	Aug	Sep	Oct	Nov	Dec

Painting and wildlife courses in Constable country

Flatford Mill lies in the heart of Constable country on the Suffolk–Essex border and hosts one of the most comprehensive and long-running programmes of arts and environment courses in the UK. The centre's buildings, particularly the Mill and Willy Lott's House, are instantly recognisable from many of the painter's works. Courses are specialised and diverse, ranging from traditional crafts such as calligraphy and spinning, through to digital imaging. Much of the photography and painting takes its inspiration from the rich mosaic of lowland landscapes, wildlife habitats and historical places; these are also the source for the natural history courses, which include bird ringing, bird song and mammals

Contact	Practical information	Group size: 6–15
Edward Jackson	Duration: 2–3 days	Price range: under £50
Flatford Mill Field Centre	Level: beginner,	Unsuitable for children
East Bergholt	intermediate & advanced	Pets not welcome
Suffolk CO7 6UL	Non-residential	
Tel: 0845 3307368		
Web: www.field-studies-council.org/flatfordmill	Courses available in:	

Jan	Feb	Mar	Apr	May	Jun	Jul	Aug	Sep	Oct	Nov	Dec

East Anglia

Landscape painting in the reading rooms at Holkham Hall

Holkham Hall is a beautiful stately home on the North Norfolk coast, close to many idyllic villages, fishing ports and beaches. It hosts a landscape drawing and painting course, and it's from the impressive Reading Rooms that you'll record the local landscape: statues, lakes, monuments and buildings. Your days will take the form of tutor-led workshops, with one-to-one guidance and assistance, and practical demonstrations. Running for more than ten years, these courses are relaxed and sociable; students return home with their own work of art. Stained glass courses at nearby Fakenham High School also provide an inspirational break.

Contact	Practical information	Group size: 6–15
Christine Chalk	Duration: 2–3 days	Price range: under £50
Holkham Hall	Level: beginner,	Unsuitable for children
The Old Rectory	intermediate & advanced	Pets not welcome
21 Oak Street	Non-residential	
Fakenham		
Norfolk NR21 9DX		
Tel: 01328 851223	Courses available in:	
Email: fakenham.adult.edu@norfolk.gov.uk		

Jan	Feb	Mar	Apr	May	Jun	Jul	Aug	Sep	Oct	Nov	Dec

Furniture workshops overlooking the village green

Learn to enhance your furniture on a course at The Studio, the converted stables of a 17th-century coach house overlooking Beyton's village green. Morning demonstrations and talks are followed by practical sessions on painting, distressing, glazing and finishing. Tutor June Leask has spent 15 years painting and restoring antique furniture, and her courses have been featured in 'Country Living' magazine. Jane's introductory course covers basic furniture repair and painting on day one, followed by more advanced finishes – crackle glazing, marbling and tortoise shell – on day two. She also runs courses in French polishing and repairing of wood finishes. Bury St Edmunds and Lavenham are a few miles away.

Contact	Practical information	Price range: £100–£500+
June Leask	Duration: 2–10 days	Prices include: meals &
The Studio	Level: beginner &	paints, aprons, rubber
Bridge House	intermediate	gloves
The Green	Non-residential	Unsuitable for children
Beyton	Group size: 3–10	Pet-friendly
Bury St Edmunds		
Suffolk IP30 9AJ	Courses available in:	
Tel: 01284 700009 or 01359 270 037		

Jan	Feb	Mar	Apr	May	Jun	Jul	Aug	Sep	Oct	Nov	Dec

RUSH MATTERS, COLESDEN

Crafting rushes from the banks of the Great Ouse

Based in the studio of a converted granary beside a 14th-century tithe barn, Felicity Irons' rush-crafting courses attract people from around the world. Recommended by virtually every British broadsheet newspaper, as well as Country Living and World of Interiors, Felicity's courses celebrate a longstanding English tradition that is both rewarding and fun. Using English bulrushes that Felicity harvests by hand on the banks of the Great Ouse, you will learn to weave basketry, tableware and floor matting; the content of any particular course is tailored to what participants want to do. One of the leading practitioners in her field, Felicity's work has been featured in the film Gladiator, and she has produced commissions for the Globe Theatre, the National Trust, Anoushka Hempel and David Mellor Designs.

What's special?

This is inspirational and productive: you learn a new skill in an idyllic location and in summer you work outdoors. Courses are tailored to meet the individual student's needs and you get to take home the fruits of your labours – mats, hats, bags, baskets or a fully seated chair.

Eating & sleeping

B&B at Franklins of Thorncote, Thorncote Green (01767 627345) and Church Farm, Roxton (01234 870234). For food, try the Victoria Arms or nearby Cornfields restaurant. The meals on Felicity's courses are excellent.

Directions

Leave the A1 at the A421 (towards Bedford); right after 300 yards to Chawston; left at crossroads into Colesden Road. 1 ? miles to Grange Farm on the right. Map available.

In the area

Bedford, Oundle and Huntingdon all have wonderful farmers' markets. Cambridge is nearby. Grafham Water reservoir has lots of walks.

Contact

Felicity Irons
Rush Matters
Grange Farm Workshops
Grange Farm, Colesden
Bedford, Bedfordshire MK44 3DB
Tel: 01234 376 419
Web: www.rushmatters.co.uk
Email: felicityirons@rushmatters.co.uk

Practical information

Duration: 2 days
Level: beginner,
intermediate & advanced
Non-residential
Group size: 3–10

Price range: £100–£150
Prices include: meals &
materials
Child-friendly
Pet-friendly

Courses available in:

Jan	Feb	Mar	Apr	May	Jun	Jul	Aug	Sep	Oct	Nov	Dec

Cooking with Galton Blackiston at Morston Hall

Morston Hall is an award-winning, 17th-century country house in the remote North Norfolk coastland. People travel far and wide to learn to cook with chef proprietor Galton Blackiston, who reveals the secrets behind his Michelin-starred restaurant in a series of demonstrations. It's a leisurely affair: after breakfast guests meet in the conservatory, before heading to the kitchen to witness how the day's meals are prepared. Courses vary, from seasonal themes to canapés, and party cooking to stocks and soups. After lunch participants can explore local attractions such as Sandringham, Langham Glassworks and boat trips to see seals. After dinner Galton joins guests to answer any questions about the day's cooking.

Contact
Galton Blackiston
Morston Hall
Morston
Holk
Norfolk NR25 7AA
Tel: 01263 741041
Web: www.morstonhall.com

Practical information
Duration: 2 days
Level: beginner
Non-residential
Group size: 6–10

Price range: £150–£300
Prices include: meals
Unsuitable for children
Pets not welcome

Courses available in:

Jan	Feb	Mar	Apr	May	Jun	Jul	Aug	Sep	Oct	Nov	Dec
										Nov	

East Anglia

Painting in a north Norfolk converted barn

Nicola Slattery has been working as a professional artist for 20 years. Her painting courses take place in a thatched barn in the heart of the Norfolk Broads – a perfect escape for city dwellers. Classes are geared towards developing ideas and imagination, taking subjects such as favourite quotes, old photographs and dreams as starting points. Each day begins with demonstration and discussion before participants start on their own piece. Courses include 'Adventures with Acrylic', 'Art from the Imagination', 'Mixed Media', 'Discover Printmaking' and a week-long 'Art Adventure' holiday where you try lots of different materials and on-location work. A stay in the converted farmhouse B&B opposite comes highly recommended.

Contact
Nicola Slattery
Grove Farm
Reps
Great Yarmouth
Norfolk NR29 4PS
Tel: 01493 748833
Web: www.nicolaslattery.com

Practical information
Duration: 2–7 days
Level: beginner &
intermediate
Residential & non-residential
Group size: 3–10

Price range: £100–£500+
Prices include: meals,
accommodation & materials
Unsuitable for children
Pets not welcome

Courses available in:

Jan	Feb	Mar	Apr	May	Jun	Jul	Aug	Sep	Oct	Nov	Dec
	Feb	Mar	Apr	May	Jun	Jul	Aug	Sep	Oct		

Stained glass, drawing, painting and pottery in a Norfolk barn

Running for 20 years as a gallery and course venue with a great programme of arts events, the 17th-century Old Barn Studios are set within a pretty courtyard and cottage garden in a village dating back to Saxon times. Founder Jane Ironside has been a practising artist and gallery-owner for nearly 40 years, her comprehensive and innovative array of arts and crafts courses structured around morning demonstrations followed by hands-on practice. A range of visiting experts, who enjoy working with people of differing abilities, lead the sessions in an informal and friendly atmosphere. Classes include 'Stained Glass', 'Raku Pottery', 'Papermaking', 'Lino Printing without a Press', 'Watercolours', 'Still Life' and 'Drawing'.

Contact
Jane Ironside
Old Barn Studios
The Street
Kettlestone
Norfolk NR21 0JB
Tel: 01328 878762
Web: www.oldbarnstudios.org.uk

Practical information
Duration: 2–4 days
Level: beginner &
intermediate
Non-residential

Group size: 6–15
Price range: £100–£300
Prices include: materials
Unsuitable for children
Pets not welcome

Courses available in:

Jan	Feb	Mar	Apr	May	Jun	Jul	Aug	Sep	Oct	Nov	Dec
				May	Jun	Jul	Aug	Sep			

© The Wayland Partnership

THE WAYLAND PARTNERSHIP, WATTON

Photography, sketching and more in the Wayland area

Wayland Weekends has a range of exciting weekend activities centring on the market town of Watton and its 13 neighbouring rural parishes. Wayland's unique village communities, with their attractive cottages and medieval churches, are ideal places to relax. Using specialist tutors, courses comprise two complementary day workshops, so that you can develop a skill from different angles or in different habitats, over a weekend. Courses, which offer a wide and unique range of arts and environment disciplines, involve tutorials, workshops, one-to-one critiques, demonstrations, site visits, discussion sessions and team-building skills.

Courses

Courses planned for 2005 include:

♦ Bird watching with Chris Day and the RSPB- 21/22 May
♦ Creative Writing with Caroline Gilfillan- 20/21 August
♦ Photography Skills with Graham Portlock- 2/3 July
♦ Autumn Illustration with Reinhild Raistrick- 1/2 October

What's special?

The Wayland Partnership offers tailored packages embracing a range of pastimes using local specialists. Courses are highly focused, but with an emphasis on relaxed learning and sociability, enabling participants to pick up new skills or enhance existing ones. Attractive gift vouchers are also available.

Eating & sleeping

There is a huge variety of accommodation in the Wayland area, from rural caravan sites to farmhouse B&Bs. An accommodation guide can be sent out. The day price includes a two-course lunch at a pub restaurant, and The Wayland Partnership can book accommodation and evening meals at no extra cost.

Directions

Wayland is some 20 miles west of Norwich (B1108) on the A1075 linking Thetford and Dereham. There are coach services to and from London and rail links can be easily accessed at Thetford.

In the area

The Wayland area contains the ancient Wayland Wood, where the Babes in the Wood legend originates. The Peddars Way footpath also runs through the area and the monthly Farmers' Market and Wayland Church Tours are ideal for visitors.

Contact

The Wayland Partnership Development Trust
High Street, Watton
Norfolk IP25 6AR
Tel: 01953 883915
Web: www.wayland.org.uk/site/waylandweekends
Email: claire@wayland.org.uk

Practical information

Duration: 2 days
Level: beginner,
intermediate & advanced
Non-residential

Group size: 11-20
Price range: £40-£110
Prices include: meals,
insurance & transportation

Courses available in:

Jan	Feb	Mar	Apr	May	Jun	Jul	Aug	Sep	Oct	Nov	Dec

This project is part-financed by the European
Union. European Regional Development Fund

Furniture restoration in a medieval village

Jonathan White has been restoring furniture for 20 years and teaching the subject – to novices and experts alike – for ten. He will guide you through every facet of furniture refinishing from stripping to French polishing, together with associated techniques including staining, colouring and grain filling. Once these basic skills are mastered, you'll have the chance to apply them to items of furniture in order to develop your confidence and expertise. His courses include 'French polishing', 'Veneering' and 'Chair Caning'. Set in an idyllic medieval village with a church, windmill and fantastic restaurants nearby, classes take place in a period chapel house with en-suite accommodation.

Contact
Jonathan White
Paragon School of Furniture Restoration
11–13 Town Street
Thaxted
Essex CM6 2LD
Tel: 01371 832032
Web: www.paragoncourses.co.uk

Practical information
Duration: 3–5 days
Level: beginner &
intermediate
Residential & non-residential
Group size: 3–10

Price range: £200–£500
Prices include: meals & all
materials
Unsuitable for children
Pets not welcome

Courses available in:

Jan	Feb	Mar	Apr	May	Jun	Jul	Aug	Sep	Oct	Nov	Dec

Intense drawing and painting courses in the Waveney Valley

The Red House sits on the edge of the water meadows of the Waveney Valley, whose Georgian market towns and adjacent coast have inspired landscape artists for centuries. Taught by established painters, including Hugo Grenville, who runs the courses with wife Sophie, these intensive drawing and painting breaks build skills through exercises and colour studies, providing students with technical expertise and intellectual stimulation. Classes are taken in a specially designed studio in the grounds of the 18th-century farmhouse and include 'Elements of Oil Painting', 'Liberating Colour', 'Tone and Colour', 'The Art of Landscape' (situated in the Waveney Valley) and 'Southwolk Seascapes' (depending on the weather). There is accommodation nearby.

Contact
Sophie Grenville
Red House Studios
The Red House
Mendham
Nr Haleston
Suffolk IP20 0JD
Tel: 01379 586224
Web: http://82.112.116.40

Practical information
Duration: 4 days
Level: intermediate &
advanced
Non-residential

Group size: 6–15
Price range: £300–£400
Prices include: meals
Unsuitable for children
Pets not welcome

Courses available in:

Jan	Feb	Mar	Apr	May	Jun	Jul	Aug	Sep	Oct	Nov	Dec

Painting and craft courses in converted granary

Situated in an idyllic cluster of converted granaries and malthouses overlooking the River Alde, Snape Maltings is a charming complex with shops, pubs, restaurants, concert hall and art gallery. The diverse array of craft and painting courses aims to be both didactic and recreational, and they have been running for over 20 years. Led by experienced tutors – most are practising artists and craftsmen – courses such as 'Starting Watercolour', 'Wonderful Ways with Willow', 'Watercolour Tricks of the Trade' and 'Mosaics for Gardens and Conservatories' take place in a converted granary overlooking the river, with many of the painting classes taken outside.

Contact
Melanie Thurston
Snape Maltings
Nr Saxmundham
Suffolk IP17 1SR
Tel: 01728 688303.
Web: www.snapemaltings.co.uk

Practical information
Duration: 2–5 days
Level: beginner &
intermediate
Non-residential

Group size: 6–15
Price range: £50–£300
Unsuitable for children
Pets not welcome

Courses available in:

Jan	Feb	Mar	Apr	May	Jun	Jul	Aug	Sep	Oct	Nov	Dec

Metalwork and ceramics in a 17th-century farm

There is possibly nowhere in the country that combines such a diverse range of concerns and initiatives as Wysing Arts. Housed in a 17th-century farm set in 11 acres of South Cambridgeshire countryside, it is a unique centre devoted to projects that unite contemporary visual art with science, technology and ecology. Running for over 15 years, courses are intensive and creative, allowing you to concentrate on a diverse range of materials as you acquire a new skill. Courses vary from metalwork (forging, welding and metal manipulation) to stained glass, from ceramics masterclasses to kiln building in the grounds; but all are led by professional artists and experts.

Contact
Sherry Dobbin
Wysing Arts
Fox Road
Bourn
Cambridge CB3 7TX
Tel: 01954 718881
Web: www.wysingarts.org

Practical information
Duration: 2–7 days
Level: beginner,
intermediate & advanced
Residential & non-residential
Group size: 6–20

Price range: £100–£400
Prices include: meals &
materials
Unsuitable for children
Pets not welcome

Courses available in:

Jan	Feb	Mar	Apr	May	Jun	Jul	Aug	Sep	Oct	Nov	Dec

Lincoln

Boston

Leicester

The East Midlands

The charms of this region include the Peak District National Park where various of the courses take place, Lincoln with its cathedral, and Rutland Water with its water sports. Courses in the East Midlands have a strong craft focus and we can offer stone masonry, blacksmithing, curtain making, sewing and mosaics among a diverse roster of workshops and retreats.

Sewing workshops in picturesque village

Seamstresses who are all fingers and thumbs should investigate the sewing courses offered by Alison Smith in the pretty village of Ashby-de-la-Zouch. The two- or three-day courses take place above Alison's fabric shop and are divided into dressmaking, tailoring, corsetry and others. Sewing machines are provided, but you should bring your own fabric or purchase some from downstairs. Beginners' courses focus on general techniques, advanced courses on wedding dresses, speed tailoring, pattern making and sewing lingerie. Lunch is included; for other needs, Ashby-de-la-Zouch has a pub, a restaurant and a number of farmhouse B&Bs (plus a castle, a 15th-century church and a small museum...).

Contact
Alison Smith
Alison Victoria School of Sewing
71 Market Street
Ashby-de-la-Zouch
Leicestershire LE75 1RU
Tel: 01530 416300
Web: www.schoolofsewing.co.uk

Practical information
Duration: 2-3 days
Level: beginner,
intermediate & advanced
Non-residential

Group size: 2-10
Price range: £100-£400
Prices include: lunch
Unsuitable for children
Pets not welcome

Courses available in:

Jan	Feb	Mar	Apr	May	Jun	Jul	Aug	Sep	Oct	Nov	Dec

Watercolour and flower-painting in Derbyshire country houses

Since 1992, Anna Maule has been offering five-day painting courses at country houses around Derbyshire including lovely Alison House near Cromford. Students have a choice of landscape painting courses, which explore the dramatic landscapes of Derbyshire, and flower painting courses, which take place on location and in the studio, covering techniques for painting wildflowers and floral still lifes. Absolute beginners are welcome and painters with some experience can learn more advanced techniques - the focus is on creative growth, so be prepared to try new things when you paint. Guests stay on site, and home-cooked meals are provided, but you should bring your own paints and other art materials.

Contact
Anna Maule
Art for All
14 Bren Way
Hilton
Derbyshire DE65 5HP
Tel: 01283 730207
Web: www.art-for-all.net

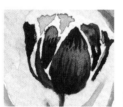

Practical information
Duration: 5 days
Level: beginner & intermediate
Residential
Group size: 2-10

Price range: £200-£300
Prices include: meals &
accommodation
Unsuitable for children
Pets not welcome

Courses available in:

Jan	Feb	Mar	Apr	May	Jun	Jul	Aug	Sep	Oct	Nov	Dec

Embroidery and needlework in a Georgian manor house

Laceby Manor is an imposing Georgian manor house set in two acres of attractive grounds, providing a cheerful location for the embroidery and needlework courses run by Artisan reTREATs. The atmosphere is informal, and students are free to select course topics when they arrive, either single projects or a range of new sewing skills. The courses cover various sewing skills, including cross-stitch, hardanger embroidery and pulled and drawn threadwork. There is accommodation (and sauna) in the manor house, and all meals are included. Alternative therapies are available for an additional fee, and in the evenings you can walk in the surrounding countryside or play a round of golf next door.

Contact
Beryl Lee
Artisan reTREATs
Laceby Manor
Laceby
Lincolnshire DN37 7EA
Tel: 01472 872217
Email: artisan.retreats@lineone.net

Practical information
Duration: 2 days
Level: beginner,
intermediate & advanced
Residential
Group size: 2-10

Price range: £150-£200
Prices include: meals,
accommodation and
materials
Unsuitable for children
Pets not welcome

Courses available in:

Jan	Feb	Mar	Apr	May	Jun	Jul	Aug	Sep	Oct	Nov	Dec

COLD HANWORTH FORGE, NEAR WELTON

Blacksmithing in a traditional forge

One of just a handful of old-fashioned forges still operating in the country, Cold Hanworth is run by blacksmith Bob Oakes, who has 25 years' experience of traditional iron-working techniques. With the heat and sparks, this is an invigorating and hands-on experience where each of the eight students works on their own individual forge hearth. And it's not male-dominated: women are extremely welcome.

Courses
The beginners' courses require no experience and are ideal for anyone tired of sitting behind a desk. They cover introductory techniques, and you'll make a piece of ironwork to take home. The advanced courses - for people with some metal-working experience - teach more complicated skills such as pattern welding, forging blades and the production of floral patterns and scrolls. New arts courses are planned for 2005.

What's special?
The two-and-a-half-day beginners' course is an excellent introduction to the essential blacksmith skills. You'll learn how to operate the forge, and heat and shape metal to create a professionally finished piece of metalwork.

Eating & sleeping
Meals are provided at the nearby inn. Accommodation options include farmhouse B&Bs in Hackthorn, camping at Welton Manor Park and self-catering holiday cottages, among them a converted steam mill.

Directions
By car, drive north from Lincoln on the A46 and turn left at Snarford or Falsingworth. The forge is a few miles along in Cold Hanworth. Or train to Lincoln then taxi (about 9 miles).

In the area
Walking in Willingham Woods and over the Lincolnshire Wolds; historic Lincoln, with its famous cathedral and castle; Rand Park Farm - outdoor centre for kids.

Contact
Bob Oakes
Cold Hanworth Forge
Cold Hanworth
Near Welton
Lincolnshire LN2 3RE
Tel: 01673 866700
Web: www.teachblacksmithing.com/courses.php
Email: boboakes@teachblacksmithing.com

Practical information
Duration: 2 days
Level: beginner,
intermediate & advanced
Non-residential
Group size: 2-10

Price range: £200–£300
Prices include: meals &
materials
Unsuitable for children
Pets not welcome

Courses available in:

Jan	Feb	Mar	Apr	May	Jun	Jul	Aug	Sep	Oct	Nov	Dec

Cookery courses on the Derbyshire Dales borders

This small hotel is housed in a twin-gabled Victorian townhouse on the outskirts of Chesterfield. The hotel has an unusual restaurant with just one table, and chef Nick Buckingham runs regular cooking courses year round for hotel guests. Tuition is provided on a one-to-one basis for single students or couples, and the day-long courses cover either preparation of entire meals or specific topics such as bread-making, pasta, vegetables and vegetarian cooking, stocks and sauces, meat, shellfish and desserts. You can take several days consecutively to make up a longer course. Most students stay at the hotel, just a five-minute drive from the Derbyshire Dales.

Contact
Nick and Tina Buckingham
Buckingham's Hotel
85 Newbold Road
Newbold, Chesterfield
Derbyshire S41 7PU
Tel: 01246 201041
Web: www.buckinghams-table.com

Practical information
Duration: 2–5 days
Level: beginner & intermediate
Residential & non-residential
Group size: 1–2

Price range: £100–£300
Prices include: meals &
accommodation
Unsuitable for children
Pets not welcome

Courses available in:

Jan	Feb	Mar	Apr	May	Jun	Jul	Aug	Sep	Oct	Nov	Dec

Woodworking courses in a Peak District mill

Set against the dramatic backdrop of the Peak District National Park, the old mill at Millers Dale has been offering courses in wood-turning and other wood carving techniques for more than 20 years. Over 5000 students have passed through the doors, but classes are restricted to four people to ensure personal attention. The company offers a huge range of courses for beginners and professionals - popular options include freehand carving, turning wood on a lathe, furniture-making and building a guitar - and all tools and materials are provided. Students are fully covered for accidents, and accommodation and evening meals are available in a B&B opposite the Mill.

Contact
Eve Middleton
Craft Supplies Ltd
The Mill
Millers Dale, Buxton
Derbyshire SK17 8SN
Tel: 01298 871636
Web: www.craft-supplies.co.uk

Practical information
Duration: 2–3 days
Level: beginner,
intermediate & advanced
Non-residential

Group size: 2–4
Price range: £150–£300
Prices include: materials
Unsuitable for children
Pets not welcome

Courses available in:

Jan	Feb	Mar	Apr	May	Jun	Jul	Aug	Sep	Oct	Nov	Dec

Dry stone walling and hedge-laying weekends

This Derbyshire community college offers some unusual courses in traditional countryside crafts, along with a more familiar selection of arts, crafts and skills courses. The two-day dry-stone walling and traditional hedge-laying courses are ideal if you have a garden to landscape. On the former, you'll learn how to lay the traditional self-supporting walls seen all over Derbyshire, while the hedge-laying course covers the production of hand-woven hedgerows. Courses take place at the training farm in Broomfield, or up on the dales on a hill farm owned by the college. See the Conservation and Countryside section of the website for the latest dates.

Contact
Patrick Mountain
Derby College
Broomfield Hall Campus
Morley Ilkeston
Derbyshire DE7 6DN
Tel: 01332 520200
Web: www.derby-college.ac.uk

Practical information
Duration: 2 days
Level: beginner &
intermediate
Non-residential

Group size: 6–15
Price range: £50–£100
Unsuitable for children
Pets not welcome

Courses available in:

Jan	Feb	Mar	Apr	May	Jun	Jul	Aug	Sep	Oct	Nov	Dec

Outdoor navigation in the Hope Valley

Set deep in the Derbyshire Dales, this small country youth hostel is an excellent base for exploring the Peak District. As well as more rugged outdoor courses, the centre offers navigation weekends where you can learn map reading and compass work. The countryside walks take you through various landscapes, and it's all certified by the National Navigation Awards Scheme. There are courses for beginner, intermediate and advanced walkers, and a reasonable level of fitness is required. Equipment is provided, but you should bring suitable clothing. The courses include two nights' accommodation at the Edale hostel, where most people prepare their own meals.

Contact
Rob James
Edale YHA Hostel
Rowland Cote
Nether Booth
Edale, Hope Valley
Derbyshire S33 7ZH
Tel: 01433 670302
Web: www.yha.org.uk

Practical information
Duration: 2–3 days
Level: beginner,
intermediate & advanced
Residential
Group size: 2–10

Courses available in:

Jan	Feb	Mar	Apr	May	Jun	Jul	Aug	Sep	Oct	Nov	Dec

Price range: £100–£150
Prices include:
accommodation
Unsuitable for children
Pets not welcome

Jewellery workshops in a converted barn

If you've ever felt inspired to create your own jewellery, it's worth investigating the highly professional courses offered by In the Studio in Kegworth. All the tutors at this modern studio are professional jewellers, and all equipment is provided, although there may be an additional charge for some expensive materials. Beginners and intermediate courses cover a wide range of skills or you can study advanced topics such as engraving, stone-setting, metal-casting and making wedding rings. Accommodation is in a cosy Georgian cottage next door to the studio and breakfast is included. There are several pubs and restaurants in the village for lunch and evening meals.

Contact
Teresa Speer
In the Studio
59 High Street
Kegworth
Derbyshire DE74 2DA
Tel: 01509 569890
Web: www.inthestudio.co.uk

Practical information
Duration: 2–5 days
Level: beginner,
intermediate & advanced
Residential
Group size: 2–10

Courses available in:

Jan	Feb	Mar	Apr	May	Jun	Jul	Aug	Sep	Oct	Nov	Dec

Price range: £150–£500
Prices include: meals,
accommodation & materials
Unsuitable for children
Pets not welcome

Yoga retreats in a stately home

Keythorpe Hall would not look out of place in a period drama. This vast Georgian mansion was rescued from dereliction in the 1970s and returned to its original splendour by the current owners. The house is surrounded by open countryside, providing a wonderfully serene location for weekend courses in yoga and other alternative therapies. Daily tuition is provided in hatha yoga and deep relaxation techniques, and the courses include a relaxing remedial massage from a qualified practitioner. Beginners are welcome and experienced practitioners can join advanced classes that focus on deep relaxation and meditative breathing. Prices include all meals and accommodation in the stately home.

Contact
Sarah Cawkwell
Keythorpe Yoga
The Cottage, Stackley House
Stretton Road
Great Glen, Leicester
Leicestershire LE8 9GP
Tel: 011259 3748
Web: www.keythorpeyoga.co.uk

Practical information
Duration: 2 days
Level: beginner &
intermediate
Residential
Group size: 6–20

Courses available in:

Jan	Feb	Mar	Apr	May	Jun	Jul	Aug	Sep	Oct	Nov	Dec

Price range: £200–£300
Prices include: meals &
accommodation
Unsuitable for children
Pets not welcome

East Midlands

DERBYSHIRE ARTS, MATLOCK

Art courses in the Derbyshire Dales

Pear Tree Farm overlooks the beautiful Lea Brook and is the very image of a Derbyshire hill farm with its own 76 acres of picturesque pasture and woodland. Owners Alan and Sue Barber have recently established an arts centre here as part of a farm diversification project, and offer an impressive variety of residential courses. This is a family-run business with accommodation provided in a new extension to the farmhouse. Non-participants are welcome as it's also a functioning B&B.

Courses
The 2005 schedule includes painting with watercolours, pastels and oils; stone sculpture; and print and clay techniques. There is excellent tuition from internationally respected artists such as Keith Fenwick, Charles Evans, Hazel Lale, Terry Harrison, Michael Kitchen, Tim Rose, John Wheeldon, Rob Wareing, and wildlife artist Linda Wain. All levels of ability are catered for and each tutor has a different style from illustrative to fluid and bold – if in doubt, ring Sue for advice.

What's special?
Sandy Hillyer's mixed media course, which focuses on abstract art, is special because she pushes people into contemporary styles and ways of thinking about art that are new to them, as does Maggie Slingsby with her print class and mixed media (wire and mod-rock) sculpture. Irene Brierton offers small groups a rare chance to experience an evening badger-watching.

Eating & sleeping
There are eight new double en-suite rooms, two of which have disabled facilities. All meals are provided, and it's proper farmhouse cooking.

Directions
M1 junction 28: A38 towards Derby. Then A610 to Ambergate. Right at T-junction onto A6. Right at traffic-light in Cromford. After 2 miles turn left to Lea and the farm is half a mile along on the left.

In the area
It's an area of outstanding natural beauty and historical connections – Florence Nightingale, Mary Queen of Scots and Derwent Valley Mills World Heritage Site. You can walk to Dethick, Lea Gardens, Cromford Canal and Matlock Bath (with cable cars to the Heights of Abraham). Chatsworth House is 30 minutes by car.

Contact
Alan and Sue Barber
Derbyshire Arts
Pear Tree Farm
Lea Bridge
Matlock
Derbyshire DE4 5JN
Tel: 01629 534 215
Web: www.derbyshire-arts.co.uk
Email: sue@derbyshire-arts.co.uk

Practical information
Duration: 2–5 days
Level: beginner,
intermediate & advanced
Residential & non-residential
Group size: 3–15

Price range: £200–£500+
Prices include: meals,
accommodation & art
materials
Child-friendly
Pets not welcome

Courses available in:

| Jan | Feb | Mar | Apr | May | Jun | Jul | Aug | Sep | Oct | Nov | Dec |

Photo © Derbyshire Arts

Arts, crafts and skills in an imposing country house

Knuston Hall has a pedigree going back to the Domesday Book, although the current buildings date from the 1760s. This imposing country house, in 40 acres of wooded grounds, was the setting for H E Bates's novel Spella Ho, and offers a vast range of short courses covering arts, crafts, music and personal development. Meals and accommodation are usually included, but you can arrange your own. There are two-day courses most weekends and longer courses lasting up to seven days in summer. The programme changes from year to year but usually includes painting, drawing, sewing, tai chi, pilates, folk music, singing, writing and wine appreciation. Full listings on the website.

Contact
Eamonn Flanagan
Knuston Hall
Irchester
Wellingborough
Northamptonshire NN29 7EU
Tel: 01933 312104
Web: www.knustonhall.org.uk

Practical information
Duration: 2–7 days
Level: beginner,
intermediate & advanced
Residential & non-residential
Group size: 1–15

Price range: £100–£400
Prices include: meals,
accommodation & some
materials
Child-friendly
Pets not welcome

Courses available in:

Jan	Feb	Mar	Apr	May	Jun	Jul	Aug	Sep	Oct	Nov	Dec

Painting and drawing in pretty country garden

Set in a lovely floral garden in the designated conservation village of East Langton, Langton Studios offers popular courses in watercolour painting, pastels and drawing. Courses are led by Mary Rodgers, who specialises in depictions of village life and floral scenes, with teaching in studio or garden. Weekend courses in painting and drawing run throughout the year, and there are also two- and three-day summer courses from July to August, including speciality courses for children. Life drawing classes with a guest tutor are planned for 2005. Many students bring a packed lunch, but meals can also be taken at the nearby pub. Mary can provide a list of local B&Bs.

Contact
Mary Rodgers
Langton Studios
Main Street
East Langton
Market Harborough
Leicestershire LE16 7TW
Tel: 01858 545365
Web: www.langtonstudios.com

Practical information
Duration: 2–3 days
Level: beginner &
intermediate
Non-residential
Group size: 2–10

Price range: £50–£100
Prices include:
accommodation and
materials
Child-friendly
Pets not welcome

Courses available in:

Jan	Feb	Mar	Apr	May	Jun	Jul	Aug	Sep	Oct	Nov	Dec

Archaeology and history weekends with local experts

This historical and archaeological foundation is devoted to promoting the history of Lincolnshire and offers a wide selection of weekend courses run by local historians and archaeologists. Based at the Lincoln Cathedral Centre, it is housed in the old Sub-Deanery – modern interior, 13th-century exterior. Courses cover various aspects of Lincolnshire history and some include tours of historical sites around the county. Subjects include Roman Britain, the history of Lincoln, writing historical fiction, medieval villages and Lincolnshire churches and chapels. The schedule changes every year: check the website for details. Prices include accommodation in local B&Bs and hotels, plus wine and meals, or you can make your own arrangements.

Contact
Lindum Heritage
7 Ridgeway
Nettleham
Lincolnshire LN2 2TL
Tel: 01522 851388
Web: www.lindumheritage.co.uk

Practical information
Duration: 2 days
Non-residential
Group size: 2–15

Price range: £50–£200
Prices include acommodation
and meals
Unsuitable for children
Pets not welcome

Courses available in:

Jan	Feb	Mar	Apr	May	Jun	Jul	Aug	Sep	Oct	Nov	Dec

East
Midlands

Stone-carving in the heart of the Peak District

Based at the National Stone Centre on the edge of the Peak District National Park, Living Stones offers a variety of short courses in rock sculpture. The location couldn't be more appropriate -the centre occupies a 50-acre quarry, with an educational centre highlighting the history of the 330-million-year-old rock. The courses, taught by local sculptor Carole Kirsopp, provide a rare opportunity to try real rock carving with a mallet and chisel, and no previous experience is required. For meals, there is a snack bar at the centre and several cafés in nearby Wirksworth. Outside of class hours, you can collect fossils and minerals from the old quarry workings.

Contact
Carole Kirsopp
Living Stones Sculpture Workshop
204 Derby Rd
Swanwick, Alfreton
Derbyshire DE55 1AD
Tel: 01773 540452
Web: www.livingstonessculptureworkshop.co.uk

Practical information
Duration: 2–5 days
Level: beginner &
intermediate
Non-residential

Group size: 2–10
Price range: £50–£100
Prices include: materials
Unsuitable for children
Pets not welcome

Courses available in:

Jan	Feb	Mar	Apr	May	Jun	Jul	Aug	Sep	Oct	Nov	Dec
			Apr	May	Jun	Jul	Aug	Sep	Oct		

Conservation courses in a Victorian country house

Set in an attractive Victorian country house in the Peak District National Park, this is one of the leading centres for the study of environmental management in the UK, and it also offers a wide selection of more leisurely arts and crafts courses. These cover subjects such as popular arts, handicrafts, bird-watching, botanical illustration, landscape painting, navigation and natural history. Two of the most interesting options are courses in the Peak District's archaeology and geology. Prices include accommodation at Losehill Hall, plus meals and materials. The house is set in 27 acres of gardens and grounds, within easy walking distance of classic Peak District countryside.

Contact
Stephen Jenkinson
Losehill Hall
Peak District National Park Study Centre
Castleton
Hope Valley
Derbyshire S30 2WB
Tel: 01433 620373
Web: www.peakdistrict.org/studybreaks

Practical information
Duration: 2–7 days
Level: beginner &
intermediate
Residential & non-residential
Group size: 2–20

Price range: £150–£400
Prices include: meals &
accommodation & materials
Unsuitable for children
Pets not welcome

Courses available in:

Jan	Feb	Mar	Apr	May	Jun	Jul	Aug	Sep	Oct	Nov	Dec
Jan	Feb	Mar	Apr	May	Jun	Jul	Aug	Sep	Oct	Nov	Dec

Gourmet cooking in a lovely old manor house

As its name suggests, this gourmet cookery school is housed in a stately 17th-century manor house on the outskirts of Nottingham. Once a staging post for travellers (including Dick Turpin) on the Fosse Way, today the house hosts courses led by Cordon Bleu-trained teacher Claire Tuttey. There are gourmet weekends, which focus on preparing the perfect dinner party; five-day beginners' courses, which cover kitchen hygiene, menu planning and core cooking skills; four-day courses in vegetarian cookery or preparing game; and an indulgent chocolate weekend that focuses on cakes, chocolates and deserts. Accommodation is provided in the stylishly decorated Georgian mansion and students eat the gourmet meals that they prepare.

Contact
Claire Tuttey
The Manor School of Fine Cuisine
Old Melton Road
Widmerpool
Nottinghamshire NG12 5QL
Tel: 01949 81371
Web: www.manorcuisine.co.uk

Practical information
Duration: 2–5 days
Level: beginner,
intermediate & advanced
Residential & non-residential
Group size: 6–15

Price range: £150–£500+
Prices include: meals &
accommodation.
Unsuitable for children
Pets not welcome

Courses available in:

Jan	Feb	Mar	Apr	May	Jun	Jul	Aug	Sep	Oct	Nov	Dec
Jan	Feb	Mar	Apr	May	Jun	Jul	Aug	Sep	Oct	Nov	Dec

MERRICK & DAY, GAINSBOROUGH

Curtain-making courses with industry experts

Merrick & Day believe that making curtains is an art, not simply an activity. Their courses cover all aspects, from designing curtains to fit a particular window and making Roman blinds, to advanced techniques such as draping swags. People who take the courses are interior designers, curtain-makers and home sewers: all levels of experience are welcome. Stitching is done by hand and any machining will be done by Merrick & Day staff.

Courses
The intensive three-day Curtain Design and Make-Up course covers all aspects of curtain design and make-up. Day courses focus on specific topics such as designing window treatments and creating interlined curtains, valances, blinds, pelmets and swags. Courses take place in a modern work room at Redbourne Hall, an elegant 18th-century country house.

What's special?
All the courses are small and friendly but have the benefit of being held in a professional workroom setting. The condensed three-day course is suitable for those who want to know more about the art of designing and making curtains. The 10 individual day courses are run consecutively so they can be taken separately or as a two-week course.

Eating & sleeping
It's a five-minute drive to the Red Lion Hotel (01652 648302) on Redbourne village green. This is a traditional coaching inn, with spacious rooms and cordon bleu meals. Alternatively Briggate Lodge (01652 650770, ten minutes' drive) has a spa and gym.

Directions
Junction 4 off M180; follow A15 south to Redbourne turn-off. Hall driveway leads from the roundabout on the village outskirts. Complimentary morning and afternoon pick-ups from Newark train station and Red Lion Hotel, or taxi from Scunthorpe.

In the area
Lincoln with its stunning cathedral and castle is a short drive away, or you can walk along the banks of the Humber near the dramatic Humber Bridge.

Contact
Catherine Merrick
Merrick & Day
Redbourne Hall
Redbourne
Gainsborough
Lincolnshire DN21 4JG
Tel: 01652 648814
Web: www.merrick-day.com
Email: sales@merrick-day.com

Practical information
Duration: 2–10 days
Level: beginner,
intermediate & advanced
Non-residential
Group size: 1–20

Price range: £50–£300
Prices include: lunch,
materials
Unsuitable for children
Pets not welcome

Courses available in:

Jan	Feb	Mar	Apr	May	Jun	Jul	Aug	Sep	Oct	Nov	Dec

Photographing nature in the Peak District

Lee Mott is one of a handful of Craftsmen of the Guild of Photographers in the UK. He offers an interesting selection of nature and landscape photography courses in his favourite British landscape, the Derbyshire Dales. Students are grouped according to experience, with days spent mainly on location experimenting with different techniques. Participants should bring their own camera, a cable release and plenty of film or digital storage media; some equipment is available to borrow. Transport is by comfortable jeep and the price covers accommodation (in selected hotels) and all meals. You will have to tramp through fields and woodland to get the best photos, so bring suitable clothing.

Contact
Lee Mott
Nature Photography Courses
The Studio
198 Birchwood Lane
Somercotes, Alfreton
Derbyshire DE55 4NP
Tel: 01773 609874
Web: www.naturephotographycourses.co.uk

Practical information
Duration: 3-4 days
Level: beginner &
intermediate
Residential
Group size: 2-10

Price range: £300-£500
Prices include: meals,
accommodation & some
photography equipment
Unsuitable for children
Pets not welcome

Courses available in:

| Jan | Feb | Mar | Apr | May | Jun | Jul | Aug | Sep | Oct | Nov | Dec |

Stone masonry and carving in a converted church

Thee Orton Trust was established in 1968 to promote the stone-carving and masonry skills used in the restoration and conservation of historic buildings. The trust offers weekend courses in these skills from its headquarters in a converted church in the village of Orton. All the tutors are highly experienced stoneworkers and masons. Beginners' courses cover basic masonry and stoneworking skills, while classes for those with some experience teach advanced techniques such as freehand rock carving, drawing, setting out, lettering and tool maintenance. Lunch, tools and rock for carving are included in the price and the trust can recommend B&Bs in surrounding villages.

Contact
Richard Tyler
The Orton Trust
7 Drake Close
Rothwell
Northamptonshire NN14 6DJ
Tel: 01536 711600
Web: www.ortontrust.org.uk

Practical information
Duration: 3 days
Level: beginner,
intermediate & advanced
Non-residential

Group size: 2-10
Price range: £100-£150
Prices include: materials
Unsuitable for children
Pets not welcome

Courses available in:

| Jan | Feb | Mar | Apr | May | Jun | Jul | Aug | Sep | Oct | Nov | Dec |

Photography in the Peak District

Housed in a stately old stone farmhouse, the Peak District Photography Centre is surrounded by the brooding hills of the Peak District National Park - you could hardly pick a better location for a photography course. Tutors from a wide range of photographic backgrounds teach digital photography and image manipulation as well as traditional print photography. There are introductory courses and advanced technique courses, and students can either bring their own camera or borrow equipment. The centre offers a wide range of two- to four-day courses, covering landscape photography, studio portraits and wedding photography. Accommodation is provided in converted barns in the nearby Dove Valley Centre. Non-participants welcome.

Contact
Simon Watkinson and Elaine Neely
Peak District Photography Centre
Spout Farmhouse Studio
Reapsmoor
Longnor
Derbyshire SK17 0LG
Tel: 01298 687211
Web: www.peakphotocentre.com

Practical information
Duration: 2-4 days
Level: beginner,
intermediate & advanced
Residential
Group size: 2-10

Price range: £200-£500+
Prices include:
accommodation, lunch &
some materials
Unsuitable for children
Pets not welcome

Courses available in:

| Jan | Feb | Mar | Apr | May | Jun | Jul | Aug | Sep | Oct | Nov | Dec |

Yoga and meditation in a 17th-century farm house

Housed in a striking 17th-century village farmhouse, the Practice offers holistic retreats with daily training in primordial sound meditation (meditation with mantras) and yoga, along with revitalising ayurvedic and massage treatments. There are morning and afternoon meditation and yoga classes, catering to both beginners and experienced practitioners. The centre produces its own organic fruit and vegetables, which are used to make detoxifying guest meals, and there is a maximum of ten guests on site, ensuring a relaxed environment. Group workshops on the last day of each retreat allow guests to engage in a shared activity, such as traditional drumming. Other healing therapies are available for an additional charge.

Contact
Jo Pickering
The Practice
The Manor House
Kings Norton
Leicestershire LE7 9BA
Tel: 0116 259 9211
Web: www.retreat-co.co.uk/thepractice

Practical information
Duration: 2–5 days
Level: beginner &
intermediate
Residential
Group size: 2–10

Price range: £200–£500+
Prices include: meals &
accommodation
Unsuitable for children
Pets not welcome

Courses available in:

Jan	Feb	Mar	Apr	May	Jun	Jul	Aug	Sep	Oct	Nov	Dec
			Apr	May	Jun	Jul	Aug	Sep	Oct		

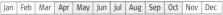

Pottery using locally mined clay

The Riddings Pottery is a small, family-run concern on the edge of the Peak District. The rambling red brick home has large gardens and several outbuildings, which contain the kilns, glaze room and various pottery wheels. Beginners are welcome and the owners provide plentiful advice if you've never used a wheel before. Tutor John Rivers mines his own clay from a local quarry and built the natural gas kilns from scratch - he can advise people who are thinking of setting up their own home pottery. The two-day courses run at weekends from February to April and September to December. B&B accommodation at the pottery is £15 per night.

Contact
John Rivers and Pat Smith
Riddings Pottery
Greenhill Lane
Riddings
Derbyshire DE55 4AY
Tel: 01773 603181
Web: www.riddingspottery.co.uk

Practical information
Duration: 2 days
Level: beginner &
intermediate
Residential & non-residential
Group size: 2–10

Price range: £100–£150
Prices include: meals,
accommodation & pottery
materials
Unsuitable for children
Pets not welcome

Courses available in:

Jan	Feb	Mar	Apr	May	Jun	Jul	Aug	Sep	Oct	Nov	Dec
	Feb	Mar	Apr					Sep	Oct	Nov	Dec

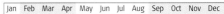

Crafts in the grounds of a 12th-century abbey

Set in the grounds of a ruined 12th-century Cistercian abbey and surrounded by 150 acres of estate land and formal gardens, Rufford Craft Centre is perfect for escaping the hubbub and getting the creative juices flowing. The centre offers an intriguing programme of 'creative activity weekends', covering a wide range of arts and crafts that includes machine embroidery, stained glass, silk dyeing, stone carving, coracle making, pot throwing and the use of paper kilns. The abbey was converted into a country house in the 17th century and the craft centre is housed in the old stable block. Staff can advise on accommodation in local B&Bs.

Contact
Helen Ackroyd
Rufford Craft Centre & Gallery
Offerton
Rufford Country Park
Newark
Nottinghamshire NG22 9DF
Tel: 01623 822944
Web: www.ruffordceramiccentre.org.uk

Practical information
Duration: 2 days
Level: beginner &
intermediate
Non-residential
Group size: 2–15

Price range: £50–£100
Prices include: lunch and
materials
Unsuitable for children
Pets not welcome

Courses available in:

Jan	Feb	Mar	Apr	May	Jun	Jul	Aug	Sep	Oct	Nov	Dec
Jan	Feb	Mar	Apr	May	Jun	Jul	Aug	Sep	Oct	Nov	Dec

East Midlands

Rug-making courses with Cilla Cameron

Rug-making used to be a common cottage industry in the UK, and Cilla Cameron is looking to revive the habit with courses at her home studio in the peaceful village of Oxton near Nottingham. She has 13 years' rug-making experience and teaches in the UK, Canada and the USA. The two-day course will teach you how to design and manufacture traditional rag rugs, including setting up a rug frame, and hooking and weaving selected fragments of fabric to create a finished design. Students are welcome to bring their own design ideas along. All materials are provided, and meals and accommodation are available locally.

Contact
Cilla Cameron
The Rug Studio
18 Elmcroft
Oxton
Nottinghamshire NG25 0SB
Tel: 0115 9655287
Web: www.ragrugsuk.co.uk

Practical information
Duration: 2 days
Level: beginner &
intermediate
Non-residential

Courses available in:

Group size: 2-10
Price range: £50-£100
Prrice include: lunch and
materials
Unsuitable for children
Pets not welcome

Jan	Feb	Mar	Apr	May	Jun	Jul	Aug	Sep	Oct	Nov	Dec
		Mar					Aug	Sep			

Willow weaving in a great farmhouse location

Set at the end of a wooded valley in the Peak District, Shatton Hall Farm is a traditional hill farm, with attractive stone outbuildings and charming gardens. The farm offers regular short courses covering various arts and crafts, including floral painting, willow weaving, clay sculpture, digital photography and field days where you can learn to identify medicinal and edible wild plants and fungi. There's a buffet lunch with wine each day and you can stay in converted cottages on the farm or make your own arrangements at local B&Bs. Materials are provided, but there may be an extra charge for more expensive ones on some of the arts courses.

Contact
Angela Kellie
Shatton Hall Farm
Bamford
Hope Valley
Derbyshire S33 0BG
Tel: 01433 620635
Web: www.peakfarmholidays.co.uk

Practical information
Duration: 2 days
Level: beginner &
intermediate
Residential & non-residential
Group size: 2-15

Courses available in:

Price range: £50-£200
Prices include: meals,
accommodation & materials
Unsuitable for children
Pets not welcome

Jan	Feb	Mar	Apr	May	Jun	Jul	Aug	Sep	Oct	Nov	Dec
				May							

Buddhism and meditation in a peaceful countryside house

The Tara Buddhist Centre is a striking red-brick country house set in peaceful grounds near Derby. The centre was established by Geshe Kelsang Gyatso, the founder of the modern Kadampa tradition of Buddhism, and it offers a regular programme of courses and retreats focusing on Buddhist learning and meditation. The centre has many long-term resident students and the atmosphere is one of quiet contemplation. There are short courses and retreats for beginners lasting just a weekend, and longer courses for experienced practitioners lasting up to a month. Prices include meals and accommodation in dormitories or private rooms, or you can use local B&Bs. Smoking and alcohol are not allowed.

Contact
Tara Buddhist Centre
Ashe Hall
Ash Lane
Etwall
Derbyshire DE65 6HT
Tel: 01283 732338 (Reception) meditate@taracentre.org.uk
Web: www.taracentre.org.uk

Practical information
Duration: 2-10 days
Level: beginner,
intermediate & advanced
Residential & non-residential
Group size: 2-20

Courses available in:

Price range: under
£50-£300
Prices include: meals &
accommodation
Unsuitable for children
Pets not welcome

Jan	Feb	Mar	Apr	May	Jun	Jul	Aug	Sep	Oct	Nov	Dec
Jan	Feb	Mar	Apr	May	Jun	Jul	Aug	Sep	Oct	Nov	Dec

Painting courses with Tim Fisher

Tim Fisher has decades of experience as a watercolour and pastel artist. He teaches at art schools all over the UK, but also offers his own short courses in landscape painting in the unspoiled countryside of Leicestershire's Wreake Valley. Beginners are welcome on the courses, which last one to three days and start with a classroom introduction to technical skills. Students then go out into the fields to paint landscapes around the village of Frisby. The price includes materials, but not lunch or accommodation. For comfortable rooms, Tim recommends the artist-friendly B&B Tole Cottage in the village of Kirby Bellars, or the more luxurious Sysonby Knoll Hotel in Melton Mowbray.

Contact
Tim Fisher
13 Hall Orchard Lane
Frisby on the Wreake
Nr Melton Mowbray
Leicestershire LE14 2NH
Tel: 01664 434340
Web: www.timfisherartist.co.uk

Practical information
Duration: 2–3 days
Residential & non-residential
Group size: 3–15

Price range: £50–£100
Unsuitable for children
Pets not welcome

Courses available in:

Jan	Feb	Mar	Apr	May	Jun	Jul	Aug	Sep	Oct	Nov	Dec

Creative watercolours with Tim Rose

Tim Rose is a working watercolour painter, specialising in buildings, gardens and urban scenes. Several times a year, he offers residential watercolour courses at scenic locations around Derbyshire, particularly Alison House near Cromford and Ingelby Gallery at Stanton-by-Bridge. Students work partly in the studios and partly on location, looking at landscapes, still-life, portraits, gardens and buildings. Courses last two to four days and take place through the summer. Materials are provided but you should bring appropriate clothing for outdoor sessions. Previous painting experience is required. Accommodation is provided at Alison House, but not at Ingelby Gallery; meals are provided on the four-day courses, but the shorter courses just include lunch.

Contact
Tim Rose
17 Plymouth Road
Sheffield
South Yorkshire S7 2DE
Tel: 0114 255 2171
Web: www.timrose.co.uk

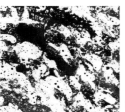

Practical information
Duration: 2–4 days
Level: beginner &
intermediate
Residential & non-residential
Group size: 11–20

Price range: £50–£400
Prices include: meals
(varies) & accommodation &
materials
Unsuitable for children
Pets not welcome

Courses available in:

Jan	Feb	Mar	Apr	May	Jun	Jul	Aug	Sep	Oct	Nov	Dec

Family-run painting holidays in a village home

Many painting courses are set in expensive country hotels, but Toynton Lodge is a small, family-run affair. Courses are designed to be intimate and personal, with a maximum of four students. Students can learn to use watercolours, pastels or oils, and courses are divided into specialist subject areas, with trips to appropriate locations around Lincolnshire. These include Windmills and Waterfalls, Boats and Beaches, Still Life and Interiors, Landscapes and Churches, and Gardens and Cottages. Your tutor is Michael Webster, a skilled watercolour and pastel artist with many years' experience of painting the Lincolnshire countryside. Accommodation and home-cooked meals are provided in a red-brick village house with an immaculate garden.

Contact
Michael Webster
Toynton Lodge Painting Holidays Toynton Lodge
Boston Road
Toynton All Saints
Spilsby
Lincolnshire PE23 5NP
Tel: 01790 752876

Practical information
Duration: 3–5 days
Level: beginner &
intermediate
Residential
Group size: 1–4

Price range: £200–£300
Prices include: meals &
accommodation & art
materials
Unsuitable for children
Pets not welcome

Courses available in:

Jan	Feb	Mar	Apr	May	Jun	Jul	Aug	Sep	Oct	Nov	Dec

East Midlands

UNIVERSITY OF NOTTINGHAM, NOTTINGHAM

Residential study tours in Lincolnshire & Derbyshire

The University of Nottingham runs an intriguing programme of residential study tours in the UK and overseas, with a focus on local history, archaeology, the arts, science and nature. The study tours are predominantly based at country hotels and residential study centres and last anything from two days to two weeks. Subjects cover everything from hands-on techniques for digital photography and opera appreciation to garden design, geology, and history and archaeology around the UK and Europe. Course handbooks and reading lists are provided for all study tours. The schedule changes every year, so contact the Study Tours department at the university for the latest listings.

Courses
Arts subjects include art and music appreciation, architecture and practical skills for artists and photographers. Science and Nature subjects include birdwatching, flora and fauna, and geology. History and Archaeology courses examine local and social history, from historic sites to the lives of famous and infamous historical figures.

What's special?
Every year, the university offers dozens of different study tours, divided into the Arts, Science and Nature, and History and Archaeology. You should be able to find something of interest in any of these categories. UK venues are mainly in Derbyshire, Lincolnshire and Northamptonshire.

Eating & sleeping
Courses focus on historical aspects and natural features so locations vary with the subject matter. All venues are selected for their proximity to relevant sites and the facilities they offer. The tours combine leisure and study and many take place at country house hotels or rural study centres. Meal inclusions are listed under the individual courses.

Directions
You should contact Study Tours directly for information on how to get to the courses. All transport during the course is provided.

In the area
As most study tours involve fieldwork in the local area, students visit plenty of local sites. You can extend your stay on most tours if you want to see more of these.

Contact
University of Nottingham
Study Tours
Centre for Continuing Education
University of Nottingham
Jubilee Campus, Nottingham
Nottinghamshire NG8 1BB
Tel: 0115 951 6526
Web: www.nottingham.ac.uk/education
Email: ce-studytours@nottingham.ac.uk

Practical information
Duration: 2–10 days
Level: beginner &
intermediate
Residential
Group size: 11–25

Price range: £100–£400
Prices include: meals,
accommodation & course
handbooks and local
transport
Unsuitable for children
Pets not welcome

Courses available in:

Jan	Feb	Mar	Apr	May	Jun	Jul	Aug	Sep	Oct	Nov	Dec

142

WRITERS' SUMMER SCHOOL, SWANWICK

Highly regarded summer school in a Georgian country house

Don't be put off by the name – the Hayes Conference Centre is a striking Georgian country house on the edge of the Derbyshire dales. The Writers' Summer School in August is one of the most popular writing courses in the country, with tuition from working writers covering a wide variety of styles. Up to 300 students attend, selecting two of the ten courses on offer, which cover writing for TV and radio, poetry, plays, detective novels, romantic fiction and other literary subjects. Students stay in the house and meals are included (many visitors rave about the food). Outside teaching hours, there are 95 acres of grounds to explore.

Contact
Jean Sutton
Writers' Summer School
10 Stag Rd
Lake
Sandown
Isle of Wright
Email: jean.sutton@lineone.net
Web: www.wss.org.uk

Practical information
Duration: 6 days
Level: beginner,
intermediate & advanced
Residential
Group size: 25+

Courses available in:

Jan	Feb	Mar	Apr	May	Jun	Jul	Aug	Sep	Oct	Nov	Dec

Price range: £200–£300
Prices include: meals &
accommodation
Unsuitable for children
Pets not welcome

XCEPTIONAL DESIGNS, NEW HOLLAND

Metalworking courses at friendly village home

Based in the fenland village of New Holland by the River Humber, Xceptional Designs offers metalworking courses for aspiring sculptors. Heavy courses are geared towards large sculptures, while Light courses concentrate on small-scale projects (jewellery and ornaments). Courses are led by former marine engineer Peter Rogers, who specialises in large kinetic sculptures, and his wife Alex Hallowes, who produces small-scale silver work. Experienced sculptors can learn advanced metalworking techniques while beginners can get their first taste of spot-welding. Soldering and welding equipment is provided, but you must provide your own scrap metal. Accommodation can be arranged at local B&Bs, or you can stay in a dorm bed at the studio.

Contact
Peter Rodgers and Alex Hallowes
Xceptional Designs
Welban House
Humber Bank West, New Holland
Lincolnshire DN19 7RY
Tel: 01469 530992
Web: www.xdes.co.uk

Practical information
Duration: 2 days
Level: beginner,
intermediate & advanced
Residential & non-residential
Group size: 2–10

Courses available in:

Jan	Feb	Mar	Apr	May	Jun	Jul	Aug	Sep	Oct	Nov	Dec

Price range: £50–£100
Prices include: welding
equipment
Unsuitable for children
Pets not welcome

ZANTIUM STUDIOS, HOPTON

Mosaic workshops in the Peak District

Mosaics are a great way to liven up your living space and Zantium Studios will teach you how to make your own, using a variety of easy to find materials, including tiles, pebbles and glass. This is a friendly and professional operation that also offers courses in painting, drawing, stained glass and other arts and crafts, with accommodation provided on site or at local B&Bs. Non-participating partners are welcome. The studio is a lovely 17th-century farmhouse set in rolling countryside, with fine views across the fields to Carsington Water. Courses last two to five days and can be customised for groups of five or more.

Contact
Alison Massey
Zantium Studios
Godfrey Hole House
Godfrey Hole
Hopton, Wirksworth
Derbyshire DE4 4DF
Tel: 01629 824377
Web: www.zantium.co.uk

Practical information
Duration: 2–5 days
Level: beginner &
intermediate
Residential & non-residential
Group size: 3–10

Courses available in:

Jan	Feb	Mar	Apr	May	Jun	Jul	Aug	Sep	Oct	Nov	Dec

Price range: £100–£300
Prices include:
accommodation & lunch and
breakfast
Unsuitable for children
Pets not welcome

UPPINGHAM SUMMER SCHOOL, UPPINGHAM

Range of short courses on a fine private school campus

Uppingham School is a prestigious independent school with many grand buildings, both historic and modern, set in 120-acre grounds. The summer school offers an impressive programme of courses in arts, crafts, music, active recreation, home and garden, modern languages, hobbies etc, plus an interesting selection of music, drama, sport and activity courses for children. It should be possible to find something to suit every member of the family. Courses make use of the school's excellent educational and leisure facilities, including a creative arts centre, brand new modern languages block and theatre. Most courses offer residential and non-residential options.

Courses
Half-day to ten-day summer courses cover an impressive range of topics, from making your own soap or cheese to watercolour painting, upholstery, tracing your ancestors, local studies, modern languages, drama, Pilates and Alexander Technique, and photography courses. See the website for listings.

What's special?
One of the most popular new courses in 2004 was portrait modelling in clay. Students learned how to create a realistic representation of a live model using clay, oxides and pigments, which equipped them to continue sculpting portraits at home. This will continue in 2005, with the new cheese-making course also expected to be particularly popular.

Eating & sleeping
Residential students (adults and children) stay and eat in school boarding houses, which offer a range of accommodation from single rooms (including some en-suite) to 13-bed dormitories. Prices below do not include accommodation or meals.

Directions
The main school building is on High Street West. Coming from the A47, follow signs to Uppingham. After the main traffic lights in the village, turn right up High St West.

In the area
Nearby Burghley House is one of England's finest country houses. Walkers can explore Welland Wood, while birdwatchers can see myriad different migratory birds on Rutland Water.

Contact
Uppingham Summer School
34 Stockerston Road
Uppingham
Rutland LE15 9UD
Tel: 01572 820800
Web: www.uppinghamsummerschool.co.uk
Email: summerschool@uppingham.co.uk

Practical information
Duration: 2–5 days
Level: beginner,
intermediate & advanced
Residential & non-residential
Group size: 2–15

Price range: £50–£150
Prices include: meals,
accommodation & some
materials
Unsuitable for children
Pets not welcome

Courses available in:

| Jan | Feb | Mar | Apr | May | Jun | Jul | Aug | Sep | Oct | Nov | Dec |

144

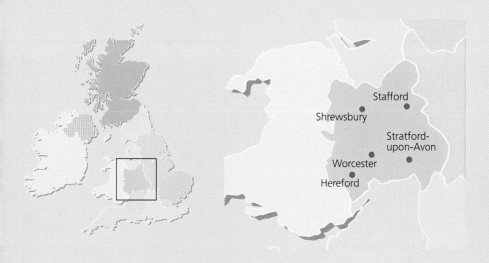

The West Midlands

As England heads towards Wales the landscape becomes more rural. After the Black Country this becomes a region of market towns and small cities – Ludlow and Shrewsbury, Hereford and Worcester. Lichfield cathedral is well worth the visit. Many of the courses here are rural-focused, teaching country pursuits. But there is also painting, cookery and even bell ringing to tempt you westwards.

Silversmithing in a 16th-century cottage

Ian Buckley has been teaching silversmithing since the 1970s and runs Bringsty Studios with his wife Sue from their 16th-century cottage in Worcester. There is a specially built silversmithing workshop on site. Set courses include the likes of 'Jewellery Making', but private tuition is also offered. Silversmithing principles covered include hollowing, sinking, seaming, soldering and polishing. Students can expect to take home a spoon, a candlestick, a ring or a photo frame. The jewellery-making courses run once a month, except January, and couples can create their own wedding rings in a special day-long course. All skill levels welcome. The city of Worcester offers excellent parks and porcelain.

Contact	**Practical information**	Price range: £100 –£200
Ian and Sue Buckley	Duration: 2 days	Prices include: lunch only.
Bringsty Arts Studio	Level: beginner,	Unsuitable for children
Bringsty Common	intermediate & advanced	Pets not welcome
Worcester	Non-residential	
Worcestershire WR6 5UJ	Group size: 3–5	
Tel: 01886 821297		
Web: www.silversmithingcourses.co.uk		

Courses available in:

Jan	Feb	Mar	Apr	May	Jun	Jul	Aug	Sep	Oct	Nov	Dec

Cooking at Caldicott Farm

Sharpen your cooking skills with a luxurious course at Caldicott Farm in the middle of the South Herefordshire countryside. Topics covered include bread making, cake baking, meat, game and fish preparation, desserts and, crucially, meal planning and organisation. The venue is a converted barn, parts of which date back to the 1600s. Food used on the courses is seasonal: there are special Christmas and Valentine courses, as well as courses incorporating local food festivals. Children over ten may take part at reduced rates, and non-cooking partners are welcome to stay and sample. Caldicott Farm is a great base from which to explore the Wye Valley and the Malvern Hills.

Contact	**Practical information**	Price range: £200–£400
Sarah	Duration: 2–3 days	Prices include: meals &
Cookaway Foodbreaks	Level: beginner,	accommodation
Caldicott Farm	intermediate & advanced	Child-friendly
Broad Oak	Residential	Pets not welcome
Herefordshire HR2 8QZ	Group size: 3–10	
Tel: 01981 580249		
Web: www.cookawayfoodbreaks.co.uk		

Courses available in:

Jan	Feb	Mar	Apr	May	Jun	Jul	Aug	Sep	Oct	Nov	Dec

Cooking for all in a 17th-century farmhouse

Victoria O'Neill teaches cooking classes at Pyon House, her 17th-century red-brick farmhouse in the countryside north of Hereford. She offers various day courses which can be combined with a day of personal tuition on a cooking topic of your choice to form a residential course. Most courses are demonstration only; a few are 'practical' or 'demonstration with hands on'. Scheduled day courses include 'Bread Making', 'Catering for Christmas', 'Best Kept Chef's Secrets', 'Men in the Kitchen' and 'Aga Food'. Children are specially catered for with courses divided into age groups. B&B accommodation is available on site. Hereford is very close to the beautiful Wye Valley.

Contact	**Practical information**	Price range: £100–£500+
Victoria O'Neill	Duration: 2–4 days	Prices include: meals,
Cooking with Class	Level: beginner,	accommodation &
Pyon House	intermediate & advanced	ingredients.
Canon Pyon	Residential & non-residential	Child-friendly
Herefordshire HR4 8PH	Group size: 1–10	Pets not welcome
Tel: 01432 830122		
Web: www.cookingwithclass.co.uk		

Courses available in:

Jan	Feb	Mar	Apr	May	Jun	Jul	Aug	Sep	Oct	Nov	Dec

COWSHED STUDIO, ALCESTER
Painting weekends in Warwickshire

Cowshed Studio's weekend painting courses take place in the stunning, 17th-century Ragley Hall, where broad rural vistas and formal gardens add to the charm of the hall itself. The weekend includes B&B or self-catering accommodation in country locations, the freedom of the grounds, light lunches and the chance to paint aspects of Ragley with help and tutoring in your chosen medium (guests can choose to develop whichever medium or style they wish). There are also midweek courses in watercolours, oils or acrylic at Cowshed Studio, both through the day and in the evening. Materials are included but visitors should bring their own brushes.

Contact
Gill Holway
Cowshed Studio
50 Stratford Road
Alcester
Warwickshire B49 5AS
Tel: 01789 400074
Web: www.cowshedart.co.uk

Practical information
Duration: 2–10 days
Level: beginner,
intermediate & advanced
Non-residential
Group size: 1–25

Price range: £50–£500+
Prices include: some meals
& painting materials for
most courses.
Unsuitable for children
Pets not welcome

Courses available in:

Jan	Feb	Mar	Apr	May	Jun	Jul	Aug	Sep	Oct	Nov	Dec

EASTNOR POTTERY, LEDBURY
Pottery at Eastnor Castle

Eastnor Pottery is located in the clock tower cottage in the grounds of Eastnor Castle. Tutor Jon Williams has been teaching here since 1998, running hands-on weekend workshops which cover throwing, turning, finishing, attaching and decorating. Workshop facilities include six electrically operated potter's wheels and three electric kilns and each participant is guaranteed their own wheel. Finished work may be left to be fired and can then be posted or collected at a later stage. Jon runs children's workshops, as well as special-occasion workshops such as hen parties. There are magnificent walks in the castle grounds and the Malvern Hills which surround the pottery. Participants should bring a packed lunch.

Contact
Jon Williams and Sarah Monk
Eastnor Castle
Home Farm
Eastnor, Ledbury
Herefordshire HR18 1RD
Tel: 01531 633886
Web: www.eastnorpottery.co.uk

Practical information
Duration: 2 days
Level: beginner &
intermediate
Non-residential

Group size: 3–10
Price range: £50–£100
Child-friendly
Pets not welcome

Courses available in:

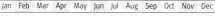

Jan	Feb	Mar	Apr	May	Jun	Jul	Aug	Sep	Oct	Nov	Dec

FARNCOMBE ESTATE CENTRE, BROADWAY
Special interests in Worcestershire

Situated on the edge of the Cotswolds, Farncombe Estate Centre offers weekend study breaks in just about everything. The emphasis is on lifelong learning, so expect to flex your visual and critical skills whether you opt for art or Zen. Guests can explore the 1780 mansion house and its large grounds, from where you can see the Black Mountains and the Wrekin on a good day, or enjoy the bar, games room, tennis court and other facilities. Weekend courses offer tuition in Art History and Appreciation; Body, Mind and Spirit; Living the Land; Music Appreciation; Practical Arts, Crafts and Photography; Singing and Voice; and Writing, Literature and Theatre.

Contact
William Redway
Farncombe Estate Centre
Broadway
Worcestershire WR12 7LJ
Tel: 0845 2308590
Web: www.farncombeestate.co.uk

Practical information
Duration: 2–3 days
Level: beginner,
intermediate & advanced
Residential & non-residential
Group size: 6–25+

Price range: £150–£500+
Prices include: meals &
accommodation
Child-friendly
Pet-friendly

Courses available in:

Jan	Feb	Mar	Apr	May	Jun	Jul	Aug	Sep	Oct	Nov	Dec

West
Midlands

FILBERT SPLOSH, LEINTWARDINE OR CRADLEY

Painting and drawing with Filbert Splosh

Filbert Splosh, the alter ego of Paul Priestley, has been hosting art experiences for two years. Prior to this he was a successful art teacher who also wrote novels and built a car in his spare time. With a dash of theatrical flair, lashings of fun and a very inspirational approach Filbert has a unique method for teaching art. He hosts a variety of painting and drawing courses for all abilities, turning those who cannot draw straight lines into artists. The venues are the village halls of the picturesque and historic villages of Leintwardine and Cradley.

Courses
Course titles include 'Expressive Painting Weekend', 'Seated Figure Weekend', 'Introduction to Oil/Acrylics Painting', 'Drawing for Beginners' and 'Inspirational Drawing'. The painting/drawing media vary and are often specific to the course – e.g. graphite, pastels, watercolours. Courses can usually be combined together as participants wish.

What's special?
The 'Portrait Painting Weekends' cover traditional and modern styles and participants are encouraged to explore both before creating a full-scale painting on the second day. Models are of varying ages and both genders.

Eating & sleeping
Lower Buckton (01547 540532) in Leintwardine offers groups of six exclusive use of house and grounds; nearby Ludlow has four Michelin-starred restaurants. Cradley is five miles from Malvern where the Bredon House Hotel (01684 566990) has spectacular views.

Directions
Leintwardine is 6 miles west of Ludlow. The village hall is opposite the church on the A4113 in Leintwardine. Cradley Village Hall is approached from the A4103, between Storridge and Stifford's Bridge. The hall is next to the church in the centre of the village.

In the area
Ludlow, near Leintwardine, dates back to 1086 and has a castle, medieval streets and superb dining. The Malvern Hills offer excellent hiking and a thriving arts scene which attracts a host of top performances.

Contact	Practical information	Price range: £50–£200
Paul Priestley	Duration: 2–4 days	Prices include: lunch only
Filbert Splosh	Level: beginner,	and some materials
Ashfield	intermediate & advanced	Child-friendly
Luston, Leominster	Non-residential	Pet-friendly
Herefordshire	Group size: 3–15	
Tel: 01568 617433		
Web: www.filbertsplosh.co.uk	Courses available in:	
Email: filbertsplosh@talk21.com		

Jan	Feb	Mar	Apr	May	Jun	Jul	Aug	Sep	Oct	Nov	Dec

Further education a Cadbury family home

Fircroft College in Birmingham is a former Cadbury family home on six acres of land. Courses offered here include Creative Writing, Digital Photography, Enjoying Film and Successful Fundraising, and there are many other business and information technology related courses. Participants are awarded a nationally recognised Certificate of Accreditation at the end of the courses, which are free to UK permanent residents who do not have a degree or professional qualification. Accommodation and meals are provided on site, and special diets are catered for. Childcare is provided on weekends and school holidays where possible for children aged between three months and 12 years.

Contact
Michael Conway Jones
Fircroft College of Adult Education
1018 Bristol Road
Selly Oak, Birmingham
West Midlands B29 6LH
Tel: 01214 720116
Web: www.fircroft.ac.uk

Practical information
Duration: 2–4 days
Level: beginner,
intermediate & advanced
Residential
Group size: 6–20

Price range: under £50
Prices include: meals &
accommodation
Child-friendly
Pets not welcome

Courses available in:

Jan	Feb	Mar	Apr	May	Jun	Jul	Aug	Sep	Oct	Nov	Dec

Bell-ringing in Shropshire

For something a little different, feed your inner campanologist on a bell-ringing holiday. Fire Ring have been running courses for five years from a purpose-built teaching belfry in a barn in South Shropshire. This has eight dumbbells, connected to a simulator, which feel and sound exactly like real bells. Training is followed by a visit to other towers in the area. The courses include 'Beginners and Improvers', 'Plain Bob Doubles' and 'Minor, and Plain Hunt'. There's also a Fire Ring holiday which visits 20 towers in Herefordshire, Shropshire and Wales. B&B is supplied locally, at Great House, with other meals pre-booked in local pubs.

West Midlands

Contact
John Turney
Fire Ring
Orchard House
Hopton Heath
Craven Arms
Shropshire SY7 0QD
Tel: 01547 530470
Web: www.firering.co.uk

Practical information
Duration: 2–4 days
Level: beginner,
intermediate & advanced
Residential
Group size: 1–10

Price range: £200–£300
Prices include: meals &
accommodation
Unsuitable for children
Pets not welcome

Courses available in:

Jan	Feb	Mar	Apr	May	Jun	Jul	Aug	Sep	Oct	Nov	Dec

Crafting with wood in Telford and Wrekin

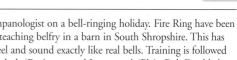

The Green Wood Trust is a charity which aims to 'promote the traditional management of broadleaved woodland through teaching traditional craft and coppice management skills'. Courses are held at Coalbrookdale, a small wood in a River Severn valley, or in several lovely woodlands nearby. Accomplished craftsmen lead courses in making various items: besom brooms, felt for rugs and yurts, charcoal, Shaker boxes, cider and chairs. By volunteering skills or energy to the Trust, participants can help pay for courses. Coalbrookdale is on the edge of Ironbridge, the birthplace of the Industrial Revolution. The old train station houses a dining room where course lunches are served.

Contact
Judy Walker
Green Wood Trust
Station Road
Coalbrookdale
Telford and Wrekin
Shropshire TF8 7DR
Tel: 01952 432769
Web: www.greenwoodtrust.org.uk

Practical information
Duration: 2–5 days
Level: beginner,
intermediate & advanced
Non-residential

Group size: 6–10
Price range: £50–£400
Prices include: meals &
lunch and some materials.
Unsuitable for children
Pets not welcome

Courses available in:

Jan	Feb	Mar	Apr	May	Jun	Jul	Aug	Sep	Oct	Nov	Dec

GREEN CUSINE, KINGTON

Green cuisine on a farmhouse in Kington

Green Cuisine's Daphne Lambert is an experienced chef and nutritionist devoted to teaching the benefits of seasonal, local and organic food. The courses take place in a restored 18th-century barn at Penrhos Court, a series of medieval farm buildings on the Welsh borders, and include much hands-on tuition.

Courses
The general 'Food and Health course covers organic growing, wholefoods, juicing, diet and the 'right fats'. The 'Women's Health' course teaches nutritional aids to help prevent menopausal problems, breast cancer, osteoporosis and other problems, while generating energy. Other courses include 'Food and Health', 'Christmas Food and Health', 'Beating Candida' and 'Mamaheaven'. Some include treatments such as aromatherapy massage.

What's special?
'A Time to Heal' is a retreat encouraging participants to take responsibility for their well-being. They arrive with a diagnosed illness or with the feeling that their life needs change, and leave with a customised diet and a deeper understanding of how to create and sustain good health.

Eating & sleeping
There is on-site accommodation in en-suite rooms in the Penrhos Hotel with views of the surrounding hills. Meals are prepared in the kitchen/juice bar – which doubles as a learning room – at the centre of the farm complex.

Directions
Penrhos is on the A44 just before the Welsh border. It is one mile east of Kington and 15 miles west of Leominster. The nearest rail station is Leominster.

In the area
Kington has a rich history dating back 1,000 years and is the starting point for the Black and White Villages trail. Walking, cycling, fishing and golf are all available nearby.

Contact
Green Cuisine
Penrhos Court
Kington
Herefordshire HR5 3LH
Tel: 01544 230720
Web: www.greencuisine.org
Email: info@greencuisine.org

Practical information
Duration: 2–6 days
Level: beginner,
intermediate & advanced
Residential
Group size: 1–15

Courses available in:

Jan	Feb	Mar	Apr	May	Jun	Jul	Aug	Sep	Oct	Nov	Dec

Price range: £200–£500+
Prices include: meals,
accommodation & yoga,
aromatherapy, massages,
colonics
Child-friendly
Pets not welcome

Ancient woodworking skills

Mike Abbott has taught woodland crafts for over two decades. His greenwood philosophy is to 'go with the grain' of the wood; to see what it offers rather than try to force it into shapes. His courses, based in Clissett's Wood near the Malvern Hills, are offered for different levels of experience. Beginners could take the three-day 'Introduction to Green Woodwork' which covers the basic principles and shows participants how to make practical goods such as candlesticks, baby rattles and spoons. Or they could join the six-day 'General Chair-making' course. Camping accommodation is available on site, or B&B recommendations can be given.

Contact
Mike Abbott
Green Woodwork
Greenwood Cottage
Bishops Frome
Worcestershire WR6 5AS
Tel: 01531 640005
Web: www.living-wood.co.uk

Practical information
Duration: 3–9 days
Level: beginner,
intermediate & advanced
Residential & non-residential
Group size: 1–10

Price range: £100–£400
Prices include: Tools &
materials on most courses.
Unsuitable for children
Pets not welcome

Courses available in:

Jan	Feb	Mar	Apr	May	Jun	Jul	Aug	Sep	Oct	Nov	Dec

Green woodworking in the Herefordshire woods

Gudrun Leitz established Green Woodwork in 1995 to teach the skills needed to turn unseasoned timber into home and garden furniture. Visitors learn how to cleave and shape wood and finish the design with pole-lathes and shavehorses. Most leave with several turned items such as candlesticks and high stools. Gudrun also runs 'development weeks' in Clissett Wood and Childer Wood. Both woods are to the west of the Malvern Hills, in an area celebrated for its rural character. Accommodation ranges between camping pitches, caravans, basic greenwood huts and B&B accommodation. Courses include 'Green Woodwork and Chair-Making', 'Make and Use a Pole-Lathe', 'Chair-Making Workshop', 'Rush-Seating', and 'Hazel and Hedgerow Chairs'.

Contact
Gudrun Leitz
Greenwood Chairs
Hill Farm
Stanley Hill
Bosbury, Ledbury
Herefordshire HR8 1HE
Tel: 01531 640125
Web: www.greenwoodwork.co.uk

Practical information
Duration: 2–9 days
Level: beginner,
intermediate & advanced
Residential & non-residential
Group size: 6–10

Price range: £100–£400
Prices include: Basic
materials & tool use
Child-friendly
Pets not welcome

Courses available in:

Jan	Feb	Mar	Apr	May	Jun	Jul	Aug	Sep	Oct	Nov	Dec

Pottery and painting in Tenbury Wells

The Martin Homer Pottery and Painting Summer School offers a superb setting in a 17th-century farmhouse. The studios are in a converted barn, where small groups of students can receive high levels of personal attention. Professional potters cover all stages of 'throwing', pulling handles and spouts, turning, modelling, glazing and firing. Your best pots will be fired, glazed and posted to you. The painting courses, aimed at all levels of experience, cover various painting media, as well as basic principles and techniques. Much of the painting will draw inspiration from the beautiful local landscapes. Accommodation is arranged nearby in one of three country houses which also provide home-cooked meals.

Contact
Martin Homer
Homer Pottery
Lower Aston House
Aston Bank
Tenbury Wells
Worcestershire WR15 8LW
Tel: 01584 781404
Web: www.homerpottery.co.uk

Practical information
Duration: 2–5 days
Level: beginner,
intermediate & advanced
Residential
Group size: 3–15

Price range: £200–£500
Prices include: meals,
accommodation & some
materials
Child-friendly
Pet-friendly

Courses available in:

Jan	Feb	Mar	Apr	May	Jun	Jul	Aug	Sep	Oct	Nov	Dec

West
Midlands

Natural therapy in Hay-on-Wye

Haytherapy offers residential weekend courses in a range of natural therapies. Founder Tina Finley is an expert in both reflexology and aromatherapy, while other therapists specialising in nutrition, Bowen technique and homeopathy will contribute to the courses where appropriate, as tutors or guest speakers. The venue is the Baskerville Hall Hotel, built in 1839, where Arthur Conan Doyle learnt of the eponymous hounds. Facilities include a swimming pool, sauna, bars, games and music rooms as well as 130 acres of grounds.

Courses
Courses include introductions to reflexology, aromatherapy, Indian head massage, sports massage and crystals, as well as a general introduction to holistic therapies. Reiki attunement weekends are available, and there is a Reiki Master Course for those wanting to pass on their skills to others. Groups of five or more can arrange a tailor-made course.

What's special?
The 'Introduction to Holistic Therapies' course covers a range of practices including aromatherapy, reflexology, acupressure, Indian head massage, nutrition, crystals and reiki. The schedule is flexible, according to the needs of the group, and leaves plenty of time for swimming and exploring the grounds.

Eating & sleeping
Accommodation ranges from camping and dormitories to luxurious executive rooms. Meals for course participants often have a French flavour. Set menus include the likes of home-made soups, roast meats with vegetables and cheesecake.

Directions
Junction 7 off M5; A4103 to Hereford; then A438 into Hay-on-Wye. Or Junction 32 off M4; take A470 north, which becomes the A438. Clyro and Baskerville Hall are to the west of Hay on the A438.

In the area
Brilliant location for outdoor pursuits such as pony trekking, canoeing on the River Wye and exploring the Brecon Beacons on foot or by bike.

Contact
Tina Finley
Haytherapy
5a King Street
Hereford
Herefordshire HR4 9BW
Tel: 01432 350054
Web: www.haytherapy.co.uk
Email: tina@haytherapy.co.uk

Practical information
Duration: 2 days
Level: beginner,
intermediate & advanced
Residential
Group size: 3–25+

Price range: £200–£500+
Prices include: meals &
accommodation
Child-friendly
Pet-friendly

Courses available in:

Jan	Feb	Mar	Apr	May	Jun	Jul	Aug	Sep	Oct	Nov	Dec

Natural dyeing by the River Wye

Jane Meredith runs weekend plant dyeing courses from her house and garden on the banks of the River Wye. She teaches guests how to dye their clothes using natural substances derived from plants, which can include anything from chamomile to stinging nettles, dyer's greenweed to onion skins. On the Saturday, guests dye a fleece, with Jane showing what type of fleece can be used, as well how to sort and wash them. On the Sunday, guests weave a peg loom mat from the fleece, which they can take home. If it's a three-day course, Jane moves on to simple weaving, felt-making and hand-spinning. B&B is available on site.

Contact
Jane Meredith
The Forge
Byford
Hereford
Herefordshire HR4 7LD
Tel: 01981 590370
Web: www.plantdyedwool.co.uk

Practical information
Duration: 2–3 days
Level: beginner,
intermediate & advanced
Residential & non-residential
Group size: 3–15

Price range: £50–£150
Prices include:
accommodation & materials.
Unsuitable for children
Pets not welcome

Courses available in:

Jan	Feb	Mar	Apr	May	Jun	Jul	Aug	Sep	Oct	Nov	Dec

Rag Rugs in Herefordshire

Dig out a stash of unwanted materials and recycle them into a work of art. Jenni Stuart-Anderson has been teaching rag rug making since 1997 and has designed at the London Art College. The craft traditionally involved the entire family working over winter evenings, and materials can range from old and unused clothes to furnishings. The courses take place at various venues, including Jenni's own home, Lower Buckton in Leintwardine and Marlborough College in Wiltshire. They cover hooking, progging and sometimes plaiting, and participants leave with a rug of their own design, such as a seat cover, as well as the skills to begin more ambitious projects.

West Midlands

Contact
Jenni Stuart-Anderson
The Birches
Middleton-on-the-Hill
Herefordshire HR6 0HN
Tel: 01568 750 229
Web: www.jenni.ragrugs.freeuk.com

Practical information
Duration: 2–6 days
Level: beginner,
intermediate & advanced
Residential & non-residential
Group size: 2–15

Price range: £50–£500+
Prices include: meals,
accommodation.
Child-friendly
Pets not welcome

Courses available in:

Jan	Feb	Mar	Apr	May	Jun	Jul	Aug	Sep	Oct	Nov	Dec

Willow basket-weaving in a country cottage

Jenny Pearce began basket weaving over ten years ago in her native Ireland and now runs workshops from her country cottage in Canon Frome. The baskets are made from unstripped willow, and each student will take home at least one. Jenny teaches both traditional and contemporary designs, using Celtic and English methods, and grows some of the willow herself as rare types can be difficult to obtain. The courses run over weekends and the price includes a substantial lunch. Jenny also runs a course specifically for oval basket-making. She can make accommodation recommendations, while the nearby market town of Ledbury offers museums and 17th-century cobbled streets.

Contact
Jenny Pearce
Vicarage Cottage
Canon Frome
Nr Ledbury
Herefordshire HR8 2TG
Tel: 01531 670574
Web: members.lycos.co.uk/willowbaskets/welcome.htm

Practical information
Duration: 2 days
Level: beginner &
intermediate
Residential & non-residential
Group size: 1–10

Price range: £50–£100
Prices include: lunch,
refreshments & materials.
Unsuitable for children
Pets not welcome

Courses available in:

Jan	Feb	Mar	Apr	May	Jun	Jul	Aug	Sep	Oct	Nov	Dec

Creative writing in the Clun Valley

Set in 30 acres of woodland in the Clun Valley, this South Shropshire venue is a beautiful site for a comprehensive list of Arvon Foundation writing courses. These include 'Starting to Write', 'Poetry', 'Horror', 'Theatre' and 'TV Drama'. Tutored courses are usually led by two accomplished writers, with a third attending mid-week to give a reading. The centre also offers a 'Writing Retreat', where participants can focus on their writing in a tranquil, dedicated space, without a tutor. Students prepare the evening meals in turn, in groups of four, and prepare their own breakfast and lunch. The Arvon Foundation runs a grant system for those who would have difficulty paying.

Contact
The John Osborne Arvon Centre
The Hurst
Clunton
Craven Arms
Shropshire SY7 0JA
Tel: 01588 640658
Web: www.arvonfoundation.org

Practical information
Duration: 2–5 days
Level: beginner,
intermediate & advanced
Residential
Group size: 11–20

Price range: £400–£500
Prices include: meals &
accommodation
Unsuitable for children
Pets not welcome

Courses available in:

Jan	Feb	Mar	Apr	May	Jun	Jul	Aug	Sep	Oct	Nov	Dec

Yoga: living well in Wolverhampton

The Parkdale Yoga Centre was set up by Anna Ingham and Peter Yates seven years ago in a Victorian house in leafy parkland. Anna combines complementary therapies such as Shiatsu with her teaching, while Peter, who has been practising yoga for over 30 years, draws on Hatha yoga and Raja yoga techniques. The weekend retreats help students to embrace the positive aspects of life and are suitable for all levels of experience. Groups are limited to eight people, with students accommodated and fed (organic vegetarian or vegan) on site. Wolverhampton is ten minutes' walk away offering museums and galleries. The Centre also runs week-long summer retreats in the Lake District.

Contact
Anna Ingham and Peter Yates
The Parkdale Yoga Centre
10 Parkdale West
Wolverhampton
West Midlands WV1 4TE
Tel: 01902 424048
Web: www.heartyoga.co.uk

Practical information
Duration: 2–7 days
Level: beginner,
intermediate & advanced
Residential
Group size: 6–15
Courses available in:

Price range: £100–£300
Prices include: meals &
accommodation
Unsuitable for children
Pets not welcome

Jan	Feb	Mar	Apr	May	Jun	Jul	Aug	Sep	Oct	Nov	Dec

Live and learn in Staffordshire

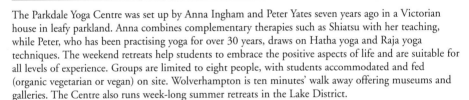

Pendrell Hall College is a Victorian country mansion hosting a rich variety of courses. Many of these are in the arts arena, with weekend courses such as 'Watercolour for Beginners', 'Life Painting' and 'Chinese-Japanese Calligraphy'. There are also beadwork courses, silk painting, music courses, complementary therapy courses, geology and astronomy, among others. Participants are often expected to arrive the evening before the course begins, when an evening meal will be provided. A list of materials is available for each course on booking. There is accommodation on site, if wanted, and all meals are provided (minus breakfast for non-residents). Nearby Wolverhampton offers museums, stately homes and galleries to explore.

Contact
Pendrell Hall College
Codsall Wood
South Staffs
Staffordshire WV8 1QP
Tel: 01902 434112
Web: www.aredu.org.uk/pendrellhall

Practical information
Duration: 2–6 days
Level: beginner,
intermediate & advanced
Residential & non-residential
Group size: 6–25+

Price range: £100–£300
Prices include: meals &
accommodation
Child-friendly
Pets not welcome

Courses available in:

Jan	Feb	Mar	Apr	May	Jun	Jul	Aug	Sep	Oct	Nov	Dec

Life outside in Shrewsbury

Set in 12 acres of woodland and grassland, the Preston Montford branch of the Field Studies Council is a glorious place to learn outdoors. There are courses about many of the area's living things, including trees, grasses, otters and dragonflies. The landscape itself is also used as a learning tool in courses on local geology and archaeology. And if learning about the landscape doesn't interest you, you could always paint it on one of the watercolour courses. All courses are marked according to participants' suggested experience level. Accommodation and meals are provided on site in the huge Queen Anne country house. Shrewsbury has medieval churches and abbeys, and a castle.

Contact
Cathy Preston
Preston Montford
Montford Bridge
Shrewsbury
Shropshire SY4 1DX
Tel: 0845 3307378
Web: www.field-studies-council.org/prestonmontford

Practical information
Duration: 2–7 days
Level: beginner,
intermediate & advanced
Residential & non-residential
Group size: 3–20

Price range: £100–£400
Prices include: meals &
accommodation
Child-friendly
Pets not welcome

Courses available in:

Jan	Feb	Mar	Apr	May	Jun	Jul	Aug	Sep	Oct	Nov	Dec

Tai Chi on a peaceful country property

Richard Farmer is the founder and principal instructor of Rising Dragon Tai Chi. He has studied for over 27 years and teaches both traditional tai chi and 'Living Transformation' courses. Courses take place at Poulstone Court, a large Victorian house set in substantial grounds which also has a large barn for practice in the event of rain. Some courses are for people who are experienced in tai chi, while the bi-annual 'Living Transformation' courses are ideal for beginners. They aim to enhance spiritual understanding through meditation, movement and discussion. The River Wye, Black Mountains and Malvern Hills are all easily accessible.

Contact
Richard Farmer
Rising Dragon Tai Chi School
Central Office & Residential Centre
Poulstone Court
Kings Caple
Herefordshire HR1 4UA
Tel: 01432 840860
Web: www.risingdragontaichi.com

Practical information
Duration: 2–5 days
Level: beginner,
intermediate & advanced
Residential
Group size: 16–25+

Price range: £150–£400
Prices include: meals &
accommodation
Unsuitable for children
Pets not welcome

Courses available in:

Jan	Feb	Mar	Apr	May	Jun	Jul	Aug	Sep	Oct	Nov	Dec

West
Midlands

Painting holidays in Herefordshire

Under the tutelage of local artist Ronald Swanick, Stable Studio offer non-residential workshops for all abilities. The fully-catered holidays include accommodation in Kington's Burton Hotel, with tuition in Ronald's studio (which has a two-acre garden), the surrounding countryside and private gardens. Typically, the group spends the morning in the studio working on techniques and finished paintings, before going into the countryside, but the exact itinerary depends on the group's needs. The non-residential workshops last for two or three days, and Ronald will help with finding accommodation. Workshops include Drawing for the Terrified, Watercolour for the Terrified, Oils and Acrylics, Drawing and Painting, and Introduction to Abstract Art.

Contact
Ronald Swanwick
Stable Studio
Eardisley Road
Kington
Herefordshire HR5 3HB
Tel: 01544 230871
Web: www.stablestudio.co.uk

Practical information
Duration: 2–6 days
Level: beginner,
intermediate & advanced
Residential & non-residential
Group size: 1–15
Courses available in:

Price range: £100–£400
Prices include: meals,
accommodation & painting
materials on most courses.
Unsuitable for children
Pet-friendly

Jan	Feb	Mar	Apr	May	Jun	Jul	Aug	Sep	Oct	Nov	Dec

THE ORCHARDS SCHOOL OF COOKERY, SALFORD PRIORS, NEAR EVESHAM

Cookery courses

Recently adjudged one of the top 25 cookery schools in the world, Orchards Cookery School offers three courses: 'Designer Dinners for Beginners', 'Chalet Cooks' and 'Off to University'. Sisters Isabel and Lucy Bomford run and teach the courses from an 18th-century Georgian farmhouse. Lucy trained and worked as a chef in Paris, so many of the recipes have a French accent.

Courses
The 'Designer Dinners for Beginners' course covers 12 different meal plans for dinner parties. The emphasis is on impressive meals with minimum stress and preparation time. The 'Chalet Cook' course can set students up for a season (or a career) in the snow. The 'Off to University' course is a great introduction to creating nourishing meals on a budget.

What's special?
'Designer Dinners for Beginners' fully equips participants with the skills and confidence to host sensational dinner parties. Covering advance preparation, complementary courses, dealing with disasters and choosing wine, each evening concludes with a dinner party feasting on the results of the day's tuition.

Eating & sleeping
Students stay in shared twins (extra for single accommodation). Breakfast is a simple meal: cook your own eggs if desired. Lunches and dinners consist of meals cooked during the course.

Directions
Off the M5, M42 or M40, onto the A46. At B439 junction, turn towards Salford Priors. After 400 yards, right into School Road. 400 yards to Orchard Farms on the left. By train: Evesham (nearest), Stratford or Redditch.

In the area
Badminton, tennis and croquet on site. Eight miles to Stratford-upon-Avon. Plus Sudeley and Warwick Castle, Ragley Hall and the Cotswolds.

Contact
Isabel Bomford
The Orchards School of Cookery
Salford Priors
Nr Evesham
Worcestershire
Tel: 01789 490 259
Web: www.orchardscookery.co.uk
Email: isabel@orchardscookery.co.uk

Practical information
Duration: 5–10 days
Level: beginner &
intermediate
Residential
Group size: 3–10
Price range: £500+

Prices include: meals, accommodation & All ingredients, equipment, apron and 'cookery file' of recipes.
Child-friendly
Pets not welcome

Courses available in:

Jan	Feb	Mar	Apr	May	Jun	Jul	Aug	Sep	Oct	Nov	Dec

Buddhist retreat for women in Shropshire

In 2005, Taraloka Buddhist Retreat Centre celebrates 20 years of retreats for women. They offer several retreats a month, with many suitable for newcomers, and focus on two foundation practices: 'Mindfulness of Breathing' and 'Metta Bhavana' (development of universal loving kindness and friendliness). Teachers are all ordained members of the Western Buddhist Order. The venue is a farmhouse with converted barns and outbuildings. Accommodation is in two loft rooms with beds for seven women in each, or there are single/shared rooms. There are facilities for disabled participants, and solitary retreats can also be accommodated. The price of the retreats is based on a suggested donation.

Contact
Hazel Baker
Taraloka Buddhist Retreat Centre for Women
Bettisfield
Whitchurch
Shropshire SY13 2LD
Tel: 0845 3304063
Web: www.taraloka.org.uk

Practical information
Duration: 2–10 days
Level: beginner,
intermediate & advanced
Residential
Group size: 1–25+

Price range: under
£50–£300
Prices include: meals &
accommodation
Unsuitable for children
Pets not welcome

Courses available in:

Jan	Feb	Mar	Apr	May	Jun	Jul	Aug	Sep	Oct	Nov	Dec

Crafts in a 17th-century farmhouse

The Threshing Barn in Staffordshire offers craft courses in the lovely surrounds of a 17th-century working farm. Courses are usually one-day long but can be combined depending on the skills you wish to learn; there are set dates for courses, but the schedule is very flexible. Each of the courses can be tailored to a particular level of skill. They include 'Willow Baskets and Garden Structures', 'Soap-making', 'Dry Flower Arranging', 'Corn Dollies' and 'Decoupage'. Special workshops are also held by accomplished fabric artists throughout the year. The Threshing Barn also sells craft materials, including dyes. Local attractions include Alton Towers theme park.

Contact
Janet Thurman
The Threshing Barn
Lower Lady Meadow Farm
Bradnop, Leek
Staffordshire ST13 7EZ
Tel: 01538 304494
Web: www.threshingbarn.com

Practical information
Duration: 2–4 days
Level: beginner,
intermediate & advanced
Non-residential
Group size: 1–10

Price range: £50–£200
Prices include: Lunch &
course materials.
Child-friendly
Pets not welcome

Courses available in:

Jan	Feb	Mar	Apr	May	Jun	Jul	Aug	Sep	Oct	Nov	Dec

West
Midlands

Life-long learning in Stoke-on-Trent

The Wedgwood Memorial College in Stoke-on-Trent has held courses for adults since 1945. The vast array of subjects covered here include alternative medicine, archaeology and architecture, art appreciation and practical art, ceramics and pottery, dance and drama, history, music, and social and political studies. Some courses may require a particular level of experience of its attendees; others can contribute to a formal qualification. The Centre has a large library and the grounds include a tennis court, sculpture garden and arboretum. Stoke-on-Trent is internationally renowned for its ceramics: there are related museums and factory tours in the city.

Contact
Judith Robinson
Wedgwood Memorial College
Station Road
Barlaston
Stoke-on-Trent
Staffordshire ST12 9DG
Tel: 01782 372105 or 01782 373427
Web: www.sgfl.org.uk/wmc

Practical information
Duration: 2–6 days
Level: beginner,
intermediate & advanced
Residential & non-residential
Group size: 11–20

Price range: £100–£200
Prices include: meals &
accommodation
Child-friendly
Pets not welcome

Courses available in:

Jan	Feb	Mar	Apr	May	Jun	Jul	Aug	Sep	Oct	Nov	Dec

Learn to heal in Stoke-on-Trent

Willow Lodge Healing Therapies offers breaks at Willow Lodge, a large house with a beautiful, spacious and colourful garden. Resident therapists Karen Aitken and Karl Hemmings offer a unique range of alternative therapies and body work aiming to improve health and fitness levels and general well-being. Participants can create individually tailored breaks, combining a therapy with yoga, qigong and t'ai chi classes. And they can also learn to administer treatments: the training in alternative therapies is open to both professional therapists and interested, enthusiastic amateurs.

Courses
Willow Lodge is the only venue in the world to offer training in the use of the Otosan Ear Cone and the Aqua Cleanse™ detoxification process. Other training courses on offer include the revolutionary new Zenergy Therapy, and also Indian Head Massage, Hopi Ear Candle, chakra balancing and reiki attunement. Therapies on offer include all of the above, plus Zenergy Therapy.

What's special?
Aqua Cleanse™ is designed as a mind and body detoxification. It involves immersion of the feet into warm water in specially designed equipment and works by targeting unhealthy cells. The treatment can counteract problems such as arthritis, hangovers, insomnia and menstrual pain.

Eating & sleeping
Tollgate Hotel and Leisure Centre (0870 787 5800) is recommended for accommodation and food, as is The White House Hotel (01782 642460). There are several local B&Bs.

Directions
Follow the A50 past Longton; right at intersection into Trentham Road (A5035), and Church Road is on the right just past School Lane. Nearest rail station is Stoke.

In the area
Trentham Gardens to the south of Stoke-on-Trent, has 400 acres of woodlands, a lake and Italian gardens, plus live music in the summer. Alton Towers is less than 15 miles away.

Contact
Karen Aitken
Willow Lodge
96 Church Road, Blurton
Stoke-on-Trent
Staffordshire ST3 3BB
Tel: 0845 226 3132
Web: www.healinglodge.co.uk
Email: info@healinglodge.co.uk

Practical information
uration: 2-7 days
Level: beginner,
intermediate & advanced
Non-residential
Group size: 1-10

Price range: £50-£500+
Unsuitable for children
Pets not welcome

Courses available in:

Jan	Feb	Mar	Apr	May	Jun	Jul	Aug	Sep	Oct	Nov	Dec

Painting in a 14th-century Tudor house

Weobley Art Centre hosts weekend and week-long residential courses in watercolours and drawing at the 14th-century Old Corner House in the village of Weobley. There are plenty of fine historic houses, ancient farms, wide valleys and distant blue hills to inspire the budding painter. Weekend courses (£245) concentrate on watercolour techniques, while the Watercolour Week (£495) combines painting excursions with studio sessions. Other week-long courses, such as the popular 'Drawing and Watercolour for the Beginner' course, introduce painters to the fundamentals of drawing and painting, and take them in stages to a finished watercolour study. All courses include studio tuition in perspective, composition and, where relevant, colour mixing.

Contact
Bob Kilvert
Weobley Art Centre
The Old Corner House
Broad St, Weobley
Herefordshire HR4 8SA
Tel: 01544 318548
Web: www.watercolouratweobley.com

Practical information
Duration: 2–6 days
Level: intermediate & advanced
Residential & non-residential
Group size: 3–15

Price range: £200–£500
Prices include: meals & accommodation
Unsuitable for children
Pet-friendly

Courses available in:

Jan	Feb	Mar	Apr	May	Jun	Jul	Aug	Sep	Oct	Nov	Dec

Quaker courses in Birmingham

Woodbrooke is the former home of George Cadbury of chocolate fame. It is a huge Georgian edifice built in 1930 with ten acres of grounds and its own lake. Cadbury was a Quaker and his property is now the UK's Quaker Study Centre. Although courses are mainly centred on themes of interest to Quakers, such as spiritual journeys and Quaker history, Woodbrooke welcomes people of every or no religion. Course titles include 'Art and Conflict', 'Circle Dance for the Winter Solstice' and 'A New Year Retreat for Women'. Accommodation is provided on site, as are meals, and some of the ingredients are grown in the garden.

Contact
Leonorah
Woodbrooke Quaker Study Centre
1046 Bristol Road
Birmingham
West Midlands B29 6LJ
Tel: 0121 4725171
Web: www.woodbrooke.org.uk

Practical information
Duration: 2–4 days
Level: beginner, intermediate & advanced
Residential & non-residential
Group size: 6–25+

Price range: £100–£300
Prices include: meals & accommodation
Unsuitable for children
Pets not welcome

Courses available in:

Jan	Feb	Mar	Apr	May	Jun	Jul	Aug	Sep	Oct	Nov	Dec

West Midlands

Middlesborough

Scarborough

York

Leeds

Kingston-
upon-Hull

Sheffield

Yorkshire

One of the most charismatic of English counties, home to beautiful, medieval York with its huge Gothic cathedral; lively Leeds; the famous North York moors and dales; the east coast with Whitby and Scarborough; plus Brontë and Herriot country. You might like to try a cookery course in a county famous for its pies, tarts, puddings and cheeses; or use the scenery to help you unwind, relax and release some of your creative potential through painting, writing or – why not – working with sheepdogs.

Arts, crafts and stained glass in the Yorkshire Dales

Arkleside is a 17th-century barn which has been converted for use as an art studio. Set at the end of a quiet lane in a village in the heart of Coverdale, surrounded by farmland and wild moors, it's the perfect setting for naturally-inspired creativity. Local artists run courses in the making of stained glass, and pieces created by students can be fired in the kiln. After lessons in the craft's theory, students get to work designing their piece of glass. Once the design has been approved, they can cut the glass and lead it to produce the finished piece. There is accommodation available within the barn or in nearby alternatives.

Contact
Barbara Johnston
Arkleside Art Studio
New Lathe
Horsehouse, Leyburn
North Yorkshire DL8 4TU
Tel: 01969 640463
Web: www.arklesideart.co.uk

Practical information
Duration: 3–5 days
Level: beginner
Residential
Group size: 3–10

Price range: £150–£200
Prices include: meals
Unsuitable for children
Pets not welcome

Courses available in:

Jan	Feb	Mar	Apr	May	Jun	Jul	Aug	Sep	Oct	Nov	Dec

Challenging writing courses in Ted Hughes' former home

Ted Hughes' former home in 20 acres of Yorkshire countryside, Lumb Bank is now a writers' commune and workshop where participants cook communally and share bedrooms. Teaching involves a mixture of group exercises, one-to-one feedback and talks, but you will also read and listen to others' work. Tutors are all published authors and the guest writer is often an author of note. Subjects treated in the Start to Write course include characterisation, plot, setting, structure and subject matter. Approximately 25 courses run each year, encompassing all forms of writing, from poetry to songwriting. Grants of up to £250 are available for those on low incomes.

Contact
Ann Anderton
The Arvon Foundation
The Ted Hughes Arvon Centre
Lumb Bank
Heptonstall, Hebden Bridge
West Yorkshire HX7 6DF
Tel: 01422 843714
Web: www.arvonfoundation.org

Practical information
Duration: 6 days
Level: beginner,
intermediate & advanced
Residential
Group size: 6–20

Price range: £150–£500
Prices include: meals &
accommodation
Unsuitable for children
Pets not welcome

Courses available in:

Jan	Feb	Mar	Apr	May	Jun	Jul	Aug	Sep	Oct	Nov	Dec
			✓	✓		✓			✓	✓	

Handmade books in a Quaker barn

Bainside Arts Barn is a Quaker-owned building which provides a space for a huge variety of arts-based courses. One of the more interesting courses teaches Amish quilting, where students make either a cushion cover or a wall hanging and learn both machine- and hand-sewing techniques. Lunch, made from local produce, is provided on site, and there are pubs and restaurants for dinner. Other courses include painting, drawing, mosaic-making, felting and writing. Children are free to participate in the courses, particularly older children doing painting, drama and poetry, and there are some family days planned for younger children. There are bursaries available to cover part of the cost.

Contact
Ros Handley
Bainside Arts Barn
Bainbridge
Wensleydale
North Yorkshire DL83EF
Tel: 01969 650 070
Web: www.bainside-arts.org.uk

Practical information
Duration: 2 days
Level: beginner
Non-residential
Group size: 6–10

Price range: under
£50–£100
Child-friendly
Pet-friendly

Courses available in:

Jan	Feb	Mar	Apr	May	Jun	Jul	Aug	Sep	Oct	Nov	Dec
	✓										

Cookery courses at a famous Yorkshire tea room

The Betty's Certificate Course is a cookery course suitable for everyone from novice cooks wanting to build up a repertoire, to those seeking confidence for entertaining. It takes place at Betty's Cookery School on the outskirts of Harrogate. On each of the first eight days, students learn to make a breakfast dish, canapé and starter (all of which they eat), and then in the afternoon, a main course and dessert (also eaten). There are separate days for bread and pasta making, as well as time in the classroom to take the Basic Food Hygiene certificate and learn about budgeting, entertaining, planning and cooking on a large scale.

Contact
Lesley Wilde
Betty's Cookery School
Hookstone Park
Hookstone Chase, Harrogate
North Yorkshire HG2 7LD
Tel: 01423 814016
Web: www.bettyscookeryschool.co.uk

Practical information
Duration: 10 days
Level: beginner &
intermediate
Non-residential

Group size: 1–20
Price range: £500+
Prices include: meals
Child-friendly
Pets not welcome

Courses available in:

Jan	Feb	Mar	Apr	May	Jun	Jul	Aug	Sep	Oct	Nov	Dec

Building conservation: lime week

This course is suitable for anyone with an interest in building conservation – in particular anyone with an old house that they would like to restore. The first day is spent in lectures at York's majestic Kings Manor, a building used by Henry VIII where students learn about lime, its use in historic buildings and its chemical make-up. The next three days are spent at the open-air Ryedale Folk Museum, where course participants help restore old buildings. Practical work will be dictated by what is required at the time, but can include work on both the fabric of the walls and the interiors. Accommodation is provided in a local Quaker house.

Contact
Pam Ward
Centre for Conservation
Dept of Archaeology
University of York
The King's Manor
York
North Yorkshire YO1 2EP
Tel: 01904 433963

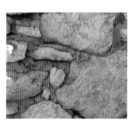

Practical information
Duration: 4 days
Level: beginner
Residential
Group size: 1–20

Price range: £300–£400
Prices include: meals &
accommodation
Unsuitable for children
Pets not welcome

Courses available in:

Jan	Feb	Mar	Apr	May	Jun	Jul	Aug	Sep	Oct	Nov	Dec

Tracking dinosaur footprints on the Scarborough coast

Join Professors Mike Romano and Martin Whyte in mapping the Yorkshire coast as it was in the Jurassic era. After some initial training, you spend your days down on the shoreline searching for dinosaur footprints (usually brontosaurus and tridactyl). Each day, you are assigned different tasks, and each evening there is a debrief to review what has been discovered. Although under-16s are not allowed on the course, family members can stay in the hotel and take part in other activities. Earthwatch run a number of courses throughout the world, focusing on ecological issues and covering everything from bush fires in Australia to ancient Thai civilisations.

Contact
Claudia Eckhardt
Earthwatch
267 Banbury Road
Oxford
Oxfordshire OX2 7HT
Tel: 01865 318831
Web: www.earthwatch.org.uk

Practical information
Duration: 5 days
Level: beginner
Residential
Group size: 6–10

Price range: £200–£300
Prices include: meals &
accommodation
Unsuitable for children
Pets not welcome

Courses available in:

Jan	Feb	Mar	Apr	May	Jun	Jul	Aug	Sep	Oct	Nov	Dec

Yorkshire

Summer school for musicians of all abilities

Ellso is the East London Late Starters Orchestra, and is a forum for string musicians of all abilities to come together to make music. The week-long summer school, held in a beautiful Palladian mansion, Bretton Hall near Wakefield, is for everyone, from those who haven't played for years to those who have played more recently. Over the course of the week, musicians will participate in full orchestral ensembles, chamber groups, coaching sessions and other options from Baroque to jazz to improvisation. Instruments can be provided if necessary. Dinner is at 7pm every day and there is a chance for informal music-making in the bar each evening until midnight.

Contact
Jenny Lloyd
East London Late Starters Orchestra (ELLSO)
1 Yew Tree Close
Harringey
London N22 7UY
Tel: 020 8881 5192
Web: www.ellso.easynet.co.uk

Practical information
Duration: 6 days
Level: beginner,
intermediate & advanced
Residential & non-residential
Group size: 6-20

Price range: £150-£300
Prices include: meals &
accommodation
Unsuitable for children
Pets not welcome

Courses available in:

Jan	Feb	Mar	Apr	May	Jun	Jul	Aug	Sep	Oct	Nov	Dec
						Jul					

Design your own garden with Elaine Newington-Ward

Elaine runs her garden-design courses on demand all year round. Half the time is spent on the ground plan and hard landscaping, the other half on soft landscaping and planting. People on a four- or five-day course may have time to produce colour and project management plans. There is no practical element, but there are plenty of opportunities to look at the work that's been done in Elaine's own garden. Non-participating partners are welcome to stay in the house while another family member is on the course. Bed and breakfast and lunch are provided, and the local pub serves dinners.

Contact
Elaine Newington-Ward
2 Pendle View
Giggleswick
Settle
North Yorkshire BD24 0AZ
Tel: 01729 824169
Web: www.designyourowngarden.co.uk

Practical information
Duration: 2-5 days
Level: beginner
Residential
Group size: 1-5

Price range: £200-£300
Prices include: meals &
accommodation
Unsuitable for children
Pets not welcome

Courses available in:

Jan	Feb	Mar	Apr	May	Jun	Jul	Aug	Sep	Oct	Nov	Dec
Jan	Feb	Mar	Apr	May	Jun	Jul	Aug	Sep	Oct	Nov	Dec

Furniture restoration with John Boddy

This introduction to furniture restoration takes place in purpose-built workshops adjacent to John Boddy's Fine Wood and Tool Store in the town of Boroughbridge. Participants bring their own piece of furniture to restore, and can learn to repair chair frames, restore drawer fronts and table-top splits, remove water damage from table tops and lift veneers. After completing the structural work, the repair is coloured and polished to blend with the original. Other courses on offer include gilding, veneering, finishing, chair caning, carving and French polishing. Overnight accommodation is available at a selection of local, period hotels all within a five-minute walk.

Contact
John Boddy
Fine Wood and Tool Store Ltd
Riverside Sawmills
Boroughbridge
North Yorkshire YO51 9LJ
Tel: 0870 3814486

Practical information
Duration: 2-3 days
Level: beginner
Non-residential
Group size: 3-5
Price range: £150-£200

Prices include: meals &
materials, equipment,
protective clothing
Unsuitable for children
Pets not welcome

Courses available in:

Jan	Feb	Mar	Apr	May	Jun	Jul	Aug	Sep	Oct	Nov	Dec
Jan	Feb	Mar	Apr	May	Jun	Jul	Aug	Sep	Oct	Nov	Dec

Learning to work with sheepdogs

Golcar Farm is a working sheep farm which offers a taste of farming life on its Sheepdog Experience. The first morning is spent learning how to work and communicate with the sheepdog. Then, after lunch in the local pub, it's back to the field to put all the training into practice. The second day provides an opportunity either for consultations about training problems or to explore the local moors on a guided walk or pony trek. Accommodation is not provided, but there are B&Bs and holiday cottages at the end of the farm lane, and there is plenty to do in the local area for non-participating family members.

Contact	**Practical information**	Group size: 1–10
Barbara Sykes	Duration: 2 days	Price range: £50–£200
Mainline Border Collie Centre	Level: beginner	Unsuitable for children
Golcar Farm, Spring Lane	Non-residential	Pet-friendly
Eldwick, Nr Bingley		
West Yorkshire BD16 3AU		
Tel: 01274 564163	Courses available in:	
Web: www.bordercollies.co.uk		

Jan | Feb | Mar | Apr | May | Jun | Jul | Aug | Sep | Oct | Nov | Dec

Painting in Malham

Five different painting courses are held each year at Malham, with attendants staying at the field centre, a Georgian country house leased from the National Trust. You paint at various local beauty spots, such as the moors around Settle. Some materials are provided by the tutor, but students would be expected to bring others with them (they are given a list before arriving). The Field Studies Centre runs a huge variety of courses at the centre, many concurrently, so it is possible for families/couples/groups of friends to do different courses in the same week. These include spinning and mushroom foraging and cooking. Alternatively, a non-participant could just pay for accommodation.

Contact	**Practical information**	Price range: £200–£300
Susan Johnson	Duration: 5 days	Prices include: meals &
Malham Tarn Field Centre	Level: beginner,	accommodation
Field Studies Council Head Office	intermediate & advanced	Child-friendly
Montford Bridge	Residential	Pets not welcome
Preston Montford, Shrewsbury	Group size: 6–15	
Shropshire SY4 1HW		
Tel: 01743 852100	Courses available in:	
Web: www.field-studies-council.org		

Jan | Feb | Mar | Apr | May | Jun | Jul | Aug | Sep | Oct | Nov | Dec

Painting and pottery at pretty countryside B&B

Val Freestone offers residential painting courses at her pretty B&B in the countryside between York and Harrogate. Courses can be tailor-made and arranged either as an intensive two-day session or over a longer period, combining painting with free time. Courses focus on a combination of landscape and still life, and students are taught the basics of acrylics and watercolour, brushes and colours. Various picturesque villages and rivers nearby offer subject matter for landscape work. There is an option for an evening slideshow and a lecture in art history. For the more experienced artist, Val is happy to take classes painting historic buildings in York or Knaresborough.

Contact	**Practical information**	Price range: £150–£200
Val Freestone	Duration: 2–4 days	Prices include:
Mayfield	Level: beginner,	accommodation &
Kirk Hammerton	intermediate & advanced	equipment if necessary
York	Residential	Unsuitable for children
North Yorkshire YO5 8DQ	Group size: 2–5	Pets not welcome
Tel: 01423 330660		
Email: cvf@mayfieldbnb.co.uk	Courses available in:	

Jan | Feb | Mar | Apr | May | Jun | Jul | Aug | Sep | Oct | Nov | Dec

Yorkshire

Relaxation workshop weekend on the Moors

Come to the moors to spend two delicious days learning about relaxation techniques and self-therapy. The Orange Tree is a former Victorian general store and Post Office which has been converted into a haven of tranquillity on the North York moors. The ethos is escape and relaxation, and the food is all vegetarian, with much of the produce home-grown. In the mornings, course members will learn a variety of techniques from posture and breathing to self-massage, meditation, visualisation and crystal therapy. After lunch on Saturday, enjoy complementary therapies and a sauna, or explore miles of beautiful moor land. Non-participating partners are welcome.

Contact
Rob Davies
The Orange Tree
Rosedale East
Rosedale Abbey, Nr Pickering
North Yorkshire YO18 8RH
Tel: 01751 417219
Web: www.theorangetree.com

Practical information
Duration: 2 days
Level: beginner
Residential
Group size: 1–20

Price range: £150–£200
Prices include: meals &
accommodation
Unsuitable for children
Pets not welcome

Courses available in:

Jan	Feb	Mar	Apr	May	Jun	Jul	Aug	Sep	Oct	Nov	Dec

Stress management weekend in relaxing countryside

Park Lodge is the charming setting for this stress management weekend. With fully equipped treatment rooms, spa and acres of Yorkshire farmland, it is the ideal place to unwind and learn how to redress problems in your work/life balance. The course starts by identifying the causes and symptoms of stress, and then teaches participants natural therapies to help combat it. The first day focuses on teaching, while on the second day students work with qualified therapists to help overcome specific problems, and receive relaxing treatments to ensure that they leave the weekend feeling rejuvenated and ready to put their learning into practice.

Contact
Julie Saunders
Park Willow Ltd
Park Lodge
Park Ave
Wortley Village, Sheffield
South Yorkshire S35 7DR
Tel: 0114 883158
Web: www.parkwillow.co.uk

Practical information
Duration: 2 days
Level: beginner
Non-residential
Group size: 6–10

Price range: £150–£300
Prices include: meals
Unsuitable for children
Pets not welcome

Courses available in:

Jan	Feb	Mar	Apr	May	Jun	Jul	Aug	Sep	Oct	Nov	Dec

Dry-stone walling with a Master

These introductory courses to dry-stone walling take place either on the picturesque Otley Chevin or in the grounds of St Peter's Church in Rawdon. Under the instruction of a master dry-stone waller, course members take down and then rebuild a section of wall. Deconstructing shows how the wall was constructed, and then in the rebuilding process students learn how to put down solid foundations, build the wall up and finish the top. More advanced courses are available for those who have completed this introduction. Participants should bring packed lunches and drinks, but all other equipment is provided, including safety goggles. Many small hotels and B&Bs offer accommodation locally.

Contact
Richard Kitchen
Richard Kitchen
8 St John's Court
Yeadon, Leeds
West Yorkshire LS19 7FW
Tel: 0113 250 7190
Web: www.cetera.co.uk/otley-dales-dswa

Practical information
Duration: 2 days
Level: beginner
Non-residential
Group size: 6–20

Price range: under
£50–£100
Prices include: equipment
Child-friendly
Pet-friendly

Courses available in:

Jan	Feb	Mar	Apr	May	Jun	Jul	Aug	Sep	Oct	Nov	Dec

Rug-making in the heart of the Yorkshire Dales

Set in the heart of Herriot country, Reeth makes a picturesque spot for learning the traditional art of rag rug making. In her fully equipped studio, Heather Ritchie offers tailor-made courses which begin with an introduction on what – and what not – to do, followed by an explanation of the fabrics and tools. Practical work follows: designing a rug, drawing it on to the hessian backing and then working on the rug and progressing as far as possible. There are further courses for those wanting more advanced training or to learn about dyeing techniques. Heather can accommodate four students in her B&B, or there are other B&Bs in the village.

Contact
Heather Ritchie
Shades of Heather
The Garden Studio
Greencroft
Reeth, Richmond
North Yorkshire DL11 6QT
Tel: 01748 884 435
Web: www.rugmaker.co.uk

Practical information
Duration: 2–3 days
Level: beginner &
intermediate
Residential & non-residential
Group size: 3–10

Courses available in:

Jan	Feb	Mar	Apr	May	Jun	Jul	Aug	Sep	Oct	Nov	Dec

Price range: £50–£100
Prices include: fabrics &
equipment
Unsuitable for children
Pets not welcome

Wine-tasting in the Yorkshire Dales

The Stone House Hotel is a traditional Yorkshire country house hotel hosting three-day wine-tasting courses. Your days are spent exploring the local Wensleydale area, your evenings enjoying a selection of New World wines. The course is run by Derek Smedley, the hotel sommelier and a Master of Wine for 30 years, who explains the flavours and textures of the wine. The first night concentrates on South America, with Australian and South African wines on the following two. Four-course dinners use mainly local produce, washed down with wines tasted during the lesson. In winter the hotel runs other courses, such as painting, sketching, photography, lace-making, embroidery, backgammon, whisky-tasting and sheepdog-training.

Contact
Mr Taplin and Mr Westwood
Stone House Hotel
Sedbusk
Hawes
North Yorkshire DL8 3PT
Tel: 01969 667 571
Web: www.stonehousehotel.co.uk

Practical information
Duration: 3 days
Level: beginner
Residential
Group size: 6–15

Courses available in:

Jan	Feb	Mar	Apr	May	Jun	Jul	Aug	Sep	Oct	Nov	Dec

Price range: £200–£300
Prices include: meals &
accommodation
Child-friendly
Pet-friendly

Yorkshire

Rosemary Shrager at Swinton Park Cookery School

This well-respected cookery school is part of Swinton Park, a luxurious country house hotel in Masham. Courses are run by Rosemary Shrager, whose traditional style of cookery concentrates on British food, although there are also courses in French and Italian cookery. Students spend their mornings cooking lunch, their afternoons watching further demonstrations or doing practical work and their late afternoons enjoying the hotel's other facilities. Dinner is served in the cookery school's private dining room. There is a wide variety of courses, taught over one, two or four days as the students want. Subjects include modern British, bread, fish, desserts, back to basics, dinner parties, summer food and classic cookery.

Contact
Rosemary Shrager
Swinton Park Cookery School
Masham
Ripon
North Yorkshire HG4 4JH
Tel: 01765 680900
Web: www.swintonpark.com/cookery

Practical information
Duration: 2–4 days
Level: beginner,
intermediate & advanced
Residential
Group size: 2–10

Courses available in:

Jan	Feb	Mar	Apr	May	Jun	Jul	Aug	Sep	Oct	Nov	Dec

Price range: £500+
Prices include: meals &
accommodation
Unsuitable for children
Pets not welcome

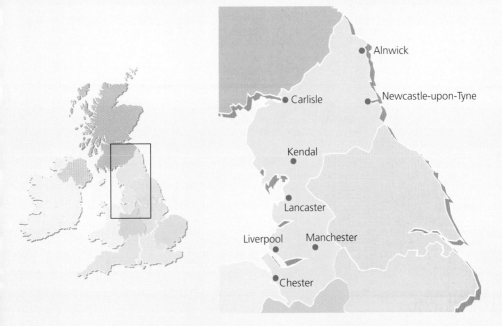

Alnwick

Carlisle

Newcastle-upon-Tyne

Kendal

Lancaster

Liverpool   Manchester

Chester

The North of England

Where to start? The countryside, perhaps is not a bad place: from the crags of the Lake District to the wilderness of Northumberland, the North of England showcases myriad variations on the theme of beautiful landscapes which make suitable backdrops for an array of courses in walking, birdwatching, photography and others. Towns include historic Durham and Chester, and Newcastle and Manchester, while Hadrian's Wall and the Angel of the North should keep your camera happy. This is a region whose constituent parts all have distinct cultures and local identities; food, literary and arts and crafts traditions will colour many of the courses that you do here.

Say cheesemaking: how to make Cheddar, Cheshire and more

An insight for all cheese-lovers into the complexities of cheese. Chris Ashby has 12 years' experience in cheese-making and runs a variety of courses at Reaseheath College just outside Nantwich, Cheshire. The Basic course covers ingredients and the mechanisms that change milk into cheese. The Soft Cheese course, which may or may not follow on from this, introduces fresh soft (eg feta and mozzarella), mould-ripened, bacterial-ripened and blue cheeses. The Yogurt and Fermented Products course explains milk, shelf life and the fermenting processes. Reaseheath owns a large area of farmland, a nine-hole golf course and a fishing lake, and students can use these for a reduced fee. Accommodation recommendations available.

Contact
Chris Ashby
A B Cheesemaking
7 Daybell Close
Bottesford, Nottingham
Nottinghamshire NG13 0DQ
Tel: 01949 842867
Web: www.abcheesemaking.co.uk

Practical information
Duration: 3 days
Level: beginner,
intermediate & advanced
Non-residential

Group size: 6–20
Price range: £400–£500
Unsuitable for children
Pets not welcome

Courses available in:

Jan	Feb	Mar	Apr	May	Jun	Jul	Aug	Sep	Oct	Nov	Dec

Silversmithing and Jewellery construction

Formerly a Victorian country house, Alston Hall is set in landscaped gardens only a few miles from Preston and an hour from Blackpool. To the north and east you will find unbridled moorland and gentle pastureland, and the area provides excellent walking country. Alston Hall has just celebrated its Golden Jubilee as a place of learning and is open 51 weeks of the year, attracting a broad range of people to around 800 day, evening and residential courses. A small selection for 2005 includes: Silversmithing and Constructing Jewellery, Yoga, Drawing for the Faint-Hearted, Constructive Beadwork, Japanese Reiki, Glass Workshops and Fiction Writing.

Contact
Vincent Ashworth
Alston Hall College
Alston Hall Lane
Longridge
Preston
Lancashire PR3 3BP
Tel: 01772 784661
Web: www.alstonhall.com

Practical information
Duration: 3 days
Level: beginner,
intermediate & advanced
Residential
Group size: 6–15

Price range: £100–£200
Prices include: meals &
accommodation
Unsuitable for children
Pets not welcome

Courses available in:

Jan	Feb	Mar	Apr	May	Jun	Jul	Aug	Sep	Oct	Nov	Dec

Bring your guitar out of the bedroom for a weekend

Beckfoot Country House stages a range of guitar-playing weekends for those with some basic knowledge of the instrument. Hosted by experts who are both exceptional players and qualified, enthusiastic teachers, the courses are primarily aimed at hobby players. Courses include a Back to Basics weekend, which covers practising techniques, basic lead and rhythm techniques, a little theory and a lot of playing. Rock, jazz, blues, country, bass and guitar maintenance workshops are also available. Beckfoot is in the Lowther Valley, an unspoilt area of the Lake District with fine views and plenty of outdoor activities for non-participants and those taking time off from practising.

Contact
Beckfoot Country House
Helton
Penrith
Cumbria CA10 2QB
Tel: 01931 713241
Web: www.beckfoot.co.uk

Practical information
Duration: 3 days
Level: beginner,
intermediate & advanced
Residential

Group size: 3–10
Price range: £300–£400
Prices include: meals &
accommodation
Child-friendly
Pets not welcome

Courses available in:

Jan	Feb	Mar	Apr	May	Jun	Jul	Aug	Sep	Oct	Nov	Dec

BREAD MATTERS, PENRITH

The pleasures, art and spirituality of bread making the organic way

The brain child of former BBC producer Andrew Whitley, Bread Matters aims to give novices, enthusiasts and culinary professionals a better understanding of the baking process. Andrew founded the Village Bakery, which has been producing organic bread in the wood-fired ovens for nearly 30 years. The MasterClass includes a visit to the local watermill, source of all the bakery's flour in the early days.

Courses
The two-day fundamental course spends one day on the basics then one day teaching more specialised bread forms such as sourdough and ciabatta. Other two-day courses include Italian Baking, using Italian organic flour to make 'biga' dough; Gluten-Free to accommodate the growth in food intolerance; Perfect Sourdoughs and Leavens; and Baking without Yeast. The five-day MasterClass is also open to all abilities.

What's special?
More than just organic baking, the courses – described by Andrew as "the thinking person's baking courses" – explore the politics, health and spirituality of food in an informal way. The most popular course is Bread Matters Fundamental, which is open to all levels of experience.

Eating & sleeping
Guest houses within walking distance include Greenholme (Edith James 01768 881436) and Meadowbank (Margaret Morton 01768 881652). Or the Temple Sowerby House Hotel (01768 361578) is 15 minutes' drive. Lunches are taken in the organic restaurant and the Shepherds Inn does evening meals.

Directions
9 miles from Junction 40 on the M6, on the A686 between Penrith and Alston. The West Coast Line between Euston and Glasgow serves Penrith where there is a taxi rank.

In the area
The site is at the foot of the Pennines, in the Eden Valley with its pretty market towns and villages. The quieter North Lakes are half an hour's drive, Hadrian's Wall is 40 minutes.

North of England

Contact
Andrew Whitley
Bread Matters
The Village Bakery
Melmerby, Penrith
Cumbria CA10 1HE
Tel: 01768 881899
Web: www.breadmatters.com
Email: andrew@breadmatters.com

Practical information
Duration: 2–5 days
Level: beginner,
intermediate & advanced
Non-residential
Group size: 6–15

Price range: £300–£500+
Prices include: lunch; 5-day
course includes 1 evening
meal
Child-friendly
Pets not welcome

Courses available in:

Jan	Feb	Mar	Apr	May	Jun	Jul	Aug	Sep	Oct	Nov	Dec

BIRDWATCH NORTHUMBRIA, VARIOUS LOCATIONS IN NORTHUMBERLAND

Relaxed birdwatching tours in Northumbria

Founder Mark Winter started by offering Northumberland tours to friends but quickly expanded to guiding anyone new to birdwatching. Courses vary according to venue, but include at least one full day of guided birdwatching, with Mark introducing participants to the birds of Northumbria. The courses are ideal for those who might be intimidated by serious birdwatchers or who feel they do not know enough about local wildlife to participate. They take place in different parts of the region (Cheviot Hills, Beadnall, Alnwick – you decide) and so focus on different types of bird, such as waders, ducks, woodland birds, wintering birds, summer birds.

Contact
Mark Winter
Birdwatch Northumbria
Felton
Northumberland NE65 9DQ
Tel: 01670 783 451
Web: www.birdwatchnorthumbria.co.uk

Practical information
Duration: 2–3 days
Level: beginner
Residential & non-residential
Group size: 1–10

Price range: £50–£400
Unsuitable for children
Pets not welcome

Courses available in:

Jan	Feb	Mar	Apr	May	Jun	Jul	Aug	Sep	Oct	Nov	Dec

BLENCATHRA FIELD STUDIES CENTRE, KESWICK

Walking and sketching in the Lake District

Aimed at beginners, this four-day course combines the pleasures of walking in the Lakes with the fun of capturing their beauty on paper. Although primarily using pencil and watercolours, participants are encouraged to develop their personal style with a range of other media. Nigel Gerke, who runs the course, is a landscape gardener and art tutor, roles that he combines with his love of walking. The centre operates in partnership with the Lake District National Park Authority and faces a wonderful southern Lakeland panorama. The grounds provide a habitat for much wildlife, including red squirrels. Other courses include Drawing and Painting a Summer Landscape, Mosses and Liverworts, and Landscape Photography.

Contact
Nigel Gerke
Blencathra Field Studies Centre
Threlkeld
Keswick
Cumbria CA12 4SG
Tel: 0176 8779601
Web: www.field-studies-council.org/blencathra

Practical information
Duration: 3–8 days
Level: beginner &
intermediate
Residential
Group size: 6–25

Price range: £150–£400
Prices include: meals &
accommodation
Child-friendly
Pets not welcome

Courses available in:

Jan	Feb	Mar	Apr	May	Jun	Jul	Aug	Sep	Oct	Nov	Dec

THE BRIGHTLIFE CENTRE, ANDREAS

Chakra healing: full package break on the Isle of Man

The Brightlife Centre on the Isle of Man has earned a reputation as a place of personal development and holistic learning set in a truly relaxing atmosphere. Located on the outskirts of Andreas village, it has beautifully decorated rooms, well-maintained gardens and can cater to all dietary needs. Facilities include a 'floatroom suite', therapy room and Betar Machine. All courses are taught by recognised professionals including Pete Cowen, a regular life coach on GMTV. Courses include Past Life Regression, Yoga and DIY Life Coaching. All are suitable for any ability and prices are fully inclusive of flights from the UK mainland, transfers on the island, accommodation and meals.

Contact
Frank Dunphy
The Brightlife Centre
Ramsey Rd
Andreas
Isle of Man IM7 4EN
Tel: 01624 880318
Web: www.brightlife.com

Practical information
Duration: 3–5 days
Level: beginner,
intermediate & advanced
Residential
Group size: 6–20

Price range: £200–£400
Prices include: meals &
accommodation
Unsuitable for children
Pets not welcome

Courses available in:

Jan	Feb	Mar	Apr	May	Jun	Jul	Aug	Sep	Oct	Nov	Dec

BURTON MANOR, NESTON

Summer school at Burton Manor

Burton Manor is a short-stay residential college set in 30 acres of its own grounds and formal gardens, with views of the Dee Estuary and Welsh Hills. Built in the late 19th century, this listed building was home to one of William Gladstone's sons. Now it hosts courses throughout the year, the highlight being their excellent summer school

Courses
The eight-day summer school is open to all levels of experience with classes taught by experienced tutors. All participants will be taught in withdrawal groups before coming together for tutorials, demonstrations and discussions. A wide variety of media and subjects will be covered. Courses include Woodcarving for all, Sourcing your Family History, Writing a Screenplay and Willow Basket Making.

What's special?
The Creative Writing course is aimed at all abilities and levels of experience; the only requirement is a desire to express yourself in the written word. The course will focus on how to create poetry and prose, especially through observation and word choice. Time is spent in workshops, discussions, exercises and personal observations as well as practical criticism of published work. Rosie Ford, the teacher, is a published author.

Eating & sleeping
Accommodation is provided on site in 44 basic but comfortable rooms. There are public rooms, a bar and a music room with minstrels' gallery offering wonderful views across the Dee Estuary and Welsh Hills beyond.

Directions
Follow the M56 to its end, then signs for Queensferry and North Wales. A540 towards Hoylake. At fourth lights turn left on Dunstan Lane. Burton Manor is in Burton village on the left. By rail, change at Liverpool Lime Street for Hooton. From Hooton take F58 bus or taxi (0151 336 3999).

In the area
Liverpool and Chester are both near. Burton is a picturesque village and nearby is Haddon Woods, a National Trust site.

Contact
Rosie Ford
Burton Manor
Neston
Cheshire
Tel: 0151 336 5172
Web: www.burtonmanor.com
Email: jan.hooper@burtonmanor.com

Practical information
Duration: 8–3 days
Level: beginner &
intermediate
Residential
Group size: 6–25

Price range: £200–£500+
Prices include: meals &
accommodation
Unsuitable for children
Pets not welcome

Courses available in:

Jan	Feb	Mar	Apr	May	Jun	Jul	Aug	Sep	Oct	Nov	Dec

North
of England

Loom-weaving: design, create and wear

The six-day weaving course at Castle Head is aimed at those wishing to develop their skills in fabric weaving and cloth design. Janet Phillips, an experienced teacher and published author, will provide the tuition and all the materials necessary to complete the course, whether you make a designer scarf or experimental sample. The centre is located between Morecambe Bay and the Lakeland fells in 20 hectares of grounds, yet close to the motorway network and mainline railway. Other courses include Exploring Historical Gardens in the Lake District, Hill-walking and Sketching in the Lake District, Drawing and Painting Trees, Basket-Weaving, and History of Lakeland Steam Transport.

Contact
Janet Phillips
Castle Head Field Centre
Field Studies Council
Grange over Sands
Cumbria LA11 6QT
Tel: 0845 330 7364
Web: www.field-studies-council.org/castlehead

Practical information
Duration: 3-6 days
Level: beginner &
intermediate
Residential
Group size: 6-25

Price range: £300-£500
Prices include: meals &
accommodation
Child-friendly
Pets not welcome

Courses available in:

Jan	Feb	Mar	Apr	May	Jun	Jul	Aug	Sep	Oct	Nov	Dec

Craft and gardening in a Victorian railway station

The Garden Station offers a range of courses, mostly in gardening, but also in arts and crafts and food. It is based in the old Langley Railway Station, a light, airy building with beautiful gardens. The station, built in 1867, was closed in the 1950s then restored by Jane Torday from 1999. Courses include: a printmaking workshop where participants create lino cuts focusing on garden and plant images; Botanical Art Days; Medieval Flora and Fauna – a discussion of flora and fauna depicted in medieval churches and medieval attitudes to flora and fauna; and willow workshops such as Willow Birdhouses and Angels and Figurines from Willow.

Contact
Jane Torday
The Garden Station
Langley
Hexham
Northumberland NE47 5LA
Tel: 01434 684 391
Web: www.thegardenstation.co.uk

Practical information
Duration: 2 days
Level: beginner,
intermediate & advanced
Non-residential

Group size: 1-15
Price range: under £50
Unsuitable for children
Pets not welcome

Courses available in:

Jan	Feb	Mar	Apr	May	Jun	Jul	Aug	Sep	Oct	Nov	Dec

Get your hands dirty on a pottery course

These pottery courses are for people with little or no experience of earthenware and stoneware. Taught by working potters Dick and Barbara Wright, who have over 20 years' experience behind them, the courses cover all aspects of pottery making and allow participants to learn at their own speed. Mornings are spent learning techniques, while afternoons are free for students to continue potting (until 10.30pm if they're keen!) or explore the area. The setting is special, as students study and sleep in a 17th-century building; it is in west Cumbria, near Eskdale, Wasdale and Ennerdale, and local attractions include Muncaster Castle and the Ravenglass Estuary.

Contact
Dick and Barbara Wright
Gosforth Pottery
Hardingill House
Gosforth
Cumbria CA20 1HA
Tel: 019467 25296
Web: www.potterycourses.co.uk

Practical information
Duration: 2-6 days
Level: beginner &
intermediate
Residential
Group size: 3-10

Price range: £200-£500
Prices include: meals &
accommodation
Unsuitable for children
Pets not welcome

Courses available in:

Jan	Feb	Mar	Apr	May	Jun	Jul	Aug	Sep	Oct	Nov	Dec

THE CORDON VERT COOKERY SCHOOL, ALTRINCHAM

Cooking at the home of vegetarianism

Vegetarian courses have been held at the Vegetarian Society's headquarters on the edge of the Cheshire countryside near Manchester since 1982. Professional tutors run relaxed courses for cooks of all abilities, including professionals, and provide a chance for you to start from scratch, improve your repertoire or even explore opening your own vegetarian café. The school is internationally recognised and provides the Cordon Vert Diploma qualification.

Courses
Courses served up here include the Mediterranean-themed Alfresco Days, Wild Mushroom weekends, Foundation Workshop (four days to learn vegetarian nutrition and menu planning), Creative Gourmet, Dairy Free & Delicious, and Around the World Workshop, among many others.

What's special?
Cordon Vert's courses are aimed at all ability levels and are open to anyone with an interest in vegetarian cooking. Meat eaters are very welcome too; in fact they make up 50 per cent of the students. The tuition is intensive but strongly geared towards informality, fun and creativity.

Eating & sleeping
There are 12 rooms, all with en-suite bathrooms, and food is plentiful. There are no alternative hotels within walking distance, but there are a couple of local pubs offering a good selection of beers.

Directions
Junction 7 off M56 towards Altrincham (A56). Parkdale is on the right after the junction with the B1560. There are trains and trams to Altrincham Interchange from Manchester's Piccadilly and Victoria stations.

In the area
There are two National Trust properties nearby: Dunham Massey and Tatton Park. Central Manchester is around 20 minutes by tram from Altrincham station.

Contact
Lyn Yarwood
The Cordon Vert Cookery School
The Vegetarian Society
Parkdale
Dunham Road
Altrincham
Cheshire
Tel: 0161 925 2014
Web: www.vegsoc.org/cordonvert
Email: cordonvert@vegsoc.org

Practical information
Duration: 2–8 days
Level: beginner,
intermediate & advanced
Residential & non-residential
Group size: 6–15

Price range: £300–£500+
Prices include: meals & accommodation
Unsuitable for children
Pets not welcome

Courses available in:

Jan	Feb	Mar	Apr	May	Jun	Jul	Aug	Sep	Oct	Nov	Dec

Black and white photography in beautiful rural location

Grove Farm is an 18th-century farmhouse within the original boundaries of Raby Castle, close to the lovely village of Staindrop and the town of Barnard Castle. Joann Thompson organises various courses at the farm, which has been her husband's family home since childhood. Highly experienced tutors include Jeff Teasdale, an award-winning freelance photographer with over 35 years' experience. He runs 'Photography in Teesdale' and 'Landscape Photography' courses, both aimed at improving basic camera skills and turning landscapes into superb photographs. There's also a 'Creative Writing' course concentrating on writing basics and the appreciation of character and setting, and there are plans for pencil and charcoal and Japanese woodblock printing courses.

Contact
Joann Thompson
Grove Farm Art Breaks
Grove Farm
Staindrop, Darlington
County Durham DL2 3LN
Tel: 01833 660327
Web: www.grovefarmbreaks.co.uk

Practical information
Duration: 2–3 days
Level: beginner &
intermediate
Residential & non-residential
Group size: 1–10

Price range: under
£50–£300
Prices include: meals &
accommodation
Unsuitable for children
Pets not welcome

Courses available in:

Jan	Feb	Mar	Apr	May	Jun	Jul	Aug	Sep	Oct	Nov	Dec

Expert guides and lectures at Hadrian's Wall

Michael Binns and Janet Elsworth organise tailor-made tours of Hadrian's Wall for groups of all sizes. They aim to give visitors an insight into the history of the area, and guide them to the most worthwhile places. Tours are led by university teachers in Roman Frontier Studies and take visitors to almost every accessible part of the wall, including excavations, mile castles and turrets. You can see two or three of the major sites in one day, the central section in three days, and the entire system in ten. Tours can be accompanied by illustrated evening talks on sites or background historical topics. Excursions around Alnwick and Durham are also offered.

Contact
Michael Binns
Hadrian's Wall Heritage Tours
15 Redewater Road
Newcastle Upon Tyne
Northumberland NE4 9UD
Tel: 0191 2744451
Web: www.hadrians-wall.co.uk

Practical information
Duration: 2–10 days
Level: beginner,
intermediate & advanced
Residential & non-residential
Group size: 1–25+

Price range: £200–£500+
Prices include: meals &
accommodation
Unsuitable for children
Pets not welcome

Courses available in:

Jan	Feb	Mar	Apr	May	Jun	Jul	Aug	Sep	Oct	Nov	Dec

Huge range of courses at a mansion on Bassenthwaite Lake

Now beautifully restored, Higham Hall was built in 1828 for railway pioneer Thomas Hoskin. The location at the northern end of Bassenthwaite Lake makes it an ideal place to relax and learn a new skill. The hall is set in four acres of informal Victorian gardens and has a library, bar, tennis court, putting green and croquet lawn. There is accommodation in the house, self-catering cottage or campsite, or you can stay off site. The mansion offers 250 courses throughout the year covering a broad spectrum of subjects: Wine tasting, Working with Silver, People Sketching & Painting, Basketwork, Enamelling, Learning to Dance, Upholstery, Yoga... to name but a few.

Contact
Alex Alexandre
Higham Hall College
Bassenthwaite Lake
Cockermouth
Cumbria CA13 9SH
Tel: 017687 76276
Web: www.highamhall.com

Practical information
Duration: 3 days
Level: beginner &
intermediate
Residential
Group size: 6–10

Price range: £150–£200
Prices include: meals,
accommodation; self
catering available
Child-friendly
Pet-friendly

Courses available in:

Jan	Feb	Mar	Apr	May	Jun	Jul	Aug	Sep	Oct	Nov	Dec

DONALD GUNN, VARIOUS LOCATIONS IN NORTHUMBERLAND

Dry stone walling courses in Northumberland

Dry stone walling – building walls using stones but not mortar – is a dying craft in the UK and its traditions and techniques have developed over thousands of years. These courses provide one of few opportunities for beginners to learn the skill. The locations are various spots around Northumberland, but all are taught by Donald Gunn. He is a highly qualified craftsman with 19 years' experience who also arranges farmhouse breaks and is a certified instructor with the Drystone Walling Association (DWSA).

Courses
On the beginners' course participants learn the basic techniques and how to build walls, sheep stells and circles. There are also 'de-stress' courses aimed at business people, plus women's courses and professional certification courses. Certification includes NVQ and DWSA professional tests, in case dry stone walling becomes more than a passing interest. Donald is also going to offer a range of new activities including wood-carving, stone-carving and stained glass-making.

What's special?
Do your bit to resurrect a dying craft and leave a positive mark on the landscape. If you've always wanted to know how those traditional walls were built, here's your chance. The course will equip you with the skills to try building a garden wall at home.

Eating & sleeping
After confirming the exact location of your course, the organiser will be happy to arrange accommodation in a variety of establishments according to requirements.

Directions
The course organiser will be able to give you directions to the specific location.

In the area
Major visitor attractions in Northumberland include Hadrian's Wall, Dunstanburgh Castle, Lindisfarne Priory and Holy Island. Towns and villages to visit include Warkworth and Alnwick.

Contact
Donald Gunn
2 Rayheugh Farm Cottages
Chathill
Northumberland
Tel: 01668 219818
Web: drystone-walls.com
Email: dgunnwalls@hotmail.com

Practical information
Duration: 2–3 days
Level: beginner,
intermediate & advanced
Non-residential

Group size: 1–10
Price range: 50–300
Unsuitable for children
Pets not welcome

Courses available in:

Jan	Feb	Mar	Apr	May	Jun	Jul	Aug	Sep	Oct	Nov	Dec

North
of England

Creative writing at Highgreen Manor

Various courses take place in the outbuildings of the Grade II listed Highgreen Manor. The manor is located in beautiful surroundings close to Hexham, and its outbuildings have been restored and converted into offices, a flat for the artist in residence and a studio – courses take place in The Dovecote, a former stable and loft. Courses include visual arts, creative writing and yoga, run by experienced teachers including Susan Elderkin (writing), Oliver Bevan (painting) and Sophy Hoare (yoga). Course titles include Writing for the Hell of It, Ways of Seeing (painting) and Poetry - As Written, As Read. When not studying, you can visit Hadrian's Wall, Kielder Forest and the Cheviot Hills.

Contact
Susan Elderkin
Highgreen Arts
28 Batoum Gardens
London W6 7QD
Tel: 020 7602 1363
Web: www.highgreen-arts.co.uk

Practical information
Duration: 2–3 days
Level: beginner &
intermediate
Residential

Group size: 1–10
Price range: £300–£400
Prices include: meals &
accommodation
Unsuitable for children
Pets not welcome

Courses available in:

Jan	Feb	Mar	Apr	May	Jun	Jul	Aug	Sep	Oct	Nov	Dec

Cookery courses at Horsley Hall

Horsley Hall is a lovely 17th-century manor house hotel situated in the Horsley Valley on the south side of the River Wear, a suitable location for the wide range of cookery courses run by Liz Curry. She is the proprietor of Horsley Hall and has more than 30 years' experience in the catering industry. Her courses take place in professionally equipped kitchens and include topics such as 'Cake Decorating', 'Festive Favourites with a Twist', 'Summer Entertaining' and Indian-themed 'Buffet Food'. There are also courses for men only. The hotel is close to visitor attractions such as Beamish Museum and High Force Waterfall. Accommodation costs between £55 and £145 per night.

Contact
Liz Curry
Horsley Hall
Eastgate
Bishop Auckland
County Durham DL13 2LJ
Tel: 01388 517239
Web: www.horsleyhall.co.uk

Practical information
Duration: 2–4 days
Level: beginner &
intermediate
Residential & non-residential
Group size: 1–25+

Price range: £50–£500+
Prices include: meals &
accommodation
Unsuitable for children
Pets not welcome

Courses available in:

Jan	Feb	Mar	Apr	May	Jun	Jul	Aug	Sep	Oct	Nov	Dec

Falconry in the spectacular Leaplish Water Park

The Bird of Prey Centre is located in the forest and lakeside surroundings of Kielder Water and has one of the largest collections of birds in the north of England. They run two one-day falconry courses that can be taken on consecutive days. The Introduction to Falconry teaches the basics of bird care, including holding the bird, oiling the jesses, attaching the swivel and tying the Falconer's Knot. Bird Management is more advanced, looking at buying, housing and training a bird for free flight. Participants can gain experience flying birds within Kielder's grounds, and there is plenty for non-participants to do, including ferry cruises, walks and water sports.

Contact
Kielder Water Bird of Prey Centre
Leaplish Waterside Park
Nr Bellingham
Northumberland NE48 1AX
Tel: 01434 250400
Web: www.birds-ofprey.com

Practical information
Duration: 2 days
Level: beginner &
intermediate
Non-residential

Group size: 1–15
Price range: £50–£200
Unsuitable for children
Pets not welcome

Courses available in:

Jan	Feb	Mar	Apr	May	Jun	Jul	Aug	Sep	Oct	Nov	Dec

KNOBBLY STICK MEN, KENDAL

Leisurely walking with expert local guides

Peter Jackson and John Nicholls are the Knobbly Stick Men, two well-informed, experience hill-walkers who lead walks through the Lake District. As you walk, they will share their considerable knowledge of local geology, history, flora and fauna. Although some fitness is required, the holidays are not aimed at endurance walkers, and each day usually covers between 5 and 12 miles. And if you want a day off to relax or explore, that's fine. Walks include the six-day Ullswater Skyline; eight days in the Wasdale area; and the five-day "Walking the easy way", centred on Morecambe Bay. They can also organise unguided walks.

Contact
Peter Jackson and John Nicholls
Knobbly Stick Men
5 Whitbarrow Close
Kendal
Cumbria LA9 6RR
Tel: 01539 737576
Web: www.knobblystick.com

Practical information
Duration: 3–8 days
Level: beginner &
intermediate
Residential
Group size: 3–10

Price range: £400–£500+
Prices include: meals,
accommodation & guides
and local transport
Unsuitable for children
Pets not welcome

Courses available in:

Jan	Feb	Mar	Apr	May	Jun	Jul	Aug	Sep	Oct	Nov	Dec

MANJUSHRI CENTRE, ULVERSTON

Buddhist meditation classes in the tranquil Lake District

These weekend courses are both for newcomers to meditation and for those wanting to develop their understanding of the subject. The main study programmes take place in the morning, with participants learning to meditate and to understand the basics of Buddhism. Afternoons are free to enjoy the surroundings. The resident teacher is Gen-la Samden, an English monk who has practised and taught meditation around the world. Conishead Priory was founded in 1160, then demolished and rebuilt in the 19th century in the Victorian Gothic style. Set in 70 acres of gardens and woodlands, it is the first centre of its kind in England, receiving guests from all over the world.

Contact
Gen-la Samden Gyatso
Manjushri Centre
Conishead Priory
Ulverston
Cumbria LA129QQ
Tel: 01229 584029
Web: www.manjushri.org.uk

Practical information
Duration: 3 days
Level: beginner &
intermediate
Residential
Group size: 25+

Price range: £50–£100
Prices include: meals &
accommodation
Unsuitable for children
Pets not welcome

Courses available in:

Jan	Feb	Mar	Apr	May	Jun	Jul	Aug	Sep	Oct	Nov	Dec

MILLER HOWE HOTEL & RESTAURANT, WINDERMERE

Learn the resident chef's special secrets in The Lakes

The Miller Howe Hotel has been running November cookery courses for over 20 years. They show how to host the perfect dinner party, teaching five or six alternatives for each course, with the emphasis on meals that can be prepared well in advance of guests' arrival. People of all abilities are welcome to a friendly and creative learning environment. Chef and tutor Paul Webster is a Master Chef of Great Britain who spent three years working with Marco Pierre White. The quality of the teaching and the relaxed atmosphere mean that some participants return year after year. Free time is made available for exploring the surrounding Lakeland countryside.

Contact
Miller Howe Hotel & Restaurant
Rayrigg Rad
Windermere
Cumbria LA23 1EY
Tel: 015394 42536
Web: www.millerhowe.com

Practical information
Duration: 3 days
Level: beginner &
intermediate
Residential
Group size: 6–10

Price range: £400–£500+
Prices include: meals &
accommodation
Unsuitable for children
Pets not welcome

Courses available in:

Jan	Feb	Mar	Apr	May	Jun	Jul	Aug	Sep	Oct	Nov	Dec

LAKELAND PHOTOGRAPHIC HOLIDAYS, KESWICK

Picture and destination perfect: photographing the Lake District

John and Gail Gravett are professional photographers who run photography holidays in the Lake District. The holidays offer full-day excursions, personalised coaching, advice on locations and fully equipped darkrooms, plus same-day processing of pictures ready for slide show and digital presentations and constructive feedback. The courses are based at Fern Howe which has comfortable lounges, wonderful food and formal gardens leading to five acres of woodland overlooking Bassenthwaite and Skiddaw. Wildlife visitors include deer, red squirrels and badgers. With its splendid views and easy access to the Lakes, this location not only makes for great photography but provides a stunning backdrop to a relaxing holiday.

Courses
There are seven-day, generalised Photographic Holiday Workshops, running weekly from February through to December, plus more specialised five-day courses including: 'Limited Walking Break'; 'Black and White Photography', covering basic exposure through to processing and printing; and 'Getting to Grips with Digital', covering camera maintenance, exposure, memory cards and computer software.

What's special?
The Holiday Workshops are the most popular courses. Open to all levels of competence, they use a variety of media and offer full-day excursions to suit participants' mobility and requirements. Topics include landscape and close-up photography, covering exposure and composition, plus working with slides and digital.

Eating & sleeping
The courses are fully inclusive, with packed lunches provided on field trips. Gail, a certified cook, produces all the meals and can cater for vegetarians and special diets. All rooms, save one single, are en-suite and individually decorated.

Directions
Junction 40 off the M6; A66 towards Cockermouth. 2 miles after Keswick, left into Braithwaite village (B5292). Turn right opposite the Royal Oak. Left after 300 yards to Fern Howe. Will meet trains at Penrith.

In the area
Plenty of walks and drives in the Lake District. Cockermouth has good shopping plus the Jennings Brewery tour. Rheged is also nearby – a unique complex of speciality shops, IMAX cinema and mountaineering exhibitions.

Contact
John & Gail Gravett
Lakeland Photographic Holidays
Fern Howe
Braithwaite, Keswick
Cumbria CA12 5SZ
Tel: 01768 778459
Web: www.lakelandphotohols.com
Email: info@lakelandphotohols.com

Practical information
Duration: 4–7 days
Level: beginner,
intermediate & advanced
Residential
Group size: 6–10

Price range: £200–£500
Prices include: meals,
accommodation &
excursions
Child-friendly
Pets not welcome

Courses available in:

Jan	Feb	Mar	Apr	May	Jun	Jul	Aug	Sep	Oct	Nov	Dec

Twitching weekends in the Lake District

These birdwatching breaks are run throughout the year at the convenience of participants, with itineraries dictated by season, weather, tides and guests' target birds. Expert tuition is available from Mike Robinson, who has 15 years' serious birding experience. Mike and wife Annie run the courses from their home outside Beetham, an ideal birding base. The breaks are very informal and the evenings can be spent in the family home discussing the day's events and enjoying the birding multi-media library. This area of the UK has many birding sights, including the Kent Estuary, the RSPB reserve at Leighton Moss and England's only pair of nesting golden eagles.

Contact
Mike Robinson
North West Birds
Barn Close
Beetham
Cumbria LA7 7AL
Tel: 015395 63191
Web: www.nwbirds.co.uk

Practical information
Duration: 2–4 days
Level: beginner,
intermediate & advanced
Residential
Group size: 3–5

Price range: £150–£400
Prices include: meals &
accommodation
Unsuitable for children
Pets not welcome

Courses available in:

Jan	Feb	Mar	Apr	May	Jun	Jul	Aug	Sep	Oct	Nov	Dec

Painting and drawing on the Northumbrian coast

The Old School Arts Centre was founded in 1997 in a building which dates from 1876, and offers excellent facilities for painting, including a studio and a sitting room. It's located in the middle of Alnmouth, a small village on the north Northumberland coast, whose beautiful surroundings provide ample opportunities for outdoor painting and drawing. Courses can be tailor-made and include watercolours, pastels, drawing, and pen and ink. All are geared towards teaching basic skills but are not just aimed at beginners. Courses start at £40 per day and are non-residential, although there are numerous hotels and B&Bs nearby. Speak to the organisers about weekend courses.

Contact
Judi Hill
The Old School Arts Centre
Foxton Road
Alnmouth
Northumberland NE66 3NH
Tel: 01665 830999
Web: www.alnarts.fsnet.co.uk

Practical information
Duration: 2–5 days
Level: beginner &
intermediate
Non-residential

Group size: 1–10
Price range: under
£50–£200
Unsuitable for children
Pets not welcome

Courses available in:

Jan	Feb	Mar	Apr	May	Jun	Jul	Aug	Sep	Oct	Nov	Dec

North
of England

Create your own stone carving in the Cheshire countryside

Potters Steve Marr and Andrew Pollard not only make and sell their own work at the Pottery Barn but encourage other craftspeople to host courses beneath the shop. The result is an array of stimulating courses running throughout the year. Peter Price runs a two-day stone-carving course. Then there are courses in 'Green Man' stone carving – a Medieval tradition based on a human figure symbolising man's connection to the earth, plus workshops in coracle building and longbow making. The Barn is in the Cheshire countryside on the banks of the Trent and Mersey Canal, and lunch in the local pub is included in the price.

Contact
Peter Price and Andrew Pollard
The Potters Barn
Roughwood Lane, Hassall Green
Sandbach
Cheshire CW11 4XX
Tel: 01270 884080
Web: www.thepottersbarn.f2s.com

Practical information
Duration: 2 days
Level: beginner &
intermediate
Non-residential

Group size: 3–15
Price range: £150–£200
Unsuitable for children
Pets not welcome

Courses available in:

Jan	Feb	Mar	Apr	May	Jun	Jul	Aug	Sep	Oct	Nov	Dec

PEAT OBERON'S SCHOOL OF BLACKSMITHING, STOCKTON-ON-TEES

Learn the art of blacksmithing

Peat Oberon, who is based at the School of Blacksmithing attached to Preston Hall Museum, was once a schoolteacher, but has been a full-time blacksmith since 1980. He has taught courses since 1990 and likes to show his students relevant examples and techniques before getting them working as soon as possible. Participants learn not only about the forge environment but also the history and background of the craft.

Courses
The three-day beginners' course is aimed at those who have not handled metals before and teaches basic blacksmithing and ironworking skills, as well as efficient and safe tool use. Other courses are geared more towards those with previous experience and will teach subject such as making your own tools, design for blacksmiths and making leaves.

What's special?
The three-day beginners' course introduces people to a skill which has now all but died out. Using drawing down, splitting and punching techniques, participants will make objects like a rat tail poker, a ram's head toasting fork and a decorative bracket for a hanging basket.

Eating & sleeping
The three-star Best Western Parkmore Hotel and Leisure Club (01642 786815) is nearby. Stockton Swallow Hotel (01642 679721) is two miles away. Lunch, home-made by Peat's wife, is included.

Directions
Preston Hall Museum is located near Stockton-on-Tees and can be reached via the A66 (from Darlington or Middlesbrough) or the A19. From these roads, follow the brown tourist signs for Preston Hall Museum (via the A135 off the A66 or the A67 off the A19).

In the area
The museum also has 'Butterfly World', an animal enclosure and a mini-golf course. For outdoors fun there's rafting on the River Tees and hiking in the Yorkshire Dales. For shopping, head to the Metro Centre in Gateshead.

Contact
Peat Oberon
Peat Oberon's School of Blacksmithing
Preston Hall Museum
Yarm Road
Stockton-on-Tees
County Durham
Tel: 01642 785543
Web: www.school-of-blacksmithing.co.uk
Email: peat@school-of-blacksmithing.co.uk

Practical information
Duration: 3 days
Level: beginner,
intermediate & advanced
Non-residential
Group size: 1–10

Price range: £200–£300
Prices include: lunch
Unsuitable for children
Pets not welcome

Courses available in:

Jan	Feb	Mar	Apr	May	Jun	Jul	Aug	Sep	Oct	Nov	Dec

ROSES AND CASTLES, AUDLEM
Folk art of the canals painting break

A folk art with an unknown origin, Roses and Castles is the term for the hand-painted pictorials seen on the sides and accessories of traditional narrow boats. This is ideal both for boat-owners and land-lubbers, as participants paint on to items they bring themselves. The first day is spent in discussion, practice and painting of the backgrounds. On the second day, the top layer of decoration is added. If time allows, students can also try lining-out, graining and lettering. Tutored and organised by Anne Luard and Jane Marshall, these relaxed workshops have been taking place for seven years in a converted stable near the Macclesfield Canal.

Contact
Anne Luard and Jane Marshall
Roses and Castles
The Old Stables
Bottom Lock
Audlem
Cheshire CW3 0HA
Tel: 01625 614845
Web: www.calara.co.uk/RosesandCastles.htm

Practical information
Duration: 2–10 days
Level: beginner &
intermediate
Non-residential

Group size: 2
Price range: £50–£100
Unsuitable for children
Pets not welcome

Courses available in:

Jan	Feb	Mar	Apr	May	Jun	Jul	Aug	Sep	Oct	Nov	Dec
			Apr	May		Jul	Aug				

ROTHAY MANOR HOTEL, AMBLESIDE
Picture perfect: learn and enjoy photographing the Lakeland landscapes

This landscape photography course is aimed at beginner and more experienced photographers alike. Three days are spent outdoors (some walking may be required) and there are also discussions, appraisals and evening talks. Group numbers are limited to ensure personal attention, and non-participants are welcome. The course is taught by Martin Silvester, a member of the Royal Photographical Society, and his wife Elaine. Rothay Manor Hotel is an elegant country house hotel built in 1825 in the heart of the Lake District. Other courses available here include Fine Art and Antiques, Gardening (with visits to local gardens), and Lakeland History, Architecture, Literature and Landscapes (five nights).

Contact
Nigel Nixon
Rothay Manor Hotel
Ambleside
Cumbria LA22 0EH
Tel: 015394 33605
Web: www.rothaymanor.co.uk

Practical information
Duration: 5 days
Level: beginner &
intermediate
Residential

Group size: 6–15
Price range: £400–£500+
Prices include: half board –
no lunch
Child-friendly

Courses available in:

Jan	Feb	Mar	Apr	May	Jun	Jul	Aug	Sep	Oct	Nov	Dec
	Feb	Mar	Apr						Oct		

THE TUFTON ARMS HOTEL, APPLEBY IN WESTMORLAND
Fishing for the budding angler (or unsuccessful fisherman...)

John Pape has been teaching fly-fishing for 25 years and runs courses on the River Eden. He'll show you where and when to fish, river etiquette, how flies work and much more. Each day begins at 10.30am and continues even after dinner. John only teaches small groups to ensure a suitable level of personal attention. You can borrow most equipment, but you do need waders or wellington boots and a fishing licence from the Post Office. Accommodation is provided at the splendid Tufton Arms Hotel, in the market square of Appleby in Westmorland, and they will freeze your catch ready to take home. For non-participants, the Lake District and Yorkshire Dales are nearby.

Contact
Nigel Milsom and Paul Zissler
Market Square
The Tufton Arms Hotel
Appleby in Westmorland
Cumbria CA16 6XA
Tel: 017683 51593
Web: www.tuftonarmshotel.co.uk

Practical information
Duration: 4 days
Level: beginner &
intermediate
Residential
Group size: 3–5
Courses available in:

Price range: £400–£500
Prices include: half board;
packed lunch £5 per day
Child-friendly
Pet-friendly

Jan	Feb	Mar	Apr	May	Jun	Jul	Aug	Sep	Oct	Nov	Dec
				May	Jun	Jul	Aug				

Unleash your latent mystical powers as a Medium

These residential mediumship courses are intensive but enjoyable. They are ideal for both newcomers and improvers, and can lead to further stages of mediumship development. Students are encouraged to progress at their own pace in a warm, caring environment. Val Cunningham-Simm is the founder and principal of the school and delivers the highest level of training through her group of tutors. The main house of this Quaker retreat was completed in 1834 and is located in the Lake District near Grasmere, with stunning views of the local fells.

Courses

The best-attended course is the five-day Mediumship Development, which is aimed at people wishing to learn more about areas such as Psychic Awareness, Clairvoyance, Psychic Art, Healing, Auras, Energies, Clairaudience, Clairsentience, Understanding Angels and Altered States. Following this, students may be invited to take part in the more advanced Diploma Courses. There are also beginners' weekend courses in Manchester, Chester, Lancaster, Birmingham and Surrey.

What's special?

The intensive Mediumship Development course is suitable for all levels of experience. Days are spent investigating Auro Fields, Soul Readings, Energies, Psychic Work and much more.

Eating & sleeping

Accommodation is in Glenthorne Country Guest House (01539 435 389), which has 25 en-suite rooms plus lounges and a games room, but no bar. The menus are interesting and varied, with vegetarians well catered for.

Directions

Leave the M6 at junction 36 towards Kendal (A590). Follow signposts for Windermere (A591) until Grasmere. Two minutes' walk from the centre of Grasmere. By rail, to Windermere from Oxenholme Junction or Manchester Airport, then bus to Grasmere.

In the area

Maps can be borrowed for walks around the Lake District. Ambleside is a short drive away, for shops and a cinema. Those with an interest in Wordsworth will enjoy nearby find Rydal Mount and Dove Cottage.

Contact

Val Cunningham-Simm
UK School of Mediumship
96 Birchley Rd
Wigan
Tel: 01744 893555
Web: www.ukschoolofmediumship.com
Email: info@ukschoolofmediumship.com

Practical information

Duration: 2–5 days
Level: beginner & intermediate
Residential

Group size: 3–20
Price range: £50–£500
Prices include: meals & accommodation
Unsuitable for children
Pets not welcome

Courses available in:

Jan	Feb	Mar	Apr	May	Jun	Jul	Aug	Sep	Oct	Nov	Dec

"Hey girl, take a walk on the wild side" guided walks for women

These Photographic/Walking holidays around Borrowdale in the Lake District are for women only and suitable for all levels of walking and photographic ability. Daily walks cover four to five miles without much climbing, and Jax Murray, the course leader, takes a gentle and very relaxed approach. Walkers will photograph landscapes and close-up subjects – rocks, plant life and animals – with instruction on light and composition. Where possible, processing is done locally so results can be discussed *in situ*. Accommodation may be limited for non-participants, although if there is room there are other outdoor activities nearby. Walking Women also run Natural History walks with specialist guides.

Contact
Walking Women
22 Duke St
Leamington Spa
Warwickshire CT32 4TR
Tel: 01926 313321
Web: www.walkingwomen.com

Practical information
Duration: 3 days
Level: beginner &
intermediate
Residential
Group size: 2-10

Price range: £150-£200
Prices include: breakfast and
packed lunch
Unsuitable for children
Pets not welcome

Courses available in:

Jan	Feb	Mar	Apr	May	Jun	Jul	Aug	Sep	Oct	Nov	Dec
	Feb	Mar	Apr	May		Jul	Aug	Sep	Oct		

Yoga and walking

This holiday course combines yoga, workshops and walks. Yoga classes take place throughout the day, and workshop subjects include chakras, mantras, homeopathy, healing and Qi Gong. In the afternoons, there are guided walks, while the evening offers further workshops, yoga practice and group activities. Philip Xerri trained in India in 1980 and has been teaching yoga ever since. He has developed his own integrated style of teaching and is also qualified in massage and reflexology. The course takes place at a Gothic-style mansion set in its own landscaped grounds overlooking Coniston Water. The atmosphere is definitely more house party than hotel.

Contact
Philip Xerri
Yoga Quests
20 Portland St
Lancaster
Lancashire LA1 1SZ
Tel: 01524 381154
Web: www.yogaquests.co.uk

Practical information
Duration: 6 days
Level: beginner &
intermediate
Residential
Group size: 6-25+

Price range: £300-£400
Prices include: meals &
accommodation
Unsuitable for children
Pets not welcome

Courses available in:

Jan	Feb	Mar	Apr	May	Jun	Jul	Aug	Sep	Oct	Nov	Dec
			Apr								

North
of England

Holyhead

Colwyn Bay

Caenarfon

Aberyswyth

Camarthen

Pembroke

Swansea

Cardiff

Wales

Wales is a land famous for its valleys and its hills, with three picturesque national parks - Snowdonia in the north, the Pembrokeshire Coast in the south west, and the Brecon Beacons in the south east. Add in the Gower Peninsula, the Black Mountains, and myriad castles and you have a country rich in photographic and painting potential. A high proportion of our Welsh courses are in some way spiritual and are concerned with yoga, meditation, healing or some other means to bring calm into your life.

Alternative therapies off the North Wales coast

Vivien Candlish set up the Anglesey Healing Centre in 1989 and has been teaching Reiki there since 1992. In addition, she offers 'Hopi Ear Candle Therapy' and a weekend called 'A Course in Miracles' which aims to increase spiritual awareness. Personal and group retreats can be tailor-made at any time of the year, with a different therapy each day. Accommodation and home-grown vegetarian food are offered on site, and there is an extensive library plus log fires to read before. The centre is on Anglesey, off the North Wales coast, and there are many historical sites and much coastline to be explored.

Contact	**Practical information**	Price range: £100–£500+
Vivien Candlish	Duration: 2–10 days	Prices include: meals &
Anglesey Healing Centre	Level: beginner,	accommodation
Llangoed	intermediate & advanced	Child-friendly
Beaumaris	Residential	Pets not welcome
Anglesey LL58 8PB	Group size: 1–10	
Tel: 01248 490814		
Web:www.angleseyhealingcentre.co.uk	Courses available in:	

Jan	Feb	Mar	Apr	May	Jun	Jul	Aug	Sep	Oct	Nov	Dec

Activities on Anglesey

Anglesey Interest Breaks in Brynsiencyn hold courses for many different tastes. Wildlife, art (e.g. Chinese brush painting), riding, reiki, sculpture, weaving, art and books are just some of the subjects on offer. They can also cater to a maximum of six people designing their own course. Courses are all available in Welsh and disabled visitors are welcome. Lunch and transportation is included if the course is off site. Accommodation is provided in a converted barn with six acres of grounds, and there is a heated swimming pool open between May and October. Anglesey offers riding, fishing and coastal castles, as well as glorious beaches.

Contact	**Practical information**	Price range: £200–£500+
Kevin and Alison Wood	Duration: 2–7 days	Prices include: meals,
Anglesey Interest Breaks	Level: beginner,	accommodation & all
Pont Dic	intermediate & advanced	materials
Brynsiencyn	Residential	Unsuitable for children
Anglesey LL61 6SJ	Group size: 3–10	Pets not welcome
Tel: 01248 430907		
Web: www.interestbreaks.co.uk	Courses available in:	

Jan	Feb	Mar	Apr	May	Jun	Jul	Aug	Sep	Oct	Nov	Dec

Pottery in Pembrokeshire National Park

Artist and tutor Anna Kavanagh runs residential pottery weeks at Trallwyn Cottages in the Pembrokeshire National Park. She limits the groups to four people and all skill levels are welcome. Days are set aside for potting, firing and glazing so that all creations are ready to take home at the end of the week. Terracotta and stoneware clays are used separately and are not mixed during the same course. The cottages include a converted cowshed, a 300-year-old farmhouse and a cottage studio – all surrounded by moors, mountains, wild ponies and sheep. Non-participating partners may stay if guest numbers are low.

Contact	**Practical information**	Prices include:
Anna Kavanagh	Duration: 4–10 days	accommodation & some
Ashera Pottery	Level: beginner,	meals and materials
Mynachlogddu	intermediate & advanced	provided.
Clynderwen	Residential	Child-friendly
Pembrokeshire SA66 7SE	Group size: 1–10	Pet-friendly
Tel: 01994 419278	Price range: £200–£500	
Web: http://home.clara.net/trallwyn/POTTERY_TEACHING.html		

Jan	Feb	Mar	Apr	May	Jun	Jul	Aug	Sep	Oct	Nov	Dec

Photography in Pembrokeshire

Len Bateman has 35 years' experience as a professional photographer and runs courses spanning wedding photography, landscapes and seascapes, natural history photography and digital photography. Courses are geared to different levels of photographic experience and most contain references to digital photography. Each course gives information specific to the subject: composition, seeing the light, planning the shoot, use of filters, etc. The venue is in the Pembrokeshire National Park in the 19th-century Old School House, which has a fully equipped photographic studio and accommodation. Some courses allow participants to bring their partner free of charge, as well as children at a reduced rate.

Contact	**Practical information**	Price range: £200–£500+
Len Bateman	Duration: 2–4 days	Prices include: meals &
Bateman Studios	Level: beginner,	accommodation
The Old School House	intermediate & advanced	Child-friendly
Walton West, Haverfordwest	Residential	Pet-friendly
Pembrokeshire SA62 3UA	Group size: 2–10	
Tel: 01437 781117		
Web: www.photocourses.co.uk	Courses available in:	

Jan	Feb	Mar	Apr	May	Jun	Jul	Aug	Sep	Oct	Nov	Dec

Painting in a converted chapel in Snowdonia

Ann and Chris Fellows set up Brush Strokes in the Snowdonia National Park over six years ago. Having been taught by Carlo Sdoya, Ann tutors many of the courses herself, but visiting artists also teach throughout the year. Students paint in the studio (a converted chapel) and the surrounding National Park, where there are lakes, rivers, mountains and a castle to provide inspiration. Courses include 'Watercolours for Beginners', 'Patterns and Colours in Modern Painting', 'Castles of Snowdonia', 'Brush, Colour and Welsh Water' and 'Loose and Juicy Watercolours'. Some courses teach in one medium (e.g. watercolour, acrylics or oils) while others use mixed media.

Contact	**Practical information**	Price range: £50–£200
Ann Fellows	Duration: 2–4 days	Prices include: meals & light
Brush Strokes	Level: beginner,	lunch only included.
Capel Isa	intermediate & advanced	Unsuitable for children
Dolwyddelan	Non-residential	Pet-friendly
Conwy	Group size: 3–15	
North Wales LL25 0TJ		
Tel: 01690 750488	Courses available in:	
Web: www.brush-strokes.org		

Jan	Feb	Mar	Apr	May	Jun	Jul	Aug	Sep	Oct	Nov	Dec

'Destination life centre' in Powys Mansion

Buckland Hall is a huge mansion built in 1898 and set in 60 acres of gardens and parkland. Its owners think of it as a 'destination life centre' and the courses offered reflect that idea. Individual breaks aim to improve spiritual, mental and physical well-being. The courses are run by external companies and each combines activities such as yoga, meditation, relaxation and massage. There are 29 en-suite bedrooms in Buckland Hall as well as extensive communal areas and a games room. The food is vegetarian, locally produced and organically farmed where possible. This area of the Brecon Beacon National Park has plenty of walking and cycling opportunities.

Contact	**Practical information**	Price range: £50–£400
Buckland Hall	Duration: 2–10	Prices include:
Bwylch	Level: intermediate &	accommodation
Brecon	advanced	Unsuitable for children
Powys LD3 7JJ	Residential & non-residential	Pets not welcome
Tel: 01874 730276	Group size: 2–25	
Web: www.bucklandhall.co.uk		
	Courses available in:	

Jan	Feb	Mar	Apr	May	Jun	Jul	Aug	Sep	Oct	Nov	Dec

Wales

Hatha Yoga in Carmarthenshire

Ruth Richards has been teaching yoga for 20 years. Hatha yoga, which is the main focus of these weekends, aims to realign the body using physical and breathing exercises, and guided meditation and massage will also be practised. The yoga begins at 10am each day, finishing at 4pm with breaks for lunch and afternoon tea. Courses include home-cooked meals and accommodation at Cae Iago, a converted 19th-century farmhouse. Rooms have two or three beds – partners and children are welcome to stay, though there are no childcare facilities. Llandeilo has its own 12th-century castle with magnificent grounds including a protected deer park with a herd of fallow deer.

Contact
Ruth Richards
Cae Iago Yoga
Brisken House
26 Carmarthen Street
Llandeilo
Carmarthenshire SA19 6AN
Tel: 01558 822053
Web: www.caeiago.co.uk/yoga.htm

Practical information
Duration: 2 days
Level: beginner,
intermediate & advanced
Residential
Group size: 6-10

Courses available in:

Jan	Feb	Mar	Apr	May	Jun	Jul	Aug	Sep	Oct	Nov	Dec
										Nov	

Price range: £150-£200
Prices include: meals &
accommodation
Child-friendly
Pets not welcome

Green living in Machynlleth

The Centre for Alternative Technology has been running for 25 years and is hailed as Europe's Leading Eco-centre. Its aim is to 'inspire, inform and enable' people to live sustainably. Courses focus on subjects such as using renewable sources of energy ('How to Build a Wind Turbine'), environmentally friendly building ('The Solar House'), blacksmithing and organic gardening. Prices include accommodation and vegetarian meals, and there are also campsites and B&B alternatives close by. The Centre is four miles north of Machynlleth in mid Wales with nearby attractions including King Arthur's Labyrinth and Powys Castle and Gardens.

Contact
Laura Snowball
Centre for Alternative Technology (CAT)
Machynlleth
Powys SY20 9AZ
Tel: 01654 705950
Web: www.cat.org.uk

Practical information
Duration: 2-5 days
Level: beginner,
intermediate & advanced
Residential
Group size: 6-25+
Price range: £100-£500+

Prices include: meals,
accommodation & most
materials included.
Unsuitable for children
Pets not welcome

Courses available in:

Jan	Feb	Mar	Apr	May	Jun	Jul	Aug	Sep	Oct	Nov	Dec

Tailored holidays in Pembrokeshire

The Clynfyw Countryside Centre is run on environmentally friendly lines, and its courses cover traditional subjects such as watercolour painting, green woodturning, charcoal production and pottery. They focus on presenting traditional subjects in a contemporary way, and participants choose which classes to take. The centre filters waste water through a reed bed system, heats with waste wood and uses photovoltaic panels to convert daylight to electricity. Their organic farmland is used to rear Duroc pigs, Welsh Black cattle and winter tack sheep. The local area offers riding, cheese making and salmon fishing, with the Pembrokeshire Coast National Park and Ceredigion Heritage Coast both within 15 miles.

Contact
Jim
Clynfyw Countryside Centre
Abercych, Boncath
Pembrokeshire SA37 0HF
Tel: 01239 841236
Web: www.clynfyw.co.uk

Practical information
Duration: 2-5 days
Level: beginner, intermediate
& advanced
Residential & non-residential
Group size: 3-25+

Courses available in:

Jan	Feb	Mar	Apr	May	Jun	Jul	Aug	Sep	Oct	Nov	Dec

Price range: under £50-£400
Prices include: call in advance
Child-friendly
Pets not welcome

Creative arts by the sea

Coleg Harlech and the Workers' Educational Association (North Wales) specialise in teaching adults who missed out on earlier education. Their centre in the Snowdonia National Park overlooks the coast and offers many short residential courses in the arts and humanities. Accommodation is available in the Halls of Residence, but students can also self-cater off site, using the restaurant if desired. Courses last two to seven days and include 'Digital Photography', 'Orchestral Summer School', 'Landscape Painting' and 'Welsh Summer School'. Students do not need any formal education qualifications or training. The Harlech area boasts a castle, a theatre and the National Park.

Contact
Coleg Harlech
Harlech
Gwynedd LL46 2PU
Tel: 01766 781900
Web: www.harlech.ac.uk

Practical Information
Duration: 2-7 days
Level: beginner &
intermediate
Residential
Group size: 6-25

Price range: £100-£400
Prices include: meals &
accommodation
Unsuitable for children
Pets not welcome

Courses available in:

Jan	Feb	Mar	Apr	May	Jun	Jul	Aug	Sep	Oct	Nov	Dec

Painting in the mountains of Snowdonia

The Cors y Garnedd Art Centre offers courses in various drawing and painting media in the beautiful surrounds of southern Snowdonia. Participants work either in the studio (a converted barn) or in one of the National Park locations on courses such as 'Painting Clean and Fresh Watercolours', 'Impressionistic Line and Wash', 'Pastels, Oils, Watercolours, Acrylics', 'Pastels and Watercolours' and 'Oils'. Many of the tutors are professional artists and all have substantial teaching experience. Accommodation is in Cors y Garnedd, a traditional 16th-century Welsh Longhouse or the 17th-century Ty Isaf, with its stone walls and oak beams. In the evenings, four-course meals with complimentary wine are eaten together in Cors y Garnedd.

Contact
Merle Gibbs
Cors y Garnedd Art Centre
Llanfachreth
Dolgellau
Gwynedd LL40 2EH
Tel: 01341 422627
Web: www.painting-courses.co.uk

Practical information
Duration: 3-10 days
Level: beginner,
intermediate & advanced
Residential & non-residential
Group size: 3-10

Price range: £400-£500+
Prices include: meals &
accommodation. Unsuitable
for children
Pets not welcome

Courses available in:

Jan	Feb	Mar	Apr	May	Jun	Jul	Aug	Sep	Oct	Nov	Dec

Creative courses in various Welsh locations

Located on the Welsh border and in Wales, four studios form part of 'Creative Days'. These are The Old Vicarage in Llansilin; Machinations in Llanbrynmair, with its riverside workshops; the Thomas Shop Studio in Penybont, on the River Ithon; and the Mirage Glass Studio, a craft complex at Llangedwyn Mill. There are four main subject areas: 'Art and Design' includes stained glass and bonsai; 'Textiles' includes gold threadwork and Japanese embroidery; 'Celebrating Traditional Skills' will have you hedge-laying or making panpipes and rain sticks; and 'Chase the Dream' offers 'Out of this World' poetry and 'I'd Love to Run a B&B''. Each venue offers accommodation on site or close by.

Wales

Contact
Pam Johnson
Creative Days
The Old Vicarage
Llansilin
Oswestry
Shropshire SY10 7PX
Tel: 01691 791345
Web: www.creativedays.co.uk

Practical information
Duration: 2-3 days
Level: beginner,
intermediate & advanced
Residential & non-residential
Group size: 2-10

Price range: £100-£200
Unsuitable for children
Pets not welcome

Courses available in:

Jan	Feb	Mar	Apr	May	Jun	Jul	Aug	Sep	Oct	Nov	Dec

GLANHELYG HOLIDAYS, CARDIGAN
Painting on a Victorian property in rural Dyfed

Glanhelyg Holidays specialise in oil and watercolour courses for small groups of painters. Their facilities include accommodation in a Victorian house, a fully equipped studio with abundant natural light, a chalet-style gallery set in the woods, and three and a half acres of peaceful grounds. Two instructors (Caroline Pont and Sylvia Jones) specialise in watercolours and one (Maria Shakespeare) in oils. Glanhelyg is also available for non-painting groups: the studio space is ideal for creative meetings, meditation and yoga. The house can sleep six and local accommodation can be recommended. Beyond Glanhelyg, the Pembrokeshire Coast path begins at Cardigan, and there are plenty of cliff-top walks and sandy coves.

Contact
Caroline Pont
Glanhelyg Holidays
Glanhelyg
Llechryd
Cardigan
Dyfed SA43 2NJ
Tel: 01239 682119
Web: www.glanhelyg.co.uk

Practical information
Duration: 2–6 days
Level: beginner &
intermediate
Residential & non-residential
Group size: 1–10

Courses available in:

Jan	Feb	Mar	Apr	May	Jun	Jul	Aug	Sep	Oct	Nov	Dec

Price range: £150–£400
Prices include: meals &
accommodation
Unsuitable for children
Pet-friendly

THE GLYNHIR ESTATE, LLANDYBIE
Arts and crafts by the Black Mountains

The Glynhir Estate dates from the 1600s and offers courses in painting, sculpture, photography and quilting. Tuition is relaxed and can cater to different levels of experience. Painting courses range from one to ten days; quilting courses are four days and suitable for beginners and experienced participants alike; photography courses last a weekend and non-participating partners are welcome. The sculpture course is much longer at five weeks. There are four bedrooms in the main house or self-catering accommodation in the converted cottages. The estate has its own waterfall, walled gardens and parkland, with peacocks, ducks, geese and chicken roaming the yard. The surrounding area offers riding, golf and Black Mountain rambles.

Contact
Justine
The Glynhir Estate
Glynhir Road
Llandybie
Ammanford
Dyfed SA18 2TD
Tel: 01269 850438
Web: www.theglynhirestate.com

Practical information
Duration: 2–10 days
Level: beginner,
intermediate & advanced
Residential
Group size: 3–25+

Courses available in:

Jan	Feb	Mar	Apr	May	Jun	Jul	Aug	Sep	Oct	Nov	Dec

Price range: £100–£500+
Prices include: meals (if not
self-caterd) &
accommodation.
Child-friendly
Pet-friendly.

HEARTSPRING, LLANSTEFFAN
Healing weekends in Carmarthen

Heartspring offers healing mini-breaks and tailored retreats. Based in the conservation village of Llansteffan on the Carmarthenshire coast, it's a place to indulge in holistic therapies. The breaks are individually tailored and the therapy list is vast: meditation tuition, Gaian healing, Alexander technique, living foods and detox advice, aromatherapy, Indian head massage, Swedish massage, counselling, reflexology, deep tissue massage and profound relaxation. Food is organic vegan and served in the dining room, or guests can self-cater in the kitchen. Healing mini-breaks include two nights' B&B, evening meals and three healing sessions. The house is a five-minute walk from the beach and Llansteffan has an ancient church and Norman castle.

Contact
Maddie
Heartspring
Hill House
Llansteffan
Carmarthenshire SA33 5JG
Tel: 01267 241999
Web: www.heartspring.co.uk/whatson.htm

Practical information
Duration: 2–10 days
Level: beginner,
intermediate & advanced
Residential & non-residential
Group size: 1–10

Courses available in:

Jan	Feb	Mar	Apr	May	Jun	Jul	Aug	Sep	Oct	Nov	Dec

Price range: £100–£500+
Prices include: meals,
accommodation & Optional
meals & accommodation.
Child-friendly
Pets not welcome

HAFAN-Y-COED, ABERCRAF

Spiritual awareness in the Brecon Beacons

In the south of the Brecon Beacons National Park under the Sleeping Giant mountain is Hafan-y-Coed, a residential 'Awareness Centre'. 'The Land of Beginning Again' has its own small lake and acres of green countryside and woodland, and during the summer months much of the course work takes place outdoors. There is a natural circle of trees and a labyrinth made of Welsh stone, which is used for meditation and prayer and is continually added to by guests. The atmosphere is both tranquil and friendly: it is a place for learning, and for putting down new roots.

Courses

Courses include 'Trance Mediumship', focusing on strengthening spiritual links; 'Mediumship and Psychic Art'; a 'Christmas Special Week'; and Native American, Indian, Pagan and circle dancing. Other courses in subjects such as tai chi, yoga and 'Eastern Traditions' focus on self-development. Occasionally there's an 'Experimental Week', working with trance and séance.

What's special?

Hafan-y-Coed is open to individuals and groups, and is not affiliated with any religion. Some of the courses are spiritually inclined, such as 'Psychic Art', which allows participants to channel skills such as drawing, writing and playing music.

Eating & sleeping

The two main buildings at Hafan-y-Coed have 21 bedrooms (no en-suites) with communal lounge rooms. Meals are made with locally produced fresh food such as Welsh lamb and mint sausages. All diets are catered for.

Directions

M4: junction 45 on to A4067 towards Abercraf. M5: junction 8 on to M50, follow A40 past Abergavenny, then left onto A4067 into the Brecon Beacons. Hafan-y-Coed is off the A4067 just north of Abercraf village. Nearest station: Neath.

In the area

Hafan-y-Coed is in the Brecon Beacons National Park, with over 500 square miles to cycle, walk, fish, climb and cave. Craig-y-Nos Castle and the National Showcaves Centre for Wales are both less than three miles away.

Contact	Practical information	Price range: £100–£200
Carole Sharp	Duration: 2–5 days	Prices include: meals &
Hafan-y-Coed	Level: beginner,	accommodation
Heol Tawe	intermediate & advanced	Child-friendly
Abercraf	Residential & non-residential	Pet-friendly
Swansea	Group size: 6–25+	
Tel: 01639 730985		
Web: www.hafanycoed.com	Courses available in:	
Email: hyc@btconnect.com		

Jan	Feb	Mar	Apr	May	Jun	Jul	Aug	Sep	Oct	Nov	Dec

Wales

Painting and drawing in Welshpool

David Wynn and Jenny Nimmo set up the Henllan Mill Summer School in 1982. David specialises in tutoring beginners by introducing them to different media – watercolour, charcoal, pencil and pastel – while encouraging them to 'see' with an artist's eyes. He also tutors experienced artists. Students are requested to bring examples of past work to share and discuss. There are three studios on site and the mill has quaint outdoor terrain for painting, including the mill itself, the river, ponds, sheds and animals, as well as a landscape of woods and hills. Accommodation is possible at the mill or in one of the nearby farm B&Bs.

Contact
David Wynn and Jenny Nimmo
Henllan Mill
Llangynyw
Welshpool
Powys SY21 9EN
Tel: 01938 810269
Web: www.henllanmill.co.uk

Practical information
Duration: 5–10 days
Level: beginner,
intermediate & advanced
Residential &

non-residential
Group size: 3–10
Price range: £100–£300
Unsuitable for children
Pets not welcome

Courses available in:

Jan	Feb	Mar	Apr	May	Jun	Jul	Aug	Sep	Oct	Nov	Dec

Outdoor photography in Snowdonia

Jean Napier has lived and worked in the Snowdonia National Park as a professional photographer and tutor for ten years – and she's also a qualified mountain leader. Her courses take place outdoors as much as possible to make the most of the scenery. Although specialising in black and white prints, she tutors in the creative and technical aspects of all types of film. Participants are required to bring their own camera and equipment, as well as a small collection of previous work to share and discuss. Accommodation is in the 19th-century mansion of Plas Tan y Bwlch, whose gardens include semi-wild areas for flora and fauna.

Contact
Jean Napier
Plas Tan y Bwlch
Maentwrog
Blaenau Ffestiniog
Gwynedd LL41 3YU
Tel: 01766 590324/334
Web: www.jean-napier.com

Practical information
Duration: 2 days
Level: beginner,
intermediate & advanced
Residential
Group size: 6–15
Price range: £100–£150

Prices include: meals,
accommodation &
transportation to sites for
photography
Unsuitable for children
Pets not welcome

Courses available in:

Jan	Feb	Mar	Apr	May	Jun	Jul	Aug	Sep	Oct	Nov	Dec

Basket-weaving weekends in Powys

Lois Grindey is a traditional willow-basket maker and teacher. She is dedicated to keeping the willow-weaving tradition alive and is well versed in its natural and social history: the patterns and techniques learnt on the courses date back hundreds of years. Participants are guaranteed to take home at least one basket with them, and are given written instructions at the end of the course to help them weave their own. Lunch and refreshments are provided and Lois can recommend local accommodation and meal venues. Located in mid Wales, the area is excellent for birds of prey - including the red kite - and the Brecon Beacons National Park is nearby.

Contact
Lois Grindey
Kibsey Craft
Pen-Y-Pound
Llawr-Y-Glyn
Caersws
Powys SY17 5RW
Email: lois@kibseycraft.co.uk
Web: www.kibseycraft.co.uk

Practical information
Duration: 2 days
Level: beginner,
intermediate & advanced
Non-residential
Group size: 3–10

Price range: £50–£100
Prices include: meals &
Lunch only.
£10 charge for materials.
Child-friendly
Pet-friendly

Courses available in:

Jan	Feb	Mar	Apr	May	Jun	Jul	Aug	Sep	Oct	Nov	Dec

Tibetan Yantra yoga

John Renshaw is a qualified Yantra yoga instructor and has been teaching its principles for 18 years. He runs weekend workshops and longer retreats at a converted barn in Kunselling, part of a centre owned by the Dzogchen Community near the Brecon Beacons. Introductory yantra weekends are suitable for both beginners and those with prior experience. They focus on breathing as an essential element of meditation, introducing eight particular exercises; this combines with physical movement to co-ordinate body and mind. There are longer workshops for those who have completed the introduction. Accommodation is offered on site, although students may need to share bedrooms. Further local accommodation is recommended on request.

Contact
Peter White
Kunselling Retreat Centre
Dzogchen Community UK
Nr Crickadarn
Powys LD2 3AJ
Email peterwhite@i12.com
Web: http://myweb.tiscali.co.uk/ringses/dzogchen/yantra/

Practical information
Duration: 2 days
Level: beginner,
intermediate & advanced
Residential
Group size: 6–20

Price range: £100–£150
Prices include: meals,
accommodation & Evening
meal £5 extra
Unsuitable for children
Pets not welcome

Courses available in:

Jan	Feb	Mar	Apr	May	Jun	Jul	Aug	Sep	Oct	Nov	Dec

Buddhist centre with yoga, meditation and tai chi

The Lam Rim Buddhist Centre near the Black Mountains was founded in 1978 to provide spiritual leader Ven Geshe Damchö with a place to teach and practise. Pentwyn Manor is the central building, surrounded by eight and a half acres of gardens and woodland, and a converted coach house can accommodate course participants if desired. The food provided is supplemented by the on-site garden and is vegetarian. Courses range over tai chi, yoga and meditation as well as specific topics relating to spirituality, awareness and breath. Examples include: 'The Courage to Love', 'Learning to Live Without Fear', 'Tai Chi Weekend' and 'Spreading Peace and Kindness to All Beings'.

Contact
Lam Rim Buddhist Centre
Pentwyn Manor
Penrhos
Raglan, Usk
Monmouthshire NP15 2LE
Tel: 01600 780383
Web: www.lamrim.org.uk

Practical information
Duration: 2–5 days
Level: beginner,
intermediate & advanced
Residential & non-residential
Group size: 6–25+

Price range: £50–£300
Prices include: meals &
accommodation
Unsuitable for children
Pets not welcome

Courses available in:

Jan	Feb	Mar	Apr	May	Jun	Jul	Aug	Sep	Oct	Nov	Dec

Alternative therapies in Carmarthen

Malindi is a natural healing and teaching centre which focuses on improving mental, emotional, physical and spiritual well-being. Established in the Carmarthen countryside in 2001, the Centre offers numerous alternative therapies such as aromatherapy, herbal nutrition, Alexander technique and colour light therapy - taught by tutors from all over the world. There are daily classes in meditation, yoga (including yoga for pregnant women) and holistic support for cancer sufferers. Courses include 'Native American Ceremony', 'Advanced Crystal Energy Weekend', 'The Living Celtic Spiritual Tradition' and 'Yoga Weekend'. Nearby Carmarthen is a traditional Welsh market town and the Gwili steam railway is a lovely way to see the Carmarthen hills.

Contact
Stephanie
Malindi Natural Healing and Teaching Centre
Cynwyl Elfed
Carmarthen
Carmarthenshire SA33 6SY
Tel: 01559 371511
Web: www.malindi.co.uk

Practical information
Duration: 2–5 days
Level: beginner,
intermediate & advanced
Non-residential
Group size: 3–25+

Price range: £50–£500
Prices include: meals
(light buffet lunch) &
accommodation
Child-friendly
Pets not welcome

Courses available in:

Jan	Feb	Mar	Apr	May	Jun	Jul	Aug	Sep	Oct	Nov	Dec

Wales

Falconry in the heart of Wales

Steve and Helen Smith set up Mid Wales Falconry in 1999 and now have 20 birds which they fly every day. Residents include owls, falcons, hawks and vultures. Children are very welcome, especially on the shorter course which covers basic bird training, handling and management. Longer courses include time with a professional falconer and bird first aid, as well as falcon tracking, tradition and terminology. Accommodation is either on site in the self-catering Mews Holiday Cottages or in nearby B&Bs. Horses can also be looked after, should you wish to bring one. Welshpool is home to the Andrew Logan Museum of Sculpture and Powis Castle and gardens.

Contact
Steve Smith
Mid Wales Falconry
Pen-y-Bryn
Castle Caereinion,
Welshpool, Powys
SY32 9AS
Tel: 01938 850265
Web: www.midwalesfalconry.co.uk

Practical information
Duration: 2–5 days
Level: beginner &
intermediate
Residential &
non-residential
Group size: 1–10

Courses available in:

Jan	Feb	Mar	Apr	May	Jun	Jul	Aug	Sep	Oct	Nov	Dec

Price range: £150–£500
Prices include: meals
(breakfast only) &
accommodation
Child-friendly
Pet-friendly

Fly-fishing in North Wales

North Wales Fly-Fishing School classes take place in the freshwater rivers and lakes of North Wales as well as in the sea. Introductory meetings and theory sessions happen at the 18th-century Plas Coch Hotel in Bala, where course participants enjoy a special room rate. Courses are geared to particular fish, including 'Trout', 'Sea Trout', 'Salmon', 'Grayling & Bass' and 'Pollack'. Courses are mainly one to three days long, but full-week packages with mixed seasonal fishing can be arranged to improve your casting and fly-fishing knowledge. For non-fishing partners and family Bala is the largest naturally occurring body of water in Wales, offering water sports and a narrow-gauge railway.

Contact
Robert Glynn
North Wales Fly Fishing School
4 Hillam Road
Wallasey
Gwynedd CH45 8LE
Tel: 0702 111 4746
Web: www.nwalesflyfishingschool.com

Practical information
Duration: 2–7 days
Level: beginner,
intermediate & advanced
Non-residential
Group size: 1–20

Courses available in:

Jan	Feb	Mar	Apr	May	Jun	Jul	Aug	Sep	Oct	Nov	Dec

Price range: £200–£500+
Prices include: tickets for
the waters
Child-friendly
Pet-friendly

Bird-watching rambles and fungi forays in Powys

The Elan Valley in mid Wales is a particularly good location for spotting birds of prey and collecting mushrooms. Daniel Butler and Welsh red kite expert Tony Cross lead a 'Raptor Rambles' break to help you track down birds such as red kites, goshawks, merlins, owls and peregrine falcons in their natural habitats. Daniel, a passionate fungi expert, also hosts 'Fungi Foray' courses to learn about and locate mushrooms and toadstools. Prices include accommodation and meals at the Elan Valley Hotel. Raptor Rambles prices include local transport and entry to the Gigrin Farm Kite Feeding Station. Fungi Foray breaks take place in autumn only.

Contact
Darren Bell
Raptor Rambles
Tan-y-Cefn
Rhayader
Powys LD6 5PD
Tel: 01597 811168
Web: www.raptor-rambles.co.uk

Practical information
Duration: 2 days
Level: beginner,
intermediate & advanced
Non-residential
Group size: 6–10

Courses available in:

Jan	Feb	Mar	Apr	May	Jun	Jul	Aug	Sep	Oct	Nov	Dec

Price range: £150–£300
Prices include: meals,
accommodation & local
transportation & entry to
Gigrin Farm
Child-friendly & pet-friendly

Buddhist meditation in the Samatha tradition

Samatha, pronounced 'Sa-matter', means calm. Samatha Buddhist meditation weekends are aimed at newcomers and focus on creating calm and clearing the mind. There are usually two instructors, and the weekend involves individual and group meditation, teaching, walks and light activity. The Samatha Centre is located in mid Wales, with accommodation on site in a converted farmhouse. There is no charge for the tuition itself, only for accommodation, and participants may be asked to help with the preparation of meals. Most courses last a weekend, although occasionally they take a week. After the introductory course, participants can join a local Samatha group or keep in contact with one of the tutors.

Contact
The Samatha Centre
Greenstreete
Llangunllo
nr Knighton
Powys LD7 1SP
Web: www.samatha.org

Practical information
Duration: 2–5 days
Level: beginner
Residential
Group size: 3–15

Price range: under £50–£100
Prices include: meals &
accommodation
Unsuitable for children
Pets not welcome

Courses available in:

Jan	Feb	Mar	Apr	May	Jun	Jul	Aug	Sep	Oct	Nov	Dec

Holistic health dowsing

Ute Eden has been practising dowsing since 1994 and established the School of Holistic Dowsing in 2001. She describes dowsing as a 'life laundry', physically, emotionally and spiritually. Her courses at the Malindi Centre aim to enable people to help themselves by applying dowsing to every aspect of their lives. The foundation course introduces students to pendulum dowsing and applications, as well as exploring nutrition, regeneration and bach flower remedies. They are spread over two weekends: the first covers theory and practice; the second focuses on regeneration and Bach flower remedies. Ute usually holds two to four courses a year, though more can be arranged on demand.

Contact
School of Holistic Dowsing
Rhyd Galed
Talley
Llandeilo SA19 7AQ
Tel: 01558 685417
Web: www.schoolofholisticdowsing.co.uk

Practical information
Duration: 3–6 days
Level: beginner
Residential

Group size: 3–15
Price range: £200–£400
Unsuitable for children
Pets not welcome

Courses available in:

Jan	Feb	Mar	Apr	May	Jun	Jul	Aug	Sep	Oct	Nov	Dec

Weaving, spinning and dyeing in Cilgerran

Snail Trail Handweavers run courses in weaving and dyeing, with spinning if appropriate. They are based in the small town of Cilgerran at Penwenallt Farm, a four-acre smallholding with accommodation in a Georgian farmhouse. The studio is well equipped with weaving tools, and students can realise their own designs: achievable items include bags, rugs, wall hangings, fabrics and accessories. Tutor Martin Weatherhead can teach a variety of weaving techniques, including Ikat, and everyone will be weaving from day one. The dyeing course covers both synthetic and natural dyes, with materials for the latter collected in the local area. Cilgerran has its own castle and the Cardigan Bay has spectacular coastline.

Contact
Martin Weatherhead
Snail Trail Handweavers
Penwenallt Farm
Cilgerran
Cardigan
Dyfed, SA19 7AQ
Tel: 01239 841228
Web: www.snail-trail.co.uk

Practical information
Duration: 7 days
Level: beginner,
intermediate & advanced
Residential
Group size: 3–10

Price range: £400–£500
Prices include: meal &
accommodation
Child-friendly
Pets not welcome

Courses available in:

Jan	Feb	Mar	Apr	May	Jun	Jul	Aug	Sep	Oct	Nov	Dec

Wales

William Gladstone's Library in Hawarden

St Deiniol's Library, Britain's only residential library, was founded in 1898 by William Gladstone. Its mission is 'to encourage research and promote education in theology, intellectual history and 19th- century studies'. Residential courses fall within these themes and they include 'Dining with Babette: film, hospitality and human transformation', 'Radical Christianity', 'Greek in a Week', 'The Pre-Raphaelites' and 'The Conversation: doing theology at the movies'. Accommodation and vegetarian meals are included in course prices – participants stay on site in recently refurbished bedrooms. Hawarden has two castles – Euloe Castle, a ruin probably dating back to the 1200s, and Hawarden Castle, where Gladstone lived and died.

Contact
Mr Morris
St Deiniol's Library
Church Lane, Hawarden
Flintshire CH5 3DF
Tel: 01244 532350
Web: www.st-deiniols.org

Practical information
Duration: 2-7 days
Level: beginner,
intermediate & advanced
Non-residential
Group size: 1-20

Price range: £200–£500+
Prices include: tickets for
the waters
Child-friendly
Pet-friendly

Courses available in:

Jan	Feb	Mar	Apr	May	Jun	Jul	Aug	Sep	Oct	Nov	Dec

Stone-carving in Powys

Lottie and William O'Leary are stone carvers who moved to Powys in 1992 to set up their 'Stone carving and Memorials' workshop. Their courses run from Friday lunchtime to Sunday evening, with design ideas honed on the first day, before the chiselling begins: students have a choice from limestone, slate and sandstone. Stones are chipped outdoors, weather permitting, and all participants should leave with their own carving. Tuition is intensive as there is a maximum of six people per course. Lunch is provided, and locally produced organic food is staple. Powys has its own splendid castle to visit, cycling is popular and the Brecon Beacons are close by.

Contact
Lottie and William O'Leary
Stone Carving and Memorials
Upper House
Knuclas
Knighton
Powys LD7 1PN
Tel: 01547 528792
Web: www.stonecarving.co.uk

Practical information
Duration: 2-7 days
Level: beginner,
intermediate & advanced
Non-residential
Group size: 1-20

Price range: £200–£500+
Prices include: Tickets for
the waters included.
Child-friendly
Pet-friendly

Courses available in:

Jan	Feb	Mar	Apr	May	Jun	Jul	Aug	Sep	Oct	Nov	Dec

Learn to swim in Cardigan Bay

The only residential swimming course in the UK, 'Swimming Without Stress' offers intensive swimming lessons over several days. The venue is a swimming pool in Cardigan Bay which is part of Brongwyn Holidays. Qualified swimming instructors use the Alexander Technique and the Shaw Method to make students comfortable in the water. They tailor lessons to individual needs, with a maximum of three lessons per day lasting 40 minutes or an hour. The school also has special weekend courses for the nervous swimmer. Students can self-cater on site or use local B&Bs. Cardigan Bay's attractions include dolphin watching, the Pembrokeshire coastal path and the market town of Cardigan.

Contact
Ian and Cheryl Cross
Swimming Without Stress
Olive Cottage
St Dogmaels
Pembrokeshire SA43 3HP
Tel: 01239 613789
Web: www.swimmingwithoutstress.co.uk

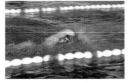

Practical information
Duration: 2-4 days
Level: beginner,
intermediate & advanced
Residential & non-residential

Group size: 1
Price range: £50–£500+
Child-friendly
Pet-friendly

Courses available in:

Jan	Feb	Mar	Apr	May	Jun	Jul	Aug	Sep	Oct	Nov	Dec

Upholstery at Teify View in Ceredigion

Myra Cazalet has been running week-long upholstery courses at Teify View since 1990. Beginners can bring a drop-in seat, a pin-stuffed seat and a sprung dining chair, all to be completed during the week, and can use their own fabrics if they wish. Principles covered include stuffing, springing, webbing, re-covering and shallow buttoning. Courses are limited to five students, and there is a six-week upholstery diploma for those hoping to start a career. Accommodation is either in the main house or a converted barn cottage, and Myra provides breakfast and lunch; evening meals are self-catered. Teify View is near Newcastle Emlyn and the sandy Ceredigion coast.

Contact
Myra Cazalet
The Traditional Upholstery Workshop
Teify View, Llandyfriog
Newcastle Emlyn
Ceredigion SA38 9HB
Tel: 01239 711265
Web: www.upholsterycourses.com

Practical information
Duration: 5 days
Level: beginner,
intermediate & advanced
Residential
Group size: 1-5

Price range: £400-£500
Prices include: lunch &
accommodation.
Unsuitable for children
Pets not welcome

Courses available in:

Jan	Feb	Mar	Apr	May	Jun	Jul	Aug	Sep	Oct	Nov	Dec

Sustainable crafts and creative health in Snowdonia

Trigonos is a not-for-profit organisation in the Nantlle Valley which runs various courses, many with a sustainable focus. Weaver and textile artist Eta Ingham-Lawrie, who exhibits work throughout the UK and Europe, tutors weaving, knitting and dyeing courses here. Other courses include 'Building Health' using the Alexander Technique and creative exploration, and 'From Garden Weed to Herbal Cure'. The property has a walled garden, a stream, meadows and woodlands and prides itself on its home-cooked food – the dining room offers views of the Snowdonia mountains and lake Llyn Nantlle Uchaf. The local area offers many attractions from spectacular walks and medieval castles to swimming and theatre.

Contact
Trigonos
Plas Baladeulyn
Nantlle
Caernarfon
Gwynedd LL54 6BW
Tel: 01286 882388
Web: www.trigonos.org

Practical information
Duration: 2-3 days
Level: beginner,
intermediate & advanced
Residential & non-residential
Group size: 3-25
Price range: £100-£300

Prices include: meals,
accommodation & most
materials
Child-friendly
Pets not welcome

Courses available in:

Jan	Feb	Mar	Apr	May	Jun	Jul	Aug	Sep	Oct	Nov	Dec

Bird-watching and fishing in Gwynedd

Tynycornel Hotel has stood in the Snowdonia National Park on the shore of the Tal-y-Llyn Lake since 1844. It is a sensational venue for fishing and birdwatching and guests have priority access to the Tal-y-Llyn Lake, which the hotel owns. Manager Tom Rowlands and his brother David were born and bred in the area and can customise your stay to include guided visits to the best fishing and birdwatching spots. You can even bring your dog. Fish caught in the local waters include brown trout, sea trout, salmon and bass. Birds in the area include red kites, merlin, peregrine falcons, eider ducks, cormorants, wading birds and geese.

Contact
Tom Rolands
Tynycornel Hotel
Tal-y-Llyn
Tywyn
Gwynedd LL36 9AJ
Tel: 01654 782282
Web: www.tynycornel.co.uk

Practical information
Duration: 2-10 days
Level: beginner,
intermediate & advanced
Residential
Group size: 1-25+

Price range: £100-£500+
Prices include: meals &
accommodation
Child-friendly
Pet-friendly

Courses available in:

Jan	Feb	Mar	Apr	May	Jun	Jul	Aug	Sep	Oct	Nov	Dec

Wales

Craft breaks in the Carmarthen countryside

The focus on a Waunifor Crafty Break is creativity and relaxation. The company was established in 2000 by Lisette Chesshire, who makes and sells her own pottery, and she teaches alongside Jackie Henshall. Their courses include mosaics, 'Pottery and Clay Modelling', 'Glass Painting, Bead Jewellery and Card Making', 'Willow Sculpture for Beginners' and a 'Christmas Crafts Weekend'. Tailor-made courses can include any of these. Accommodation is available in traditional Welsh stone cottages and meals can be provided if necessary. There are five acres of grounds, with Victorian walled garden, pond and woodland walks. For non-participating partners there are many outdoor activities locally, such as canoeing, fishing and red kite spotting.

Contact
Lisette Chesshire
Waunifor Crafty Breaks
Waunifor Estate
Maesycrugiau
Carmarthenshire SA39 9LX
Tel: 01559 395437/247
Web: www.craftybreaks.com

Practical information
Duration: 2–10 days
Level: beginner,
intermediate & advanced
Residential &
non-residential

Group size: 1–10
Price range: £100–£500+
Prices include:
accommodation & lunch.
Child-friendly
Pet-friendly

Courses available in:

Jan	Feb	Mar	Apr	May	Jun	Jul	Aug	Sep	Oct	Nov	Dec

Scotland

Hugely popular with tourists on account of its rugged scenery and picture-postcard landscapes, Scotland makes an excellent place to 'get away from it all' on a weekend course – or for longer. Add in the whisky, the music, the golf and the Celtic culture, and reasons for visiting Scotland seem endless. It's an excellent place for outdoorsy courses that take you to some of the less visited regions and islands, as well as for those based in Edinburgh that allow you to enjoy the varied charms of the capital city.

Writing and poetry courses near Inverness

If you are serious about writing and poetry, you should consider the Moniack Trust's highly respected courses at Moniack Mhor, a traditional croft house with Highland vistas aplenty. Outdoor enthusiasts will love this part of Scotland, with Loch Ness nearby, Kiltarlity village two miles away and Inverness 14. Throughout the summer, in partnership with the Arvon Foundation, Moniack hosts courses in subjects ranging from Crime Writing and Writing for Children to Poetry and Playwriting. Tutors include novelist Val McDermid and BAFTA award-winning playwright Alan Plater. You can also focus on Starting to Write, Writing from Life, Writing for Television, Life Story, Fiction and Novel Writing.

Contact
Sophia Fraser
Arvon Foundation
Moniack Mhor
Teavarran, Kiltarlity
Beauly
Inverness-shire IV4 7HT
Tel: 01463 741675
Web: www.arvonfoundation.org

Practical information
Duration: 5–7 days
Level: beginner,
intermediate & advanced
Residential
Group size: 3–10

Price range: £400–£500+
Prices include: meals &
accommodation
Unsuitable for children
Pets not welcome

Courses available in:

Jan	Feb	Mar	Apr	May	Jun	Jul	Aug	Sep	Oct	Nov	Dec
					Jun	Jul	Aug	Sep			

Ceramic classes with seasonal themes

People interested in hobby crafts won't find a more reliable place to learn in Scotland. Bothy Ceramics was established in 1985 and is Scotland's premier supplier of hobbyist materials. The course programme reflects seasonal festivities so expect classes dedicated to creating ceramic pieces with Christmas and Easter-related themes. Alongside tuition, they will offer advice on setting up your own ceramics business and can organise a tailored course. The business lies a short distance outside the pretty village of Guildtown. There are lots of gentle walks in the area including one through Blairmuir Wood where you'll find standing stones. Perth has some excellent hotels including Parklands and Sunbank House.

Contact
Lorna
Bothy Ceramics Ltd
Cambusmichael
Guildtown
Perthshire PH2 6BN
Tel: 01821 640320
Web: www.bothyceramics.fsnet.co.uk

Practical information
Duration: 2–3 days
Level: beginner,
intermediate & advanced
Non-residential
Group size: 3–10

Price range: £50–£200
Unsuitable for children
Pets not welcome

Courses available in:

Jan	Feb	Mar	Apr	May	Jun	Jul	Aug	Sep	Oct	Nov	Dec
Jan		Mar	Apr							Nov	Dec

Art courses in a seaside studio

Bridge House Art has an excellent reputation for its art courses. The well-equipped studio in the seaside town of Ullapool offers courses in fine art, drawing, painting, printmaking and textiles. There is also a stained glass weekend workshop, suitable for beginners and experts alike, where participants design and produce small panels, windows and shaped pieces using leaded and copper foil techniques. Ullapool is a great base for exploring the dramatic wilderness of the northwest Highlands – it has lots of excellent restaurants and all types of accommodation from hostels to luxury hotels. You could also hop on a ferry from the port here to Stornaway on the Isle of Lewis.

Contact
Eleanor White
Bridge House Art
Old Moss Road
Ullapool
Ross-shire IV26 2TG
Tel: 01854 612281

Practical information
Duration: 2 days
Level: beginner
Non-residential
Group size: 6–10

Price range: under
£50–£100
Child-friendly
Pet-friendly

Courses available in:

Jan	Feb	Mar	Apr	May	Jun	Jul	Aug	Sep	Oct	Nov	Dec
Jan	Feb		Apr			Jul		Sep	Oct	Nov	Dec

Art courses in a seaside studio

Bridge House Art has an excellent reputation for its art courses. The well-equipped studio in the seaside town of Ullapool offers courses in fine art, drawing, painting, printmaking and textiles. There is also a stained glass weekend workshop, suitable for beginners and experts alike, where participants design and produce small panels, windows and shaped pieces using leaded and copper foil techniques. Ullapool is a great base for exploring the dramatic wilderness of the northwest Highlands – it has lots of excellent restaurants and all types of accommodation from hostels to luxury hotels. You could also hop on a ferry from the port here to Stornaway on the Isle of Lewis.

Contact
Eleanor White
Bridge House Art
Old Moss Road
Ullapool
Ross-shire IV26 2TG
Tel: 01854 612281

Practical information
Duration: 2–7 days
Level: beginner,
intermediate & advanced
Non-residential

Group size: 2–15
Price range: £100–£400
Child-friendly
Pets not welcome

Courses available in:

Jan	Feb	Mar	Apr	May	Jun	Jul	Aug	Sep	Oct	Nov	Dec

Falconry and fishing at Gleneagles

If you would like to handle hawks in the grounds of one of Scotland's most prestigious hotels, then this course is a must. Gleneagles' professional falconers will guide you through the basics of handling and flying Harris hawks. And you can combine this with one of the other activities available: there's an equestrian centre, superb fishing, off-road driving and shooting – not to mention a famous golf course and health spa. This darling of the Scottish hotel scene has a rich history and a luxurious ambience. There are lavish suites fit for world leaders and 270 well-appointed bedrooms. Gleneagles is in the Highland foothills an hour's drive from Glasgow and Edinburgh.

Contact
British School of Falconry and
   Fishing at Gleneagles
The Gleneagles Hotel
Auchterarder
Perthshire PH3 1BR
Tel: 0800 389 3737
Web: www.gleneagles.com

Practical information
Duration: 2–3 days
Level: beginner,
intermediate & advanced
Residential

& non-residential
Group size: 1–5
Price range: £500+
Child-friendly
Pets not welcome

Courses available in:

Jan	Feb	Mar	Apr	May	Jun	Jul	Aug	Sep	Oct	Nov	Dec

Learn to pipe at Scotland's oldest piping school

The School of Piping is the oldest teaching establishment for Scotland's national instrument. You can expect top-quality tuition and guidance from the staff: Robert Wallace, the college principal is one of Scotland's leading professional pipers. Students are shown every aspect of good piping – technique, expression and sound – and can also work towards the Institute of Piping exams. At the museum and library visitors can examine the evolution of the instrument and its social importance. The college is less than a mile west of George Square, within easy reach of Glasgow's stylish attractions, and has a list of nearby hotels and guesthouses.

Contact
College of Piping
16–24 Otago St
Glasgow
Strathclyde G12 8HJ
Tel: 0141 334 3587
Web: www.college-of-piping.co.uk

Practical information
Duration: 2–10 days
Level: beginner,
intermediate & advanced
Non-residential
Group size: 2–10

Price range: £50–£400
Prices include: meals &
accommodation
Unsuitable for children
Pets not welcome

Courses available in:

Jan	Feb	Mar	Apr	May	Jun	Jul	Aug	Sep	Oct	Nov	Dec

Scotland

ARDIVAL HARPS, STRATHPEFFER

Play the harp in the Highlands

Ardival Harps has a worldwide reputation as a maker of Scottish harps. These range from the Pictish lap harps, on which beginners first learn, to the traditional floor-standing folk harps or clarsachs. Ardival also makes wire-strung harps and the mysterious buzzing bray harps of the Renaissance. Students have the chance to play simple tunes on all of these instruments. They will learn from a specialist about their historical development and hear them expertly played. Those who feel truly inspired can pursue their interest by purchasing or hiring an instrument.

Courses
The four-day Harp Holidays beginners' course takes place at Orchard House in the grounds of the magnificent Castle Leod. The courses are run by Bill Taylor, who has an international reputation as a player, recording artist and teacher of historical and traditional harp music.

What's special?
Previous beginners have valued the extensive knowledge of harp history and harp music that Bill shares with students. Students have also appreciated his versatility and patience as a teacher of groups. Residential courses are available for more experienced players.

Eating & sleeping
Homemade lunches provided each day. For evening meals try the Brunstane Lodge Hotel (01997 421261) in Strathpeffer and Café India (01349 862552) in Dingwall. Strathpeffer has all sorts of accommodation; Scoraig Guest House (01997 421532) is a favourite.

Directions
Castle Leod drive is 1/4 mile east of Strathpeffer. Once inside the gate, take the second drive on the left, signposted 'Orchard House & Ardival Harps'. Alternatively, fly/rail/bus to Inverness and take local bus 27 to Strathpeffer. Or rail to Dingwall and taxi/bus.

In the area
In Strathpeffer the Victorian Spa Pavilion has been lovingly restored and is a centre for dances and concerts. There are beautiful walks, relaxed or energetic, in all directions.

Contact	**Practical information**	Price range: £150–£200
Bill Taylor	Duration: 4 days	Prices include: meals &
Ardival Harps	Level: beginner,	lunch only
Orchard House	intermediate & advanced	Unsuitable for children
Castle Leod	Non-residential	Pets not welcome
Strathpeffer, Ross-shire	Group size: 3–10	
Tel: 01997 421260		
Web: www.ardival.com	Courses available in:	
Email: info@ardival.com	Jan Feb **Mar Apr May Jun Jul Aug** Sep Oct Nov Dec	

ARIUNDLE CENTRE, STRONTIAN

Craft workshops in the Western Highlands

The Ariundle Centre is known for its workshops and craft community and has been running courses since the 1970s. Run by the Campbell family, it was originally known as Cozy Knits but a change of emphasis led them to change the name. They are based near the village of Strontian, whose name derives from a Gaelic word meaning 'Point of the Fairies'. The mineral strontian was discovered in the lead mines here in the 1790s and subsequently named after the village, and there's an exhibition at Ariundle exploring the mining history.

Courses
During the week you can drop in and get a taste for some of the skills, while the weekend course list includes batik, stained glass, wool-spinning and decorating mirrors. There's also beginners' watercolour, basket-making, pottery, felting, constructed textiles and paper-making.

What's special?
The enthusiastic tutors have many years' experience, making the courses very popular indeed. The batik and basket-making courses go from strength to strength: they manage to encourage creativity from the most unlikely participants and are frequently sold out well in advance.

Eating & sleeping
The bunkhouse has various en-suite rooms catering for couples and groups of up to six. All courses include healthy meals, with candlelit dinners served from 6.30pm. Alternatively, there are some excellent hotel restaurants nearby.

Directions
Take the A82 to the Corran Ferry; turn left off the ferry toward the small village of Strontian. The centre is on the edge of the Ariundle Oakwoods.

In the area
It is a short drive from the landscapes of Glencoe and Glen Nevis, and on the nearby Ardnamurchan peninsula you may see deer, otters and eagles. Fort William is the nearest town.

Contact
Kate Campbell
Ariundle Centre
Strontian
Argyll PH36 4JA
Tel: 01967 402279
Web: www.ariundle.co.uk
Email: info@ariundle.co.uk

Practical information
Duration: 2–5 days
Level: beginner,
intermediate & advanced
Residential & non-residential
Group size: 3–10

Price range: under
£50–£150
Prices include: meals &
accommodation
Child-friendly
Pet-friendly

Courses available in:

Jan	Feb	Mar	Apr	May	Jun	Jul	Aug	Sep	Oct	Nov	Dec

Scotland

Scottish musical and cultural courses at Stirling University

If you're interested in Scottish and Gaelic culture, the courses at the University of Stirling might strike a chord. The university has a fantastic choice of short and summer courses covering subjects from accordion playing to archaeology. Courses are categorised into three groups: Scottish History, Culture, Society & Natural Heritage; Creative Arts; and Music and Dance. People staying on the handsome campus within the verdant 360-acre Airthrey Estate have access to many facilities including golf, theatre, swimming and cinema and there's great walking nearby as well as fishing. Stirling, the former capital of Scotland, is full of cultural, historical and leisure attractions.

Contact
Margery Stirling
DAICE
Airthrey Castle
University of Stirling
Stirling, Stirlingshire FK9 4LA
Tel: 01786 467951
Web: www.daice.stir.ac.uk/sss/index.htm

Practical information
Duration: 2–5 days
Level: beginner,
intermediate & advanced
Residential

& non-residential
Group size: 3–20
Price range: £50–£300
Unsuitable for children
Pets not welcome

Courses available in:

Jan	Feb	Mar	Apr	May	Jun	Jul	Aug	Sep	Oct	Nov	Dec

Recording scavenging birds on the Ross of Mull

Head over to the island of Mull to take part in a fascinating and valuable Earthwatch project led by ecologist Dr Paul Howarth. Each year four 'teams' are given the chance to learn about and record the behaviour of predatory and scavenging birds on the Ross of Mull. Field studies and lectures focus on the populations of various birds of prey including golden eagles, buzzards, kestrels, hen harriers, ravens and short-eared owls. Participants are also likely to see other species around the island habitats, including deer, otters, dolphins and seals. Accommodation is in shared rooms in a secluded former gamekeeper's cottage near the sea at the heart of the research site.

Contact
Dr Paul Howarth
Eagles of Mull, Earthwatch
267 Banbury Road
Oxford
Oxfordshire OX2 7HT
Tel: 01865 318838
Web: www.earthwatch.org/europe/discovery/eagles.html

Practical information
Duration: 6 days
Level: beginner,
intermediate & advanced
Residential
Group size: 3–10

Price range: £400–£500
Prices include: meals &
accommodation
Child-friendly
Pets not welcome

Courses available in:

Jan	Feb	Mar	Apr	May	Jun	Jul	Aug	Sep	Oct	Nov	Dec

Cookery and food writing in a converted stable

If you're an aspiring chef or you just fancy learning some new culinary tricks, the Edinburgh School of Food and Wine will have a course to suit your needs. You'll be looked after by a friendly and experienced team in a former coaching house amid the leafy grounds of Newliston House 12 miles west of Edinburgh. Choose from the range of short, fun courses: for the novice cook there is the Survival Course which teaches basic skills, whilst for more experienced cooks the week-long Advanced Course is an ideal refresher. Budding food columnists might like the Food Writing Course, which includes visits to restaurants, hotels and manufacturers.

Contact
Jill Davidson
Edinburgh School of Food and Wine
The Coach House
Newliston, Nr. Edinburgh
Midlothian EH29 9EB
Tel: 0131 333 5001
Web: www.esfw.com

Practical information
Duration: 5 days
Level: beginner &
intermediate
Non-residential

Group size: 6–20
Price range: £300–£500
Prices include: meals
Child-friendly
Pets not welcome

Courses available in:

Jan	Feb	Mar	Apr	May	Jun	Jul	Aug	Sep	Oct	Nov	Dec

Spiritual workshops at the Findhorn Foundation

Founded in 1962, the Findhorn Community today consists of holistic businesses and initiatives linked by a 'shared positive vision for humanity and the earth'. Their core programme of week-long workshops explores largely spiritual themes encompassing ideas about self-awareness and living in a community. And there is an eco-village which runs an education programme about sustainability and ecology. Core Programme workshops include Ecovillage Experience Week, Business Experience Week, Japanese Experience week, Exploring Community Life, Life Purpose, Findhorn Garden Week and Spiritual Practice. There are many shorter workshops (2-6 days) including Biodanza, Astroshamanic Healing and Letting Go. Accommodation is available in the village of Findhorn and in nearby Forres.

Contact
Findhorn Foundation
The Park
Findhorn
Forres
Moray IV36 3TZ
Tel: 01309 690311
Web: www.findhorn.org

Practical information
Duration: 2–10 days
Level: beginner,
intermediate & advanced
Residential & non-residential
Group size: 2–25+

Price range: £50–£500+
Prices include: meals &
accommodation
Child-friendly
Pet-friendly

Courses available in:

Jan	Feb	Mar	Apr	May	Jun	Jul	Aug	Sep	Oct	Nov	Dec

Fishing with Forbes of Kingennie

Kingennie has some of the best coarse-, bait- and fly-fishing waters in North-East Scotland, attracting around 10,000 anglers each year. Tuition is available for beginners and seasoned anglers alike and can be structured to your needs, be it for a few hours or a couple of days. Fisheries manager Neil Anderson is a registered Scottish Game Anglers Trout Fly-Fishing Instructor (SGAIC) and can offer advice on all aspects of the sport. The Angus countryside is well worth exploring, as is recently rejuvenated Dundee, which boasts the highly acclaimed Dundee Contemporary Arts, the McManus Galleries and the 'Discovery', used for Captain Scott's 1901 Antarctic Expedition.

Contact
Neil Anderson
Forbes of Kingennie
Kingennie
Broughty Ferry
Dundee, Angus DD5 3RD
Tel: 01382 350777
Web: www.forbesofkingennie.com

Practical information
Duration: 2–10 days
Level: beginner,
intermediate & advanced
Residential & non-residential

Group size: 1
Price range: £50–£500+
Child-friendly
Pet-friendly

Courses available in:

Jan	Feb	Mar	Apr	May	Jun	Jul	Aug	Sep	Oct	Nov	Dec

Artistic courses at a prestigious art school

The Glasgow School of Art's Easter programme and Summer School are based at the prestigious Rennie Mackintosh building, one of the city's most iconic structures. Courses are held on the main campus as well as at the magnificent House for an Art Lover, a Mackintosh-designed building on the south side of the city. The curriculum is divided into Drawing and Painting, Sculpture and Ceramics, and Design and Photography, with tuition coming from invited lecturers, professional artists and academic staff. Courses include 'Decoration on Clay', 'Volcanic Art', 'Japanese Printmaking and Papermaking', 'Millinery Workshop', 'Urban Landscapes', 'Introduction to Raku' and 'Embroidered Textiles'. The college has a list of recommended accommodation.

Contact
Glasgow School of Art
167 Renfrew Street
Glasgow
Strathclyde G3 6RQ
Tel: 0141 353 4500
Web: www.gsa.ac.uk

Practical information
Duration: 5–10 days
Level: beginner,
intermediate & advanced
Non-residential

Group size: 3–20
Price range: £100–£300
Unsuitable for children
Pets not welcome

Courses available in:

Jan	Feb	Mar	Apr	May	Jun	Jul	Aug	Sep	Oct	Nov	Dec

Scotland

CASTLE OF PARK, CORNHILL

Painting and creative writing courses in Aberdeenshire

Castle of Park is a stunning 16th-century castle with lovingly restored bedrooms, en-suite bathrooms and wonderful grounds. It hosts painting courses aimed at both beginners and experienced painters, with the rich natural landscapes and marine environments nearby providing inspiring subject matter. Seasonal changes in the parkland's flora and fauna make each painting course unique. Most are watercolour-focused, although other media, notably pastels, are taught as well. There are also various creative writing courses on topics ranging from romance to TV scripts and novels. The castle is located near the Moray coast just an hour's drive from Aberdeen in a great spot for outdoor enthusiasts and whisky aficionados. It also has its own small lake, croquet lawn and woodland walks.

What's special?
In two words: the tutors. Mariana Robinson brings an innovative approach to her flower painting; Margaret Evans is a highly regarded pastels expert; Muriel Owen, John Christian, Keith Fenwick and Anne Lang are vastly experienced and popular tutors; and Colin Bradley specialises in an exciting new medium, pastel pencils. This year's international dimension is provided by Danish artist Annelise Pio Hansen.

Eating & sleeping
The accommodation varies from grand suites to intimate bedrooms. Pre-dinner drinks are served in the Georgian drawing room with an Adam fireplace, and candlelit meals (with complimentary wines) are prepared from the finest local ingredients.

Directions
From Aberdeen, take the A96 to Keith, then the road towards Banff. Castle of Park lies just to the south of Cornhill village. Course participants can be picked up at Aberdeen airport/station.

In the area
Dramatic scenery, famous distilleries and some of the best salmon rivers in the world are all within easy reach. Highlights include 17th-century fishing villages and harbours, the Moray coastline and the ruins of Findlater Castle.

Contact
Bill and Lois Breckon
Castle of Park
Cornhill
Aberdeenshire AB45 2AX
Tel: 01466 751111
Web: www.castleofpark.net
Email: info@castleofpark.net

Practical information
Duration: 3–6 days
Level: beginner,
intermediate & advanced
Residential
Group size: 6–15

Price range: £500+
Prices include: meals &
accommodation
Unsuitable for children
Pet-friendly

Courses available in:

Jan	Feb	Mar	Apr	May	Jun	Jul	Aug	Sep	Oct	Nov	Dec

EDINBURGH COLLEGE OF ART SUMMER SCHOOL, EDINBURGH

Edinburgh College of Art Summer School

The prestigious Edinburgh College of Art runs some excellent week-long courses in July and August. As well as portfolio building courses for students wanting to go to art college, they offer many other courses run by highly qualified tutors. Students are able to learn at their own pace and are given plenty of individual attention in small groups. Much of the teaching is done from the north-facing studios with their huge windows looking towards the castle, which is within walking distance. The courses are particularly sociable and provide an excellent way of meeting like-minded people.

Courses
Weeklong courses include Ceramics, Drawing, Fashion, Graphic Design, Painting, Jewellery Photography, Printmaking, Sculpture, Textiles, Millinery and Stained Glass.

What's special?
The 'Drawing with Colour and Mixed Media' course provides an excellent forum for developing your talents in many artistic fields. Highly experienced paper artist and painter Chrissie Heughan is an inspirational tutor and always full of encouragement.

Eating & sleeping
Students are eligible for discount rates at various hotels nearby, including the Novotel across the road. Further information is available through the Summer School office.

Directions
The college is on Lady Lawson Street in the city centre and is most easily accessed via Lauriston Place. Lothian Bus numbers 23, 27, 35 and 45 stop outside. Car parking nearby is available through the college.

In the area
The college lies on the edge of the Old Town, near the trendy Grassmarket area, famed for its eclectic shopping, restaurants and nightlife. There are numerous museums and art galleries in close proximity. The Summer School also coincides with many of the festivals which take place in August.

Contact	**Practical information**	Price range: £100–£400
Katy Taylor	Duration: 2–5 days	Prices include: most extra-
Edinburgh College of Art Summer School	Level: beginner,	curricular activities; some
Summer School Office	intermediate & advanced	materials
Centre for Continuing Studies	Non-residential	Unsuitable for children
Edinburgh College of Art	Group size: 3–20	Pets not welcome
Lauriston Place, Edinburgh		
Tel: 0131 221 6109		
Web: www.eca.ac.uk		
Email: continuing.studies@eca.ac.uk	Courses available in:	

Courses available in:

Jan	Feb	Mar	Apr	May	Jun	Jul	Aug	Sep	Oct	Nov	Dec
						Jul	Aug				

Bird-watching in the Highlands and on the Islands

'BBC Wildlife' and 'Bird Watching' magazines are frequent users of Heatherlea, which gives some indication of its standing in the wildlife world. Each itinerary is meticulously planned and involves visits to some of Europe's most stunning wild places. Expert guides will teach the techniques used by wildlife professionals to get the best views of Scotland's feathered species. The popular 'Spring in Scotland' holiday includes a trip to Mull and the Moray Coast to see animals including eagles, ptarmigans, capercaillies and otters. Week-long courses throughout the year offer visits to spectacular locations in the Highlands and islands, including Skye, Lewis and Orkney. Accommodation is in the nearby Mountview Hotel.

Contact
Kevin and Caryl Shaw
Heatherlea Birdwatching
Mountview Hotel
Nethybridge
Inverness-shire PH25 3EB
Tel: 01479 821248
Web: www.heatherlea.co.uk

Practical information
Duration: 7–10 days
Level: beginner,
intermediate & advanced
Residential

Group size: 3–15
Price range: £500+
Prices include: meals
Unsuitable for children
Pets not welcome

Courses available in:

Jan	Feb	Mar	Apr	May	Jun	Jul	Aug	Sep	Oct	Nov	Dec

Fly-fishing school in the Highlands

There can't be many wilder places to fish in Britain than the Assynt area of Sutherland. Camma Loch is a magnificent spot to escape the modern world and there are plenty of opportunities to try other outdoor activities. Courses cater for anglers from the absolute novice to the more experienced, and can be customised to suit individual requirements. A typical syllabus might include angling safety and wading, tackle and line selection, casting practice, basic knots, leader making and fly selection. The six-day Spring Salmon Fishing course on the Lower Oykel costs £525 for accommodation and meals at Oykel Bridge Hotel, and £290 for all tuition and fishing.

Contact
Stephen Smith
Highland School of Fly Fishing
Resallach House
Elphin
Assynt
Sutherland IV27 4HH
Tel: 01854 666 334
Web: www.flyfishing-scotland.net/home.html

Practical information
Duration: 2–7 days
Level: beginner,
intermediate & advanced
Residential & non-residential
Group size: 1–10

Price range: £300–£500+
Prices include: meals &
accommodation
Child-friendly
Pet-friendly

Courses available in:

Jan	Feb	Mar	Apr	May	Jun	Jul	Aug	Sep	Oct	Nov	Dec

The healing qualities of flower essences

A trip to the beautiful Isle of Gigha ('ghee-ah') is a special undertaking. It is just six miles in length, 1.5 miles wide and lies three miles off the coast of Kintyre, to which it is linked by frequent ferries. Once there, Achamore House makes the perfect place to explore the healing qualities of flower essences. The courses are quite long (four to seven days) to ensure ample reward for the effort required to get there, and look at the uses of so called 'vibrational essences'. Guests can enjoy the 50 acres of gardens created to showcase Sir James Horlick's rhododendrons, and plans are afoot to build an orchid greenhouse.

Contact
International Flower Essence Repertoire (IFER)
Achamore House
Isle of Gigha
Argyll & Bute PA41 7AD
Tel: 01583 505385
Web: www.healingflowers.com/gigha.htm

Practical information
Duration: 4–7 days
Level: beginner,
intermediate & advanced
Residential
Group size: 3–15

Price range: £200–£500+
Prices include: meals &
accommodation
Unsuitable for children
Pets not welcome

Courses available in:

Jan	Feb	Mar	Apr	May	Jun	Jul	Aug	Sep	Oct	Nov	Dec

Traditional Scots cooking courses in the Garden of Skye

Renowned cook and writer Claire Macdonald runs short cookery courses on the Isle of Skye. Alongside her husband, the High Chief of Clan Donald, Claire has established Kinloch Lodge as a much sought-after small hotel. Her courses and demonstrations extol the virtues of cooking food 'in season' using the best Skye produce. The three-day course combines cookery with time for relaxing in the beautiful surroundings: there are two mornings of demonstrations where Claire imparts her cookery knowledge and prepares seasonal meals. The nutrient-rich, warm waters of the Gulf Stream make this part of the island relatively mild – it is famous for its tropical plants and enchanting fishing villages.

Contact
Claire Macdonald
Lady Claire Macdonald's Food and Cooking
Kinloch Lodge
Sleat
Isle of Skye
Inverness-shire IV43 8QY
Tel: 01471 833333
Web: www.claire-macdonald.com

Practical information
Duration: 3 days
Level: beginner,
intermediate & advanced
Residential
Group size: 3–15

Price range: £300–£500
Prices include: meals &
accommodation
Unsuitable for children
Pets not welcome

Courses available in:

Jan	Feb	Mar	Apr	May	Jun	Jul	Aug	Sep	Oct	Nov	Dec

Whisky tasting and education in Fife

You'll learn everything you need to know about whisky making on this superb three-day course. Soak up casks of knowledge about grist recipes and barley mashing – and perhaps enjoy the odd dram along the way. There is even the chance for some hands-on experience of the distilling process. The recently built facilities of Ladybank Company of Distillers Club are your state-of-the-art venue and the price includes nine litres of your newly made cask-strength whisky and a bottled sample. Edinburgh is 40 miles away, and the Fife coastal path offers many scenic jaunts. Golf courses are two-a-penny in this part of the world.

Contact
Ladybank Whisky School
Ladybank Company of Distillers Club Ltd
21-23 Hill Street
Edinburgh
Midlothian EH2 3JP
Tel: 0845 450 1885
Web: www.whiskyschool.com

Practical information
Duration: 2–3 days
Level: beginner,
intermediate & advanced
Non-residential

Group size: 2–10
Price range: £300–£500
Prices include: meals
Unsuitable for children
Pets not welcome

Courses available in:

Jan	Feb	Mar	Apr	May	Jun	Jul	Aug	Sep	Oct	Nov	Dec

Art courses in the Northwest Highlands

Couldoran House is set in some spectacular Highland scenery: the Torridon hills are not far away and the Isle of Skye may be glimpsed from the estate's mountains. Art classes are led by experienced artists with numbers limited to ensure individualised tutoring. There are daily forays into the hills and around the lochs, often using an all-terrain vehicle. The Landscape Painting course concentrates on different media, the Watercolour Painting course on expressionism. In Walk and Sketch, you'll explore the scenery armed with various sketching materials, including waterproof paper. Accommodation is available in Couldoran itself and nearby B&Bs, and there's lots of fishing and photographic opportunities around the estate.

Contact
Gillian Pattinson
Loch Carron Estate
Couldoran House
Strathcarron
Ross-shire IV54 8UY
Tel: 01520 733227
Web: www.lochcarronestate.com

Practical information
Duration: 2–6 days
Level: beginner,
intermediate & advanced
Residential & non-residential
Group size: 2–10

Price range: £200–£500+
Prices include: meals &
accommodation
Child-friendly
Pets not welcome

Courses available in:

Jan	Feb	Mar	Apr	May	Jun	Jul	Aug	Sep	Oct	Nov	Dec

Scotland

Thai cookery classes in Edinburgh

Rujira Yuenboon Herd (or Ru, as she is known) is a self-styled 'Thai culinary artist'. Her charm, enthusiasm and hard work have created a highly respected cookery school which has gained many plaudits and been featured in magazines and on TV.

Courses

The school specialises in traditional Thai cuisine and combines intensive learning with a relaxed atmosphere; teaching is either one-to-one or for very small groups. Each day's tuition involves the preparation of between five and seven dishes, and the first session includes a talk on traditional Thai ingredients and their uses. Another course looks at fruit and vegetable carving: students learn how to create leaves and flowers, then make an intricate food sculpture. Tailored courses can be arranged for beginners or professionals and classes take place in mornings, afternoons and evenings to suit individual students. One-day courses are available.

What's special?

Ru has come up with a winning formula where each day is well structured, with little time wasted on long breaks. The school not only provides a platform for learning Thai cookery, it also ensures students learn techniques to a professional standard. No time is wasted with tidying and washing up and Ru is confident that the format is unique in Britain.

Eating & sleeping

Edinburgh is full of high-quality eating and sleeping establishments, from B&B to five-star hotels. Please contact the school for more information.

Directions

The school is located on the southern outskirts of Edinburgh only a few miles from the city centre. Waverley and Haymarket stations are approximately 3 miles from the school, which is on a main bus route served by Lothian Buses no. 7 and 37 (and other buses to Penicuik)

In the area

Liberton is a fascinating area with many attractions including the Royal Observatory, the Braid Hills golf course and the beautiful 15th-century Roslyn Chapel. The Braid Hills and Braidburn offer walking opportunities galore.

Contact

Rujira Yuenboon Herd (Ru)
Krua Thai Cookery School
19 Liberton Brae
Edinburgh
Midlothian EH16 6AQ
Tel: 0131 664 3036
Web: www.kruathai.co.uk
Email: kruathai@globalnet.co.uk

Practical information

Duration: 2–5 days
Level: beginner,
intermediate & advanced
Non-residential
Group size: 1–5

Price range: £150–£500+
Prices include: meals &
ingredients
Unsuitable for children
Pets not welcome

Courses available in:

Jan	Feb	Mar	Apr	May	Jun	Jul	Aug	Sep	Oct	Nov	Dec

Spiritual and artistic workshops in the Moray countryside

This well-established community in the Moray countryside east of Inverness runs a comprehensive programme of workshops covering spiritual, healing and artistic themes. The handsome Victorian mansion has excellent facilities and gardens and is a peaceful place for those seeking a break. As well as courses on reiki, music and dance there is a course for golfers seeking a more spiritual path to glory – 'Fairway to Heaven'. There are also longer courses on, for example, T'ai Chi, Puppet Making with Story, and Music and Dance. Hotspots in the surrounding area include beaches at Nairn and Findhorn Bay as well as countless nature reserves and mountain walks.

Contact
Newbold House
111 St Leonards Road
Forres
Moray IV36 2RE
Tel: 01309 672 659
Web: www.newboldhouse.org/artstudio.html

Practical information
Duration: 2–10 days
Level: beginner,
intermediate & advanced
Residential & non-residential
Group size: 2–15

Price range: £100–£300
Prices include: meals &
accommodation
Child-friendly
Pets not welcome

Courses available in:

Jan	Feb	Mar	Apr	May	Jun	Jul	Aug	Sep	Oct	Nov	Dec

Cooking with Nick Nairn in the Trossach foothills

The Nick Nairn Cook School, in the Trossach foothills, is highly regarded for its state-of-the-art facilities and fun atmosphere. You'll improve your culinary skills under the guidance of celebrity chef Nick Nairn and his Michelin-starred team while enjoying plenty of opportunities for socialising. Outdoorsy types will want to tramp the local hills, including Ben Lomond. You can mix and match classes – e.g. two days of Italian and then a day of French – since there are many to choose from. The subjects of the recreational classes range from formal dining to Italian, while the masterclass series covers just about everything. There's a variety of hotels and B&Bs in the area including Gleneagles.

Contact
Nick Nairn
Nick Nairn Cook School
Port of Menteith
Stirling
Stirlingshire FK8 3JZ
Tel: 01877 389900
Web: www.nicknairncookschool.com

Practical information
Duration: 2–10 days
Level: beginner,
intermediate & advanced
Residential & non-residential
Group size: 6–15

Price range: £150–£500+
Prices include: meals &
accommodation
Unsuitable for children
Pets not welcome

Courses available in:

Jan	Feb	Mar	Apr	May	Jun	Jul	Aug	Sep	Oct	Nov	Dec

Thinking visually with photographer Philip Dunn

Philip Dunn has over 40 years' experience as a professional photographer, and the courses he runs in south-west Scotland are fun and highly effective. They are suitable both for photographers looking to forge a career and for those just pursuing a hobby. Their principal aim is to teach participants how to think visually; the subject matter varies according to students' needs, from the surrounding landscapes to indoor studies of local craftsmen, and inspiration comes from the Galloway countryside and Solway coast. Students can continue their studies at home by accessing the course notes on the Photoactive website. There is a choice of accommodation in the fishing village of Kirkcudbright.

Contact
Philip Dunn
Treesbank
Tongland Road
Kirkcudbright
Dumfries DG6 4UU
Tel: 01557 331343
Web: www.photoactive.co.uk/index.htm

Practical information
Duration: 2–5 days
Level: beginner,
intermediate & advanced
Residential

& non-residential
Group size: 1–5
Price range: £100–£500+
Child-friendly
Pet-friendly

Courses available in:

Jan	Feb	Mar	Apr	May	Jun	Jul	Aug	Sep	Oct	Nov	Dec

Scotland

217

Landscape photography in Scotland's most rugged mountains

Photograph Scotland is run by John McKinlay, one of Scotland's leading professional landscape photographers. He allows a maximum of five people on each course so everyone gets lots of individual attention. For a taster you should try the two-day introductory landscape photography course based at Glenbruach Country House in the magnificent Trossachs. The other courses happen in Scotland's most rugged mountains, in Glencoe, Skye, Wester Ross, the Isle of Barra and the Ardnamurchan peninsula, which is the most westerly point on the British mainland, and participants stay in carefully chosen hotels. Scenery aside, there are many other places of interest worth visiting at each location.

Contact	Practical information	Price range: £150–£500+
John McKinlay	Duration: 2–6 days	Prices include: meals &
Photograph Scotland	Level: beginner,	accommodation
Trossachs Road	intermediate & advanced	Child-friendly
Aberfoyle	Residential & non-residential	Pets not welcome
Trossachs FK8 3SW	Group size: 1–5	
Tel: 01877 382613	Courses available in:	
Web: www.photographscotland.com		

Jan	Feb	Mar	Apr	**May**	Jun	Jul	Aug	**Sep**	**Oct**	Nov	Dec

Creative workshops on the Trotternish Peninsula

Quiraing Lodge is a large Victorian house that is the base for a well-established and varied programme of courses. It lies in an acre of garden overlooking Staffin Bay, on Skye's spectacular Trotternish peninsula, an area perfect for outdoor enthusiasts and photographers. The photography course at Quiraing concentrates on a number of themes, from natural history to digital and black-and-white. And there is a large darkroom and library available. Meals use the best local produce and vegetarians are welcome. All tutors are enthusiastic experts in their fields, and other courses include Bookbinding, Coptic Binding, Raku Ceramics, Land Art and Sand Drawing, Environmental Dance and Yoga Retreat.

Contact	Practical information	Price range: £100–£500+
Sam Gardener	Duration: 2–9 days	Prices include: meals &
Quiraing Lodge	Level: beginner,	accommodation
Staffin	intermediate & advanced	Child-friendly
Isle of Skye	Residential & non-residential	Pet-friendly
Inverness-shire IV51 9JS	Group size: 2–15	
Tel: 01470 562330		
Web: www.portmanteau.co.uk/quiraing	Courses available in:	

Jan	Feb	Mar	Apr	May	Jun	Jul	Aug	Sep	Oct	Nov	Dec

Cooking and decoupage at Ruthven House

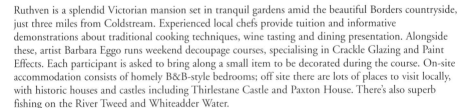

Ruthven is a splendid Victorian mansion set in tranquil gardens amid the beautiful Borders countryside, just three miles from Coldstream. Experienced local chefs provide tuition and informative demonstrations about traditional cooking techniques, wine tasting and dining presentation. Alongside these, artist Barbara Eggo runs weekend decoupage courses, specialising in Crackle Glazing and Paint Effects. Each participant is asked to bring along a small item to be decorated during the course. On-site accommodation consists of homely B&B-style bedrooms; off site there are lots of places to visit locally, with historic houses and castles including Thirlestane Castle and Paxton House. There's also superb fishing on the River Tweed and Whiteadder Water.

Contact	Practical information	Price range: £300–£400
Francis Gradidge	Duration: 3 days	Prices include: meals &
Ruthven House	Level: beginner,	accommodation
Coldstream	intermediate & advanced	Unsuitable for children
Berwickshire TD12 4JU	Residential	Pets not welcome
Tel: 0845 644 8304	Group size: 3–10	
Web: www.bordersovernight.co.uk	Courses available in:	

Jan	Feb	Mar	Apr	**May**	Jun	Jul	**Aug**	Sep	Oct	Nov	Dec

Retreat set in gardens at the foot of Ben Ghobhlach

If you wish to escape the stresses of modern life and learn new skills, Shanti Griha in remote Wester Ross ticks all the boxes. This professionally run retreat is set in enchanting gardens at the foot of Ben Ghobhlach, 300 yards from the seashore. The surrounding wilderness provides outdoor enthusiasts with plenty to see and do. The croft house has comfortable accommodation, or there is a small cabin for absolute peace and jaw-dropping views. Organic food and drink is locally sourced: a spring provides the water. The varied programme includes meditation, wind power, Thai massage, Discover Your Voice (singing lessons), yoga and Ayurvedic diet, and dry stone dyking.

Contact
Brian and Kathrin Cooper
Shanti Griha Retreat Centre
Scoraig
Dundonnell
Ross-shire IV23 2RE
Tel: 01854 633260
Web: www.shantigriha.com

Practical information
Duration: 5–10 days
Level: beginner,
intermediate & advanced
Residential

Courses available in:

Group size: 3–10
Price range: £300–£500+
Prices include: meals &
accommodation
Unsuitable for children
Pets not welcome

Jan	Feb	Mar	Apr	May	Jun	Jul	Aug	Sep	Oct	Nov	Dec

Nature tours of Britain's northernmost points

Shetland Wildlife Holidays aim to give once-in-a-lifetime adventures to people who wish to avoid touristy hotspots and get close to Britain's most northerly habitats. Trips include a wildlife photography course and adventures in Fair Isle. You might watch killer whales, photograph phalaropes feeding at your toes and visit one of the world's most impressive 'seabird cities'. Some fitness is required, although the excursions are not strenuous, and the small group size means that there's lots of personal attention from the experts. Transport within Shetland (including boat trips) and guide fees are included. Guests can stay in guesthouses or hotels at Sumburgh and Baltasound.

Contact
Hugh Harrop
Shetland Wildlife Tours
Longhill Maywick
Shetland ZE2 9JF
Tel: 01950 422483
Web: www.shetlandwildlife.co.uk

Practical information
Duration: 5–10 days
Level: beginner,
intermediate & advanced
Residential
Group size: 3–15

Courses available in:

Price range: £300–£500+
Prices include: meals,
accommodation & transport
in Shetland
Unsuitable for children
Pets not welcome

Jan	Feb	Mar	Apr	May	Jun	Jul	Aug	Sep	Oct	Nov	Dec

Photography in dramatic Highlands surroundings

The stunning landscapes of Skye and various Highland locations supply the inspiration on these popular photography holidays. The 'Landscape Course' takes place on Skye and topics covered include composition, lighting, exposure, filters and depth of field. Alternatively there is a 'holiday programme' which offers more freedom for the experienced photographer. Course organiser Steve Terry has over 20 years' experience as a photographer and photography teacher. His waterside B&B and self-catering apartment offer a choice of accommodation on the Skye-based courses. When not behind the camera, climbers and walkers should head to the Cuillin mountains which are ten miles from the Skye in Focus HQ. One-on-one workshops also available.

Contact
Steve and Gill Terry
Skye in Focus
The Skye Picture House
Ard Dorch, Broadford
Isle of Skye
Inverness-shire IV49 9AJ
Tel: 01471 822264
Web: www.skyeinfocus.co.uk

Practical information
Duration: 7–10 days
Level: intermediate &
advanced
Residential & non-residential
Group size: 1–10

Courses available in:

Price range: £500+
Prices include: meals &
accommodation
Unsuitable for children
Pets not welcome

Jan	Feb	Mar	Apr	May	Jun	Jul	Aug	Sep	Oct	Nov	Dec

Scotland

SABHAL MÒR OSTAIG, SLEAT

Gaelic language, music and song on Skye

There can be no more beautiful spot in Scotland in which to master the Gaelic language or learn a traditional musical instrument. Sabhal Mòr Ostaig lies in Sleat, in the southern part of the Isle of Skye, its climate warmed by the Gulf Stream, which makes it possible to grow tropical plants. The College has superb facilities and various types of accommodation. It has been running short courses for over 30 years now, and is renowned for its vibrancy: ceilidhs and other organised activities make it a fun and sociable place to stay.

Courses
As well as Gaelic language for all levels, they run courses in musical instruments such as the fiddle, Scottish pipes, cello and accordion. They also offer courses in step-dance, Gaelic song and painting.

What's special?
The Fiddle Week has been running since 1987 and world-renowned fiddler Alasdair Fraser focuses on bringing out players' creative sides. Fèis an Eilein, an annual 10-day music and cultural festival hosted by the College every July, is also an excellent time to attend a course. Social events include informal ceilidhs and workshops, and a College ceilidh takes place each Thursday, where participants get the chance to perform.

Eating & sleeping
All rooms have en-suite facilities. For £100 per night there is a penthouse suite in the tower. Wholesome lunches and dinners are served in the dining room. Alternatively, the College has a list of local B&Bs and self-catering properties.

Directions
By ferry: A851 toward Broadford. By bridge: A87 toward Broadford, then toward Armadale on A851. Bus: from Inverness and Glasgow to Broadford. Rail: to Kyle and Mallaig.

In the area
Outdoor activities range from gentle nature trails to alpine standard mountaineering. There are boat trips to view seals and dolphins, horse-riding, and nearby Armadale Castle is worth visiting for its gardens.

Contact
Elsie Maclean
Sabhal Mòr Ostaig
Sleat
Isle of Skye
Tel: 01471 888240
Web: www.smo.uhi.ac.uk/smo/cg
Email: cg@smo.uhi.ac.uk

Practical information
Duration: 2–5 days
Level: beginner,
intermediate & advanced
Residential & non-residential
Group size: 3–20

Courses available in:

Jan	Feb	Mar	Apr	May	Jun	Jul	Aug	Sep	Oct	Nov	Dec
	Feb	Mar	Apr	May	Jun	Jul	Aug	Sep	Oct	Nov	

Price range: £100–£300
Prices include:
accommodation
Child-friendly
Pets not welcome

Wildlife-watching in Scotland's untamed wilderness

Speyside Wildlife claims that 'wildlife-watching is for everyone, not just for dedicated enthusiasts' and it is this ethos of accessibility that makes it popular with pros and public alike: Bill Oddie is a regular. The tours cover vast areas of Scotland's largely untouched wilderness from Speyside up to Shetland. Meals use the finest Highland produce, and all accommodation, transport and guiding is likewise arranged. If you choose the Speyside week you'll stay in a beautifully converted barn at Ballintean; while at Rothiemurchus, in the Cairngorms National Park, baiting at the wildlife-watching cabin attracts pine martens and badgers

Contact
Sally Dowden
Speyside Wildlife Holidays
Garden Office
Inverdruie House
Inverdruie, Aviemore
Inverness-shire PH22 1QH
Tel: 01479 812498
Web: www.speysidewildlife.co.uk

Practical information
Duration: 2-10 days
Level: beginner,
intermediate & advanced
Residential
Group size: 1-15

Courses available in:

Jan	Feb	Mar	Apr	May	Jun	Jul	Aug	Sep	Oct	Nov	Dec

Price range: £500+
Prices include: meals &
accommodation
Unsuitable for children
Pets not welcome

Pottery and art with Topham Vickers

Topham Vickers is an innovative artist who works with ceramics and mixed media. His interest in ancient Middle Eastern and African bush ceramics adds a refreshing twist to the usual style of pottery lesson. Throughout the year he runs courses from his studio in the village of Minnigaff, teaching coil and slab-building techniques (no throwing) inspired by Middle Eastern and African ceremonial and functional ceramic making. Decent local accommodation is available in the area, from four-star hotels and B&Bs to hostels. There are many castles worth visiting and stacks of historical references to Robert the Bruce.

Contact
Topham Vickers
Mill Cottage
Millcroft Road
Minnigaff
Newton Stewart
Galloway DG8 6PJ
Tel: 01671 403399
Web: www.tophamvickers.co.uk

Practical information
Duration: 2-10 days
Level: beginner,
intermediate & advanced
Non-residential

Courses available in:

Jan	Feb	Mar	Apr	May	Jun	Jul	Aug	Sep	Oct	Nov	Dec

Group size: 1-5
Price range: £150-£500+
Child-friendly
Pet-friendly

Yoga courses in one of Europe's largest purpose-built studios

Union Yoga in central Edinburgh specialises in the teaching of Ashtanga Vinyasa yoga and has a range of gentle but challenging courses to suit all abilities. The main studio has 2000 square feet of bamboo-floored space, making it one of the largest purpose-built yoga studios in Europe. The team has been put together by Brian Cooper, who has been practising yoga for 35 years and is an advanced Ashtanga practitioner. There are week-long beginners' courses each month which gently guide students through the foundations of the sequence. All postures are broken down and explained. There are many other workshops and events each week, and personalised courses can be arranged.

Contact
Brian Cooper
Union Yoga Centre
25 Rodney Street
Edinburgh
Midlothian EH7 4EL
Tel: 0131 5583334
Web: www.unionyoga.co.uk

Practical information
Duration: 2-10 days
Level: beginner,
intermediate & advanced
Non-residential

Courses available in:

Jan	Feb	Mar	Apr	May	Jun	Jul	Aug	Sep	Oct	Nov	Dec

Group size: 1-20
Price range: £50-£500+
Unsuitable for children
Pets not welcome

Scotland

Open studies summer courses at University of Edinburgh

The University of Edinburgh's Open Studies Summer School programme is mightily impressive in terms of the quality and range of subjects. Edinburgh is a wonderful city to visit in July and August, what with the Edinburgh Tattoo and the Edinburgh Festival, so why not combine tourism with a spot of learning? You'll be dazzled by the choice: Archaeology, Art & Architecture, Computing, Creative Writing, Film & Media Studies, History, Languages & Cultures, Literature, Music & Dance, Personal Development & Health, Philosophy & Religion, Science & Nature and Society & Politics. The Office of Lifelong Learning (OLL) advises participants on the accommodation available, and the university campus has basic lodgings if needed.

Contact
John Woodhead
University of Edinburgh
Office of Lifelong Learning (OLL)
11 Buccleuch Place
Edinburgh, Midlothian EH8 9LW
Tel: 0131 6504400
Web: www.lifelong.ed.ac.uk

Practical information
Duration: 5–10 days
Level: beginner,
intermediate & advanced
Non-residential

Courses available in:

Jan	Feb	Mar	Apr	May	Jun	Jul	Aug	Sep	Oct	Nov	Dec

Group size: 11–20
Price range: £100–£200
Unsuitable for children
Pets not welcome

Tiles and textiles in an idyllic fishing village

The Wild Tiles centre in the idyllic Sutherland fishing village of Helmsdale provides teaching in a range of arts and crafts. Jan Kilpatrick, who runs the courses, is a practising artist specialising in mosaic and textile work. Weekend courses introduce making mosaics for an outdoor space, tapestry work using paper, or batik and tie-dyeing. The emphasis is on using eclectic objects and vivid colours. There are five-day summer courses covering similar themes: Mad about Mosaic and Textile Illuminations. Accommodation is available in-house in the cheerily decorated Skylight House. Helmsdale provides a wealth of inspiring scenes, and apart from walking-oriented attractions, the area has salmon fishing and golf courses.

Contact
Jan Kilpatrick
Wild Tiles
Skylight House
Helmsdale
Sutherland KW8 6JA
Tel: 01431 821 672
Web: www.wildtiles.co.uk

Practical information
Duration: 2–5 days
Level: beginner,
intermediate & advanced
Residential

Courses available in:

Jan	Feb	Mar	Apr	May	Jun	Jul	Aug	Sep	Oct	Nov	Dec

& non-residential
Group size: 2–5
Price range: £50–£200
Child-friendly
Pet-friendly

Photography holidays and workshops in Cairngorms National Park

Wildshots specialises in photographic adventure holidays and workshops in the Scottish Highlands. Visitors stay in a house-party environment at the converted steading (large stables) at the northern end of Glenfeshie in the foothills of the Cairngorms. The surrounding countryside contains pristine pine and birch woodland, and the River Feshie is close by. Photographers can use the many temporary and permanent hides in the extensive grounds and alongside the lochan: you'll snap close-up photos of great spotted woodpeckers, red squirrels, crested tits, roe deer and ospreys. There are around five carefully researched holiday courses per year: Summer Scotland, Wild Scotland (Summer), Autumn Gold, Wildlife Photography and Creative Photography Workshop.

Contact
Pete and Amanda Cairns
Wildshots
Ballintean, Glenfeshie
Kingussie
Inverness-shire PH21 1NX
Tel: 01540 651352
Web: www.wildshots.co.uk

Practical information
Duration: 2–6 days
Level: beginner,
intermediate & advanced
Residential
Group size: 6–15

Courses available in:

Jan	Feb	Mar	Apr	May	Jun	Jul	Aug	Sep	Oct	Nov	Dec

Price range: £200–£500+
Prices include: meals &
accommodation
Unsuitable for children
Pets not welcome

Trout fishing tuition in a private loch

Fishing purists will tell you that fly-fishing is the most challenging fishing technique and Speyside is one of the most sought-after places to enjoy its intricacies. Willowbank runs fly-fishing courses for all abilities on two serene private lochs which have wild brown trout as well as stocked rainbow and brook trout. Loch McLeod lies in remote moor land while Loch Dallas is less wild and is visited by ospreys. Willowbank can also arrange salmon fishing tuition on the River Spey plus complete packages to fish the Castle Grant beat. Grantown-on-Spey has a host of nearby natural attractions including the Cairngorms National Park. Excellent accommodation is available in Willowbank Guest House.

Contact
Anne and Chris Hirst
Willowbank
High Street
Grantown-on-Spey
Inverness-shire PH26 3EN
Tel: 01479 872089
Web: www.willowbankguesthouse.co.uk

Practical information
Duration: 2–10 days
Level: beginner,
intermediate & advanced
Residential & non-residential
Group size: 2–5

Price range: under
£50–£400
Child-friendly
Pets not welcome

Courses available in:

Jan	Feb	Mar	Apr	May	Jun	Jul	Aug	Sep	Oct	Nov	Dec

Expert painting courses in stunning surroundings

Wood of Shaws is a country estate by the River Deveron in rural Aberdeenshire, which has charmed painters and visitors for over 10 years. The aim of their art courses is to improve observation, tonal skills and painting abilities: in short, you get expert advice in stunning surroundings. The courses take place from May to early October, with a couple on the West Coast and on Skye for those seeking the most dramatic landscapes. Hosts Mary and Michael Kitchen provide superb food and plenty of suggestions for days out. There are countless castles, fishing villages and rugged landscapes, and Michael has an in-depth knowledge of where to fish.

Contact
Michael and Mary Kitchen
Wood of Shaws Studio & Gallery
Alvah Banff
Banff
Banffshire AB45 3UL
Tel: 01261 821223
Web: www.woodofshaws.co.uk

Practical information
Duration: 2–6 days
Level: beginner,
intermediate & advanced
Residential & non-residential
Group size: 1–10

Price range: £150–£500
Prices include: meals &
accommodation
Unsuitable for children
Pets not welcome

Courses available in:

Jan	Feb	Mar	Apr	May	Jun	Jul	Aug	Sep	Oct	Nov	Dec
				May	Jun	Jul	Aug	Sep	Oct		

Scotland

FOUR WINDS INSPIRATION CENTRE, EDINBURGH

Crafts and environmental pursuits in Edinburgh

Four Winds Inspiration Centre is an environmental education and craft-based charity set in attractive Edinburgh surroundings. The centre runs a wide range of craft classes for participants who want to try out some of the traditional and innovative activities on offer, plus a popular programme of courses exploring the uses of native plants and herbal remedies. The centre is awash with fascinating things to see and cultural initiatives, and produces custom-designed carved furniture, sculptures and playground items.

Courses
Craft courses offered here include Wood and Stone Carving, Willow Plant Frames & Garden Sculptures, Basket Weaving, Mosaic, Greenwood Working, Rustic Furniture, Raku Ceramic Firing, Batik and Hand-Building Ceramics. Herbal classes include Making Tinctures, Herb Drying, Making Creams & Ointments and Ladies' Herbal. Whilst the vast majority of courses are one-day, occasional weekend courses are offered and each spring Four Winds holds a week-long course relating to small, wind turbine design, construction and operation.

What's special?
Amongst their fantastic range of craft classes is the ever-popular mosaic class taken by Jan Kilpatrick: all manner of fragmented materials including broken plates, tiles and glass are transformed into colourful decorative art pieces for the home and garden. Alternatively, Raku ceramic firing shows pupils a fascinating and highly effective way of firing ceramics using copper glazes.

Eating & sleeping
There is a wide selection of hotels and bed & breakfast establishments in the area, with price ranges to suit all budgets. Stockbridge is a popular area nearby with many cafés and restaurants. Ask for recommendations.

Directions
Plenty of local buses serve the Inverleith Park area of Edinburgh, or you can take a taxi from the station or airport.

In the area
The Royal Botanical Gardens are nearby and worth exploring, the architecturally renowned New Town has smart squares and upmarket shopping, while the Old Town has cobbled streets and alleys brimming with history.

Contact
Four Winds Inspiration Centre
The Pavilion
Inverleith Park Arboretum Place
Edinburgh
Midlothian EH3 5NY
Tel: 0131 332 2229
Web: www.four-winds.org.uk
Email: info@four-winds.org.uk

Practical information
1–6 days
Level: beginner,
intermediate & advanced
Non-residential

Group size: 6–15
Price range: £40–£300
Child-friendly
Pet-friendly

Courses available in:

Jan	Feb	Mar	Apr	May	Jun	Jul	Aug	Sep	Oct	Nov	Dec

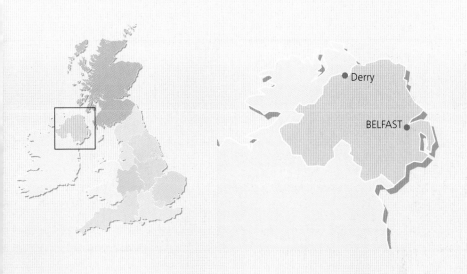

Northern Ireland

Less commonly visited by tourists from England, Scotland and Wales than Eire to the south, Northern Ireland offers natural delights such as Giants Causeway, the Sperrin Mountains and Co. Fermanagh's magnificent Lough Erne with its great fishing. There are beautiful coastal villages near Portrush and three thriving cities – Belfast, Londonderry and Armagh. Belfast, in particular, is a vibrant, welcoming place that is starting to attract increasing numbers of visitors.

Fly-fishing school in a stately country mansion

Colebrook Park is the 1820 home of Viscount and Viscountess Brookeborough who have renovated it to combine a traditional atmosphere with modern comforts. Accommodation is provided in luxurious en-suite rooms, but this is very much a 'house for paying guests', not a hotel. There are lots of activities on offer: fly-fishing, clay-pigeon shooting, archery, stalking, golf, canoeing, mountain biking and others. The fly-fishing courses, taught by a qualified instructor, are particularly special. The nearby rivers and hill loughs contain many trout and pike, and you spend the weekend learning to cast, first on grass, then river and lake, before starting to fish properly. Fly-tying tuition also available.

Contact
Viscount Brookeborough
Colebrooke Park Fly Fishing School
Colebrooke Park Estate
Brookeborough
Co. Fermanagh BT94 4DW
Tel: 028 8953 1402
Web: www.colebrooke.info

Practical information
Duration: 3 days
Level: beginner,
intermediate & advanced
Residential & non-residential
Group size: 3–10

Price range: £300–£400
Prices include: meals &
accommodation
Unsuitable for children
Pets not welcome

Courses available in:

Jan	Feb	Mar	Apr	May	Jun	Jul	Aug	Sep	Oct	Nov	Dec
			Apr	May	Jun	Jul	Aug	Sep			

Painting workshops with Dermot Cavanagh

Dermot Cavanagh was teaching painting classes at a technical college in Belfast in the early 1990s before starting weekend watercolour workshops from his own home. As these workshops grew in popularity, he set up a studio at the Argory National Trust Property near Moy in Co. Tyrone. In 1997 he first presented the Awash with Colour series on BBC Northern Ireland and the show has continued to develop since then. His courses cover materials, colour mixing, perspective and washes. Attractions in the area include walking in the scenic Sperrin Mountains and archaeological sites such as the Beachmore Stone Circles. Accommodation can be organised in nearby guest houses.

Contact
Dermot Cavanagh
Rhoneview Studio
30 Seyloran Lane
Moy
Co. Tyrone BT71 7EH
Tel: 028 8778 4166
Web: www.dermotcavanagh.com

Practical information
Duration: 2–3 days
Level: beginner,
intermediate & advanced
Non-residential
Group size: 6–20

Price range: £150–£300
Prices include: Lunch is
provided at the 2-day
workshops
Unsuitable for children
Pets not welcome

Courses available in:

Jan	Feb	Mar	Apr	May	Jun	Jul	Aug	Sep	Oct	Nov	Dec
Jan	Feb	Mar	Apr	May	Jun	Jul	Aug	Sep	Oct	Nov	Dec

Painting courses near the Giant's Causeway

Mary and Joe McFadden are professional artists who offer individually tailored painting courses from their Antrim B&B. Mary is a recent AA Landlady of the Year and the B&B is a delight, scenically located at the bottom of Glendun, one of the historic Glens of Antrim, and offering varied breakfasts all made from organic produce. Courses are organised on an adhoc basis, with participants joined into small groups as appropriate. You can study for as many days as you wish and combine tuition with 'days off' exploring. You can also stay in the Drumkeerin Camping Barn, which has accommodation for 16. Local attractions include the Giant's Causeway and many castles and forts.

Contact
Mary and Joe McFadden
Drumkeerin
201a Torr Road
Cushendun
Co. Antrim BT44 0PU
Tel: 028 2176 1554
Web: www.drumkeerinbedandbreakfast.co.uk

Practical information
Duration: 2–7 days
Level: beginner,
intermediate & advanced
Residential
Group size: 1–5

Price range: £50–£400
Prices include: breakfast &
accommodation
Child-friendly
Pets not welcome

Courses available in:

Jan	Feb	Mar	Apr	May	Jun	Jul	Aug	Sep	Oct	Nov	Dec
Jan	Feb	Mar	Apr	May	Jun	Jul	Aug	Sep	Oct	Nov	Dec

BELLE ISLE SCHOOL
OF COOKERY, ENNISKILLEN

Cookery courses at a renowned countryside school

This state-of-the-art cookery school is located in the grounds of Belle Isle Castle on Upper Lough Erne, an area renowned for its unspoilt countryside. The school is run by Monaghan chef Liz Moore whose approach mixes modern techniques with traditional Irish recipes. Families and children are welcome on special weekend courses, and tennis, boating, fishing, shooting and golf are available.

Courses

Belle Isle provides many different types of courses throughout the year, from weekend to week-long, as well as specialist courses on wine. And for aspiring chefs, there's an intensive, month-long course in September. Other courses - all of them seasonal - include Dinner Party Special, Game Cooking, Winter Wonders, Soups & Stews and Christmas Special.

What's special?

Liz Moore is both highly talented and very down to earth, so you get practical instruction as well as plenty of inspiration. And the situation is as spectacular as the teaching: Belle Isle is on Lough Erne and the specially built cookery school overlooks the lake and the mountains.

Eating & sleeping

All residential course prices include accommodation in either a courtyard apartment or estate cottage. For a supplement, you can stay in Belle Isle Castle during the castle cooking weekends. Bookings are made through the main school.

Directions

Enniskillen 8 miles, Dublin 105 miles, Belfast 72 miles, Donegal 47 miles - excellent directions on website. In Lisbellaw village, turn left at the Wild Duck Inn. Continue straight on till you reach a T-junction. Turn left; pass church and small lake on the left. 200 yards past lake, turn right at the house (on the right, with a red telephone kiosk outside) to Belle Isle.

In the area

The splendid Castle Coole is close by, as are Florence Court, Marble Arch Caves, Belleek Pottery, Crom Estate, Enniskillen Castle and the Giants Causeway.

Contact
Andrea Law
Belle Isle School of Cookery
Lisbellaw
Enniskillen
Co. Fermanagh
Tel: 028 6638 7231
Web: www.irish-cookery-school.com
Email: info@irishcookeryschool.com

Practical information
Duration: 2–7 days
Level: beginner,
intermediate & advanced
Residential
Group size: 3–10

Price range: £200–£500+
Prices include: meals &
accommodation
Child-friendly
Pet-friendly

Courses available in:

Jan	Feb	Mar	Apr	May	Jun	Jul	Aug	Sep	Oct	Nov	Dec

Northern
Ireland

Handloom weaving workshops

Karen Hay-Edie is a handloom weaver whose tweeds, fabrics and rugs are inspired by the landscape around her – Carlingford Lough, the Mourne Mountains and the Cooley Mountains. She has spent many years in this family business making hand-woven place mats, cushion covers, rugs, wall-hangings and throws. The workshop has branched out into five-day handloom weaving courses, tutored by Karen and Leonara Dand, also a master weaver. No previous experience is necessary, and participants (each with their own loom) may choose from a wide range of colours and yarns. There are six looms with warps set up for a range of items such as rugs, hangings, cushions, mats etc.

Contact
Karen Hay-Edie
Mourne Textiles
86 Old Killowen Road
Newry
Co. Down BT34 3AE
Tel: 028 4173 8373
Web: www.adcrafts.info/mournetextiles.htm

Practical information
Duration: 5 days
Level: beginner,
intermediate & advanced
Non-residential
Group size: 2–10

Price range: £200–£300
Prices include: lunch & all
materials
Child-friendly
Pet-friendly

Courses available in:

Jan	Feb	Mar	Apr	May	Jun	Jul	Aug	Sep	Oct	Nov	Dec

Ireland

With a literary tradition from the lap of the gods, vibrant cities and some spectacular landscapes, Ireland is a wonderful place to do a course – and there are many cheap flights from the UK. The beautiful Burren plateau in Co. Clare is a popular area for landscape-oriented courses; Dublin makes a superb destination for a short break; and Cork is the European Capital of Culture for 2005. Some courses have a particularly strong Irish flavour and will enfold participants in the country's literary, musical and cultural traditions.

Exploring rambles and ruins on Achill Island

The Achill Archaeological Field School runs the Deserted Village Project on Achill Island, off the West coast of Ireland. The Project studies the post-medieval settlement at Slievemore and is based in the village of Dooagh ten kilometres from Achill Sound. Courses cover various aspects of archaeology: Introduction to Archaeology is aimed at amateurs and would-be students, and covers excavation methodology, surveying, planning and archaeological drawing; Ceramics in Archaeology covers the identification and classification of ceramics; and there is a three-day Archaeology Taster course for beginners. Self-catering accommodation is provided in dormitories and holiday houses. Possible activities include riding, surfing and scuba diving.

Contact
Maura Ryan
Achill Archaeological Field School
Achill Folklife Centre
Dooagh
Achill Island
Co. Mayo
Tel: 098 43564
Web: www.achill-fieldschool.com

Practical information
Duration: 3–5 days
Level: beginner &
intermediate
Residential
Group size: 1–25+

Price range: €200–€500+
Prices include:
accommodation
Unsuitable for children
Pets not welcome

Courses available in:

Jan	Feb	Mar	Apr	May	Jun	Jul	Aug	Sep	Oct	Nov	Dec
		Mar	Apr	May	Jun	Jul	Aug	Sep			

Crafts in a secluded country house

Run by the Irish Countrywomen's Association, An Grianán is a country house in a secluded location close to the River Boyne estuary. You can enjoy a huge range of courses here, from art and crafts to cookery, alternative therapies and bridge. Courses to sample include Aromatherapy, Beading & Embroidery, Painting on Plates/Fabric and Practical Gardening. Accommodation is available in single or shared rooms inside the house or in luxurious bungalows in the grounds. There are gardens and walks in the grounds, and Termonfechin village is five miles to the north. Other activities include the beach, golf, fishing, horse riding, historical sites and shopping in Drogheda.

Contact
Ann Flanagan
An Grianán
Termonfechin
Co. Louth
Tel: 041 9822119
Web: www.an-grianan.ie

Practical information
Duration: 3–5 days
Level: beginner &
intermediate
Residential & non-residential
Group size: 6–15

Price range: €100–€300
Prices include: meals &
accommodation
Child-friendly
Pets not welcome

Courses available in:

Jan	Feb	Mar	Apr	May	Jun	Jul	Aug	Sep	Oct	Nov	Dec
Jan	Feb	Mar	Apr	May	Jun	Jul	Aug	Sep	Oct	Nov	Dec

Fishing in Lough Corrib and the River Cong

The Ashford Castle estate, which dates back to 1228, was completely renovated in 1970, and is now regarded as one of the top hotels in Ireland. Accommodation is luxurious and the restaurant is run by Michelin-starred chef Stefan Matz. The hotel runs a fly-fishing school in conjunction with the Orvis Fly-Fishing Company, and courses can be several days long, covering all aspects of fly-fishing from casting to tying knots. Salmon and brown trout fishing in nearby Lough Corrib is regarded as some of the best in Europe. Other activities include golf, falconry, riding, clay shooting, tennis, archery, pony and trap tours, and health and beauty treatments.

Contact
Frank Costello
Ashford Castle
Cong
Co. Mayo
Tel: 094 9546003
Web: www.ashford.ie

Practical information
Duration: 3 days
Level: beginner &
intermediate
Residential & non-residential
Group size: 3–10

Price range: €500+
Prices include: lunch
Child-friendly
Pets not welcome

Courses available in:

Jan	Feb	Mar	Apr	May	Jun	Jul	Aug	Sep	Oct	Nov	Dec
Jan	Feb	Mar	Apr	May	Jun	Jul	Aug	Sep	Oct		

Cookery and entertaining at renowned seaside school

The Allen family moved into Ballymaloe House in 1948 and went on to establish the now famous hotel and restaurant. They opened the Cookery School in 1983 where they run courses in many types of cookery and entertaining. These are taught by Darina Allen and other restaurant chefs, some of whom trained in London with the likes of Raymond Blanc, while others trained in Thailand. Accommodation is available in well-equipped self-catering cottages in converted 18th-century farm buildings and the school's garden setting is no less splendid than the food. Ballymaloe's course inventory includes an Intensive Introductory Wine Course, Brilliant Breads, Thai, Vietnamese and Malaysian Flavours, and Modern Entertaining.

Contact
Tim & Darina Allen
Ballymaloe Cookery School
Ballymaloe House
Shanagarry, Midleton
Co. Cork
Tel: 021 4646785
Web: www.cookingisfun.ie

Practical information
Duration: 2–5 days
Level: beginner
Residential & non-residential
Group size: 21–25+

Price range: €300–€500+
Prices include: lunch only
Child-friendly
Pets not welcome

Courses available in:

Jan	Feb	Mar	Apr	May	Jun	Jul	Aug	Sep	Oct	Nov	Dec

Simple traditional cookery at Berry Lodge

Dating from 1775, Berry Lodge is a modernised family home with Victorian-style bedrooms, which hosts a variety of cookery courses. The programme includes introductory weekends and longer speciality courses, all with an emphasis on simple, traditional recipes. Courses to sample include Basic Techniques of Cookery (three days); Men in the Kitchen (two days); and A Taste of Irish Cookery, Entertaining with Style or Harvest Vegetarian - these last three provide one day of cookery and two nights' accommodation. Berry Lodge is located close to the Cliffs of Moher, the Burren and the famous golf links at Lahinch and Doobeg, and the area is excellent for walking and fishing.

Contact
Rita Meade
Berry Lodge Cookery School
Annagh
Miltown Malbay
Co. Clare
Tel: 065 708 7022
Web: www.berrylodge.westclare.net

Practical information
Duration: 2–3 days
Level: beginner &
intermediate
Residential & non-residential
Group size: 3–10

Price range: €150–€400
Prices include:
accommodation & some
meals (call for details).
Child-friendly
Pet-friendly

Courses available in:

Jan	Feb	Mar	Apr	May	Jun	Jul	Aug	Sep	Oct	Nov	Dec

Introduction to birdwatching techniques

Birdwatch Ireland (BWI) is Ireland's main voluntary conservation organisation and their remit is the protection of wild birds and their habitats. They do this through research, conservation projects, policy development and lobbying, and they manage or own several reserves. They also educate, and run two- to five-day courses at the Cape Clear Bird Observatory on Cape Clear Island off Ireland's southern tip. Courses, which include introductory and improved birdwatching, wildlife photography and field study, combine outdoor field trips with lectures, and participants must expect some rugged walking. They should also bring equipment such as binoculars, field notebook and cameras. Accommodation and meals, plus whale- and dolphin-watching, are all available locally.

Contact
Declan Murphy
Birdwatch Ireland
Rockingham House (HQ)
Newcastle
Co. Wicklow
Tel: 01 281 9878
Web: www.birdwatchireland.ie

Practical information
Duration: 2–5 days
Level: beginner,
intermediate & advanced
Residential & non-residential

Group size: 6–15
Price range: €50–€200
Unsuitable for children
Pet-friendly

Courses available in:

Jan	Feb	Mar	Apr	May	Jun	Jul	Aug	Sep	Oct	Nov	Dec

Ireland

BURREN COLLEGE OF ART, BALLYVAUGHAN

Art and photography in the grounds of Newtown Castle

The Burren College of Art sits in the grounds of 16th-century Newtown Castle in the rural setting of the Burren, an area of great historical and natural interest. Opened in the mid 1990s, it specialises in fine art education for undergraduates and graduates, but during the summer runs a range of week-long courses which explore nature through photography, drawing, painting and sculpture. Some courses involve travel around the Burren and to the Aran Islands, and participants are encouraged to draw on the local environment, its history and culture for inspiration – as did the likes of Yeats and Synge. One month artist residencies are also available.

Courses
There are one-week courses in painting, drawing, sculpture and photography, all aimed at different experience levels, from professional artists to complete beginners. Courses are kept small to ensure individual attention and all the tutors are practising artists. A new international art forum will focus on the theory and current practices of art criticism.

What's special?
The Botanical Painting course is particularly popular because the Burren is such a wonderful floral environment, where Alpine plants grow alongside Mediterranean. The intensive portfolio course for school-leavers is popular among teenagers, while art teachers can also find some refreshing courses.

Eating & sleeping
Core House B&B (+353 65 7077310); Ballyvaughan Lodge Guesthouse (7077292); Hylands Burren Hotel (7077037), Gregans Castle Hotel (7077005). Food of the Arts Café on campus, Holywell Italian Cafe just behind, and Pier Head Restaurant in Kinvara.

Directions
45 minutes from Galway and 45 from Ennis, off N67. Contact the college for more details. Or bus from Galway to Ballyvaughan village (just over a mile from the college).

In the area
Spectacular Burren landscape and shoreline all around. Visit the Cliffs of Moher, Aillwee Caves, the Aran Islands and Doolin for its music. Plus Coole Park, Corcomroe Cistercian Abbey and many ancient sites.

Contact
Eleanor Franklin
Burren College of Art
Newtown Castle
Ballyvaughan
Co. Clare
Tel: 065 7077200
Web: www.burrencollege.ie
Email: ailsa@burrencollege.ie

Practical information
Duration: 5 days
Level: beginner,
intermediate & advanced
Non-residential

Group size: 3–15
Price range: £300–£500
Unsuitable for children
Pets not welcome

Courses available in:

Jan	Feb	Mar	Apr	May	Jun	Jul	Aug	Sep	Oct	Nov	Dec

Music and creative energy workshops

The Boghill Centre is a residential activity centre located in 50 acres of natural bog setting close to the Burren in Clare. A large range of workshops are offered in subjects such as Tai Chi, Meditation, Yoga, Massage, Dance, Voice Work and Pottery. There's also a traditional music course, suitable for players of all standards and all traditional instruments, and a week-long creative energy workshop. There's a range of accommodation options and non-participants are welcome to stay. Kilfenora village, where traditional music is available in the pubs, is three miles away, and the towns of Doolin and Ennis, and the Aran Islands are within striking distance.

Contact
Boghill Centre
Boghill
Kilfenora
Co. Clare
Tel: 065 7074644
Web: www.boghill.com

Practical information
Duration: 3–7 days
Level: beginner,
intermediate & advanced
Residential
Group size: 25+

Courses available in:

Price range: €100–€400
Prices include: meals &
accommodation.
Child-friendly
Pets not welcome

Jan	Feb	Mar	Apr	May	Jun	Jul	Aug	Sep	Oct	Nov	Dec

Painting the Burren landscape

The Burren Painting Centre is located in the O'Neill's Town House in the Clare town of Lisdoonvarna. The house was built in the early 1900s by the grandfather of John O'Neill, who now runs the centre with his wife Chris. They offer an assortment of courses – all tutored by working artists – teaching the use of watercolours, oils, acrylics, pen or ink to paint landscapes and seascapes. The emphasis is on outdoor painting, with excursions to various Burren locations, and some courses go to the Aran Islands. There is accommodation in the O'Neill's Town House (non-participants welcome) and much beautiful scenery to explore in the area.

Contact
Chris O'Neill
Burren Painting Centre
O'Neills Town House
Lisdoonvarna
Co. Clare
Tel: 065 7074208
Web: www.burrenpaintingcentre.com

Practical information
Duration: 2–6 days
Level: beginner,
intermediate & advanced
Residential & non-residential
Group size: 6–20

Courses available in:

Price range: €150–€500+
Prices include:call for
details.
Unsuitable for children
Pets not welcome

Jan	Feb	Mar	Apr	May	Jun	Jul	Aug	Sep	Oct	Nov	Dec

Yoga centre in the scenic West

The centre offers weekend and week-long workshops in different forms of Yoga, Pilates, holistic health, meditation and Buddhist teaching, and all Yoga teachers are fully qualified practitioners. The centre, with its two acres of grassy and wooded grounds, is located on the scenic west coast of Ireland, 50 minutes' drive from Shannon Airport. Accommodation is in single or shared rooms for up to eight people and vegetarian food is prepared by a gourmet chef. Courses include an Ashtanga and Meditation week, Lyengar and Meditation, Bikram Yoga, Vegetarian Cooking, and Pilates. Other activities include swimming, walking, horse riding and sailing.

Contact
Dave Brocklebank
Burren Yoga and Meditation Centre
Lig do Scith
Cappaghmore
Kinvara
Co. Galway
Tel: 091 637680
Web: www.burrenyoga.com

Practical information
Duration: 3–7 days
Level: beginner,
intermediate & advanced
Residential & non-residential
Group size: 11–15

Courses available in:

Price range: €200–€500+
Prices include: meals &
accommodation
Unsuitable for children
Pets not welcome

Jan	Feb	Mar	Apr	May	Jun	Jul	Aug	Sep	Oct	Nov	Dec

Ireland

CHRYSALIS HOLISTIC CENTRE, DONARD
Spiritual renewal an hour from Dublin

Located one hour from Dublin in the tranquil Wicklow countryside, Chrysalis comprises a converted 18th-century rectory, wooden chalet, two hermitages, sauna, craft shop, organic garden and beautiful landscaped gardens. A varied programme of workshops and retreats are based on the theme of 'time out', personal discovery and spiritual growth, and tutors are all experienced therapists in their fields. They include Reiki Master Margaret Brady, James D'Angelo, a leading authority on sound healing therapy, and body psychotherapist John Doyle. Courses available include Uncovering Your True Self, Yoga and Reflexology, the Alexander Technique, Personality Styles and Work Life Balance, and Healing with the Voice.

Contact	**Practical information**	Price range: €200–€500+
Claire Harrison	Duration: 3–5 days	Prices include: meals &
Chrysalis Holistic Centre	Level: beginner	accommodation
Donard	Residential	Unsuitable for children
Co. Wicklow	Group size: 11–25	Pets not welcome
Tel: 045 404713		
Web: www.chrysalis.ie	Courses available in:	

Jan	Feb	Mar	Apr	May	Jun	Jul	Aug	Sep	Oct	Nov	Dec

CLOONA HEALTH CENTRE, WESTPORT
Holistic, energising programmes in a renovated mill

The Cloona Health Centre was founded in 1970 by Sonia Kelly, who had a strong interest in eastern philosophies and yoga. Located in an old woollen mill in the Mayo countryside, three miles from Westport, it is now run by Sonia's son and his wife. Three- and five-day Energising Programmes are facilitated by experienced therapists and practitioners. Each day has two hours of morning yoga, a one-hour guided walk with instruction on walking and movement skills, and an evening sauna and massage. Accommodation is provided in oak-furnished rooms. Five-day courses run from March to October, costing €495, while a three-day programme runs from October to January, costing €315.

Contact	**Practical information**	Price range: €300–€500
Dhara Kelly	Duration: 3–5 days	Prices include: meals &
Cloona Health Centre	Level: beginner,	accommodation
Westport	intermediate & advanced	Unsuitable for children
Co. Mayo	Residential	Pets not welcome
Tel: 098 25251	Group size: 6–15	
Web: www.cloona.ie		
	Courses available in:	

Jan	Feb	Mar	Apr	May	Jun	Jul	Aug	Sep	Oct	Nov	Dec

THE COTTAGES, BETTYSTOWN
Painting courses with a leading botanical artist

The Cottages are six 300-year-old holiday cottages owned by one of Ireland's leading botanical artists, Susan Sex, and they are the base for three-day watercolour painting courses tutored by top Irish artists. Susan herself teaches Botanical Watercolour for Intermediate/Advanced Painters; then there is Watercolour for Beginners/Improvers; Watercolour Travelling Sketches; and Intermediate Watercolour Skills and Techniques. The self-catering cottages are close to stunning beaches on Ireland's north-east coast and have been renovated to a very high standard. They have oak-beamed ceilings, open fireplaces, and farmhouse-style kitchens. Resident painters can enjoy full board from Friday evening to Monday evening. Non-residents also welcome.

Contact	**Practical information**	Price range: €200–€500
Susan Sex	Duration: 3 days	Prices include: meals &
The Cottages	Level: beginner,	accommodation.
Seabank	intermediate & advanced	Child-friendly
Bettystown	Residential & non-residential	Pets not welcome
Co. Meath	Group size: 6–15	
Tel: 041 9828104		
Web: www.cottages-ireland.com	Courses available in:	

Jan	Feb	Mar	Apr	May	Jun	Jul	Aug	Sep	Oct	Nov	Dec

DELPHI LODGE FLY FISHING SCHOOL, LEENANE

Fly fishing in the wilds of Connemara

The Peter O'Reilly Fly Fishing School is located at Delphi Lodge, an 1830s country house in Connemara. Peter, who is a member of the Association of Professional Game Angling Instructors, started his school over 15 years ago and has written widely on angling. This is a wonderful place to learn as there is salmon fishing in the Bundorragh River (20 productive pools) and in the lakes. The basic courses cover river and lake fishing; wet/dry fly fishing, casting, knotting and boat management skills. Tuition is also available for more experienced anglers, while small groups ensure that participants receive personal attention.

Courses
The lodge places great emphasis on informality and community – it does not consider itself a hotel – and everyone eats together with owner Peter Mantle. There are 12 rooms, or you can choose one of the estate's cottages for more privacy.

What's special?
It is special for the combination of expert tuition from one of Ireland's finest game angling instructors and the ambience of a country house situated in remote splendour in the wilds of Connemara.

Eating & sleeping
All guests stay in the hotel, where some rooms overlook the lake. Fabulous food is prepared by chef Cliodhna Prendergast, who recently won an award for Best Chef in the West of Ireland.

Directions
From Galway, N59 towards Clifden Right at Maam Cross. Left at T-junction in Maam. Right in Leenane towards Westport. Left after two miles to Delphi/Louisburgh. Six miles to Lodge.

In the area
Mountains for the hill walkers; sandy beaches for the sedentary. Gardens and crafts at Kylemore Abbey. Westport and Galway are lively, cosmopolitan towns.

Contact
Carole Eyles
Delphi Lodge Fly Fishing School
Leenane
Co Galway
Tel: 095 42222
Web: www.delphi-salmon.com
Email: delfish@iol.ie

Practical information
Duration: 3–7 days
Level: beginner,
intermediate & advanced
Residential
Group size: 3–10

Price range: €500+
Prices include: meals &
accommodation
Unsuitable for children
Pets not welcome

Courses available in:

Jan	Feb	Mar	Apr	May	Jun	Jul	Aug	Sep	Oct	Nov	Dec

Ireland

Writing courses overlooking Dingle Bay

Dingle Writing Courses was established in 1996 by Nicholas McLachlan and Abigail Joffe, in a purpose-built centre in Inch overlooking Dingle Bay. Led by published authors such as Clare Boylan and Andrew O'Hagan, the courses give writers a literary experience while allowing them to share their work with others and receive professional criticism. The format allows for individual and group exercises, and private writing time. Past courses have included Poetry, Fiction, Travel writing, Memoir, Scriptwriting and Writing the Landscape. The centre has a garden, and accommodation is mainly provided in shared bedrooms (single rooms in separate B&Bs), with meals provided by a resident chef.

Contact
Nicholas McLachlan and Abigail Joffe
Dingle Writing Courses
Ballintlea
Ventry
Co. Kerry
Tel: 066 915 9815
Web: www.dinglewritingcourses.ie

Practical information
Duration: 2 days
Level: beginner,
intermediate & advanced
Residential & non-residential
Group size: 6-15

Price range: €300–€400
Prices include:
accommodation & some
meals
Child-friendly
Pet-friendly

Courses available in:

Jan	Feb	Mar	Apr	May	Jun	Jul	Aug	Sep	Oct	Nov	Dec

Yoga and meditation retreats at a Tibetan Buddhist centre

Dzogchen Beara is a Tibetan Buddhist Retreat Centre under the spiritual direction of Sogyal Rinpoche, author of the Tibetan Book of Living and Dying. Overlooking the Atlantic on Cork's Beara Peninsula, the centre offers courses encouraging quiet reflection, healing and renewal through meditation and yoga. Courses are suitable both for students of Tibetan Buddhism and those just wanting to rest. A small number of dormitory beds and shared cottages are available on site, and there are hotels and B&Bs nearby. Courses include Creating a New Reality; Vajrasattava and Guru Yoga; An Introduction to Meditation; Discovering the True Nature of Love; and Compassionate Companionship.

Contact
Dzogchen Beara
Garranes
Allihies
Co. Cork
Tel: 027 73032
Web: www.dzogchenbeara.org

Practical information
Duration: 3-7 days
Level: beginner,
intermediate & advanced
Residential & non-residential
Group size: 25+

Price range: €100–€200
Prices include: meals
Unsuitable for children
Pets not welcome

Courses available in:

Jan	Feb	Mar	Apr	May	Jun	Jul	Aug	Sep	Oct	Nov	Dec

Intensive yoga study with experienced specialised tutors

The East Clare Yoga Centre is run by the Sturton family in the grounds of their home at Boru Oak Lodge. Susanne Sturton is a qualified Iyengar yoga teacher who has practised for 10 years, and she teaches with other tutors such as Judith Richards (25 years a yoga teacher). The centre uses a purpose-built yoga studio, with accommodation on site. Susanne's husband Paul and his parents look after the food side, cooking organic, vegetarian meals. The grounds consist of two acres of mature gardens near Raheen Wood and close to Lough Derg. Much traditional music is available in pubs in the area and there are many woodland and hillside walks.

Contact
Susanne Sturton
East Clare Yoga Centre
Boru Oak Lodge
Raheen Road
Tuamgraney
Co. Clare
Tel: 061 640923
Web: www.eastclareyoga.com

Practical information
Duration: 3-5 days
Level: beginner,
intermediate & advanced
Residential
Group size: 6-15

Price range: €200–€500
Prices include: meals &
accommodation
Unsuitable for children
Pets not welcome

Courses available in:

Jan	Feb	Mar	Apr	May	Jun	Jul	Aug	Sep	Oct	Nov	Dec

Creative and alternative pottery courses on the Mizen Peninsula

The Ewe Art Centre, located on the beautiful Mizen Peninsula on the Atlantic Coast, is the working home of artist Sheena Wood and contains a workshop and gallery. Sheena offers a wide range of clay courses, from Pottery and Throwing to Clock Making, Mirror Making and Candle Holder Making. Small group courses (five to ten people) can be arranged in Acrylic Painting and Mixed Media, Creative Garden Design and others. Three- to five-day courses involve classes in the mornings and free afternoons, and the fee includes a week's self-catering accommodation. Other activities nearby include hill walking, pony trekking, golf, tennis and whale watching.

Contact
The Ewe Art Centre
Tooreen
Glengarriff
West Cork
Tel: 027 63840
Web: www.theewe.com

Practical information
Duration: 3–5 days
Level: beginner &
intermediate
Residential
Group size: 3–10

Price range: €200–€400
Prices include:
accommodation
Child-friendly
Pets not welcome

Courses available in:

Jan	Feb	Mar	Apr	May	Jun	Jul	Aug	Sep	Oct	Nov	Dec

Film production at the heart of Temple Bar

Filmbase is an organisation which offers support and training to independent and low-budget film-makers. Founded in 1987, it has recently relocated to new premises in the heart of Temple Bar. The company offers affordable training, equipment and studio hire, information, support and advice, and also lobbies on behalf of filmmakers. Their courses, both long and short, cover all areas of film production, from scriptwriting and directing to camera operation, sound and lighting. The Irish Film Institute is located nearby, with daily screenings of independent and foreign films. Accommodation is available in many hotels nearby, some of them luxurious.

Contact
Vanessa Gildea
Filmbase
Curved Street Building
Temple Bar
Dublin 2
Co. Dublin
Tel: 01 6796716
Web: www.filmbase.ie

Practical information
Duration: 2–4 days
Level: beginner,
intermediate & advanced
Non-residential

Group size: 3–20
Price range: €100–€300
Unsuitable for children
Pets not welcome

Courses available in:

Jan	Feb	Mar	Apr	May	Jun	Jul	Aug	Sep	Oct	Nov	Dec

Playwriting courses and drama workshops in Temple Bar

The Fishamble Theatre Company aims to present new work of the highest standards and is dedicated to the discovery, development and production of new plays. Their annual summer weekend playwriting course covers all aspects of the craft, including uses of the imagination, openings, structures, plot, characterisation and dialogue. Many practical examples and stimulating exercises will be given, and there is an opportunity for participants to have their script workshopped and read to the public in the nearby Project Arts Centre. The company is located in Temple Bar, Dublin's cultural quarter, with many hotels and attractions in the area.

Contact
Gavin Kostick
Fishamble Theatre Company
Shamrock Chambers
1/2 Eustace Street
Dublin 2
Co. Dublin
Tel: 01 6704018
Web: www.fishamble.com

Practical information
Duration: 3 days
Level: intermediate
Non-residential

Group size: 6–10
Price range: €150–€200
Child-friendly
Pets not welcome

Courses available in:

Jan	Feb	Mar	Apr	May	Jun	Jul	Aug	Sep	Oct	Nov	Dec

Ireland

Ceramics crafts courses with a professional potter

Marcus O'Mahony runs various pottery courses from his fully-equipped studio in the Waterford countryside near Lismore. A member of the Craft Potters Association, he has been a full-time potter for the past ten years and teaches at Dublin's National College of Art and Design. He specialises in two particular forms of the art – salt-glaze and wood-firing.

Courses

Marcus runs pottery weekends throughout the year which introduce beginners to the practices of throwing and hand-building. In May and June he runs seven-day, full-board salt-glaze courses (€850) and in July a ten-day, full-board wood-fire course (€1250). These longer courses are aimed at those who already have (minimal) experience. The wood-fire course is particularly interesting for potters who have previously only used gas kilns.

What's special?

Marcus is hugely enthusiastic about the fact that all people have the potential to do something creative with clay. On the beginners and improvers weekends he will draw this potential out of you, using other tutors as necessary to ensure personal attention. Prices listed below are for these weekends.

Eating & sleeping

There is excellent accommodation on site, either in the farmhouse or the apartment above the studio (€35 per person per night). Both of these can be hired separately from the courses. All courses include excellent home-made lunches. The longer courses are all-inclusive with three-course dinners, wine and accommodation as well. Buggy's and The Bride View are recommended local restaurants.

Directions

You can fly cheaply to Cork airport, from where Marcus can pick you up. By car, the pottery is three miles west of Lismore; see the map on the website.

In the area

Nearby Lismore is an attractive town on the Blackwater River; its castle is particularly renowned. The Atlantic Ocean and its beaches are ten miles away, and there are plentiful hiking, riding, fishing and golfing possibilities in this rural area.

Contact

Marcus O'Mahony
Glencairn Pottery
Lismore
Co. Waterford
Tel: 058 56694
Web: www.marcusomahony.com
Email: info@marcusomahony.com

Practical information

Duration: 2–10 days
Level: beginner,
intermediate & advanced
Residential & non-residential
Group size: 6–10

Price range: €100–€150
Prices include: lunch
Unsuitable for children
Pets not welcome

Courses available in:

Jan	Feb	Mar	Apr	May	Jun	Jul	Aug	Sep	Oct	Nov	Dec

THE FOXFORD LODGE, FOXFORD
Painting at a luxury guesthouse in Mayo

The Foxford Lodge is a luxury guesthouse with a nautical theme: a Galway Hooker mast, complete with sail, greets you in the entrance hall. The guesthouse hosts residential painting courses tutored by experienced artists. Watercolour painting courses include the three-day Get a Handle on Watercolour and the seven-day Capture Summer. Or there's acrylic painting, silk painting and oil painting. Fishing tuition can be arranged, and there is excellent fishing in the River Moy and several lakes. Accommodation is in comfortable, en-suite rooms and there is much fresh home cooking and baking. The lodge is located near the Ox Mountains and the Foxford Way, making it an excellent base for hill walking.

Contact
Brigid and Harry Feeney
The Foxford Lodge
Pontoon Road
Foxford
Co. Mayo
Tel: 094 9257777
Web: www.thefoxfordlodge.ie

Practical information
Duration: 2–7 days
Level: beginner &
intermediate
Residential
Group size: 6–10

Price range: €200–€500+
Prices include: meals &
accommodation
Child-friendly
Pets not welcome

Courses available in:

Jan	Feb	Mar	Apr	May	Jun	Jul	Aug	Sep	Oct	Nov	Dec

THE GAIETY SCHOOL OF ACTING, DUBLIN
Weekend courses in cultural Temple Bar

The Gaiety School of Acting was set up in 1986 by its chairman, Joe Dowling, who has been the Artistic Director of the Abbey Theatre and is Managing Director of Dublin's Gaiety Theatre. The school is directed by Patrick Sutton, who has worked as an actor and artistic director in Ireland, England and France. As well as full-time courses, there is a varied programme of weekend and week-long courses at this Temple Bar location. Weekend workshops include Make a 'Short' Short Movie, a Voice Weekend and Stage Combat. Four-day Easter workshops include Improvisation for Adults. Week-long summer workshops include Acting for Camera and TV Presentation for Adults.

Contact
Patrick Sutton
The Gaiety School of Acting
Sycamore Street
Temple Bar, Dublin 2
Co. Dublin
Tel: 01 6799277
Web: www.gaietyschool.com

Practical information
Duration: 2–5 days
Level: beginner,
intermediate & advanced
Non-residential

Group size: 6–20
Price range: €150–€500+
Child-friendly
Pets not welcome

Courses available in:

Jan	Feb	Mar	Apr	May	Jun	Jul	Aug	Sep	Oct	Nov	Dec

GREEN WOOD CHAIRS, SKIBBEREEN
Furniture-making courses in relaxed country environment

Alison Ospina founded Greenwood Chairs in 1996 and specialises in hazel wood chair-making at her studio, the Wooden House, near Skibbereen in West Cork. She uses a sustainable method of coppicing to manage her hazel woodland. In addition to a one-day taster course, she runs a three-day chair-making course where students make a hazel wood chair to bring home. The environment in the workshop is very peaceful as participants learn to use a range of hand, not machine, tools. No previous experience of woodwork is necessary and the techniques are easy to learn. Accommodation is available in many B&Bs and hotels in Skibbereen, which is a lively market town.

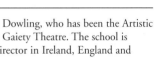

Contact
Alison Ospina
Green Wood Chairs
The Wooden House
Rossnagoose
Skibbereen
Co. Cork
Tel: 028 21890
Web: http://gofree.indigo.ie/~greenwud

Practical information
Duration: 3 days
Level: beginner,
intermediate & advanced
Non-residential
Group size: 1–2

Price range: €300–€400
Prices include: A light lunch
is provided.
Child-friendly
Pet-friendly

Courses available in:

Jan	Feb	Mar	Apr	May	Jun	Jul	Aug	Sep	Oct	Nov	Dec

Ireland

Clare Island yoga retreats

The Clare Island Yoga Retreat Centre started in 2001 when Christophe Mouze and his wife Ciara Cullen started running retreats in a community hall. Since then they have built a studio and renovated their traditional island cottage to provide accommodation. French-born Christophe gave up a career in IT to train as an Iyengar yoga teacher, while Ciara has a background in dance. The centre offers yoga and meditation retreats. Many are run by visiting teachers, with some suitable for beginners/all levels and others for advanced students only. Food is organic and students will enjoy high-quality vegetarian cooking. Tuition is sometimes paid for by donation (€5–€12 per hour) or by working.

Contact
Ciara and Christophe Mouze
The Healing Path
Ballytoughey
Clare Island
Co. Mayo
Tel: 098 25412 or 087 2504845
Web: www.yogaholidays.net/clare/index.htm

Practical information
Duration: 4–10 days
Level: beginner,
intermediate & advanced
Residential
Group size: 6–20

Price range: €200–€500+
Prices include: meals,
accommodation
Unsuitable for children
Pets not welcome

Courses available in:

Jan	Feb	Mar	Apr	May	Jun	Jul	Aug	Sep	Oct	Nov	Dec

Whale-watching workshops with conservation group

The Irish Whale and Dolphin Group was set up in 1990 in order to establish Ireland's first sighting and stranding scheme. The group, which is committed to the conservation of whales, dolphins and other cetaceans, organises weekend whale watching courses on Cape Clear Island in Co. Cork, run by group secretary Padraig Whooley. Courses include workshops on identifying cetaceans, and field trips with cliff- and boat-based whale watches. As much time as possible is devoted to outdoor activities, although participants are expected to attend the workshops and slideshows. Cape Clear Island is also a paradise for wild birds and there is a bird observatory, which has some self-catering accommodation.

Contact
Padraig Whooley
The Irish Whale and Dolphin Group
Gortagrenane
Castlefreke
Clonakilty, Co.Cork
Tel: 023 31911
Web: www.iwdg.ie

Practical information
Duration: 2 days
Level: beginner &
intermediate
Non-residential

Group size: 11–20
Price range: €50–€100
Child-friendly
Pets not welcome

Courses available in:

Jan	Feb	Mar	Apr	May	Jun	Jul	Aug	Sep	Oct	Nov	Dec

Intensive creative writing courses in the centre of Dublin

The Irish Writers' Centre was founded in 1991 to nurture writing and an audience for literature through a varied programme of readings, workshops, lectures and seminars. It runs week-long summer workshops and weekend courses on all aspects of writing, using tutors who are experienced and often well-known authors, poets, playwrights and journalists. The Centre is located next to the Irish Writers' Museum, close to O'Connell Street and Dublin city centre with all its cultural attractions, shops and parks. Accommodation is available nearby in many hotels. Courses include: Intensive Creating Writing; Writing for Profit; Crime Writing; The Art and Craft of Writing; Poetry and Prose.

Contact
Ian Oliver
The Irish Writers' Centre
19 Parnell Square
Dublin 1
Co. Dublin
Tel: 01 8721302
Web: www.writerscentre.ie

Practical information
Duration: 2–5 days
Level: beginner,
intermediate & advanced
Non-residential

Group size: 3–20
Price range: €150–€500
Child-friendly
Pets not welcome

Courses available in:

Jan	Feb	Mar	Apr	May	Jun	Jul	Aug	Sep	Oct	Nov	Dec

Cookery in a unique and beautiful island setting

Island Cottage is a very intimate, unusual cookery school and restaurant in a beautiful location on Hare Island in West Cork. It was set up in 1989 by husband-and-wife cookery enthusiasts John Desmond and Ellmary Fenton. John, who has written cookery books, trained as a chef at the Ritz in Paris and was appointed Professeur de Cuisine at the École de Cuisine La Varenne Paris. The school specialises in one- or two-day courses for two people (€225 pp), while five-day, one-to-one courses are also available for individuals during July and August (€650 including accommodation). The school is located amid fantastic scenery with many beaches and walks in the area.

Contact
John Desmond and Ellmary Fenton
Island Cottage Cookery School
Island Cottage
Heir Island
Skibbereen
Co. Cork
Tel: 028 38102
Web: www.islandcottage.com

Practical information
Duration: 2–5 days
Level: beginner,
intermediate & advanced
Residential
Group size: 1–2

Courses available in:

Jan	Feb	Mar	Apr	May	Jun	Jul	Aug	Sep	Oct	Nov	Dec

Price range: €200–€500+
Prices include: meals &
accommodation
Unsuitable for children
Pets not welcome

Courses for alternative lifestyles

The Kerry Alternative Technology farm opened to the public in 2004. Here the Donoghue family try to live in a manner which respects the environment and complies with ethical values. They have two wind turbines, plus solar panels and other systems for power. And they keep goats and grow vegetables in organic gardens. The weekend courses cover topics like alternative power generation, organic gardening, composting and alternative living. Accommodation is in basic but comfortable rooms – don't expect hot baths every day – and organic vegetarian meals are provided. The farm is located in stunning scenery close to the Ring of Kerry. Sneem village has several pubs.

Contact
Bob and Cath Donoghue-Barnes
Kerry Alternative Technology
Gortagowan
Sneem, Killarney
Co. Kerry
Tel: 064 45563
Web: www.kerryat.com

Practical information
Duration: 2 days
Level: beginner,
intermediate & advanced
Residential & non-residential
Group size: 3–10

Courses available in:

Jan	Feb	Mar	Apr	May	Jun	Jul	Aug	Sep	Oct	Nov	Dec

Price range: €150–€200
Prices include: meals &
accommodation
Unsuitable for children
Pets not welcome

Pottery and art in converted stables and coach house

The Kinsale Pottery and Art School was set up by Adrian Wistreich in 2000 in a converted coach house and stables in the grounds of Olcote Farm near Kinsale. Adrian has been involved in several adult education programmes and runs the school with the assistance of part-time teachers who are graduates in a range of specialist disciplines. There are two- or five-day courses in various arts and crafts, including pottery, oil painting, sculpture, stained glass, printing, leatherwork, chair-making and mosaics. In July and August, several children's art and crafts camps are run in parallel with five-day ceramics courses for adults. Accommodation is available in Kinsale.

Contact
Adrian Wistreich
Kinsale Pottery and Art School
Olcote, Ballinacurra
Kinsale
Co. Cork
Tel: 021 477 7758
Web: www.kinsaleceramics.com

Practical information
Duration: 2–5 days
Level: beginner,
intermediate & advanced
Non-residential
Group size: 6–10

Courses available in:

Jan	Feb	Mar	Apr	May	Jun	Jul	Aug	Sep	Oct	Nov	Dec

Price range: €150–€300
Prices include: lunch &
materials
Child-friendly
Pets not welcome

Ireland

Weekend craft courses near the River Nore

Lavistown House was built in 1810 and is set among trees and gardens just three miles from Kilkenny, close to the River Nore. There are weekend courses in a range of art and crafts such as landscape painting and basket making, and several outdoor-focused courses including identifying mushrooms or wild flowers. Accommodation is provided in shared bedrooms (participants provide their own sheets or sleeping bag) or you can choose to stay in local B&B accommodation. Home-produced meals are cooked for the participants, but everyone shares in the washing-up. The food is also sold locally; particularly well-known are Lavistown cheese and the high quality sausages.

Contact
Olivia Goodwillie
Lavistown House
Lavistown
Kilkenny
Co. Kilkenny
Tel: 056 65145
Web: www.lavistownhouse.ie

Practical information
Duration: 3 days
Level: beginner,
intermediate & advanced
Residential & non-residential
Group size: 11–20

Price range: €100–€200
Prices include: meals &
accommodation
Unsuitable for children
Pets not welcome

Courses available in:

Jan	Feb	Mar	Apr	May	Jun	Jul	Aug	Sep	Oct	Nov	Dec

Summer courses in Dublin

The National College is Ireland's best known establishment for art and design education, offering the largest range of related degrees. Founded in the 18th century, it sits in the Liberties, the oldest part of Dublin, a short walk from the city centre. The Centre for Continuing Education in Art and Design offers a summer programme of week-long courses on painting, drawing, photography, crafts and design. Courses are taught by fully qualified artists and prospective students are sent a required materials list. Courses available include Intensive Study of the Figure, Colour Theory Workshop, Etching and Dry Point Technique, Non-Acid Printmaking and an Introduction to Textile Printing.

Contact
Nuala Hunt
The National College of Art and Design (NCAD)
100 Thomas Street
Dublin 8
Tel: 01 6364200
Web: www.ncad.ie

Practical information
Duration: 5 days
Level: beginner,
intermediate & advanced
Non-residential

Group size: 6–20
Price range: €150–€300
Child-friendly
Pets not welcome

Courses available in:

Jan	Feb	Mar	Apr	May	Jun	Jul	Aug	Sep	Oct	Nov	Dec

Cultural activity holidays in Donegal

The Oideas Gael Cultural Centre was founded in 1984 in the Irish-speaking part of south-west Donegal, an area with a strong tradition of music and dance. Oideas Gael aims to promote and integrate Irish language and culture using a wide range of arts, crafts, music and dance. There is a strong multi-cultural flavour here with people attending from all over the world, and courses are offered for Irish and non-Irish speakers alike. Tutors are experienced artists and musicians, such as the designer Patrick Gallagher. Courses include Celtic Pottery; Environment and Culture; Marine Painting; Bodhran Playing (traditional Irish drum); and Donegal Dancing.

Contact
Liam Cunningham and Siobhan Curran
Oideas Gael
Glencolumcille
Co. Donegal
Tel: 074 973 0248
Web: www.oideas-gael.com

Practical information
Duration: 3–7 days
Level: beginner,
intermediate & advanced
Residential & non-residential

Group size: 11–25+
Price range: €50–€150
Child-friendly
Pet-friendly

Courses available in:

Jan	Feb	Mar	Apr	May	Jun	Jul	Aug	Sep	Oct	Nov	Dec

Organic gardening and farming in the unspoilt Leitrim countryside

The Organic Centre was established in 1995 in the countryside of North Leitrim to provide training and information about organic gardening and farming. There are demonstration gardens, growing tunnels, a wetland sewage disposal system, display gardens, a willow sculpture area, an orchard and soft fruit area, and a composting display. Gardening, cooking and crafts courses are run by experienced local gardeners and crafts workers and a list of local accommodation is sent to participants. Courses include a Beginners' Guide to Growing Organic Vegetables; Learn How to Live the Good Life; Basket Making; Growing and Using Culinary and Medicinal Herbs; and Hemp Building.

Contact
Dolores Keegan
The Organic Centre
Rossinver
Co. Leitrim
Tel: 071 9854338
Web: www.theorganiccentre.ie

Practical information
Duration: 2-6 days
Level: beginner &
intermediate
Non-residential

Group size: 11-15
Price range: €100–€500
Prices include: lunch
Unsuitable for children
Pets not welcome

Courses available in:

Jan	Feb	Mar	Apr	May	Jun	Jul	Aug	Sep	Oct	Nov	Dec

Painting courses where Loughs Conn and Cullin meet

The Pontoon School of Landscape Painting is situated at the meeting point of Loughs Conn and Cullin. The location offers a range of scenery for artists: forests, bogs, hedgerows, lakes, streams and mountains. Two- or four-day summer landscape painting courses are led by artist Pat Goff, who has taught art and art appreciation for several years. Tuition in oils, watercolours, acrylics and pastels mainly takes place outdoors, with demonstrations and lectures indoors. Students are required to bring sketch books, paper and drawing materials (or these may be purchased at the studio). Residential students stay in en-suite rooms, and gourmet meals are served in the restaurant.

Contact
Pat Goff
Pontoon School of Landscape Painting
Pontoon Bridge Hotel
Pontoon
Co. Mayo
Tel: 094 9256120
Web: http://pontoon.mayo-ireland.ie/PBHotel/Hotel.htm

Practical Information
Duration: 2–4 days
Level: beginner,
intermediate & advanced
Residential & non-residential
Group size: 1–10

Price range: €100–€300
Child-friendly
Pet-friendly

Courses available in:

Jan	Feb	Mar	Apr	May	Jun	Jul	Aug	Sep	Oct	Nov	Dec

Yoga weekends in stunning Kerry countryside

Rusheens Yoga Centre was set up 12 years ago by June Durkin in a peaceful location in Kerry, near the town of Kenmare. June has been teaching yoga for 18 years, and along with other instructors she runs weekend or week-long yoga courses at the centre using an approach inspired by Vanda Scaravelli, which emphasises listening to the body and working with the breath. Attractions in the area include heritage sites and gardens, and the beautiful town of Kenmare, which is renowned for its many restaurants and excellent cuisine. Prices at Rusheens include accommodation and all meals except one group dinner in a Kenmare restaurant.

Contact
June Durkin
Rusheens Yoga Centre
Rusheens
Ballygriffin
Kenmare
Co. Kerry
Tel: 064 41669
Web: www.rusheensyogacentre.com

Practical Information
Duration: 3–7 days
Level: beginner,
intermediate & advanced
Residential
Group size: 3–10

Price range: €200–€500+
Prices include:
accommodation & some
meals
Unsuitable for children
Pets not welcome

Courses available in:

Jan	Feb	Mar	Apr	May	Jun	Jul	Aug	Sep	Oct	Nov	Dec

Ireland

Creative writing workshops in the beautiful West

Salmon Publishing is one of Ireland's main literary publishers and the Writers' Place is their beautiful premise just north of County Clare's stunning Cliffs of Moher, overlooking the Atlantic. Here students will learn about Ireland's literary life, contemporary poetry and publishing in creative writing workshops facilitated by Jesse Lendennie, who has published several guides. The weekend workshops, which are particularly suitable for beginners, cover all aspects of the craft, using written exercises and group discussions. There are many B&Bs and guest houses in the area, whose attractions include Doolin Village (the traditional music capital of Ireland), the Burren and the Aran Islands.

Contact
Jessie Lendennie
Salmon Publishing
The Writers' Place
Cliffs of Moher, Knockeven
Co. Clare
Tel: 065 7081941
Web: www.salmonpoetry.com

Practical Information
Duration: 2 days
Level: beginner &
intermediate
Non-residential

Group size: 3–10
Price range: €100–€150
Prices include: lunch
Child-friendly
Pet-friendly

Courses available in:

Jan	Feb	Mar	Apr	May	Jun	Jul	Aug	Sep	Oct	Nov	Dec

Organic and holistic courses on the South Reen peninsula

South Reen Farm is located on the cliffs of the South Reen peninsula in Co. Cork, with fabulous views of Atlantic islands. It is a peaceful, secluded location for weekend courses in the ancient Chinese art of Qi Gong (breathing). You can also arrange with health practitioners for different kinds of massage such as Japanese head massage. The farm's philosophy is organic-oriented, aiming to working with nature and replace what they remove from the soil. Self-catering accommodation is available and there is a wood-burning stove as well as central heating. There is a private beach nearby, while other local activities include whale-watching, sea kayaking, fishing and riding.

Contact
South Reen Farm
Union Hall
Co. Cork
Tel: 028 33258
Web: www.southreenfarm.com

Practical Information
Duration: 2 days
Level: beginner,
intermediate & advanced
Residential & non-residential
Group size: 6–15

Price range: €100–€150
Prices include: lunch
Child-friendly
Pet-friendly

Courses available in:

Jan	Feb	Mar	Apr	May	Jun	Jul	Aug	Sep	Oct	Nov	Dec

Traditional Irish music at an old honey farm

Tir na Meala is a small hotel and summer school located in a scenic valley near the Cork-Kerry border, which offers courses in traditional music, art, sculpture and photography. Built as a honey farm, it has been transformed into a guest house and serves Irish, Continental and Eastern cuisine, with all ingredients home-grown. Dutch and Irish instructors are professional and very experienced; Hans de Bruijn, for example, studied at the Royal Academy of Visual Arts in The Hague and has exhibited in several Dutch museums. Courses include Traditional Irish Music, Painting/Watercolours, Nature Photography, Sculpting and Gardens (guided tours of local gardens with owner Robbie Koopmans).

Contact
Geert Janssen
Tir na Meala
Coolea
Co. Cork
Tel: 026 45651
Web: www.tirnameala.com

Practical Information
Duration: 2 days
Level: beginner,
intermediate & advanced
Residential & non-residential
Group size: 6–15

Price range: €100–€150
Prices include: lunch
Child-friendly
Pet-friendly

Courses available in:

Jan	Feb	Mar	Apr	May	Jun	Jul	Aug	Sep	Oct	Nov	Dec

Customised walking and wildlife tours in Kerry

Walking Kerry is based in the village of Sneem, amid the Kerry mountains and close to the Ring of Kerry. Local guides lead walkers through the Kerry scenery on all-inclusive packages of a week or a weekend. Trails vary from the magnificent MacGillycuddy Reeks ridge walk with views of (and swimming in!) glacial lakes, to the Eagle's Peak, a hike through a historic Gaelic-speaking area. Weekend tours include two nights' B&B, evening meals and picnics, two guided walks and transfers if required. A week-long walking tour includes trails such as MacGillycuddy Reeks, the Eagle's Peak and the Skellig Experience, a boat trip to the Skellig Rocks.

Contact
Michael O'Connor
Walking Kerry
Sneem
Co. Kerry
Tel: 064 75899
Web: www.walkingkerry.com

Practical Information
Duration: 3–6 days
Level: beginner,
intermediate & advanced
Residential
Group size: 6–15

Price range: €150–€500+
Prices include: meals &
accommodation
Unsuitable for children
Pets not welcome

Courses available in:

Jan	Feb	Mar	Apr	May	Jun	Jul	Aug	Sep	Oct	Nov	Dec

index

Index by category

Arts

Food & Drink

Writing, Film & Photography

Home & Garden

Body & Soul

Outdoors

Other categories